Milton's Theological Process

Milton's Theological Process

Reading *De Doctrina Christiana* and *Paradise Lost*

JASON A. KERR

Great Clarendon Street, Oxford, OX2 6DP,
United Kingdom

Oxford University Press is a department of the University of Oxford.
It furthers the University's objective of excellence in research, scholarship,
and education by publishing worldwide. Oxford is a registered trade mark of
Oxford University Press in the UK and in certain other countries

© Jason A. Kerr 2023

The moral rights of the author have been asserted

All rights reserved. No part of this publication may be reproduced, stored in
a retrieval system, or transmitted, in any form or by any means, without the
prior permission in writing of Oxford University Press, or as expressly permitted
by law, by licence or under terms agreed with the appropriate reprographics
rights organization. Enquiries concerning reproduction outside the scope of the
above should be sent to the Rights Department, Oxford University Press, at the
address above

You must not circulate this work in any other form
and you must impose this same condition on any acquirer

Published in the United States of America by Oxford University Press
198 Madison Avenue, New York, NY 10016, United States of America

British Library Cataloguing in Publication Data

Data available

Library of Congress Control Number: 2023937272

ISBN 9780198875086

DOI: 10.1093/oso/9780198875086.001.0001

Printed and bound by
CPI Group (UK) Ltd, Croydon, CR0 4YY

Links to third party websites are provided by Oxford in good faith and
for information only. Oxford disclaims any responsibility for the materials
contained in any third party website referenced in this work.

For John K. Hale

For Kristine, Julia, and Elijah

Contents

List of Figures	viii
Acknowledgments	ix
List of Abbreviations	xi
Note on Sources	xiii
Introduction: Reading *De Doctrina Christiana*	1

PART ONE: SCRIPTURE AND ECCLESIOLOGY

1. Scripture and Literary Form	37
2. Human Capacity and Scriptural Interpretation	66
3. Theology and the Church	108

PART TWO: THE SON OF GOD

4. The Form of Book I Chapter 5, "On the Son of God"	143
5. The Son of God and Milton's Church	169

PART THREE: *PARADISE LOST*

Interlude: On *De Doctrina Christiana* and *Paradise Lost*	203
6. The Process of *Paradise Lost*	209
Conclusion: On Milton and Theology	246
Appendix: The Manuscript of *De Doctrina Christiana*	251
Bibliography	275
General Index	289
Index of Biblical Passages	298

List of Figures

0.1. *DDC*, 211, a densely recopied page with further revisions in the margin; it is part of the two folios (pp. 209–16) tipped into I.16   30

1.1. *DDC*, 307a, the Picard version of this page   57

2.1. Detail from *DDC*, 224–25, where a mismatched catchword indicates a folio recopied to align with already existing material   74

2.2. Detail from *DDC*, 222–23: the deleted passage   77

2.3. Detail from *DDC*, 223 showing the marginal insertion of a headword   101

2.4. Detail from *DDC*, 229 showing a marginal insertion   102

4.1. Detail from *DDC*, 71 showing Skinner's marginal insertion   161

6.1. Detail from *DDC*, 204 showing the belated second coming   222

A.1. Highly embellished large hand; detail from *DDC*, 333   253

A.2. Moderately embellished, boldface large hand; detail from *DDC*, 362   253

A.3. Moderately embellished large hand without boldface; detail from *DDC*, 363, 422   254

A.4. Small hand for scriptural citations; detail from *DDC*, 357   254

A.5. Significantly smaller hand for scriptural citations; detail from *DDC*, 198   254

All images are from SP 9/61, The National Archives, Kew, and appear by permission of The National Archives.

Acknowledgments

This book owes its genesis first and foremost to John K. Hale, who started me thinking seriously about *De Doctrina* over meals at the Young Milton conference at Worcester College, Oxford in 2009. Thus began a long period of tutelage, collaboration, and friendship. The book simply wouldn't exist without John. Along with John, Gordon Campbell and Tom Corns have been invaluable interlocutors, especially on matters pertaining to the manuscript.

Two friends and colleagues have nudged me over the years to write this. The first is Ryan Netzley, who insisted, in the early stages, that the project had legs and has faithfully read and commented on drafts. The second is Jeff Miller, whom I also met at Oxford in 2009, and who suggested at the 2016 Renaissance Society of America conference (RSA) that I write a short book about how to read *De Doctrina Christiana*. The pleasure of conversations with Jeff has been a delightful fruit of working on this project.

Colleagues at Brigham Young University have also provided steady encouragement and feedback. Juliana Chapman, Sharon Harris, Brice Peterson, and Brandie Siegfried (late and lamented) have read drafts. Robert Hudson and Charlotte Stanford and arranged for me to deliver portions of the book as talks for the Medieval and Renaissance Studies research group. The Kennedy Center for International Studies provided funds that enabled me to visit the National Archives. Matt Wickman has been an unflagging mentor, and I have enjoyed the friendship and support of Kimberly Johnson, Kristin Matthews, and Miranda Wilcox. Deidre Green, more than anyone else, taught me to read and think like a theologian.

As with most books, this one builds on previous work. The roots of Chapter 2 lie in an article I co-published with John Hale, "The Origins and Development of Milton's Theology in *De Doctrina Christiana*, I. 17–18." *Milton Studies* 54 (2013): 181–206. The book draws briefly on the following articles of mine: in Chapter 2, "*De Doctrina Christiana* and Milton's Theology of Liberation." *Studies in Philology* 111, 2 (2014): 346–74; in Chapter 3, "Milton and the Anonymous Authority of *De Doctrina Christiana*." *Milton Quarterly* 49, 1 (2015): 23–43; and in the Conclusion, "Eve's Church." *Milton Quarterly* 55, 2 (2021): 67–81. I am grateful to the University of North Carolina Press and to

X ACKNOWLEDGMENTS

Wiley Blackwell for permission to reproduce material from these articles. I am indebted to peer reviewers both at these journals and at Oxford University Press for feedback that obliged me to strengthen arguments and sharpen my thinking. Edward Jones at *Milton Quarterly* has been an invaluable shepherd of my work on *De Doctrina Christiana* for many years now. Working with Sandhiya Babu, Henry Clarke, Eleanor Collins, and Alexander Hardie-Forsyth at Oxford University Press has been a pleasure; I am deeply indebted to their skill and professionalism.

Finally, thanks go to my family. Stephen and Nendy Kerr joined with Darryl and Bonnie Lee to purchase me a copy of the Oxford edition as a Christmas gift when I was a graduate student who couldn't afford it on my own. Julia and Elijah have grown up alongside this project, enduring such things as attempts at Duns Scotus jokes with relative good humor. Last but not least, the journey of the past many years has been much the better for having Kristine as a partner on the way.

List of Abbreviations

AL   John Milton, *The Art of Logic*, cited by page number from *Artis Logicae* (London, 1672) using the translation in Walter J. Ong, S. J., and Charles J. Ermatinger, ed. and trans. *A Fuller Course in the Art of Logic Conformed to the Method of Peter Ramus*, Vol. VIII, in Don M. Wolfe, ed. *The Complete Prose Works of John Milton*, 8 vols (New Haven, CT: Yale University Press, 1953–82).

Ames   William Ames, *The Marrow of Divinity* (London, 1642) with page numbers from *Medulla S. S. Theologiae* (London, 1629) in square brackets.

Beza   Theodore Beza's Latin New Testament, *Jesu Christi Domini nostri Novum Testamentum.* ([Geneva], 1598). The edition published in Geneva in 1559 will be cited by date.

Columbia   Frank Allan Patterson, ed., *The Works of John Milton*, 18 vols (New York: Columbia University Press, 1931–38).

DDC   John Milton, *De Doctrina Christiana*, National Archives SP 9/61 by manuscript page number, for easy reference to the Yale and Oxford editions. *DDC* in citations, "MS" in text.

JTB   Latin Bibles with contributions from Franciscus Junius, Immanuel Tremellius, and Theodore Beza, cited by year: London, 1585; Hanau, 1623–24; and Geneva, 1630.

KJV   The 1612 printing of the King James Bible (STC 2219)—the edition Milton used.

MMS   Gordon Campbell, Thomas N. Corns, John K. Hale, and Fiona Tweedie, *Milton and the Manuscript of* De Doctrina Christiana (Oxford: Oxford University Press, 2007).

OED   The *Oxford English Dictionary*, accessed at www.oed.com.

Oxford   The apparatus in John K. Hale and J. Donald Cullington, ed. and trans., *De Doctrina Christiana*, Vol. VIII, in *The Complete Works of John Milton*, ed. Gordon Campbell and Thomas N. Corns (Oxford: Oxford University Press, 2008-).

ODNB   *Oxford Dictionary of National Biography*, accessed at www.oxforddnb.com.

PL   *Paradise Lost*, quoted from the 1674 edition (London; Wing M2144) in consultation with Barbara K. Lewalski, ed., *Paradise Lost* (Oxford: Blackwell, 2007).

PRRD   Richard A. Muller, *Post-Reformation Reformed Dogmatics*, 4 vols, 2nd edn (Grand Rapids, MI: Baker Academic, 2003).

xii LIST OF ABBREVIATIONS

Sumner   Charles Sumner, trans., *A Treatise on Christian Doctrine* (Cambridge, 1825).

Wolleb   Johannes Wolleb, *The Abridgement of Christian Divinitie* (London, 1650) with page numbers from *Compendium Theologiae Christianae* (Cambridge, 1642) in square brackets.

Yale   Maurice Kelley, ed., John Carey, trans., *On Christian Doctrine*, Vol. VI, in Don M. Wolfe, ed., *The Complete Prose Works of John Milton*, 8 vols (New Haven, CT: Yale University Press, 1953–82).

Note on Sources

When I first began work on *De Doctrina Christiana*, attending to textual matters was a messy business. I needed to have the Columbia edition open for the Latin alongside the Yale edition for John Carey's translation, all while collating the textual information in both sources with the appendices of Maurice Kelley's *This Great Argument*. It inspired dreams of a Renaissance book wheel. The arrival of the Oxford edition simplified matters considerably, although Kelley's notes in the Yale edition remain valuable for their insights about theological context. Still, there is no substitute for working directly with the manuscript, and my argument rests, in places, on attention to its materiality: how messy is this page? How densely written is that?

I cite the treatise by manuscript page (e.g., "MS 194"in the text; "*DDC*, 194" in the notes), which allows for ready conference between the Oxford and Yale editions. Except where the Latin is directly at issue, I quote from the Oxford translation, giving the Latin in the notes so that readers might have it readily available as a check both on the translation and on my own arguments. With other Latin works, I likewise quote translations in the body and include the Latin in the notes.

The Oxford edition aims to reproduce the conditions of the manuscript to the extent possible, with boldface representing the large hand often used for definitions and headings, italics for the small hand used for scriptural quotations, and roman for everything else. Because variations in boldface, roman, and italic factor into my arguments about the treatise's evolving form, I retain these in my quotations, but for convenience, I do not usually italicize scriptural quotations from the treatise, neither do I give chapter titles in boldface. Unless noted otherwise, I am quoting from the Latin of the Oxford edition, in consultation with the manuscript itself.

I have retained original spelling in quoting early modern texts, except that (in English) I have regularized i/j, u/v, vv/w, and long s. I have spelled the Latin as it appears on the page.

Introduction

Reading *De Doctrina Christiana*

Why should anyone read *De Doctrina Christiana*? The two primary approaches that have animated scholarship on Milton's Latin theological treatise since its discovery in the nineteenth century—questions about its relationship to *Paradise Lost* bound up with debates about its Miltonic provenance—seem exhausted at present. In 1823, when Robert Lemon discovered the manuscript of *De Doctrina Christiana* in a cupboard at the State Paper Office, Milton's epic had established him as a pillar of English literature, and Charles Sumner's 1825 *editio princeps* accordingly elaborates connections between *De Doctrina Christiana* and *Paradise Lost* in its notes.[1] The hope that the treatise might illuminate the epic's theology soon ran into complications, however, given the tension between the heresies on evidence in the treatise (most notably in its Christology) and the epic's cultural reception as an expression of orthodoxy by readers like Thomas Burgess, Bishop of Salisbury, who used this perceived disconnect to argue against Milton's authorship of the treatise.[2] In this way, *De Doctrina Christiana* almost immediately became caught up in a culture war over Milton's theological legacy.

This culture war raged off and on for nearly two centuries, but it seems largely played out at present. The 2007 publication of *Milton and the Manuscript of De Doctrina Christiana* by a team of eminent scholars settled the authorship question to the satisfaction of most (but not all) Miltonists, and it followed two decades of scholarship that elaborated on Milton's heresies while complicating the theological relationship between the treatise and Milton's late poems to the point that Maurice Kelley's influential assertion that the treatise served as a "gloss" on *Paradise Lost* no longer seems adequate.[3] Consequently, reasons

---

[1] For an account of how the manuscript came to reside in the State Paper Office, see *MMS*, ch. 2.

[2] Thomas Burgess, *Milton Not the Author of the Lately-Discovered Arian Work* De Doctrina Christiana (London, 1829).

[3] Maurice Kelley, *This Great Argument: A Study of Milton's* De Doctrina Christiana *as a Gloss upon* Paradise Lost (Princeton, NJ: Princeton University Press, 1941). Key works include Michael Bauman, *Milton's Arianism* (Munich: P. Lang, 1987); and Stephen B. Dobranski and John P. Rumrich, eds, *Milton and Heresy* (Cambridge: Cambridge University Press, 1998). For a detailed account of the authorship debate, see David V. Urban, "Revisiting the History of the *De Doctrina Christiana* Authorship Debate and the Its Ramifications for Milton Scholarship: A Response to Falcone and Kerr," *Connotations* 29 (2020): 156–88. Urban's insistence on the freedom to read Milton's major poems independent of *De Doctrina Christiana* indicates the exhaustion of which I speak.

Milton's Theological Process. Jason A. Kerr, Oxford University Press. © Jason A. Kerr (2023).
DOI: 10.1093/oso/9780198875086.003.0001

2   MILTON'S THEOLOGICAL PROCESS

for Miltonists (to say nothing of anyone else) to turn to the treatise diminished almost to a vanishing point, notwithstanding the 2012 publication of a landmark new edition.[4]

This book proposes that the conversation around *De Doctrina Christiana* seems exhausted because the question of why anyone should read the treatise rests on unexamined assumptions about how to read it. Turning to the "How?" question shows that the treatise is far from exhausted, not only for Miltonists but also for scholars interested in the relationship between literature and theology more broadly. The "religious turn" in literary studies is hardly a new phenomenon, but the literary dimensions of overtly theological writing—the *logos* in *theology*—remain largely obscured behind a preference for texts like poems or sermons (especially when written by the likes of John Donne) that literary training equips scholars to access. Theological texts—texts devoted to working out doctrine, arguing against people of differing theological views, systematizing dogma for educational purposes, and so on—tend to function as secondary literature, useful tools for understanding literary works, not as literary works in themselves. In general, one reads *De Doctrina Christiana*, if one reads it at all, primarily with an eye to understanding other Miltonic texts.

This book sets out to articulate a methodology for reading *De Doctrina Christiana* as a literary work in its own right. In doing so, it does not attempt to sever *De Doctrina Christiana* from *Paradise Lost*.[5] Rather, it proposes that reading the treatise as literature reframes its relationship to the epic, illuminating points of both continuity and discontinuity between their literary and theological projects. My argument has three basic components: one about theological process and literary form, one about the relationship between logic and rhetoric, and one about the relationship between *De Doctrina Christiana* and *Paradise Lost*.

First, the manuscript of *De Doctrina Christiana* reveals that it is not a fixed repository of theological positions but an artifact of a theological process, a dynamic text with an apophatic dimension in addition to its cataphatic affirmations of various doctrinal points.[6] This process appears in the materiality of the manuscript, which bears abundant traces of both revision and expansion. These material traces correspond to a shift in the treatise's literary form

---

[4] See, however, John K. Hale, *Milton's Scriptural Theology: Confronting De Doctrina Christiana* (Leeds: Arc Humanities Press, 2019).

[5] *Pace* Filippo Falcone, "Milton's Consistency: An Answer to Jason Kerr," *Connotations* 29 (2020): 127; and Urban, "Revisiting the History," 173.

[6] On "apophatic" and "cataphatic," see Pseudo-Dionysius, *Mystical Theology*, ch. 3, in *The Complete Works*, trans. Colm Luibheid (New York: Paulist Press, 1987). Luibheid translates these Greek words as "negative" and "affirmative."

as it moves (in places) farther and farther away from its own stated formal intentions—relying on the methods of Ramist logic, about which more in a moment—and toward new generic territory marked by rhetorical modes of expression at odds with the Ramist project. With this shift in form comes an increasing literariness: as "Logic [. . .] open[s] her contracted palm into a gracefull and ornate Rhetorick," the Latin becomes less workmanlike, more exuberant—but, conversely, it sometimes also becomes more crabbed and cantankerous.[7] Indeed, the bursts of personal style that John K. Hale has examined in the treatise tend to arise in materially later, generically distinctive parts of the treatise, making his work in part an index of the treatise's rhetorical shift.[8] This shift toward rhetoric in terms of both genre and method makes its most prominent appearance in the chapter at the heart of the treatise's doctrinal notoriety, I.5 ("On the Son of God"), where a rhetorical argumentative structure has reduced the remaining traces of Ramist logical structure to vestiges of an earlier approach. Understanding both the treatise itself and the culture war around it thus seems to hinge, in large part, on understanding how and why that chapter came to take the form it does.

Second, as this claim about I.5 suggests, the treatise's shift toward rhetoric indicates a crisis in its theology and methodology. The epistle promises a theological treatise that will drown out its own words with the words of scripture. That the treatise does not altogether deliver on this promise is familiar enough (in the final analysis, scripture only accounts for about half of the total text), but scholarship has not yet taken sufficient account of the ways that this departure represents an unfolding evolution in the treatise's theology.[9] Indeed, the habit of reading the treatise as a relatively fixed repository of doctrinal positions precludes attending to the ways that it changed over time, which I am arguing extend beyond mere accrual of additional information to a reappraisal of its theology concerning the human role in scriptural interpretation upon which the treatise's foundational generic assumptions depend. Whereas the treatise initially set out to let scripture speak for itself, I argue that parts of its final state find Milton ruminating on the conditions under which humans (such as Jesus and Paul, but also himself) speak scripture, drawing on what he calls "the internal [scripture] of the holy spirit, which he, as a result of God's promise, has

---

[7] John Milton, *Of Education* (London, 1644), p. 6.

[8] See *MMS*, ch. 6; Hale, *Milton's Scriptural Theology*. Hale's approach is rhetorical because it centers *ethos* and style; I attend to the argumentative dimensions of early modern rhetoric.

[9] See, however, Jeffrey Alan Miller, "Milton, Zanchius, and the Rhetoric of Belated Reading," *Milton Quarterly* 47, 4 (2013): 199–219; and "Theological Typology, Milton, and the Aftermath of Writing," DPhil thesis, University of Oxford (2012), ch. 4.

4 MILTON'S THEOLOGICAL PROCESS

etched on believers' hearts as by no means to be neglected."[10] This passage represents a shift in Milton's theology that is visible materially in the manuscript, appearing on the first recto of a sheet added later to the chapter on Holy Scripture (I.30).[11] The chapter's three opening folios work through familiar Reformed points about the theology of scripture: establishing the canon, rejecting the need to ground the authority of scripture in anything resembling papal magisterium, insisting on scriptural perspicuity and sufficiency on points necessary to salvation, and so on. The second, later section of the chapter, however, offers a contrast to more staid Reformed theologians by arguing that internal scripture affords a means of correcting and expanding on external scripture that brings the risk of merely human speech powerfully into play. Milton appends to this definition of internal scripture a rare citation of his own treatise, pointing to the chapter on Christian liberty, I.27.[12] Consequently, Milton's ruminations about the potential for humans to speak scripture occur alongside the treatise's developing theology of the church and in tandem with its stridently controversial views on the Son of God. And these theological developments often play out materially in the chronological stratification of the manuscript of *De Doctrina Christiana*.

Understanding the relationship between the treatise's methodological crisis, its complex material state, and its Christology is therefore this book's central project. The contested concept that connects methodology and Christology is authority. As Milton becomes less methodologically confident in the capacity of scripture to ground theology independent of human interpretative activity, the question of human authority in theological matters gains urgency. In keeping with his longstanding interest in human freedom, Milton aims to liberate human theological speech from undue external imposition while also thinking about what it would mean for one human's theological speech to become authoritative, as a kind of scripture, for another—ruminations that are finally rhetorical, in the Ciceronian sense of using invention to seek out probable arguments.[13] Milton's position on the Son helps him to accomplish these desiderata: he frees the Son from what he understands as the ontological necessity entailed by participation in the Trinity, enabling the Son to serve as a model of a human whose liberated, internal-scriptural speech becomes authoritative for others.

---

[10] *DDC*, 394: "et internam sancti spiritus, quam is ex promissione Dei in cordibus credentium minime negligendam exaravit."

[11] See the Appendix, p. 262.

[12] *DDC*, 394: "ut supra cap. 27."

[13] Cicero, *De Inventione*, trans. H. M. Hubbell (Cambridge, MA: Harvard University Press, 1976 [1949]), I.vii.9; quoted below.

Scripture (as "internal") thus becomes the stuff of rhetoric rather than (as "external") the *prima materia* for a logically structured theology.

Milton addresses the problem of authoritative speech by appealing to a theological process rooted in ongoing conversation. This process begins by putting scripture in dialogue with itself, in keeping with Augustine's recommended practice (known as the rule of faith) of reading difficult passages of scripture by reference to "the plainer passages of the scriptures and the authority of the church."[14] This dialogue takes the literary form of the block of scriptural citations, presented cheek by jowl so as to produce doctrinal resonances that emerge from the scriptural language itself. For Augustine, scripture is primarily its own interpreter, and yet keeping interpretation grounded in truth requires the authority of the church, accumulated over time as tradition. To the Protestant Milton, who inveighed vehemently against the role of tradition in deciding theological matters, the second half of Augustine's formulation provoked a methodological challenge, especially as Milton became less and less able to avoid addressing the human role in interpretation (the danger that tradition is merely human rather than divine).[15]

Faced with the inadequacy of putting scripture in dialogue with itself, Milton was obliged to work out an alternative rule of faith that retains the dialogue of scripture with itself but adds a further layer of dialogue between scripture and the believer's own interpretative faculties. Such dialogue takes literary form as commentary and explication. Because this second layer of dialogue introduces human fallibility to the equation, a third, ecclesial layer becomes necessary. I call this layer "ecclesial" and not "ecclesiastical" because it construes the church as the vehicle for a Spirit-driven conversation among believers driven by a collective desire for truth rather than as a formal body structured by ecclesiastical authority.[16] For Milton, the "authority of the church" touted by Augustine must not refer to anything resembling the Roman *magisterium*, but rather to the collective Spirit-driven process of believers' testing each other's words until the results yield human speech that, like that of the Son of God, acquires the

---

[14] Augustine, *De Doctrina Christiana*, trans. R. P. H. Green (Oxford: Oxford University Press, 1995), III.ii.2. Augustine calls this principle the "rule of faith [*regula fidei*]," but I join with subsequent interpreters in using the phrase *analogia fidei*, which has roots in the Vulgate text of Romans 12:6. Latin: "Cum ergo adhibita intentio incertum esse perviderit quomodo distinguendum aut quomodo pronuntiandum sit, consulat regulam fidei, quam de scripturarum planioribus locis et ecclesiae auctoritate percepit."

[15] Muller argues that, at least initially, Protestants were less interested in jettisoning tradition than in restoring the correct tradition on the basis of scripture. *PRRD*, I.34. For more on Protestant—including English—use of the *analogia fidei*, see *PRRD*, II.493–97. In Milton studies, see Dayton Haskin, *Milton's Burden of Interpretation* (Philadelphia, PA: University of Pennsylvania Press, 1994).

[16] See also Stephen R. Honeygosky, *Milton's House of God: The Invisible and Visible Church* (Columbia, SC: University of Missouri Press, 1993), p. 31.

6   MILTON'S THEOLOGICAL PROCESS

force of scripture for all without any coercion or imposition. The literary form in which the treatise addresses this ecclesial conversation involves a rhetorical turn toward outright argumentation, with I.5 as by far the most developed instance.

This theological process, more than any given point of doctrine, informs the connections between *De Doctrina Christiana* and *Paradise Lost*. The treatise's shifts in style, form, and ultimately theology mean that it had become something different at the time Milton seems to have stopped working on it (around the Restoration, in 1660) than it was when he started (the dating here is less certain, but perhaps as early as the mid-1640s).[17] The strongest evidence for dating the manuscript lies in the hand of its primary amanuensis, Jeremie Picard, who did other scribal work for Milton in the years between 1658 and 1660.[18] Moreover, because the manuscript shows Picard's involvement in recopying revised and expanded portions of the treatise that were then added into his own already-existing fair copy, it seems plausible to conjecture that much of the shift I have been describing (and will describe in much greater detail) occurred during these years at the end of the 1650s—a time period that coincides with early work on *Paradise Lost* (completed 1665; first edition 1667).

Although this temporal overlap could be used to support Kelley's reading of the treatise as a gloss on the epic, as the third part of my argument, I propose a different view, grounded in the complex interaction between two unfolding literary trajectories.[19] The one moves from the classical epic tradition toward biblical and theological concerns, while the other begins in the world of biblical theology and moves toward a deeper awareness of the place that literary imagination and expression has in that world. If Milton abandoned work on *De Doctrina Christiana* at the Restoration as any hope of being able to publish it all but vanished, I suggest that he also abandoned it because the increasing literariness making its way into the manuscript meant that the genre as he had initially conceived it was becoming less and less apt for the work he needed it to do.[20] In my view, I.5 shows the genre channeling Milton's literary energies in a not particularly productive way, akin to his misguided attacks on Alexander

---

[17] Maurice Kelley dates at least one manuscript revision as late as 1669; "On the State of Milton's *De Doctrina Christiana*," *Modern Language Notes*, 27, 2 (1989): 46. He finds the marginal insertion on MS 372 similar to the document, dated 26 April 1669, acknowledging the receipt of five additional pounds from Samuel Simmons for the publication of *Paradise Lost*. Dissimilar handling of the initial "f" renders the identification implausible, however. An image of the receipt appears in Harris Francis Fletcher, ed., *Milton's Poetical Work: Facsimile Edition* (Urbana, IL: University of Illinois Press, 1943–48), II.210.

[18] *MMS*, 31–33.

[19] Kelley, *This Great Argument*, 72.

[20] On the case for Milton's abandoning *De Doctrina Christiana* at the Restoration, see Gordon Campbell and Thomas N. Corns, "*De Doctrina Christiana*: An England That Might Have Been," in *The Oxford Handbook of Milton*, ed. Nicholas McDowell and Nigel Smith (Oxford: Oxford University Press, 2009), pp. 426–27.

More in *Pro Se Defensio* (1655).[21] Perhaps, then, the explicitly literary project at which he was simultaneously laboring (*Paradise Lost*) afforded an improvisational opportunity to take up his literary-theological project in a new form—a chance to imagine the Son of God in less crabbed, less polemical terms. From this perspective, the continuities between *De Doctrina Christiana* and *Paradise Lost* have less to do with doctrinal adherence (although I remain persuaded that the epic's treatment of the Son is broadly compatible with the treatise's) than with a particular approach to the imaginative, literary potentialities in the project of scriptural interpretation, for which the Son in both works stands as the supreme model.

If the treatise struggled to find an apt formal expression for human speech that aspired to the status of scripture, the epic allows Milton greater freedom to digress from the language of external scripture, especially given the ways that epic per se combines narrative with generically normative occasions for digression and topical rumination. I will argue that Milton uses one such set of ruminations—Raphael's pronouncements on the nature of matter—to articulate on a cosmic scale the connection between Christology and the ecclesial process whereby human speech might find its way toward a more hallowed state.[22] Attending closely to the treatise's unfolding methodological wrangling with the relationship between scripture and theology thus affords a framework for thinking about how *Paradise Lost* develops the remarkably spare biblical stories of the Fall, the War in Heaven, and so on into what its proem describes as "this great Argument" (*PL* I.24). Just as Maurice Kelley invoked these words to argue for reading *De Doctrina Christiana* as a "gloss upon *Paradise Lost*," I invoke them now as I argue for a new way of reading the connections between the treatise and the epic, one oriented not by attention to doctrinal positions but to an unfolding approach to theological process that found fruition in Milton's "adventrous song" (*PL*, I.13).

Ways of Reading *De Doctrina Christiana*

The established ways of reading *De Doctrina Christiana* began, as I have suggested, immediately after its discovery, with the central question being whether

---

[21] See Gordon Campbell and Thomas N. Corns, *John Milton: Life, Work, and Thought* (Oxford: Oxford University Press, 2007), pp. 260–65. Milton continued to attack More in print even after being credibly informed that More was not the author of the treatise against which Milton was defending himself.

[22] See Hideyuki Shitaka, "Degeneration and Regeneration of Man's Language in *Paradise Lost*," *Studies in English Literature [Japan]* 62, 1 (1985): 21–24.

8 MILTON'S THEOLOGICAL PROCESS

it, in fact, shares a common theology with *Paradise Lost*. The treatise's first editor and translator, Charles Sumner, inaugurated this debate by making explicit links to the epic in the notes of his edition. Bishop Burgess disagreed, arguing that the doctrinal disparities between the two works meant that Milton could not have written *De Doctrina Christiana*. This debate hinges, in Burgess's words, on whether "the religious principles of the Work be wholly at variance with the principles professed and maintained by Milton in his youth, his middle age and his old age."[23] Although Sumner, Burgess, and their various heirs in the debate come to different conclusions, both share a way of reading *De Doctrina Christiana* that focuses on its "religious principles," understanding the treatise's theology as primarily a matter of its propositional content and the ways that its content aligns its author with various theological parties, orthodox or heretical.

By focusing on the treatise's content, however, always with an eye either to interpreting *Paradise Lost* or determining Milton's religious allegiances, this common way of reading invites neglect of the ways that literary form bears on the theology of *De Doctrina Christiana*, the ways that the treatise testily pitches itself against the genre of its nearest interlocutors (theological treatises by Johan Wolleb and William Ames), and eventually against its own stated generic intentions. This book aims to highlight the importance of literary form to understanding the treatise's theological project, arguing for a way of reading that locates the treatise's theology in the interplay of content and form, that is, in its use of literary devices and generic conventions to structure meaning. Given the treatise's participation in the broad genre of "theological treatise," questions of form come bound together with questions of methodology. By "methodology," I refer most obviously to the ways that *De Doctrina Christiana* structures its treatment of theological topics using the dialectical logic developed in the sixteenth century by Pierre de la Ramée (i.e., Petrus Ramus), although Milton's relationship with Ramism is also testy.[24] In addition, I use "methodology" to name the treatise's most fundamental operation: the derivation of doctrinal content from scripture. Attention to methodology in this latter sense involves three interconnected reading practices. First, it means learning how to read the scriptural citations that comprise almost half of *De Doctrina Christiana* instead of focusing primarily on "Milton's own words" and treating the scriptural citations either as supporting evidence or prooftexts, as when William B. Hunter writes that Milton's "main running text [. . .] reads

---

[23] Burgess, *Milton Not the Author*, 7–8.
[24] See the discussion below and in Chapter 1.

INTRODUCTION 9

meaningfully without any interruption if [the proof texts] are omitted."[25] Second, it means reading Milton's treatise alongside its primary interlocutors—Wolleb and Ames—not merely in terms of what positions they take but in terms of how they use scripture to substantiate their views and, indeed, how they understand the relationship between scripture and the theological views they voice. Finally, it means attending carefully to the theological significance of the revisions that appear on many pages of the manuscript and of the larger processes of revision that drive the manuscript's physical expansion over time.

Understanding the theological process that animates *De Doctrina Christiana* depends on developing new ways of reading that challenge the assumptions shared by Sumner and Burgess alike. These assumptions have continued to shape scholarly approaches to the treatise until the present day, but they owe to the nineteenth-century context of the treatise's discovery. One significant context—the nineteenth-century status of *Paradise Lost* as a devotional text of sorts for many readers—meant that the appearance of *De Doctrina Christiana* caused what Francis J. Mineka's study of its immediate reception calls a "shock to English religious sensibilities" and thus provoked a debate about Milton's relative orthodoxy and therefore also about his authorship of the treatise.[26] A second, more subtle context involves the emergence of *De Doctrina Christiana* after the eighteenth-century eclipse of Protestant scholastic theology as Milton practiced it, an eclipse whose most relevant manifestation, for present purposes, has to do with the function of scripture in theological work and the relationship between scripture and theological propositions. Together, these ways of reading have created impediments to understanding *De Doctrina Christiana* on its own terms.

Debates about Milton's relative orthodoxy are inevitably also about what constitutes the proper external standard for assessing orthodoxy. These debates

---

[25] William B. Hunter, Jr, "The Theological Context of Milton's *Christian Doctrine*," in *Achievements of the Left Hand: Essays on the Prose of John Milton*, ed. Michael Lieb and John T. Shawcross (Amherst, MA: University of Massachusetts Press, 1971), 270. Hunter, however, later attends insightfully to Milton's use of scripture. Further instances abound. David Masson described the treatise as "a maze of expository rivulets trickling among banks of Biblical quotations," leading some subsequent scholars to attempt to isolate the rivulets by cutting away the banks; *The Life of John Milton and History of His Time* (London: Macmillan, 1859–80), VI.822. Albert J. Th. Eisenring, for instance, omits scriptural references from his lengthy *précis* of the treatise because "Milton intended them to be merely illustrations of his speculations," holding that "they are in no way essential, as regards the development of his thought and arguments"; *Milton's De Doctrina Christiana: An Historical Introduction and Critical Analysis* (Fribourg: Society of St Paul, 1946), p. 35. Kelley argues for parallels between *De Doctrina Christiana* and *Paradise Lost* based on summaries of the treatise's chapters, and his quotations generally omit scriptural references to focus on statements of doctrinal positions; *This Great Argument*, chs 4–7.

[26] Francis E. Mineka, "The Critical Reception of Milton's *De Doctrina Christiana*," *Studies in English* 23 (1943): 116.

10 MILTON'S THEOLOGICAL PROCESS

are more about the measuring stick, in other words, than they are about Milton, although they speak to the deep and occasionally conflicting commitments that people have both to their own beliefs and to Milton. Milton himself participated in these debates about the measuring stick; as Tobias Gregory argues, for instance, he "redefined heresy so that the term would not apply to him."[27] Sometimes, the measuring stick is in plain sight, as with readers like the Unitarian William Ellery Channing, who were happy to find that the great man was their kind of heretic (i.e., their kind of orthodox): "We must, however, pause a moment to thank God that he has raised up this illustrious advocate of the long obscured doctrine of the Divine Unity."[28] Similarly, nineteenth-century Latter-day Saints (Mormons) like Orson Pratt found the treatise amenable to their own heterodox theological speculations.[29] Mineka highlights the limits to this approach, however, in this comment on an early Dissenting review of *De Doctrina Christiana*:

> The reviewer cannot resist a thrust at the Baptists, who might be (and were) rejoicing to find Milton on their side with regard to their most characteristic doctrine: the Baptists' triumph must be moderated by the fact that Milton's "extreme heterodoxy in other particulars must forever annihilate him as a theological authority."[30]

Precisely because the measuring stick is external to Milton, the only doctrinal marriage beds it can be used to build are Procrustean: either part of the believer must go or part of Milton.

In the spirit of "mere Christianity" that he adopted from Richard Baxter, C. S. Lewis tries the latter tack. Lewis accepts *De Doctrina Christiana* as Milton's and accepts it as heretical. He does not, however, accept that these facts oblige readers to find heresy in *Paradise Lost*, arguing that readers of the epic "are not only entitled but obliged to rule out any effects which his words can produce only by the aid of the *De Doctrina* or the *Zohar*, for the poem is not addressed to students of either." Rather, it "is overwhelmingly Christian. Except for a few isolated passages it is not even specifically Protestant or Puritan. It gives the

---

[27] Tobias Gregory, "How Milton Defined Heresy and Why," *Religion & Literature* 45, 1 (2013): 156, disagreeing with Janel Mueller, "Milton on Heresy," in Dobranski and Rumrich, *Milton and Heresy*, pp. 21–38.

[28] William Ellery Channing, *On the Character and Writings of John Milton* (Boston, MA, 1826), p. 34.

[29] John Rogers, "Orson Pratt, Parley Pratt, and the Miltonic Origins of Mormon Materialism," in *Milton, Materialism, and Embodiment: "One First Matter All,"* ed. Kevin J. Donovan and Thomas Festa (Pittsburgh, PA: Duquesne University Press, 2017), pp. 157–88.

[30] Mineka, "Critical Reception," 119.

great central tradition." This is not to claim Milton for any particular denomination but to claim him for Christianity as a whole—a project that, somewhat like Baxter's, involves focusing on doctrinal fundamentals and downplaying heresy.[31]

Milton is sympathetic to a form of "mere Christianity," but, unlike Baxter's (or Lewis's), his approach focuses on method rather than doctrine, in keeping with John Coffey's observation that "Milton's definition of heresy [...] was *procedural* rather than *substantive*. Heresy was about theological *method* rather than theological *content*."[32] Milton explains this emphasis on method over doctrine in *Of True Religion* (1673): "Heresie is in the Will and choice profestly against Scripture; error is against the Will, in misunderstanding the Scripture after all sincere efforts to understand it rightly: Hence it was said well by one of the Ancients, *Err I may, but a Heretick I will not be*." On this basis, Milton responds to his hypothetical Catholic opponent's question "Are Lutherans, Calvinists, Anabaptists, Socinians, Arminians, no Hereticks?" with "[A]ll these may have some errors, but are no Hereticks." Commitment to process, not doctrinal agreement, becomes the basis of a broad unity among Protestants, who err in spite of their good faith:

> It is a humane frailty to err, and no man is infallible here on earth. But so long as all these profess to set the Word of God only before them as the Rule of faith and obedience; and use all diligence and sincerity of heart, by reading, by learning, by study, by prayer for Illumination of the holy Spirit, to understand the Rule and obey it, they have done what man can do: God will assuredly pardon them.[33]

Burgess and others have read these passages as Milton's late-in-life rejection of heresies attributed to him on the basis of the treatise, but for Milton, the measuring stick for determining orthodoxy or heresy is not a given party platform of doctrinal positions but rather commitment to the process of using the "Word of God only" as the rule of faith.[34] For Thomas N. Corns,

---

[31] C. S. Lewis, *A Preface to* Paradise Lost (Oxford: Oxford University Press, 1960 [1942]), pp. 91–92, responding to Denis Saurat, *Milton: Man and Thinker* (New York: Dial Press, 1925). In 1941–44, Lewis was delivering the radio addresses that would become *Mere Christianity*.

[32] John Coffey, "A Ticklish Business: Defining Heresy and Orthodoxy in the Puritan Revolution," in *Heresy, Literature and Politics in Early Modern English Culture*, ed. David Loewenstein and John Marshall (Cambridge: Cambridge University Press, 2006), pp. 130–31. Emphasis in original. Compare John P. Rumrich, *Matter of Glory: A New Preface to* Paradise Lost (Pittsburgh, PA: University of Pittsburgh Press, 1987), pp. 7–10.

[33] John Milton, *Of True Religion* (London, 1673), p. 6.

[34] Burgess, *Milton Not the Author*, 15; compare Filippo Falcone, "Irreconcilable (Dis)Continuity: *De Doctrina Christiana* and Milton," *Connotations* 27 (2018): 98–100. Milton, however, declines to characterize Arians and Socinians as heretics, given that "they affirm to believe the Father, Son, and Holy

12 MILTON'S THEOLOGICAL PROCESS

this passage signals that "Milton's ultimate vision for the Church of England was of a wide Protestant faith community in which people may worship together while subscribing—without contention—to a wide range of doctrinal positions, united by their commitment to the foundation of religious belief on the revealed word of God."[35] Milton expresses a willingness to countenance some doctrinal disagreement without recourse to the concept of heresy, which arises only when one rejects scripture as the rule of faith.

The second half of the twentieth century, nevertheless, saw the most concerted attempts yet to claim Milton for heresy or orthodoxy per se. These efforts begin with the most important work of scholarship on De Doctrina Christiana in the twentieth century, Maurice Kelley's 1941 This Great Argument: De Doctrina Christiana as a Gloss upon Paradise Lost. As his title suggests, Kelley argues that the epic exhibits many of the treatise's heresies, notably its Christology. Kelley's work provoked responses that went beyond Lewis's approach by undertaking to argue that both De Doctrina Christiana and Paradise Lost sit within the pale of orthodoxy, an argument that depends on acknowledging the fluidity of that category in ways that allow certain minority views to coexist with more mainstream ideas. C. A. Patrides offered a rejoinder to Kelley in his 1966 Milton and the Christian Tradition, where the "tradition" in question is both patristic and Protestant.[36] Patrides subsequently joined with William B. Hunter and J. H. Adamson to produce Bright Essence (1970), which argues that the treatise's Christology proves compatible with strains of orthodoxy prevailing before the Council of Nicaea in 325 CE.[37]

All these views depended on accepting De Doctrina Christiana as Milton's until Burgess's challenge to Milton's authorship of the treatise resurfaced in the 1990s in the work of erstwhile Bright Essence collaborator William B. Hunter. A likely motivating factor in Hunter's transition from viewing the treatise as expressive of ante-Nicene orthodoxy to viewing it as a heretical document that needed to be jettisoned from the Miltonic canon was the 1987 publication of

---

Ghost, according to Scripture," rejecting Trinitarian tenets as "Scholastic notions, not to be found in Scripture"; Of True Religion, 7. Whatever Milton's view of Arianism, he defends its place in the broad Protestant church, grounded on scripture. He expresses the same view in the epistle to De Doctrina Christiana: "after the Evangelical books had finally been put together in writing, nothing can rightly be termed heresy except what conflicts with them [conscriptis demum libris evangelicis, pari ratione nihil nisi quod iis repugnat, posse iure nominari haeresin]," DDC, 4, pace William B. Hunter, Jr, Visitation Unimplor'd: Milton and the Authorship of De Doctrina Christiana (Pittsburgh, PA: Duquesne University Press, 1998), pp. 94–96.

[35] Thomas N. Corns, "Milton's Churches," in The Church and Literature, ed. Peter Clarke and Charlotte Methuen (Woodbridge: Boydell, 2012), pp. 200–201.

[36] C. A. Patrides, Milton and the Christian Tradition (Oxford: Clarendon Press, 1966), p. 15.

[37] William B. Hunter, Jr, C. A. Patrides, and J. H. Adamson, Bright Essence (Salt Lake City: University of Utah Press, 1971).

INTRODUCTION   13

Michael Bauman's *Milton's Arianism*, which undertook a thorough demolition of *Bright Essence*. Hunter's challenge resulted in a quarter-century of scrutiny directed at *De Doctrina Christiana*. Some of this scholarship brought renewed attention to Milton's heresies, finding that *Paradise Lost* did include heretical views but not always in the ways expressed in *De Doctrina Christiana*, complicating Kelley's earlier approach of reading the treatise as a gloss on the epic. Other scholarship attended to the manuscript itself, culminating in the 2007 publication of *Milton and the Manuscript of* De Doctrina Christiana, which affirmed Milton's authorship while also contextualizing his heretical views on several doctrinal points. That book acted as a preface of sorts to the 2012 Oxford edition of the treatise, in which its Latin text appeared freshly edited for the first time since Sumner in the nineteenth century.[38]

At present, the debates about Milton's heresy or orthodoxy, along with their attendant ways of reading, have lost most of their animating energy. Hunter's argument found (and still finds) its defenders, but most Milton scholars now accept Milton's authorship of *De Doctrina Christiana*.[39] Most scholars also accept that *Paradise Lost* expresses heretical views, if not always in the same ways that *De Doctrina Christiana* does. Recent work by David Urban and others has begun to approach the question of Milton's heresy with greater nuance, showing the interdependence of heretical and orthodox views in his theology.[40] I am sympathetic to this approach, which tries to counter the Procrustean quality of most attempts to claim Milton for either side, in part by trying to keep the categories themselves carefully historicized. If we must invoke the concepts of orthodoxy and heresy (as this book will from time to time), this is the way to do it.

Even so, appeals to concepts of orthodoxy invite a subtle way of misreading Milton's seventeenth-century treatise that involve changes in the theology of scripture in the intervening century and a half. This is a big topic so, in the

---

[38] The 1853 Bohn edition and the 1934 Columbia edition both rely on Sumner's text.

[39] Burgess's suggestion of the German Socinian Jeremias Felbinger as an alternative candidate for the authorship of *De Doctrina Christiana* has recently resurfaced; see James M. Clawson and Hugh F. Wilson, "*De Doctrina Christiana* and Milton's Canonical Works: Revisiting the Authorship Question," *Renaissance and Reformation* 44, 3 (2021): 151–98; compare Burgess, *Milton Not the Author*, 30–32, 56–58. Unlike Burgess, Clawson and Wilson rest their case on stylometric analysis. Stylometry, however, remains a probabilistic tool that needs to be complemented with substantive reading of the texts in question. In terms of substantive theological views, Felbinger is not an especially promising candidate for the authorship of *De Doctrina Christiana*. The views on divorce in his attested works do not, for instance, comport with those in *De Doctrina Christiana*; see *Politicae Christianae Compendium* (Bratislava, 1648), p. 5. More critically, neither does his interpretation of Psalm 2, according to which Christ is appointed Son of God by his resurrection from the dead ["destinatur Filius DEI per resurrectionem à mortuis"]; *Demonstrationes Christianae* (N.p., 1653), 30. Contrast the discussion of Psalm 2 in Chapter 4.

[40] See e.g., David V. Urban, "John Milton, Paradox, and the Atonement: Heresy, Orthodoxy, and the Son's Whole-Life Obedience," *Studies in Philology* 112, 4 (2015): 817–36.

14 MILTON'S THEOLOGICAL PROCESS

interest of brevity, I will attempt to describe succinctly what happened to the genre of the Protestant scholastic theological treatise between 1660 and 1823, drawing on Richard A. Muller's magisterial *Post-Reformation Reformed Dogmatics*.[41] Given the centrality of scripture to Milton's enterprise, I want to focus on the changing role it played in relation to the theological tenets that such treatises express, with two points of emphasis. The first is convention. The practice of gathering scriptural citations by topic did not begin with the Reformation, but the Reformation tenet of *sola scriptura* raised it to new prominence, with Philipp Melanchthon's 1521 *Loci Communes* standing as an important early example.[42] This practice readily lends itself, however, to the development of lists that become more or less conventional. Even good-faith attempts (like Milton's) to do the work for oneself can hardly escape the force of this convention, especially if one grew up under the influence of preaching and teaching shaped by it. Indeed, many of the scripture blocks in *De Doctrina Christiana* are similar, or even identical (at least in the sense of which texts they include), to the texts assembled under the same topic in other treatises.

As with most conventions, this one remained fluid around the edges, but as its core hardened, the sense that scripture serves as the cognitive foundation of theology (*principium cognoscendi theologiae*) gradually became somewhat less true in practice than it still was in theory. The assumption remained that the stated doctrine derived from the cited scriptural passages, but if the collection of passages had become mostly conventional, the interest of both readers and writers rather naturally turned to the doctrinal statements instead. This shift produced a way of reading the scriptural passages as "proof-texts [*dicta probantia*]", or as the evidence presented in support of the doctrinal conclusions, even though, in theory, the causal chain still ran in the other direction, from scripture to doctrine. This shift coincided with the development of religious rationalism beginning in the later seventeenth century and swelling in the eighteenth, a development that likewise tended toward understanding theological claims as logical propositions, at some expense to viewing them as the products of exegesis.

These ways of reading have informed approaches to *De Doctrina Christiana* since Sumner, who, in preparing his edition, sought "to expedite the translation by taking over from the English of the King James Bible all of the biblical citations."[43] This decision highlights an assumption that the treatise's primary interest lies in Milton's own words, which is only natural from most readers'

---

[41] The following condenses the argument in *PRRD*, II.

[42] Philipp Melanchthon, *Loci Communes Rerum Theologicarum seu Hypotyposes Theologicae* (Basil, 1521).

[43] Oxford, xxx.

perspectives, but which takes for granted one historically contingent way of understanding the relationship between scripture and theology—a relationship that I will be arguing changed significantly for Milton in the course of his work on the treatise.

The debates about Milton's orthodoxy, at least in their post-1823 manifestations, likewise take that relationship for granted, enabling a focus on doctrinal results that can be checked against whichever measuring stick instead of a focus on the exegetical and other processes that produced them. The kind of response that would have involved meeting Milton on the shared ground of scripture and undertaking on that basis to persuade him of his error had become unthinkable by 1823, in part because *De Doctrina Christiana* appeared on the scene as an artifact rather than as part of a living conversation but also because the theological landscape had shifted in the meantime: Milton simply does not occupy the same theological world as, say, Schleiermacher. This book does not undertake that kind of response to *De Doctrina Christiana*, but it takes as fundamental the need to develop ways of reading Milton's treatise that understand it as anticipating such a response, with scripture at the center.[44]

How to Read *De Doctrina Christiana*

This book aims, above all, to provide readers with a method for approaching *De Doctrina Christiana* as a literary work with attention to the discursive contexts that informed its production. That project requires sustained attention to the theological currents driving its shifting form, but here, it will be worth pulling back from the arboreal tangles of the chapters to get a view of the methodological forest, of what it might mean in practice to read *De Doctrina Christiana*. In the interest of both brevity and clarity, I leave illustrative examples to the chapters, aiming here for a descriptive overview.

Genre

A scholarly emphasis on reading theological texts for doctrinal content often papers over differences in genre, rhetorical purpose, or intended audience, resulting in a proliferation of -isms (Calvinism, Arminianism, Amyraldianism, etc.) understood as representing different theological parties, complete with

---

[44] For one such response, see Eisenring, who, as a professed Roman Catholic, weighs *De Doctrina Christiana* against the orthodoxies of Catholicism, Anglicanism, and Calvinism and finds that Milton is finally "no longer on the Christian side." *Milton's* De Doctrina Christiana, 154.

16 MILTON'S THEOLOGICAL PROCESS

platforms and talking points such as "hypothetical universalism," "infralapsarianism," etc. Parsing such doctrinal differences has its value, and yet the texts in which those doctrines find expression are not reducible to mere vehicles for propositional content, simultaneously too dense and too transparent to merit careful reading in literary terms.[45] Anyone who has read through Calvin's *Institutes* knows that it would be a far shorter book if articulating his doctrinal views were its only aim. And what are the implications of his having chosen to present his views in a different literary form than that of Philipp Melanchthon's already influential *Loci Communes?* Similarly, Thomas Aquinas's *Summa Theologiae* is not simply a compendium of theological views, useful for dipping into when topical questions arise; rather, as Mark D. Jordan writes, "the achievement of the *Summa* lies not so much in its particular arguments or doctrines as in its arrangement of arguments and doctrines. Its mastery lies in its structure."[46] Jordan draws attention to the ways that Aquinas's great work differs from other contemporary theological texts in *literary genre*, a difference that reading for doctrinal content alone tends to leave unremarked and perhaps even unnoticed.

The same holds for *De Doctrina Christiana*. Balachandra Rajan used the idea that *Paradise Lost* "is an epic poem and not a systematic theology" to argue that critics who "reduce to a theological study the work which Milton has shaped for us as 'an invariable planet of joy and felicity'" commit an injustice against poetry.[47] As a descriptor of genre, though, "theology" or even "theological treatise" operates on a similar level of precision as "poem": both meaningfully mark off some kinds of texts from others while also admitting of considerable internal diversity.[48] The situation calls for finer distinctions like those that enable us to mark the difference between an epic and a sonnet and, finer still, to differentiate between Italian, English, and Spenserian sonnets by recourse to rhyme scheme, logical structure, placement of the volta, and so on.

In genre, *De Doctrina Christiana* is a systematic theology structured (at least on the level of organization) according to Ramist logic. The systematic genre of *De Doctrina Christiana* usefully distinguishes it from other theological genres such as biblical commentary (see Calvin's voluminous output), practical

---

[45] See Daniel Shore, *Milton and the Art of Rhetoric* (Cambridge: Cambridge University Press, 2012), p. 10.

[46] Thomas Aquinas, *On Faith*, ed. Mark D. Jordan (Notre Dame, IN: Notre Dame University Press, 1990), p. 5.

[47] Balachandra Rajan, Paradise Lost & *The Seventeenth Century Reader* (London: Chatto & Windus, 1962), pp. 25–26.

[48] On the capaciousness of "treatise" in early modern England, even excluding technical Latin works, see Ian Green, *Print and Protestantism in Early Modern England* (Oxford: Oxford University Press, 2000), pp. 216–25.

theology (like Richard Baxter's 1673 *Christian Directory*), and also, as William Poole points out, polemical works like Milton's lost *Index Theologicus*.[49] It is more than a theological commonplace book of scriptural passages in that it aims not merely to gather them but to organize them into a logical doctrinal structure. To this end, Milton joins many post-Reformation theologians in adopting the logical system of the sixteenth-century French educational reformer Petrus Ramus for his systematic theology.[50] Ramus proposed a method for organizing knowledge dialectically by subdividing topics into their constituent parts (and then recursively subdividing the subdivisions), and his method proved wildly popular in the sixteenth and seventeenth centuries.[51] Milton's connection to Ramism appears explicitly in his *Art of Logic* (1672), whose full title adverts to its origins as a redaction of Ramus's *Dialectic* (last revised in 1572).[52] Milton's Ramism can, however, be overstated: as P. Albert Duhamel argued, Milton is more committed to the syllogism than Ramus was, and Katrin Ettenhuber has recently argued that the logic curriculum at Christ's College, Cambridge in Milton's time was no longer as stridently Ramist as it had been, with preference given instead to the logic manuals of Bartolomaeus Keckermann, which moderated some of Ramus's antipathy toward Aristotelian logic.[53] Nevertheless, the young Milton's distaste for Ramus in this period is evident, for instance, in his snide reference to "that logician of Paris [*Parisiensis ille dialecticus*]" in a 1627 letter to Thomas Young.[54]

In terms of the genre of *De Doctrina Christiana*, the central question turns on the relationship between logic and rhetoric. Ramus sought to divorce the two arts, giving priority to logic while effectively reducing rhetoric to

---

[49] *MMS*, 92; William Poole, ed., Manuscript Writings, Vol. XI, in *The Complete Works of John Milton* (Oxford: Oxford University Press, 2019), pp. 86–87.

[50] See e.g., *MMS*, 92 and Oxford, lv–lxii.

[51] See Walter J. Ong, S. J., *Ramus, Method, and the Decay of Dialogue* (Cambridge, MA: Harvard University Press, 1958).

[52] The full title is Joannis Miltoni Angli, *Artis logicae plenior institutio, ad Petri Rami methodum concinnata adjecta est Praxis annalytica & Petri Rami vita: libris duobus* (London, 1672).

[53] P. Albert Duhamel, "Milton's Alleged Ramism," *Publications of the Modern Language Association of America* 67, 7 (1952): 1044; Katrin Ettenhuber, "Milton's Logic: The Early Years," *The Seventeenth Century* 36, 2 (2021): 189 and *passim*. On Keckermann's influence, see Emma Annette Wilson, "The Classical Sceptical Origins of John Milton's Logic Terms," *Notes and Queries* 60, 1 (2013): 61–63. Mordechai Feingold argues that Ramism failed to make significant inroads into English education: "English Ramism: A Reinterpretation," in *The Influence of Petrus Ramus: Studies in Sixteenth and Seventeenth Century Philosophy and Sciences*, ed. Mordechai Feingold, Joseph S. Freedman, and Wolfgang Rother (Basel: Schwabe, 2001), pp. 127–28 and *passim*.

[54] Estelle Haan, ed., *John Milton*: Epistolarum Familiarum Liber Unus *and Uncollected Letters* (Leuven: Leuven University Press, 2019), pp. 40–41. On Milton's Cambridge-period hostility toward Ramus, see N. K. Sugimura, *"Matter of Glorious Trial": Spiritual and Material Substance in Paradise Lost* (New Haven, CT: Yale University Press, 2009), pp. 29–39.

18 MILTON'S THEOLOGICAL PROCESS

ornamentation.[55] Milton's *Art of Logic* does likewise: "But of all the arts the first and most general is logic, next grammar, and finally rhetoric, since reason can be used, and even used extensively, without speech, but speech cannot be used at all without logic."[56] *De Doctrina Christiana* privileges Ramist logic on the level of organization in the way that it proceeds from general topics to smaller ones via a process of subdivision that favors bifurcation. So, the topic of the book as a whole—Christian doctrine—divides into Book I (on faith) and Book II (on worship and charity). Book I derives faith from discussions of God's nature (I.2) and God's efficiency, the latter divided into internal (I.3–4) and external (I.5–33), and so on—easily represented by a large, bifurcating chart that captures the organization of the entire work.[57] The chapters thus organized on the chart themselves subdivide further as they take up their own subjects. Organization is, indeed, the aim: Ramus divided logic into two topics, invention and disposition, the former the art of finding arguments and the latter the art of arranging them. Milton's *Art of Logic* follows suit.[58]

If *De Doctrina Christiana* takes a Ramist approach to organizing its arguments (*dispositio*), what about finding them (*inventio*)?[59] Here, the case becomes more complex, in part because invention belongs to rhetoric as well as to logic. In logic, invention means finding the middle term that establishes the connection between two other syllogistic terms on a sound basis. The goal, as Milton puts it in *The Art of Logic*, is definition, which "occurs when it is explained what a thing is."[60] Milton explains the relationship between definition, distribution (the practical effect of *dispositio*), and invention:

> In teaching the arts definition is prior in use to distribution (for any given thing is defined before it is distributed), but by nature and in order of invention it

---

[55] Ong, *Ramus*, ch. 12; for Ramus, rhetoric is about "ornamenting orations [*Rhetorica circa orationis ornatu*[m]]": *Institutionum Dialecticarum Libri Tres* (Lyon, 1553), p. 61. Contrast Thomas Wilson: "Three thynges are required of an Orator. To teache. To delight. And to perswade": *The Arte of Rhetorique* (London, 1553), fol. 1v.

[56] *AL*, fol. A8v: "Omnium autem prima ac generalissima, Logica est; dein Grammatica, tum demum Rhetorica; quatenus rationis usus sine oratione etiam magnus, hujus sine illa potest esse nullus."

[57] See e.g., Oxford, lxvi–lxxiii.

[58] *AL*, 3: "There are thus two parts to logic: the invention of reasons or arguments, and their disposition [Logicae itaq; partes duae sunt; rationum sive argumentorum inventio, eorumq; dispositio]."

[59] Milton calls the second part of logic *dispositio* rather than *iudicium*, the term in Ramus and Downame: *AL*, 3. Contrast Ramus, *Institutionum Dialecticarum*,189–90, which explains that *iudicium* is the better term, and George Downame, *P. Rami Veromandui Regii Professories Dialecticae Libri Duo. Cum Commentariis Georgii Douname Annexis* (London, 1669), fol. b1r—the latter of which (in an earlier edition) influenced Milton's *Logic*.

[60] *AL*, 107: "Definitio est, cum explicatur quid res sit."

INTRODUCTION   19

comes later: for genus—without which (if one is available) no definition can be formed—borrows from distribution, which is the proper locus of genus.[61]

In dialectical fashion, invention occurs as the demands of definition and distribution play off against each other, until (ideally, at least) the evidence of invention disappears and all that remains is a well-disposed system of definitions that, on a grand scale, explains "what a thing is." The aim is truth, and a text called *De Doctrina Christiana* could hardly concern itself with anything else. Milton's *Logic* grants that "perfect definitions are hard to find [*inventu*]," allowing for description ("an imperfect definition, defining a thing through other arguments"), but definition remains the desideratum.[62]

In rhetoric, invention does not share the same drive toward definition. Instead of being the first of two parts, it is the first of five, according to Cicero's classification: *inventio, dispositio, elocutio, memoria,* and *pronuntiatio*.[63] Cicero defines invention as "the discovery of valid or seemingly valid arguments to render one's case plausible [*probabilem*]."[64] Invention involves generating possibilities that *might* work and judging which one best suits the occasion. Invention in this sense meets *elocutio* ("the fitting of the proper language to the invented matter") in a work like Erasmus's *De copia* (1514), which offers ways of multiplying expressive possibilities through variation: indeed, the "index of chapters" in the 1514 edition tellingly contains multiple variations on the word "variatio": *variatur, variandi, de variando, variamus,* and so on.[65] Rhetorical invention expands rather than contracts, and it aims at probability (Cicero's *probabilem*) rather than the truth of definition. As Thomas O. Sloane argues, the Ciceronian rhetorical mindset entails a diffidence about the possibility of knowing truth: "The theme of Ciceronianism is *probabilitas,* not *veritas:* most truth can never be known with certainty."[66] Thomas Wilson's influential sixteenth-century articulation—"Invencion, is a searchyng out of thynges true, or thynges likely, the which maie reasonably sette furth a matter, and

---

[61] *AL*, 107: "Definitio in tradendis artibus est usu quidem prior distributione (prius enim definitur unaquaeq; res quàm distribuitur) natura tamen & inveniendi ordine est posterior: genus enim, quo non adhibito, si quod sit, nulla definitio constitui potest, à distributione, qui proprius generis est locus, mutuum accipit."

[62] *AL*, 110: "Definitiones perfectae [...] difficiles inventu sunt [...] *Descriptio est definitio imperfecta, ex aliis etiam argumentis rem definiens.*"

[63] Cicero, *De inventione*, I.vii.9. Compare Wilson, *The Arte of Rhetorique,* fol. 3v.

[64] Cicero, *De inventione*, I.vii.9: "Inventio est excogitatio rerum verarum aut veri similium quae causam probabilem reddant."

[65] Cicero, *De inventione*, I.vii.9: "elocutio est idoneorum verborum ad inventionem accommodatio." Desiderius Erasmus, *De duplici copia rerum ac verborum* (Argentorati [Strasbourg], 1514), fols iii–vi.

[66] Thomas O. Sloane, *Donne, Milton, and the End of Humanist Rhetoric* (Berkeley, CA: University of California Press, 1985), p. 119.

20 MILTON'S THEOLOGICAL PROCESS

make it appere probable"—further emphasizes the probabilistic dimension of rhetorical invention.[67]

These two meanings of invention collide in Milton's admission that logical invention cannot, in practice, always precede disposition. Beneath the glossy logical presentation of truth, in other words, lies a process of invention that might look more rhetorical—more probabilistic—than the final product lets on.[68] This tense relationship between product and process corresponds to a debate of long standing in Milton studies about whether he is a poet of certainty whose rhetorical artifacts are self-consuming (Stanley Fish, for instance) or a poet who values what Peter Herman calls "incertitude" and therefore rhetorical *probabilitas*, although Herman only briefly discusses rhetoric.[69] *De Doctrina Christiana* seems like a text that obviously lends itself to the "certainty" side of the debate, given its drive toward definition. Nearly everyone has read it that way, as dispositive evidence that Milton held view X or view Y—or that, because Milton held view X and *De Doctrina Christiana* articulates view Y, Milton could not have written the treatise.[70] Neither is *De Doctrina Christiana* generally held as a repository of Miltonic *sententiae*; apart from the epistle, it is not especially quotable or readily mineable for rhetorical gems. This way of reading the theological treatise as having more to do with logic than rhetoric thus has substantial evidence on its side. And yet, neither is the treatise devoid of rhetoric in the Ciceronian sense of seeking probable arguments that might persuade its audience. Indeed, Cicero writes that definition can be a matter of rhetorical controversy when "there is no agreement about the essential point, not because the fact is not certain, but because the deed appears differently to different people, and for that reason different people describe it in different terms."[71] This very

---

[67] Wilson, *The Arte of Rhetorique*, fol. 3v.

[68] See John P. Rumrich, "Does Milton's God Play Dice with the Universe?," in *Milton and the New Scientific Age: Poetry, Science, Fiction*, ed. Catherine Gimelli Martin (New York and London: Routledge, 2019), pp. 108–26.

[69] Stanley Fish, *Self-Consuming Artifacts: The Experience of Seventeenth-Century Literature* (Berkeley, CA: University of California Press, 1972), ch. 5. Peter C. Herman mentions rhetoric in *Destabilizing Milton: Paradise Lost and the Poetics of Incertitude* (New York: Palgrave Macmillan, 2005), p. 26. On this bifurcating impulse in Milton studies, see William Kolbrener, *Milton's Warring Angels* (Cambridge: Cambridge University Press, 1997). A. J. A. Waldock found Milton productively divided between certitude and incertitude: *Paradise Lost and Its Critics* (Cambridge: Cambridge University Press, 1959 [1947]), pp. 19–24 and *passim*.

[70] Shore exempts *De Doctrina Christiana* from rhetorical consideration, writing, "There is little reason [. . .] to view the heterodox theological positions in the *Christian Doctrine* as elements of a larger persuasive strategy", *Milton and the Art of Rhetoric*, 11. He rejects Sloane's argument that Milton's oeuvre is "formalist" rather than "rhetorical," while nevertheless implicitly finding, with Sloane, that the theological treatise is "'methodical, almost coldly so" rather than rhetorical: Shore, *Milton and the Art of Rhetoric*, n. 28; Sloane, *Donne, Milton, and the End of Humanist Rhetoric*, 228.

[71] Cicero, *De inventione*, I.viii.11: "Quo in genere necesse est ideo nominis esse controversiam, quod de re ipsa non conveniat; non quod de facto non constet, sed quod id quod factum sit aliud alii videatur esse et idcirco alius alio nomine id appellet."

INTRODUCTION   21

issue arises in *De Doctrina Christiana* in cases where the language of a scriptural passage is not in dispute but the interpretation is, with the consequence that a treatise primarily devoted to logical *dispositio* becomes overtly rhetorical as the occasion warrants. The Christological interpretation of Psalm 2 affords the central (but far from only) case in point.

This tension between logical and rhetorical uses of invention is not absolute—searching for the right middle term all but necessitates a foray into copiousness amidst a suspension of certainty—and yet it remains a tension that plays out in *De Doctrina Christiana* on the level of literary form. The logical mode of invention in the treatise involves finding scriptural passages pertinent to a given topic. In Ramist fashion, each passage functions as an argument, which Milton defines as "that which is suited to the arguing of something."[72] The argument consists not in what the passage says per se but rather in its relevance to the topic at hand, as Milton explains: "an argument, properly speaking, is neither a word nor a thing, but a certain relevance of a thing to arguing."[73] Arguing (the act by which arguments are put to use) takes the form of definition (explaining what a thing is) and *dispositio* (arranging definitions and their accompanying arguments in a logical way). This method produces the dominant literary form of *De Doctrina Christiana*: definitions that divide into subheadings under which the relevant scriptural passages are gathered. Chapters gather relevant definitions and are themselves arranged under broader headings that organize the treatise as a whole.

The treatise's rhetorical moments manifest as exceptions to this form. Sometimes, these are brief digressions into argumentative prose, but nowhere in the treatise is rhetoric more abundantly on display than in I.5. As I argue in detail in Chapter 4, that chapter contains rudiments of Ramist *dispositio*, but its argumentative structure is rhetorical rather than logical.[74] The thread connecting these two literary forms is invention: rhetorical invention becomes necessary when the materials produced by logical invention turn out to engender controversy (recalling Cicero's point about *controversia* and definition). Sometimes, the controversy is relatively local and contained: why the definition is X and not

---

[72] *AL*, 3. "Argumentum est quod ad aliquid arguendum affectum est."

[73] *AL*, 4. "Argumentum autem propriè neq; vox est neq; res; sed affectio quaedam rei ad arguendum." See also Emma Annette Wilson, "Mapping Milton's 'Great Argument': The Literary Significance of the Argument Sections in *Paradise Lost*," in *Milton Through the Centuries*, ed. Gábor Ittzés and Miklós Péti (Budapest: L'Harmattan, 2012), pp. 129–30.

[74] Waldock notices the treatise's rhetorical moments, including in I.5; Paradise Lost *and Its Critics*, 21–22. Sloane finds I.5 argumentatively crabbed and therefore anti-rhetorical: *Donne, Milton, and the End of Humanist Rhetoric*, 227–29. For considerations of the chapter's rhetoric, see Kent R. Lehnhof, "Deity and Creation in the *Christian Doctrine*," *Milton Quarterly* 35, 4 (2001): 237–42; and Hale, *Milton's Scriptural Theology*, ch. 9.

22 MILTON'S THEOLOGICAL PROCESS

Y, as others would have it. In the case of I.5, the controversy is much larger, not simply because the anti-trinitarian views expressed in the chapter were controversial but because the controversy appears on the level of *dispositio*: does the chapter logically belong to God's internal efficiency (the Trinitarian view) or to God's external efficiency (Milton's view)?[75] This book argues that the treatise's formal excursions into rhetoric have consequences for the theological assumptions that govern it. The ensuing chapters will develop this argument; for now, it is enough to notice that the treatise has more rhetoric in it than scholarly ways of reading it have tended to acknowledge.

In fairness, scholars may not notice the rhetorical dimensions of *De Doctrina Christiana* because Milton's own statements of method either do not acknowledge them or are at pains to deny them. Indeed, Milton generally has few kind words to say about rhetoric.[76] The tension between rhetoric and logic thus ends up playing out in terms of the treatise's theology of scripture. Milton distinguishes *De Doctrina Christiana* from other works of Ramist systematics by emphasizing the centrality of scripture to its project. He explains the intended relationship between scripture and the words (his words) that constitute the Ramist logical framework when he announces a preference that "my pages' space should overflow with scriptural authorities assembled from all parts of the Bible, even when they repeat one another, and that as little room as possible be left for my own words, though they arise from the weaving together of the passages."[77] This statement eschews rhetoric in favor of treating scripture itself as the matter of argument. The most obvious consequence of this approach is the sheer bulk of scriptural quotation in the treatise. The basic form that such quotation takes is a block of assembled citations, generally presented in canonical order, pertaining to a given topic. Ideally, "the weaving together of the passages" leads fairly transparently to a summative statement of scripture's collective position on that topic. This gesture finds Milton at his most Ramist because it omits the middle term of Aristotelian syllogism and understands that simply compiling a statement constitutes a form of argumentation. Ramist logic then affords the means of organizing these statements into a coherent doctrinal structure. In Milton's hands, this systematic, logical articulation of Christian

---

[75] On rhetoric emerging to address questionable *dispositio*, see further Milton's apology for intruding the topic of sin into a chapter devoted to providence (I.8); *DDC*, 129–30. See also Rumrich, "Does Milton's God Play Dice with the Universe?," 116–17.

[76] See Sloane, *Donne, Milton, and the End of Humanist Rhetoric*, 232–34.

[77] *DDC*, 4: "satius duxi mearum quidem paginarum spatia confertis undique autoritatibus divinis etiam eadem ingerentibus redundare, meis verbis, ex ipso licet contextu scripturarum natis, loci quam minimum relinqui."

INTRODUCTION   23

doctrine can only prove properly persuasive if paired with what amounts to a reordering of the Bible intended to draw out its intrinsic doctrinal structure.

As evidenced by the fact that scripture constitutes merely half of its volume, *De Doctrina Christiana* does not adhere to these stated intentions with absolute fidelity. It is here that the treatise's rhetorical dimension comes into play. Reading the treatise turns, in large measure, on learning how to make sense of its departures from the formal and generic expectations it establishes—and working out how the treatise itself makes sense of them.

Reading the Scriptural Citations

Milton's scriptural quotations are, of course, important for their content, but they also need to be read for their language. Milton could read Greek, Hebrew, Aramaic, and Syriac (all vital to early modern biblical scholarship), but in most cases, the treatise presents the biblical text in Latin.[78] In preparing the Oxford edition, J. Donald Cullington traced most of the citations to a handful of preferred Latin Bibles, but he also found many cases where Milton offered his own translations in the interest of greater fidelity to the originals.[79] I have found a case where Milton's Latin rendering defies any scholarly rationale, perhaps because he was working from memory or perhaps because he was expressing a dynamic rather than literal translation.[80] This case seems within the bounds of the quotation practices established in the divorce tracts, but its implications for Milton's theology of scripture merit consideration.[81] Reading the citations thus begins with reading the words themselves by checking them against the resources Milton had at his disposal and considering the possible reasons that he may have had for choosing one rendering over others. Furthermore, Milton tends to quote the Bible in short snippets rather than full verses, so there is also the question of why he selected the particular words he did.

Milton's manner of deploying scriptural evidence also serves as a useful index to formal variation within the treatise. The blocks of scriptural citation appear as part of the Ramist structure that provided the treatise with its initial mode of organization. In time, however, Milton found this structure inadequate—a realization that takes the form of prose passages that are not

---

[78] Oxford, li–lv. Gordon Campbell and Sebastian P. Brock argue that Milton's amanuenses did not share his Syriac ability but instead relied on Latin translations: "Milton's Syriac," *Milton Quarterly* 27, no. 2 (1993): 76–77.

[79] Oxford, xlvii–li.

[80] I discuss this case in Chapter 1.

[81] See e.g., Peter Auger, "The Poetics of Scriptural Quotation in the Divorce Tracts," *Milton Quarterly* 54, 1 (2020): 23–40.

24 MILTON'S THEOLOGICAL PROCESS

explicitly part of the Ramist structure. Such passages are recognizable in part because of how they make use of scripture, whether by quoting and explicating passages one by one in prose argumentation or by presenting citations in a sequence curated to make a point instead of in their canonical order, according to the usual practice of the Ramist scripture blocks. Individual citations might also appear out of canonical order due to scribal error in the process of revision and recopying.

Reading Milton's Theological Interlocutors

Because Milton distinguishes his treatise from other works of Ramist systematics by his handling of scripture, reading *De Doctrina Christiana* involves learning to navigate its relationship with the works of other theologians.[82] Three pieces of evidence suggest points of comparison. First are the theologians that the treatise mentions by name, like Girolamo Zanchi, whose name appears four times—more than any other theologian. As Jeffrey Alan Miller has shown, however, these references to Zanchius were late additions to the manuscript.[83] In general, the treatise refers to other theologians in targeted, occasional ways rather than systematic ones, which limits the utility of such references to understanding the broader aims and structure of *De Doctrina Christiana*.

Second, Milton writes in 1650 of "*Cartwright* and *Fenner*" as "two of the Lernedest" "[a]mong our own Divines," including a reference to Fenner's "Book of *Theologie*."[84] Thomas Cartwright (1534/35–1603) and his protegé Dudley Fenner (*c.* 1558–87) were major English Calvinists of the sixteenth century. Both men published systematic theologies: Fenner's *Sacra Theologia* appeared in 1586 (with a preface by Cartwright), and Cartwright's *A Treatise of Christian Religion* appeared posthumously in 1616.[85] Fenner was also a notable English Ramist, publishing *The Artes of Logick and Rethorike* in Middleburgh in 1584.[86] In the case of Cartwright's book, the Ramist scheme owes to William Bradshaw's editorial repurposing of a previously published catechism.[87] The material's occasional recalcitrance to this repurposing appears in two late chapters (51 on vows and 52 on the church militant) that fit awkwardly into the overall

---

[82] On the treatise's named interlocutors, see Hale, *Milton's Scriptural Theology*, ch. 5.

[83] Miller, "Milton, Zanchius, and the Rhetoric of Belated Reading," 207–09.

[84] Milton, *The Tenure of Kings and Magistrates*, 2nd edn (London, 1650), p. 51.

[85] Dudley Fenner, *Sacra Theologia, sive Veritas quae est secundum Pietatem* ([Geneva], 1586); Thomas Cartwright, *A Treatise of Christian Religion* (London, 1616).

[86] On Fenner's Ramism, which influenced Ames's, see Ong, *Ramus*, ch. 12.

[87] See *MMS*, 94. The catechism first appeared as *Christian Religion* (London, 1611), then in a second edition as *A Methodicall Short Catechisme* (London, 1623).

organization.[88] Beyond the conventional decision to begin by discussing the Godhead, Cartwright's treatise bears little resemblance to *De Doctrina Christiana* on the level of organization. Any influence it had on Milton's treatise was occasional and topical rather than structural, to be discerned only by close comparison, given the absence of direct citation.[89]

Fenner's *Sacra Theologia* presents a more complicated case. Fenner divides his treatise into ten books, and the manuscript of *De Doctrina Christiana* carries traces of an abortive attempt at a similar division into ten parts.[90] The two works' division of topics begins to part ways, however, as early as Fenner's Book Two. Both treatises begin (in their fashion) by discussing what theology is and then proceeding to a discussion of God, divine attributes, and the Trinity (Fenner's Book I, which follows the common pattern shared by Cartwright's later treatise). Some of the topics that follow in Fenner's Book II, like creation (II.2) and governance (II.10), also appear in Milton's Part 2 (I.7, I.9–10) but not in the same sequence, or to the same ends. From Book V on, Fenner's treatise bears little resemblance to Milton's in the topics it takes up. Notwithstanding the potential commonality of a ten-part structure, Fenner's treatise, like Cartwright's, remains at best an occasional influence, and, in any case, an influence that the treatise does not cite directly.

The third and most familiar piece of evidence owes to Milton's nephew, Edward Phillips, who writes about the origins of *De Doctrina Christiana* in his *Life* of his uncle:

> The next work after this, was the writing from his own dictation, some part, from time to time, of a Tractate which he thought fit to collect from the ablest of Divines, who had written of that Subject; *Amesius*, *Wollebius*, &c. *viz.* A perfect System of Divinity, of which more hereafter.[91]

These are the English Calvinist theologian William Ames (1576–1633) and the Swiss Reformed theologian Johan Wolleb (1589–1629). Ames has the closer connection to Milton; he studied with the influential English Calvinist William

---

[88] "Vows" gets tacked on to prayer but without being included in the preceding charts for prayer. "The Church Militant" was probably supposed to be chapter 40, which an earlier chart says should address "Persons," but which, in fact, initiates the discussion of prayer: Cartwright, *A Treatise of Christian Religion*, 200.

[89] James B. Potts, Jr contrasts Milton and Cartwright: "Milton's Two-Fold Scripture," *Explorations in Renaissance Culture* 18 (1992): 95–96.

[90] See Gordon Campbell, "*De Doctrina Christiana*: Its Structural Principles and Its Unfinished State," *Milton Studies* 9 (1976): 255–56.

[91] Helen Darbishire, *The Early Lives of Milton* (New York: Barnes and Noble, 1965), p. 61. Phillips does not return to the topic "hereafter."

26   MILTON'S THEOLOGICAL PROCESS

Perkins at Christ's College, Cambridge, where he later served as tutor to Milton's eventual tutor at Christ's, William Chappell.[92] Ames spent much of his career in the United Provinces, but as his biographer notes, his heart remained with the plight of English puritanism.[93] The treatise contains a reference to "our Ames [*Amesius noster*]," with *noster* inserted above the line.[94] His relevant treatise is the *Medulla S. S. Theologiae*, first published in 1629 and appearing in English translation in 1642.

Milton's treatise owes a clearer formal debt, however, to Wolleb's *Compendium Theologiae Christianae*, first published at Basel in 1626. The Latin *Compendium* was printed in Cambridge in 1642 and again in London in 1647; an English translation by Alexander Ross appeared in 1650, with a second edition in 1660. This popular work remained a staple of theological education well into the eighteenth century. Scholars have long recognized that *De Doctrina Christiana* takes Wolleb's treatise as a starting point in many matters of both organization and content. Maurice Kelley located this debt primarily in Book II, but traces of his influence appear in Book I as well.[95]

Attending to Milton's theological interlocutors—especially Wolleb and Ames—invites an observation about the genre of *De Doctrina Christiana* that suggests a corollary way of reading. Milton's treatise and those of Wolleb and Ames have much in common, generically speaking. They are all Ramist works of systematic theology divided into two books (the first on the knowledge of God and the second on the worship of God), and within these divisions, they handle the relevant subtopics in broadly similar ways.[96] Nevertheless, Milton's

---

[92] Notwithstanding tutelage under the puritan Ames, Chappell became Arminian during his time at Christ's and eventually became the Laudian bishop of Cork and Ross: *ODNB*, "Chappell, William (1582–1649)." See further Campbell and Corns, *John Milton*, 26–27.

[93] Keith L. Sprunger, *The Learned Doctor William Ames: Dutch Backgrounds of English and American Puritanism* (Urbana, IL: University of Illinois Press, 1972), p. 1.

[94] *DDC*, 571. Hunter, *Visitation Unimplor'd*, 73–75 uses this reference to argue for a Dutch origin to the treatise. Sprunger, however, documents Ames's ongoing engagement with English religious politics; see *The Learned Doctor William Ames*, ch. 2 and ch. 4, esp. p. 80 n. 28. See also Miller, "Theological Typology," 248–65. Richard Baxter includes Ames in a list of pre-civil-war English nonconformists; *Reliquiae Baxterianae* (London, 1696), Part II, p. 256 (§25); *Reliquiae Baxterianae*, ed. N. H. Keeble, John Coffey, Tim Cooper, and Tom Charlton (Oxford: Oxford University Press, 2020), III.444.

[95] Maurice Kelley, "Milton's Debt to Wolleb's *Compendium Theologiae Christianae*," *Publications of the Modern Language Association of America* 50, 1 (1935): 156–65; T. S. K. Scott-Craig, "Milton's Use of Wolleb and Ames," *Modern Language Notes* 55, 6 (1940): 403–07; Kelley's discussion in Yale, 17–21. See, more recently, Jason A. Kerr and John K. Hale, "The Origins and Development of Milton's Theology in *De Doctrina Christiana*, I. 17–18," *Milton Studies* 54 (2013): 181–206"; Hale, "Points of Departure: Studies in Milton's Use of Wollebius," *Reformation* 19, no. 1 (2014): 69–82; Hale, *Milton's Scriptural Theology*, ch. 4.

[96] *MMS*, 97.

INTRODUCTION 27

distinctive handling of scripture in *De Doctrina Christiana* results in a significant generic difference from these near neighbors. As the titles *Medulla* and *Compendium* suggest, Ames and Wolleb aim to provide relatively concise systematic distillations of Reformed theology. Both volumes accordingly had extended lives in the world of theological education, albeit for different reasons: Wolleb in England and Europe because his was a relatively uncontroversial brief statement of Calvinist theology and Ames in New England, where the generally Congregationalist temper had more room for his sometimes idiosyncratic perspectives, for example, on the Sabbath.[97] Milton, by contrast, undertakes his treatise in hopes of working out his beliefs by "perusing and perpending the scripture of God itself with the utmost diligence, to have every single point investigated and understood for myself, by my very own care."[98] His treatise may aspire to distillation, but it has an exploratory, investigative dimension not similarly present in his interlocutors' works.

Noting the generic difference between *De Doctrina Christiana* and Wolleb's *Compendium* invites ways of reading that allow for an expanded sense of Milton's engagement with Wolleb and Ames. Doctrinal divergence makes their influence less visible than it is in the more derivative Book II, but the ensuing chapters will show concretely that Milton remains consistently and reliably engaged with their works, especially when he is in the process of figuring out how to articulate a doctrinal point where he disagrees with their conclusions.[99] This consistent engagement has ramifications for how Milton uses scripture in *De Doctrina Christiana* because part of his method for compiling lists of citations seems to have involved thinking carefully about which texts Wolleb and Ames cite and which conclusions they draw from them. This aspect of Milton's method suggests the value in cross-checking his lists of citations against pertinent places in Wolleb and Ames while considering the relative positioning of these places within their respective treatises' arrangements of theological *topoi*.[100] There is also value in considering which parts of the passages each author opts to quote and with what consequences.

---

[97] Miller, "Theological Typology," 256–59.

[98] *DDC*, 2: "ex ipsa Dei scriptura quam diligentissime perlecta atque perpensa, unumquodque habere mihimet ipsi, meaque ipsius opera exploratum atque cognitum."

[99] The copious manuscript revisions in Book II suggest that it is not altogether derivative; see Miller, "Theological Typology," ch. 4.

[100] See e.g., Hunter, "Theological Context," 275–77; Hale, "Points of Departure," *passim*.

28 MILTON'S THEOLOGICAL PROCESS

Reading the Manuscript

This book argues that reading *De Doctrina Christiana* requires attention to the complex state of the manuscript. A detailed account of its composition and provenance appears in *Milton and the Manuscript of* De Doctrina Christiana; briefly, however, a young and not altogether scrupulous man named Daniel Skinner had come into possession of the manuscript after Milton's death, along with some of Milton's state papers and sought to publish them in the United Provinces, where even the tolerant Elzevier family of printers proved unwilling to take it on. His efforts came to the attention of Joseph Williamson, Secretary of State for the Northern Department, who seized the materials and put them in the State Paper Office in Whitehall, where they remained until Robert Lemon discovered them in 1823.[101] The document runs to 745 manuscript pages and currently resides in the National Archives in Kew as SP 9/61. While pursuing publication, Skinner recopied the first fourteen chapters of the treatise. The remaining chapters are primarily in the hand of Jeremie Picard, a professional scribe with other documented connections to Milton during the years between 1658 and 1660.[102] Many of the Picard pages include revisions, either by Picard or by a range of other amanuenses who wrote on behalf of the blind Milton.

Reading the manuscript involves taking account of these revisions, but it also involves close attention to the physical manuscript itself. Maurice Kelley seems to have understood the work of Milton's primary amanuensis, Jeremie Picard, as constituting a single stratum, or a single chronological layer in the manuscript's sedimented history.[103] Subsequent research on the manuscript has yielded a more complex picture. While preparing *Milton and the Manuscript*, Gordon Campbell and Thomas N. Corns had access to the manuscript in an unbound state. They were able to gather information about the watermarks on the different papers used and, crucially, to note the different sizes to which the pages had been cut.[104] On the basis of this data, they posit that the work of Milton's primary amanuensis, Jeremie Picard, on the manuscript consists of three kinds of material strata: (1) a baseline fair copy of an earlier manuscript, divided into separate fascicules for each chapter; (2) occasional leaves that have been recopied and tipped into the fascicules (see Figure 0.1); and (3) whole fascicules that have been recopied to accommodate revisions.[105] To these, Jeffrey Alan Miller adds a

[101] *MMS*, 5–31.
[102] *MMS*, 31–33.
[103] Kelley distinguishes between Picard's "original draft" and his "additions" to it, meaning the revisions in his hand; *This Great Argument*, 42. See further Yale, 23–24.
[104] *MMS*, 47–50; compare Oxford, xxv.
[105] *MMS*, 55.

INTRODUCTION 29

fourth kind, involving pages recopied and added to the already once-recopied fascicules, and then a fifth kind, comprising Skinner's recopied chapters (of which Kelley and Miller argue, persuasively, that he recopied I.14 first).[106]

Helpful as these assessments of the manuscript's material layers are, they do not adequately capture the complexity of its final state. In the first place, I am not so confident as my predecessors that Picard completed a baseline fair copy as a coherent start-to-finish exercise. Given the sharp clarity of their distinction among Picard's three hands, I.15 and I.16 (excepting the latter's recopied middle section) plausibly stand as paradigmatic examples of Picard's initial fair copy. Weighing against this possibility, however, is the fact that they do not share paper with the rest of the treatise.[107] The difference in style between these chapters and the later chapters in Book II, which Campbell and Corns identify with their third and latest stratum, do indeed suggest copying at different times, but in the absence of evidence about what preceded these recopied pages, some caution about what constitutes evidence of sequencing is in order. Just as plausible (and perhaps more so) than the idea that Picard created an entire fair copy along the lines of I.15 is the possibility that the method of working in fascicules predates his involvement with the treatise and that he recopied chapters at various times, as occasion required. This latter possibility is suggested by the use of varying papers (identifiable in part by differences in size and watermark) but also by the variations in handwriting from fascicule to fascicule. Such variations include letter forms and especially also the distinction among hands—what the Oxford editors refer to as Picard's three "fonts," large hand (corresponding to bold), a smaller italic (for quotations), and a middling roman (for ordinary text)—which varies not only across fascicules but also within them, as when Picard sometimes uses large hand for definitions and headings but at other times for proper names or emphasis, albeit seemingly not both in a single material subsection of the manuscript.

On a more granular level than the fascicule is the folio, a four-page section consisting of a single folded sheet, and it seems that Picard often recopied not only by the fascicule but also by the folio. Evidence for this possibility appears in the two cases where scribes besides Picard recopied and replaced an entire folio: MS 549–52 in the hand of Amanuensis A; and MS 571–74 in the hand of Daniel Skinner. Milton is more likely to have directed the first instance than the second, but this may represent a post-Picard instance of a practice that was common during the period of Picard's work on the treatise. Jeffrey Alan Miller

---

[106] Kelley, *This Great Argument*, 57; Miller, "Milton, Zanchius, and the Rhetoric of Belated Reading," 201–03, 205.

[107] I.15 and the non-inserted pages of I.16 alone bear watermark W (using the sigla in *MMS*, 47–50).

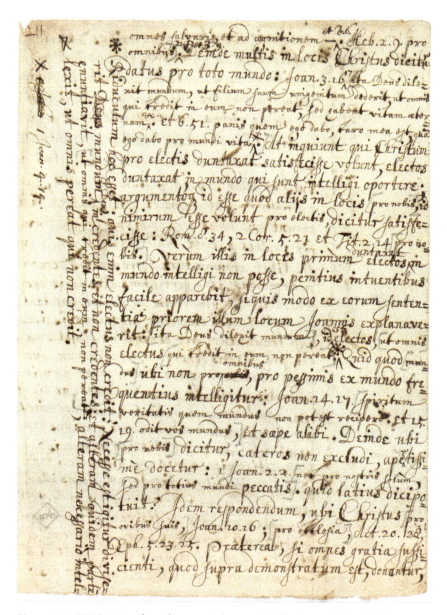

Figure 0.1 *DDC*, 211, a densely recopied page with further revisions in the margin; it is part of the two folios (pp. 209–16) tipped into I.16

argues that the folio recopied by Skinner contained a chronologically late flurry of revision involving Picard and likely others, revisions that brought a major shift in Milton's anti-Sabbatarianism.[108] Picard's participation in this practice is clear enough, with the two recopied folios in I.16 (MS 209–16) as one instance among many. Campbell and Corns have rightly drawn this feature of Picard's work to our attention, and the next logical step is to notice that it calls into question Kelley's fundamental assumption that the Picard draft represents a single, coherent project of recopying. As far as we can know (which is not far, thanks to the obscuring labors of Daniel Skinner), a complete draft in Picard's hand was the effect and perhaps even the goal, but the material evidence indicates the need for a more complex, multi-layered account of Picard's scribal involvement.

Making sense of this evidence can be difficult, but it is necessary to understanding the processes of revision and corresponding changes of mind that unfolded in the course of Milton's work on the treatise. The manuscript gives readers access to a material dimension of Milton's theological process, and it is important to notice the ways that even clean pages uncluttered by marginal or interlinear revisions provide evidence of ongoing revision, sometimes in ways that hint at insertions made in preceding material strata. The appendix to this book offers a guide to the complex stratification at work in the treatise, but I present it more in the hope of spurring further research than in any expectation of having the final word.

Reading Milton's Theology

Learning to read *De Doctrina Christiana* is ultimately a matter of using these ways of reading to track three complexly interdependent variables: literary form, theology of scripture, and theology proper. I separate theology of scripture and theology proper because Milton participates, albeit idiosyncratically, in the broader Reformed tradition that understands scripture as the foundation of theology. Part One of this book develops ways of reading the interrelationship among these variables. Chapter 1 considers the relationship between theology of scripture and literary form in the treatise in order to make methodological and theological sense of the prose passages that break from the expectations established in the epistle and the first chapter. It argues that the concepts of external and internal scripture that Milton develops in I.30 provide tools for making sense of the treatise's shifting literary form. Chapter 2 then explores the theological underpinnings of internal scripture and its attendant formal departures by examining Milton's views on the human capacity to understand and

[108] Miller, "Theological Typology," 222, 232–48.

32 MILTON'S THEOLOGICAL PROCESS

interpret scripture. Finally, Chapter 3 turns to the methodological crisis that Milton's application of internal scripture provokes, arguing that he responds by formulating a theology of the church (or ecclesiology) premised on testing the kind of human speech he is practicing. This ecclesiology turns fundamentally on the problem of authority raised by human speech—a problem that Milton had sought to avoid by using scripture to crowd his own voice off the treatise's pages. Paradoxically, Milton can imagine that his own words might become authoritative for others but at the cost of having them cease to be merely his.

Part Two of the book then turns these collective ways of reading to the treatise's most infamous theological position: its Christology. Chapter 4 takes up Milton's treatment of the Son of God in I.5, which presents an extreme case of reliance on external scripture driving the production of internal scripture as Milton rejects the doctrine of the Trinity on narrowly scriptural grounds but defends his position using a literary form that renders the Ramist structure vestigial. Chapter 5 takes up the relationship between Milton's Christology, his practice of internal scripture, and his ecclesiology, arguing that they come together in an understanding of Milton's interpretative practice as a kind of *imitatio Christi*.

Finally, after a brief interlude on the relationship between treatise and epic, in Part Three, the book brings the account of Milton's theological process developed in the first two parts to bear on *Paradise Lost*, arguing that the Christological, ecclesial approach to scripture that caused the project of *De Doctrina Christiana* to collapse in on itself finds a more apt vehicle in the epic. Chapter 6 finds Christology and ecclesiology meeting in the poem's account of matter, which plays out on a cosmic scale the process of refinement at the heart of Milton's church. The Conclusion reflects on the value of thinking patiently with things and ideas that Milton rejects, even as they, like *De Doctrina Christiana*, persist in his surviving *oeuvre*. Neglecting the parts of Milton or his career that might seem untoward or embarrassing risks idolizing the man who wrote *Eikonoklastes*—even as these neglected parts can prove quite rewarding if we will but learn how to pay attention to them.

This book does not aspire to say everything that might be said about *De Doctrina Christiana* or about its relationship to *Paradise Lost*. Unlike Kelley, my aim is not to demonstrate conclusively the consonance between the two texts. Neither do I address all the heterodox positions that Milton espouses in the treatise. My aim, rather, is to give an account of how the treatise approaches the foundations of theology, in the Reformed sense of scripture as the cognitive foundation (*principium cognoscendi*) and God as the essential foundation (*principium essendi*), with the Son of God linking the two together—albeit with results that depart significantly from Reformed norms on both counts.[109] I hope that developing and demonstrating ways of reading the treatise that are attuned to these foundational matters will open up fruitful approaches to the treatise and its relationship with the epic. As Milton put it in the epistle, "I shall mention what has proved profitable to my own studies, in case the same hope subsequently leads someone else to enter on the same way."[110] Indeed, I hope that this book's single talent will multiply manyfold in the hands of its readers.

---

[109] See Richard A. Muller, *Dictionary of Latin and Greek Theological Terms*, 2nd edn (Grand Rapids, MI: Baker Academic, 2017), s.v. "principia theologiae" and, at much greater length, *PRRD*.

[110] *DDC*, 2: "dicam enim quibus rebus profecerim, si quem fortè posthac proficiendi spes eadem ad eandem viam ingrediendam invitaverit."

PART ONE
SCRIPTURE AND ECCLESIOLOGY

1

Scripture and Literary Form

Reading *De Doctrina Christiana* involves coming to grips with the discrepancy between its stated intentions to let scripture "overflow" its pages, even at the expense of Milton's own words, and its eventual formal inclusion of extensive argumentative prose.[1] This discrepancy is more than a matter of debating what proportion of scripture would qualify as "overflowing"; it is, rather, a matter of the relationship between theology of scripture and literary form.

The foundation for this relationship appears in the chapter on Holy Scripture (I.30), where Milton speaks of a "twofold scripture: the external scripture of the written word, and the internal scripture of the holy spirit, which he, as a result of God's promise, has etched on believers' hearts as by no means to be neglected."[2] This twofold scripture manifests in the treatise as a continuum of literary forms marked by the degree of authority they assign to external scripture. On one end is the block of scriptural citations, organized under Ramist definitions and headings, whose language aspires to "arise from the weaving together of the passages."[3] On the other end are the treatise's prose passages, where Milton attempts, through rhetorical argumentation, to convey in his own words what he takes to be the sense of scripture. Understanding what is specifically literary about these forms requires delving into the curious relationship between internal scripture and rhetoric in the treatise, in conversation with Milton's views on logic and his practices of critical judgment. The more authority that Milton's own "internal scriptural" words claim for themselves, the more rhetorical they become. Because these rhetorical intrusions are at odds with both the treatise's Ramist method and the theology of scripture informing it, they precipitate a methodological and theological crisis for the treatise that will be the subject of Chapters 2 and 3.

---

[1] *DDC*, 4: "satius duxi mearum quidem paginarum spatia confertis undique autoritatibus divinis etiam eadem ingerentibus redundare, meis verbis, ex ipso licet contextu scripturarum natis, loci quam minimum relinqui."

[2] *DDC*, 394: "Duplicem enim habemus sub euangelio maximè scripturam; externam verbi scripti, et internam sancti spiritus, quam is ex promissione Dei in cordibus credentium minime negligendam exaravit."

[3] *DDC*, 4: "ex ipso licet contextu scripturarum natis."

Milton's Theological Process. Jason A. Kerr, Oxford University Press. © Jason A. Kerr (2023).
DOI: 10.1093/oso/9780198875086.003.0002

38 MILTON'S THEOLOGICAL PROCESS

For material to illustrate the treatise's range of literary forms, this chapter turns to Milton's discussion of Christian liberty in I.26–27 because the topical content of those chapters proves relevant to the questions at hand. As Chapter 3 will show, Milton's thinking about internal scripture and Christian liberty together put pressure on Augustine's rule of faith, the principle of interpretation that appeals to the "plain places of scripture" and the teaching of the church as guides to making sense of difficult passages. As we will see in the present chapter, Milton replaces this principle with the idea that "all things are in the end to be referred to the spirit and the *un*written word," that is, to the internal scripture.[4] By engaging with the treatise's thought on Christian liberty, we will be in a position to take up its views on the human capacity to interpret scripture in Chapter 2 and the ecclesiological ramifications of those views in Chapter 3.

Milton's Concept of Internal Scripture

The idea that Milton's "internal scripture" manifests in *De Doctrina Christiana* as passages of rhetorical argumentation may seem odd because internal scripture seems more like a matter of gut-level instinct or ineffable spiritual feeling than an attempt at reasoned argument intended to persuade. Indeed, Milton's *Art of Logic* distinguishes between exterior speech, "which is uttered vocally, and interior, which is only mentally conceived."[5] This distinction would seem to correspond with a verbally expressed external scripture and an internal scripture that remains non-verbal and expressed only within a person: internal scripture ventures into speech, if it ventures at all, only as testimony, never as argument.[6]

The Art of Logic, however, presents an account of reason that refuses a clear correspondence between internal speech and internal scripture. The complication arises from Milton's preference (following Ramus) for an intuitive awareness of truth. Book II proceeds from a division between axiomatic and dianoetic *dispositio*—between the logical arrangement of materials (*dispositio*) based on self-evident assertions (axioms) or on reasoned (dianoetic) methods

---

[4] *DDC*, 398: "Sic omnia demum ad spiritum atque verbum non scriptum, scriptura ipse teste referenda sunt."

[5] *AL*, 126: "Si distinguimus cum *Aristotele* sermonem in exteriorem, qui ore profertur, & interiorem, qui mente solùm concipitur."

[6] Compare John T. Connor: "The living Word, rooted in the pious heart, is a formal understanding of the interior and neither a gambit of common parlance nor ever to be confused with rhetoric's 'resistless eloquence' (*Paradise Regained* (PR) 4.266)"; "Milton's *Art of Logic* and the Force of Conviction," *Milton Studies* 45 (2006): 200.

SCRIPTURE AND LITERARY FORM   39

of deduction like syllogisms. Milton agrees with Aristotle that "an axiom often means a proposition or affirmation which is so clear that it is as it were worthy of being assented to for its own sake."[7] In Ramus, this intuitive awareness takes the form of "natural dialectic," the skill of judgment that enables a person to cut through rhetorical ornamentation and the multiplication of syllogisms to arrive at a succinct statement of an argument's matter, as when Ramus reduces Cicero's *To Milo* to the claim that ambushers and criminals may be killed.[8] Indeed, Ramus was instrumental in redefining rhetoric as an art of adornment and ornamentation instead of its classical sense as an art of argumentation. For Ramus, the logical point is what matters, not the means of its delivery: the aim is to arrive as near to wordlessness as possible.

In *The Art of Logic*, the need for words intrudes in the second half of Book II, on dianoetic ("a discourse of mind and reason") *dispositio*, which occurs "when one axiom is deduced from another," as in syllogisms.[9] The need for syllogistic reason, according to Milton, "has arisen from the weakness of the human intellect, which weakness, being unable by an immediate intuition to see in an axiom the truth and falsity of things, turns to the syllogism, in which it can judge whether they do or do not follow."[10] This is not yet rhetoric, in the Ciceronian sense of probabilistic argumentation, but words have now become necessary not just for expressing a blunt truth, as in Ramus's *précis* of Cicero's *To Milo*, but for articulating the logical connections that enable a truth to be known by the weak human intellect.[11] Judgment remains intuitive, but syllogisms provide much-needed hand-holding, whereas axioms require none. A further means of hand-holding is method, or "a dianoetic disposition of various homogeneous axioms ordered according to the clarity of their nature, from

---

[7] *AL*, 125: "Axioma saepe *Aristoteli* significat propositionem sive sententiam ita claram, ut quasi digna sit cui propter se fides habeatur."

[8] Petrus Ramus, *Institutionum Dialectorum Libri Tres* (Lyon, 1553), p. 349: "Sic Milonianam Ciceronis orationem in vnum conclusionis modum conclusam perspicies. I[n]sidiatorum & sceleratum licet interficere." Compare Walter J., Ong, S. J., *Ramus: Method, and the Decay of Dialogue* (Cambridge, MA: Harvard University Press, 1958), p. 191 (which quotes an earlier edition of Ramus); Thomas O. Sloane, *Donne, Milton, and the End of Humanist Rhetoric* Berkeley, CA: University of California Press, 1985), pp. 137–44. Connor writes of "that wordless proximity that defines logic as reason" for Milton; "Milton's *Art of Logic*," 203.

[9] *AL*, 157: "Dianoëtica est cùm aliud axioma ex alio deducitur. Vox Graeca διάνοια, mentis & rationis discursum significat."

[10] *AL*, 158: "quae quidem collectio sive deductio ab intellectûs humani imbecillitate profecta est: quae cùm rerum veritatem & falsitatem primo intuitu perspicere in axiomate non potest, ad syllogismum se confert, in quo de consequentia & inconsequentia earum judicare possit."

[11] On Ciceronian rhetoric as probabilistic, see the Introduction, pp. 19–22.

40 MILTON'S THEOLOGICAL PROCESS

which the mutual agreement of all of them is judged and embraced by the memory."[12] Method aims to extend the intuited clarity of individual axioms to a network of interrelated axioms, leaving judgment intuitive and internal.

Fundamentally, *De Doctrina Christiana* proceeds according to axiom and method. The lowest level of method is the subheading, which gathers scriptural passages whose relevance to the subheading the treatise does not typically argue or even articulate. Definitions gather subheadings, chapters gather definitions, books gather chapters, and the treatise gathers its two books, ideally producing an intuitively clear and memorable thread of connections that gives internal scripture its minimum possible verbal expression. The syllogisms that often pepper other contemporary theological works, bursting with talk of "majors" and "minors," make little to no appearance. Neither, however, does the treatise fully conform to the manner of expression that *The Art of Logic* would seem to dictate. Consider the following passage from I.5, which adopts the overtly probabilistic technique of the rhetorical question as it responds to explicitly logical claims:

> But Theologians assert that the name of Jehovah signifies two things; either the nature of God, or the fulfilment of his words and promises. If it signifies the nature and even the person of God, why should the one to whom he so often assigned words befitting God alone not be assigned the name of Jehovah too, by which name the fulfilment of those words and promises is signified?[13]

Theologians "assert"—a logic word—claims about the name "Jehovah," to which Milton responds neither with logical refutations nor with counter-assertions (testimony) that he takes to be intuitively self-evident, but with questions (three more ensue in the paragraph) designed to convince readers that his reading is more plausible than that of the Theologians. This is a rhetorical mode of speaking, not a logical one. Moreover, this rhetorical mode of speaking has come to form the chapter's organizational basis, as Chapter 4 will show.

In terms of internal scripture, such rhetorical expression emerges from the same inner, wordless conviction that motivates the logical modes of expression that also pervade the treatise. But logic alone has become inadequate to the

---

[12] *AL*, 208: "Methodus est dispositio dianoëtica variorum axiomatum homogeneorum pro naturae suae claritate praepositorum, unde omnium inter se convenientia judicatur memoriáq; comprehenditur."

[13] *DDC*, 82: "Sed nomen Iehovae duas res aiunt significare Theologi; vel Dei naturam, vel verborum ac promissionum eius impletionem: Si naturam adeoque personam Dei significat, cur cui personam atque praesentiam suam imponit, ei nomen eam significans non imponat?"

task of conveying what Milton takes to be the truth; a need for persuasion has entered the picture. John T. Connor writes that "Milton's *Art of Logic* admits a distinct aversion to verbalism and to public discourse. It seems to contemn these as the betrayal of thoughts from their only adequate security—the unuttered privacy of the mind."[14] Within this framework, speech, when it occurs, is not persuasion but testimony, witness. But *De Doctrina Christiana* does not eschew public discourse in the same way that *The Art of Logic* does. In the epistle, *De Doctrina Christiana* addresses itself to the "Universal Churches of Christ," envisioning the church as a place where doctrine is winnowed in public, and concludes with an invitation for readers to "judge of this writing according to the spirit of God guiding you."[15] The theological treatise includes both logic-based witnessing and rhetorical persuasion, rendering the interior conviction of internal scripture verbal by recourse to different discursive modes.

The treatise's assumption of rhetorical modes has to do with judgment. As discussed above, in *The Art of Logic*, Milton privileges an understanding of judgment as an intuitive recognition of an axiom's truth or falsity. In some cases, however, as indicated by the need for dianoetic means like syllogism and method, judgment needs a helping hand.[16] Again, intuitive judgment informs Milton's primary use of external scripture in the treatise: he places scriptural quotations under headings without arguing their relevance to the topic at hand, in effect treating the relationship between the gathered passages and their heading as self-evident. Rhetoric enters the picture when such self-evident connections cannot be safely assumed—and it is interesting that Milton turns to rhetoric rather than to syllogisms, as *The Art of Logic* suggests he should.[17] Intuition—in the sense of wordless mental apprehension—may still shape Milton's sense that a scriptural passage belongs to a given topic, but now he needs to explain that intuition to someone else. Identifying internal scripture with intuitive judgment means that it is present as a tacit principle of selection in the Ramist headings and scripture blocks, but it rises above the surface when the treatise undertakes persuasive argumentation, even if it assumes that the Spirit plays a role in persuading readers.

---

[14] Connor, "Milton's *Art of Logic*," 200–01.

[15] *DDC*, 1, 4, 5: "de his, prout Dei spiritus vobis praeiverit, ita iudicate."

[16] See *AL*, 129: "Falsum autem non docetur hoc modo in arte, sed judicatur: nam enuntiatio falsa non minus axioma est, quàm vera, eadem enim utrobiq; dispositio est: non idem de syllogismo ac methodo dici poterit."

[17] On Milton's mastery of classical rhetoric in a syllogistic context, see A. Robin Bowers, "Milton and Salmasius: The Rhetorical Imperatives," *Philological Quarterly* 52, 1 (1973): 64–65.

42 MILTON'S THEOLOGICAL PROCESS

The Spirit and Critical Judgment

As the principle that determines the content of the treatise (which passage goes under which heading, where additional argumentation might be needed), internal scripture thus emerges as a spiritually re-inflected cousin to the exercise of critical judgment valued among humanists. One of Milton's major departures from Ramus involves the concept of judgment. For Ramus, judgment was the second part of logic (after invention), and by this he meant (as Milton does with *dispositio*) the arrangement of the materials turned up during the process of invention. Milton disagrees, arguing that *dispositio* extends further than judgment: "Moreover, instruction in judgment teaches nothing other than to judge well, while instruction in disposition, by its function of arranging, teaches also how to reason well, whether it be by understanding, judging, disputing, or remembering."[18] As a skill subordinate to *dispositio*, Miltonic judgment determines logical connections but not what to do about them. Although Ramist logic idealizes situations where these tasks collapse into one, Milton's dissent keeps the door open for other possibilities, two of them (disputing and remembering) explicitly rhetorical.

While Miltonic judgment can include the sorts of intuitive arguments favored by Ramus, it comes overtly into play in cases where personal intuition becomes subject to interpersonal scrutiny. Such cases facilitate the testing of foundational assumptions and thus play a vital role in Milton's thinking about how the search for truth works in practice. One such instance appears in *Areopagitica* (1644), a tract that argues in favor of fostering the capacity for judgment, which can only flourish in conditions of freedom—hence the connection between the topics of internal scripture and Christian liberty. To Milton, the papacy represents the antithesis of this freedom: "the Popes of *Rome* [. . .] extended their dominion over mens eyes, as they had before over their judgments."[19] As one example of the freedom to make critical judgments, Milton cites the vision, "about the year 240," of Dionysius Alexandrinus,

a person of great name in the Church for piety and learning, who was wont to avail himself much against hereticks by being conversant in their Books; untill a certain Presbyter laid it scrupulously to his conscience, how he durst venture himselfe among those defiling volumes. The worthy man loath to give

---

[18] *AL*, 124: "doctrina deinde judicii docet nihil aliud quàm bene judicare; doctrina dispositionis pro sua disponendi parte, etiam bene ratiocinari: sive id sit intelligere, sive judicare, sive disputare, sive meminisse." Milton includes memory, which Ramus had offloaded to rhetoric.

[19] Milton, *Areopagitica* (London, 1644), p. 7.

offence fell into a new debate with himselfe what was to be thought; when suddenly a vision sent from God, it is his own Epistle that so averrs it, confirm'd him in these words: Read any books what ever come to thy hands, for thou art sufficient both to judge aright, and to examine each matter.

Perhaps as evidence of his sufficiency to judge, Dionysius tested his vision against scripture, finding that "it was answerable to that of the Apostle to the Thessalonians, Prove all things, hold fast that which is good."[20]

The story of Dionysius illustrates several salient facts about Milton's views on judgment. The first is its direct relevance to ecclesial contexts. Judgment is a human capacity ("thou art sufficient both to judge aright, and to examine each matter"), but it is charged with religious and theological implications. The "certain Presbyter" considers heretical writings unsafe to engage, even "defiling," either implying a lack of the necessary critical judgment on Dionysius's part or, more likely, indicating that critical judgment, properly exercised, would counsel avoidance rather than engagement. In Milton's view, critical judgment means being able to engage productively with potentially dangerous texts. Dionysius was reading these texts, after all, to "avail himselfe much against hereticks." Avoiding such texts risks leaving the truth undefended, which lends a specifically apologetic, polemical weight to Milton's emphasis on critical judgment, without which the church might not survive. The reference to a "certain Presbyter" gains extra punch from the context of Milton's protest against the Presbyterian-backed licensing act.

The story frames Dionysius's judgment as human and sufficient while also indicating the need for divine validation and scriptural verification. Dionysius, the story implies, had been successfully applying his judgment to heretical texts when the presbyter caused him to question. Dionysius responded by engaging with his judgment on a meta-level because the problem of self-reference rendered his capacity for judgment—his intuition—inadequate to the question. God's validating words intervene independent of Dionysius's judgment, but the turn to scripture arguably shows that judgment at work. The text that he finds, with its command to prove all things, thus validates the act of judgment that led Dionysius to seek it. The interplay between scripture and critical judgment is of central interest for thinking about *De Doctrina Christiana* and its concept of internal scripture because the exercise of judgment that brought

---

[20] Milton, *Areopagitica*, 10–11, quoting 1 Thessalonians 5:21. David Ainsworth references this passage but does not explicitly address *Areopagitica*'s engagement with the humanist concept of critical judgment: *Milton and the Spiritual Reader: Reading and Religion in Seventeenth-Century England* (New York: Routledge, 2008), ch. 1.

44 MILTON'S THEOLOGICAL PROCESS

Dionysius to 1 Thessalonians is logically prior to the text that validates it. Judgment inevitably shapes the treatise's engagement with external scripture and is, indeed, an enabling condition for such engagement because the very act of reading requires such judgment. Indeed, such judgment proves central to the concept of freedom that Milton is advancing in both *Areopagitica* and *De Doctrina Christiana*—the freedom to engage faithfully with potentially dangerous ideas. This understanding of judgment informs Milton's view that the internal, spiritual, unwritten word ultimately serves as the measuring stick of doctrinal truth.

Critical Judgment and Internal Scripture

Milton places internal scripture and critical judgment cheek by jowl in the chapter of *De Doctrina Christiana* on Holy Scripture (I.30). The discussion of internal scripture is itself an instance of the very process of rethinking that Milton uses it to theorize, appearing as it does in the last and chronologically latest stratum of the chapter's material development.[21] From the start, Milton's *dispositio* within this late stratum privileges internal scripture: his description of what it entails is longer than the corresponding description of external scripture, and the four scriptural passages he cites (Isaiah 59:21, Jeremiah 31:33–34, Acts 5:32, and 1 Corinthians 2:12) collectively emphasize the witness of the spirit, not the witness of the written word. The conclusion that follows these quotations does grant pre-eminence to the spirit but in a more measured way than the quotations anticipated: "And so today the external authority for our faith, [contained] indeed in the scriptures, is very great, and generally first, temporally; but each person has the internal authority, and likewise the supreme and preeminent one: the spirit itself."[22] Milton places external and internal scripture very nearly on par; the distinction is between *maxima* and *summa*, making it seem that the spirit's authority exceeds that of scripture only slightly.

Milton's theologizing of critical judgment occurs in this gap between the authorities of external and internal. The next section of I.30 discusses the corruption of biblical textual traditions, which was a matter of hot inter-confessional debate. Broadly speaking, the Protestant commitment to *sola scriptura* depended on the Word of God being faithfully transmitted and reliably contained in the Bible as it had come down through the centuries, whereas

---

[21] See the Appendix, p. 264.

[22] *DDC*, 395: "Itaque authoritas fidei externa est in scripturis quidem hodie maxima, et ferè prior tempore; interna verò cuique, adeóque summa atque suprema, est ipse spiritus."

SCRIPTURE AND LITERARY FORM   45

Catholic scholars were more open to the possibility that textual corruption had occurred because that indicated a need for the church to maintain doctrinal purity.[23] The growing scholarly awareness of textual variation and complexity as the seventeenth century unfolded had the effect of troubling this too-clear picture of the confessional divide. As Nicholas Hardy has shown, for instance, the Roman Index decided at times not to prohibit some Protestant works of textual scholarship precisely because they drew attention to textual corruption, even though the authors themselves had intra-confessional reasons for arguing as they did.[24] The reliability of the Hebrew Masoretic Text (down to its vowel points) was a key area of contention, but Milton adopts the standard Protestant line without hinting at the controversy:

> straight after the captivity in Babylon its guarantors and custodians [were] the priests, prophets, and other divinely instructed men—Ezra, Zechariah, Malachi, [and] others—who doubtless handed down God's holy books uncorrupted to the sanctuary and to their priestly successors; for them throughout the ages it was not only a matter of supreme scruple that nothing be changed, but also there were no grounds of suspicion causing them to make changes.[25]

Milton does not insist on the inspiration of the vowel points, but he seems content to treat the text of the Old Testament as reliable, albeit without acknowledging the questions of textual variation raised by the Septuagint and its various recensions.[26] He bases this judgment more on the rule of faith than on scholarly arguments about textual transmission: notwithstanding doubts about dating, authorship, and chronology, "very few people, if any, have expressed doubt about any doctrinal part of them," that is, the books of the Prophets and the Writings.[27] Amanuensis "B" has inserted this comment in the page's margin; on the previous page, he also crossed out "veteris testamenti" and replaced it with

[23] On Milton's involvement in debates about the precedential status of church history, see Thomas Roebuck, "Milton and the Confessionalization of Antiquarianism," in *Young Milton: The Emerging Author, 1620–1642*, ed. Edward Jones (Oxford: Oxford University Press, 2013), pp. 48–71.

[24] See e.g., Nicholas Hardy, *Criticism and Confession: The Bible in the Seventeenth Century Republic of Letters* (Oxford: Oxford University Press, 2017), pp. 218–27 (on Grotius).

[25] *DDC*, 396–97: "post Babylonicam statim captivitatem fideiussores atque custodes sacerdotes, prophetae aliíque divinitus edocti Ezra, Zacharia, Malachias, alii; qui sacros libros Dei sacrario et sacerdotibus posteris incorruptos proculdubio tradiderunt; quibus per omnes aetates et summa religio erat nequid mutaretur, et nulla suspicio quamobrem id facerent."

[26] For one window into contemporary English debates about the Septuagint, see Scott Mandelbrote, "English Scholarship and the Greek Text of the Old Testament, 1620–1720: The Impact of Codex Alexandrinus," in *Scripture and Scholarship in Early Modern England*, ed. Ariel Hessayon and Nicholas Keene (Aldershot: Ashgate, 2006), pp. 74–93.

[27] *DDC*, 397: "eorum tamen doctrinae partem ullam vel nemo vel pauci admodum in dubium vocarunt."

46 MILTON'S THEOLOGICAL PROCESS

"legis Mosaicae." These changes show Milton revising to account for the different traditional divisions of Hebrew Scripture but without significantly altering
his view of their reliability. Helpfully, however, the marginal insertion shows
that relative consensus about doctrinal stability puts to rest questions about
textual transmission.[28]

Milton is more dubious about the textual reliability of the New Testament.
He writes that it "has for many centuries had [...] diverse and diversely corrupt
custodians; [there is] no exemplar in the author's own handwriting which, in
preference to the others, we could claim as genuine."[29] In contrast to the Hebrew
Scriptures, Milton sees the New Testament as presenting problems of textual
variation without a reliable way of solving them.[30] Milton mentions scholarly attempts to rectify this corruption—"Consequently, from the handwritten
codices, the learned men Erasmus, Beza, and others published what seemed to
them most genuine"—thus alluding to one usual province for the exercise of
critical judgment.[31] For Milton, however, the scale of the problem exceeds the
remedies afforded by collating manuscript evidence and judging which readings to treat as authentic. Rather, he understands the textual uncertainty of the
New Testament as serving a larger providential purpose:

I am totally ignorant as to why by God's providence it came about that the
New Testament scripture was committed to such unsure and such slippery
custodians, unless this very fact was meant to prove that the spirit, rather than
scripture, has been offered to us as the surer guide whom we ought to follow.[32]

---

[28] On p. 518, in a later stratum of Picard's work, Milton refers to Louis Cappel, "*Spicilegium eiusdem argumenti*," in *Myrothecium Evangelicum*, ed. John Cameron (Geneva, 1632), p. 90; but Milton has
either not read or disagrees fundamentally with Cappel's *Critica Sacra* (Paris, 1650), which calls the reliability of the Masoretic Text profoundly into question; see Hardy, *Criticism and Confession*, ch. 10. The
Oxford editors conjecture that Milton used the Hebrew Bible and lexicon produced by Johannes Buxtorf
the elder, who actively opposed Cappel's work, but the matter merits further investigation: Oxford, 231
n. xxii, following Harris Francis Fletcher, *The Use of the Bible in Milton's Prose* (Urbana, IL: University
of Illinois Press, 1929), p. 81.

[29] *DDC*, 397: "multa per secula varii [...] variéque corrupti custodes fuere; autographum exemplar
prae caeteris nullum quod pro germano asserere possimus."

[30] Milton's focus remains on the corruption of canonical texts without extending into the question of
whether New Testament apocrypha (like the *Shepherd of Hermas*) ought to be canonical; contrast the
debates addressed in Nicholas Keene, "'A Two-Edged Sword': Biblical Criticism and the New Testament
Canon in Early Modern England," in Hessayon and Keene, *Scripture and Scholarship* (2006), pp. 94–
115.

[31] *DDC*, 397: "Itaque ex variis codicibus manuscriptis viri docti quod sibi germanissimum est visum
ediderunt Erasmus, Beza, et alii."

[32] *DDC*, 397: "Quod nescio sanè cur factum providentia Dei sit, ut novi testamenti scriptura cus-
todibus tam incertis támque lubricis commisa fuerit, nisi ut hoc ipsum argumento esset, certiorem nobis
propositum ducem spiritum quàm scripturam, quem sequi debeamus."

For Milton, the spirit can supply what textual collation cannot, opening the way for a carefully qualified understanding of freedom from the limitations of external scripture.

Milton's embrace of the spirit does not mean (here, at least) a rejection of scholarship and learning. Ignorance is not freedom. Rather, the corrective capacity that Milton claims for the spirit has an analogue in the practice of conjectural emendation, where an editor proposes a solution to a textual problem that cannot be addressed by other means. Such emendation was controversial in the early modern European world of scholarship, but it was, nevertheless, practiced. Anthony Grafton has shown, for instance, that Joseph Scaliger made his reputation as a young scholar in the mid-sixteenth century through his skill at conjectural emendation of classical texts.[33] John Selden likewise engaged in the practice in his 1618 *Historie of Tithes*.[34] Milton himself ventured conjectural emendations to several Shakespeare plays in his copy of the First Folio, which also evidences his practices of collation.[35] The Florentine academician Carlo Dati wrote Milton a letter (in Italian) centered on proposing an emendation to one of Tibullus's elegies, presuming Milton's interest in such matters.[36] Emendation is not an invitation to invent readings at will or to indulge the untethered freedom to make things up.[37] Even Louis Cappel, whose 1650 *Critica Sacra* sought to illustrate a broad need for conjecture by wildly expanding the set of textual variants that might point to a purer Hebrew original of the Old Testament, explicitly grounded his practice in the analogy (or rule) of faith, an appeal to the tenor of scripture as a whole.[38]

For Milton, clearly, collation of scriptural passages on doctrinal points remained a relevant theological activity, as did considerations of translation in consultation with the original languages of scripture. The amount of scholarly labor behind *De Doctrina Christiana* is astounding. In fact, it is startling how little Milton's appeal to internal scripture ultimately shapes his textual work with

[33] Anthony Grafton, *Joseph Scaliger: A Study in the History of Classical Scholarship*, Vol. I (Oxford: Clarendon Press, 1983), pp. 108–15 and *passim*.

[34] Hardy, *Criticism and Confession*, 168–69.

[35] Claire M. L. Bourne, "*Vide Supplementum: Romeo & Juliet, Hamlet*, & Seventeenth-Century Collation as Play-Reading in the First Folio," in *Early Modern English Marginalia*, ed. Katherine Acheson (New York: Routledge, 2018), pp. 222–24. See further Claire M. L. Bourne and Jason Scott-Warren, "'Thy Unvalued Booke': John Milton's Copy of the Shakespeare First Folio," *Milton Quarterly* 56, 1–2 (2022), 1–85.

[36] Columbia, XII.296–313. Of editions in the past century, Columbia alone gives Dati's Italian and full citations of the Latin passages under discussion.

[37] For a notorious exception to the rule, see Richard Bentley, *Milton's Paradise Lost. A New Edition* (London, 1732). Compare Bentley, *Dr. Bentley's Emendations on the Twelve Books of Milton's* Paradise Lost (London, 1732).

[38] Hardy, *Criticism and Confession*, 315–17; on the analogy of faith, see Dayton Haskin, *Milton's Burden of Interpretation* (Philadelphia, PA: University of Pennsylvania Press, 1994), p. 7 and *passim*.

48 MILTON'S THEOLOGICAL PROCESS

scripture in the treatise. I have found only one instance of what might be called spiritual emendation of the biblical text, in a quotation of Romans 12:2 (to be discussed below). Internal scripture manifests as prose instead because it generally involves matters of contested scriptural interpretation: the issue is not what scripture says but what it means. That gap brings the need for the spirit into view, highlighting Milton's own vulnerability as an interpreter. Both conjectural emendation and appeals to the spirit have an obvious potential to produce tendentious readings; both produce more plausible results when paired with scholarship in the usual vein.[39] Milton insists that the spirit is a "surer guide" than scripture, but his continued reliance on scripture in the face of that claim indicates an awareness of the need to make use of all available resources and of his embeddedness in a larger world of theological discourse where one must persuade others (and oneself) that particular interpretations are, in fact, plausible. His scriptural world is inescapably rhetorical, more probable than certain, which lends a communal and, indeed, ecclesial dimension to the interpretative freedom he is intent on claiming for himself.

Whereas the interconfessional war over textual corruption turned on the need (or not) for the church as a guardian of textual meaning, Milton sees in the church's custodial untrustworthiness grounds for appeal to a higher authority, even as that appeal raises concerns about the proliferation of idiosyncratic, spiritual interpretations. Milton uses argumentative prose to justify his own spiritual sense of what contested passages of scripture really mean—the "internal scripture" behind the external. In doing so, he conjures a rhetorical audience, which he imagines will evaluate his arguments based not on rhetoric alone but on "the spirit we all share."[40] Critical judgment and spiritual judgment flow together in Milton's practice and in the reception that he anticipates for his work even as the irreducible fuzziness of the latter category engenders significant methodological (and ultimately ecclesiological) reflection in the treatise. Consequently, the spiritual dimension of internal scripture, whatever that ultimately means, has identifiable literary manifestations in the treatise. Close attention to the literary forms through which Milton engages with scripture in the treatise will provide a methodological foundation for considering the question of what it means for Milton to think of the treatise's audience as a church that will evaluate his work—a delicate topic, considering that he views the Roman *magisterium* as the antithesis of the kind of critical and spiritual judgment he espouses in *De Doctrina Christiana*.

---

[39] Harry. C. Porter, "The Nose of Wax: Scripture and the Spirit from Erasmus to Milton," *Transactions of the Royal Historical Society* 14 (1964): 156.

[40] *DDC*, 49: "communemque spiritum."

External Scripture and Literary Form

The foregoing discussion of internal scripture, in terms of logic, rhetoric, and critical judgment, has laid a foundation for discussing the range of literary forms at work in *De Doctrina Christiana*. These forms involve both external and internal scripture. The treatise's primary literary form for engaging with external scripture is the block of scriptural quotations, presented in canonical order and gathered under a heading that represents part of a theological definition in the Ramist logical structure. The rationale for this literary form appears in an oft-cited passage from the epistle (already quoted in part above) where Milton distinguishes his approach to scripture in the treatise from the practice of contemporary theologians:

> And since the majority of those who have written at the greatest length on these subjects have been accustomed to fill up almost the whole of their pages with explaining their own opinions, while thrusting into the margin the scriptural passages by which all their teaching is most confirmed, with the numbers of the chapters and verses only summarily noted, I have preferred that my pages' space should overflow with scriptural authorities assembled from all parts of the Bible, even when they repeat one another, and that as little room as possible be left for my own words, though they arise from the weaving together of the passages.[41]

Milton's stated method appeals to the Protestant value of *sola scriptura*, the idea that scripture alone should form the basis of theology, but his wariness toward his own words challenges a common Protestant approach to *sola scriptura*. Protestants of the time were not opposed to interpretative prose per se, as attested by their vast literary output, including commentaries that could exceed the length of the relevant biblical books by orders of magnitude. Far from perceiving a conflict between *sola scriptura* and such writings, mainstream Reformed theology was broadly willing both to assume and to develop an exegetical tradition. Indeed, the extensive publication of commentaries shows

---

[41] *DDC*, 4:

> Cumque eorum pars maxima qui his de rebus quam plurima scripserunt, suis sensibus explicandis totas fere paginas occupare consueverint, scripturarum loca, quibus id omne quod docent maximoperè confirmatur, numeris duntaxat capitum versiculorumque strictim adnotatis in marginem extrudere, satius duxi mearum quidem paginarum spatia confertis undique autoritatibus divinis etiam eadem ingerentibus redundare, meis verbis, ex ipso licet contextu scripturarum natis, loci quam minimum relinqui.

50 MILTON'S THEOLOGICAL PROCESS

that *sola scriptura* as an ideal rests fundamentally not only on exegesis but also on the establishment of a (correct) exegetical tradition.[42]

Milton, however, writes in explicit defiance of this tradition. His readings in theology had led him to doubt the results, but also the method:

> I found with great regret that many arguments brought in those volumes by opponents were being evaded by wretched shifts, or were speciously (not solidly) answered, either by a disgusting parade of logic-chopping formulas or else by the persistent intrusion of grammarians' empty jargon; [I found] that whatever side of a question the writers were maintaining tooth and nail was often being defended with greater vehemence than validity, by misunderstanding biblical passages or snatching at fallacious inferences from them; and consequently [I found] truth at times fiercely attacked as error and heresy, and error and heresy taken for truth; [I found] them valued more from habit and partisan zeal than from the authority of the scriptures.[43]

Consequently, Milton set out to foreground "the authority of the scriptures" by correcting the methodological overreliance on "habit and zeal" that manifest, on the level of literary form, as the "disgusting" intrusions of "logic-chopping formulas" and "grammarians' empty jargon."

Restoring the authority of the scriptures to its proper place in theological writing meant allowing scripture to come far closer to speaking for itself than was normative for Protestant scholastic theology. For Milton, that meant putting blocks of quoted scripture at the heart of the treatise and making the logical machinery for arranging them "arise from the weaving together of the passages" as much as possible. But arranging scripture so that it can speak for itself (*dispositio*) requires an extraordinary amount of human labor, including the interpretative labor of determining which scriptural passages belong where in the Ramist scheme, or whether the scheme itself needs to be revised to bring it into closer harmony with scripture. In this sense, as discussed above, even the curation of external scripture amounts to an attempt to express internal

---

[42] See *PRRD*, II, ch. 7.

[43] *DDC*, 2:

> multa ibi adversariorum argumenta miserè elusa, aut elenchorum ostentatis putidè formulis aut interiectis ubique Grammaticorum inanibus vocabulis, in speciem potius quam solidè refutata, sanè dolens, reperi: quam autem ipsi partem pro vera mordicus tenerent, vel scripturae locis malè intellectis, vel consequentiis inde fallacibus arreptis, contentiosiùs esse saepè quam validiùs defensam; hinc veritatem pro errore atque haeresi nonnunquam acerrimè oppugnatam: errorem atque haeresin pro veritate habitam; consuetudine ac studio partium quam scripturarum authoritate commendatiorem.

scripture via acts of critical judgment that reveal a rhetorical element at work even in the treatise's most overtly logical literary forms. The form of the scripture block may obscure these interventions of human interpretative agency, but they are present all the same.

External Scripture as Internal Scripture

The ways of reading required by internal scripture begin, paradoxically enough, with how the treatise deploys external scripture. In Reformed theology generally, "internal scripture" refers to the way that the Spirit inscribes external scripture on the heart, in keeping with Jeremiah 31:33. Calvin, careful to steer readers away from "fanatics," emphasizes the ways that this internal scripture points continually back to the external and does not, by any means, render it superfluous. Citing Paul's urging not to "quench the spirit" (1 Thessalonians 5:19–20), Calvin writes that the Apostle

> does not loftily catch them up to empty speculations without the Word, but immediately adds that prophecies are not to be despised [. . .] What say these fanatics, swollen with pride, who consider this the one excellent illumination when, carelessly forsaking and bidding farewell to God's Word, they, no less confidently than boldly, seize upon whatever they may have conceived when snoring?

For Calvin, ultimately, "the Word is the instrument by which the Lord dispenses the illumination of his Spirit to believers. For they know no other Spirit than him who dwelt and spoke in the apostles, and by whose oracles they are continually recalled to the hearing of the Word."[44]

Milton simultaneously agrees with Calvin and parts ways with him. He agrees that internal scripture points back to the external, and he is certainly in no hurry to jettison the latter. Nevertheless, he seems to believe that the external scripture, especially given its imperfect transmission and preservation, only partially expresses the truth more amply expressed in internal scripture, which

---

[44] John Calvin, *Institutes of the Christian Religion*, ed. John T. McNeill, trans. Ford Lewis Battles (Louisville, KY: Westminster John Knox Press, 2006 [1960]), p. 96 (I.ix.3): "non sublimiter eos arripit ad inanes sine verbo speculationes: sed continuò subiicit, non sperne[n]das prophetias [. . .] Quid ad haec tumidi isti ἐνθουσιαζαί, qui hanc vnam reputant eximiam illuminationem, vbi securè omisso ac valere iusso Dei verbo, quicquid stertendo conceperint, non minus confide[n]ter quàm temere arripiunt?"; Calvin, *Institutio Christianae Religionis* (Geneva, 1559), p. 22; Geoffrey F. Nuttall surveys the range of approaches to this question among mid-seventeenth-century puritans in *The Holy Spirit in Puritan Faith and Experience* (Chicago, IL: University of Chicago Press, 1992 [1946]).

52 MILTON'S THEOLOGICAL PROCESS

is why "all things are in the end to be referred to the spirit and the *un*written word."[45]

The first level of "internal scriptural" labor in the treatise thus involves Milton's attempts to render external scripture in ways that more perfectly express the internal. Such labor appears in the treatise primarily in the form of translation because the treatise is in Latin and, with rare exception, prefers to quote scripture in that language. The treatise's reliance on the Junius–Tremellius Latin translation has been noted since Charles Sumner's *editio princeps* in 1825, and work on the question of Milton's Latin Bibles has proceeded from there, with Harris Francis Fletcher's work in the early twentieth century and J. Donald Cullington's for the Oxford edition as major instances.[46] This scholarship identifies fidelity to the original Hebrew and Greek as a driving concern: Milton would often choose the version that best comported with the original, or he would provide his own translation. How the treatise rendered most of its biblical citations can be explained using these philological methods.

The exceptions, however, show how internal scripture might be at work even in cases with clear philological explanations. The rendering of Romans 12:2 on MS 333, in the chapter on Christian liberty (I.27), simultaneously shows internal scripture at work and attempts to provide an external scriptural warrant for it. Amanuensis "M" adds this verse (interlinearly, then continued in the margin) to the sequence appearing under the heading **So that we may be slaves to God [*Ut Deo serviamus*]**. This heading points back to the definition's distinction, rooted in Romans 6, between "the slavery of sin [*servitute peccati*]" from which Christ provides freedom and the ensuing state of being slaves to God, identified with Christian liberty. As will be discussed in Chapter 2, in I.17, this verse provides an important scriptural rationale for the kind of searching and testing advocated in the epistle as well as for a theological insistence on the possibility that even unregenerate people can experience renewal of the required capacity. There, a quotation of the verse as it appears in Beza's 1598 New Testament proved sufficient to make the point: "per renovationem mentis vestrae ad hoc, ut probetis quae sit voluntas Dei—."[47] In I.27, however, Milton takes a different tack, beginning with the final words of verse 1: "rationalem cultum. et ne

---

[45] *DDC*, 398: "Sic omnia demum ad spiritum atque verbum non scriptum, scriptura ipsa teste referenda sunt."

[46] Sumner, xv–xvi; Fletcher, *The Use of the Bible in Milton's Prose*, ch. 3; Oxford, xlvii–li. An unresolved question remains regarding Milton's use of the JTB. Sumner suggested, on textual grounds, that Milton was using a 1630 Geneva edition, whereas the Oxford editors suggest, also on textual grounds, a 1623–24 edition produced at Hanau (*Hanoviae*—not Hanover, which would be *Hanoverae* or *Hannoverae*). In the cases I have checked (noted below), these two editions share the relevant variants. The matter requires further study.

[47] *DDC*, 221.

SCRIPTURE AND LITERARY FORM   53

conformemini huic seculo, sed transformemini renovatione mentis vestrae ad explorandum quaenam sit voluntas Dei illa bona et accepta, & perfecta."[48] "Reasonable worship [*rationalem cultum*]" appears as "reasonable service" in the KJV, but by choosing Beza's *cultum* over the Vulgate *obsequium*, which denotes yielding, or even subjugation, Milton instead frames this particular form of slavery as a positive one of labor and care or, more specifically, of "search[ing] out."[49] The replacement of *ut probetis* with *ad explorandum* cements the point, making the exploration of God's will the very purpose of this mental renewal.

This phrase, *ad explorandum*, is worthy of note because it has no plausible scholarly or philological basis and therefore seems to be an instance of spiritual emendation on Milton's part.[50] Milton's composition of this verse offers some insight into his broader methods, with the effect of making *ad explorandum* stand out all the more. Milton does three things. First, he follows the Vulgate— against Beza—in rendering the dissimilar Greek verbs συσχηματίζεσθε and μεταμορφοῦσθε with Latin verbs built around the common root *formare*, although he keeps Beza's *tranformare* instead of the Vulgate's *reformare*. If Milton seems to depart from the Greek, he follows the Greek (and Beza) by putting both verbs in the same mood—although he chooses the subjunctive of the Vulgate's *reformemini* over the Greek imperative reproduced by Beza. Second, in using *accepta* instead of *placens* in Beza or *beneplacens* in the Vulgate, Milton opts for a different possible translation of the Greek εὐάρεστον, perhaps finding support in Walton's renderings of the Syriac and Arabic or, closer to home, in the "acceptable" of the KJV.[51] With *ad explorandum*, though, Milton strikes out on his own. Latin has no way of directly reproducing the grammar of the Greek purposive expression εἰς τὸ δοκιμάζειν ὑμᾶς, where ὑμᾶς is the subject of the infinitive, but *ut probetis* seems like the most straightforward way of doing it: a basic subjunctive purpose clause with the pronoun

[48] *DDC*, 333: "[I urge you [...] to present your bodies [...] as [your] reasonable worship. And do not be conformed to this age, but be transformed by the renewal of your mind for exploring what exactly God's will is: that good and acceptable and perfect [will]."

[49] Charlton T. Lewis and Charles Short, *A Latin Dictionary* (Oxford: Oxford University Press, 1879), s.v. "obsequium" and "cultus."

[50] Milton was perhaps quoting from memory, but even if so, this case remains an outlier, given his general level of philological care.

[51] The use of *accepta* suggests an English rather than a Continental source for the treatise. For evidence that Milton consulted the KJV while working on the treatise, his 1612 copy of the KJV contains a marginal note in the hand of Jeremie Picard correcting the translation of Romans 15:6 in parallel with the Latin rendering on MS 56. See Thomas Fulton, *The Book of Book: Biblical Interpretation, Literary Culture, and the Political Imagination from Erasmus to Milton* (Philadelphia, PA: University of Pennsylvania Press, 2021), pp. 216–18.

54   MILTON'S THEOLOGICAL PROCESS

implied by the verb.[52] Milton's formulation drops the pronoun altogether, resulting in a less personal, more generalized purpose to the transformation being urged. Then there is the choice of word. *Probo* effectively captures the idea of testing or trying conveyed by the Greek, and while *exploro* can also have this meaning, its primary sense has more to do with searching than with testing. Thus we find Milton subtly shifting the scriptural sense in a direction reminiscent of the "Nation [. . .] so prone to seek after knowledge" portrayed in *Areopagitica*, a place where people are both "searching" and "trying all things."[53]

The questions about scripture raised by *ad explorandum* invite Milton's readers into the very process those words evoke. Milton presents these words as the words of scripture, without drawing any attention to the idiosyncratic rendering. This gesture shows a certain kind of critical judgment at work: the skill of conjectural emendation. To be sure, this is an audacious instance of emendation, given that the text in question is not a crux and is easy enough to translate from Greek into workable Latin. It therefore illustrates acutely both the double-edged quality of such emendation and what happens when Milton uses the concept of internal scripture to recast matters of textual criticism in a theological frame. Emendation offers a way of responding to textual corruption even as it can also generate and compound such corruption.[54] And, as Anthony Grafton writes about Lorenzo Valla's celebrated emendations of Livy, this skill is "a matter of talent" and, as such, "there was no generally applicable method that underlay [Valla's emendations] and that could be passed on to disciples or grasped by readers."[55] Milton is not exactly responding to textual corruption in this case; after all, he is elsewhere content to quote Beza's rendering of the verse. Rather, he seems to be responding to a sense that the biblical text could communicate its theological implications more clearly—which, ironically, puts Milton in the company of the anonymous glossator responsible for the Johannine comma (1 John 5:7), perhaps the most notorious case of textual corruption demonstrably emerging from scribal transmission.[56]

---

[52] Milton uses *ut probetis* the other four times he cites the verse, twice in I.17–18 (pp. 221, 237) and twice in I.21 (pp. 262, 266). See Michael Bauman, *A Scripture Index to John Milton's De Doctrina Christiana* (Binghamton, NY: Medieval & Renaissance Texts & Studies, 1989), p. 123.

[53] Milton, *Areopagitica*, 31.

[54] Grafton, *Joseph Scaliger*, I.31.

[55] Grafton, *Joseph Scaliger*, I.13.

[56] This verse's earliest Greek manuscript attestation (as a variant reading) dates to the tenth century, although traces of it appear in patristic writings. It likely originated as a marginal gloss that crept into the text. On the comma in the context of early modern textual criticism, see Stephen D. Snobelen, "'To Us There Is But One God, the Father': Antitrinitarian Textual Criticism in Seventeenth- and Early Eighteenth-Century England," in Hessayon and Keene, *Scripture and Scholarship*, 116–36; Rob Iliffe, "Friendly Criticism: Richard Simon, John Locke, Isaac Newton and the *Johannine Comma*," in Hessayon

For Milton, the concept of internal scripture offers a response to this conundrum. The question is whether readers ought to accept as scripture Milton's rendering of the verse and on what basis—a question that sends readers back to the "internal scripture" written on their own hearts and to the collective ecclesial process of "exploring" and testing the truth that Romans 12:2 enjoins. Milton presents the careful collation of written scripture in its entirety as necessary to the process of inward, spiritual writing. The human work is not the spiritual work (Milton is no Pelagian), but human writing becomes the occasion for the possibility of spiritual writing, on the hearts of writer and reader both, presuming that the reader is suitably engaged. In these terms, *ad explorandum* is an invitation for readers to pull out their own stacks of Bibles in various languages, weigh the options, observe that Milton departs from all precedent, and consider spiritually whether or not his rendering comports with the internal word as written on their own hearts; as Milton writes in I.30, "indeed, no one else can fruitfully interpret for [a faithful person] unless he himself also make the same interpretation for himself and his conscience."[57] *Ad explorandum* is also an invitation for writers, amidst their own uncertainties and the high probability of speaking incorrectly about God, to make the attempt anyway, with a confidence that might, in some cases, turn out to have been a not misplaced faith. Finally, it is an invitation for all who participate in Milton's abstract church to test such utterances in a spirit of openness and charity that *explorare* conveys more aptly than *probare* quite could.[58]

The case of *ad explorandum* shows that internal scripture remains operative even when the external is directly in play and even when Milton simply quotes from Junius–Tremellius or Beza. *Ad explorandum* shows that a process of critical judgment, made possible by the renewal of mind—and therefore also of intuition—described in Romans 12:2 and theologized in I.17 ("On Renewal, and also on Calling") lies behind even these more apparently straightforward citations, to say nothing of the processes of selection and arrangement that led to their inclusion in the treatise to begin with. These processes include many "external" considerations—grammar, attention to the original languages, consulting commentaries and the writings of other theologians, etc.—that collectively serve to make internal scripture broadly responsible to the larger

---

and Keene, *Scripture and Scholarship*, 137–57; Grantley McDonald, *Biblical Criticism in Early Modern Europe: Erasmus, the Johannine Comma and Trinitarian Debate* (Cambridge: Cambridge University Press, 2016).

[57] *DDC*, 391: "immo alius nemo interpretari cum fruct[u] potest, nisi ipse quoque sibi conscientiaéque suae idem interpretetur."

[58] For an instance of creative conjectural emendation that did not meet with approval (Scaliger's reading of Mark 9:49), see Hardy, *Criticism and Confession*, 190.

56   MILTON'S THEOLOGICAL PROCESS

tradition, as invoked in Augustine's rule of faith. When Milton talks of humans becoming "slaves to God," then, he does not have servility to the biblical text in mind. All readers must approach the text with the nuanced kind of freedom that critical judgment involves. Nevertheless, internal scripture remains the foundation, and I now turn to its more overt manifestations and the kinds of ecclesial adjudication that they invite.

Form and the Dialectic of Authority

In practice, Milton's own words have varying formal relationships with external scripture, and with these variations come differences in the kinds of rhetorical authority being claimed from moment to moment. Like its external cousin, internal scripture is diverse, although internal scripture is unified by its responsiveness to the external. This responsiveness qualifies Milton's claims, imbuing them always with the potential (however minimized in given instances) of needing correction. A single, heavily revised page—307a/308 (see Figure 1.1), the only page to exist in both the Picard and Skinner strata—shows these varieties of authority at work.

The treatise's prose stands at the least distance from external scripture in the headings that precede scripture blocks. On this page, the first heading initially read "for the Israelites especially [*Israelitis potissimum*]," until Amanuensis "M" changed it to "for the Israelites alone [*Israelitis duntaxat*]," in keeping with identical changes made to the definition on the preceding page.[59] This change coincides with the addition, via the left-hand margin, of a verse to the scripture block that follows: "Ps. 147:19–20: [*God declares*] *his words to Jacob*, etc., *his statutes and judgments to Israel. He has not [done] so for any [other] nation*, etc."[60] The

---

[59] See John K. Hale, *Milton's Scriptural Theology: Confronting* De Doctrina Christina (Leeds: Arc Humanities Press, 2019), pp. 33–34. Kelley argued, against Sewell, that this revision did not indicate a doctrinal change of mind, the argument resting on the presence of the "duntaxat" position in a passage in Picard's hand on pp. 320–21; Maurice Kelley, *This Great Argument: A Study of Milton's* De Doctrina Christiana *as a Gloss upon* Paradise Lost (Princeton, NJ: Princeton University Press, 1941), p. 62 (57–65), responding to Arthur Sewell, "Milton and the Mosaic Law," *Modern Language Review* 30, 1 (1935): 13–18. Kelley has not, however, accounted for the stratification of the Picard draft—the evidence suggesting that the long prose argument of pp. 320–31, with its reference to Milton's "belated" reading of Zanchius, was a later addition to the Picard copy of I.27. The ensuing reference to Ephesians 2, on which Milton appears to have been reading Zanchius's commentary, affords further evidence for the connection. See Jeffrey Alan Miller, "Milton, Zanchius, and the Rhetoric of Belated Reading," *Milton Quarterly* 47, 4 (2013): 209. For Milton's shifting views on the abolition/abrogation of the Mosaic Law, see Jeffrey Alan Miller, "Theological Typology, Milton, and the Aftermath of Writing," DPhil thesis, University of Oxford (2012), ch. 4; Jason A. Kerr, "Shifting Perspectives on Law in *De Doctrina Christiana*: A Response to Filippo Falcone," *Connotations* 28 (2019): 131–37.

[60] *DDC*, 307a: "Psal. 147. 19. 20. *verba sua Iacobo* &c. *statuta et iudicia sua Israeli non sic ulli genti* &c."

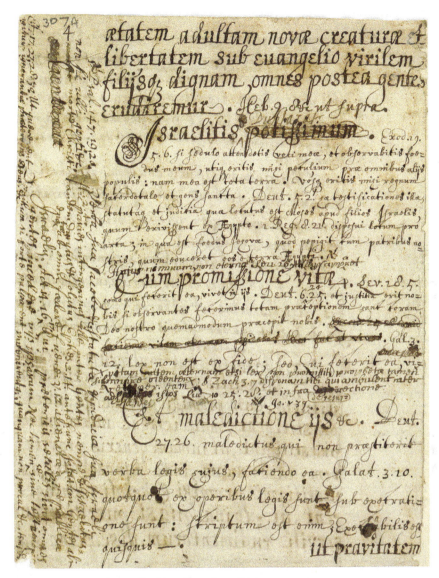

Figure 1.1 *DDC*, 307a, the Picard version of this page

preceding passages indicated primarily that Israel had received the covenant from God, only referencing any particular status attached to that receipt in Exodus 19:5–6, which assures that God will make a diligent and obedient Israel "a special possession in preference to all other peoples."[61] Both *potissimum* and

---

[61] *DDC*, 307a: "peculium prae omnibus aliis populis."

58 MILTON'S THEOLOGICAL PROCESS

duntaxat are compatible with this passage, but the verse from Psalm 147 obliges the narrower reading, and so Milton has his amanuensis make the change. The authority of the treatise's own words thus proves highly responsive to external scripture in this instance. Its words are liable to falsification by the emergence of a single contrary verse—hence the work of further searching in the Bible and resulting adjustments to the headings. There, the treatise speaks with as little of its own authority as possible; its words may technically qualify as internal scripture, but only barely.

Unsurprisingly, then, much of the treatise's work entails addressing scriptural passages that might be read as falsifying its headings. Such work is necessarily less submissive to the biblical text, indicating a more assertive form of authoritative appeal to internal scripture. In the passage at hand, Psalm 147:19–20 actually begins a longer insertion. Aside from a bare (and somewhat puzzling) reference to Romans 2:4, the next part of the insertion is a prose sentence that references but does not quote Ephesians 2:14: "This wall of partition, namely, that between gentiles and Israelites, was at length torn asunder and destroyed by Christ's death, Eph. 2:14." The next sentence then sets up an additional selection of scriptural passages: "Before its destruction gentiles were alienated from the whole covenant," followed by quotations from Ephesians 2:12, Acts 14:16–17, and Acts 17:27–8, 30.[62] These passages, presented out of canonical sequence, bear a different relation to the preceding prose than the citations prior to this insertion bear to the heading. Whereas the heading aims to express the tenor of the scriptures gathered under it, this bit of prose is devoted to arguing, on scriptural grounds, that the heading actually expresses the tenor of scripture. The scriptures following this prose thus serve more overtly than their preceding cousins to bolster the prose's claim to the status of internal scripture. This status turns on the way that the prose, rather than being responsive to scripture in the manner of the heading, serves to shore up the heading against potential scriptural pushback. The prose does not entirely claim this assertive force for itself, adducing as it does some scriptural passages of its own.

Unlike the scripture blocks in the Ramist scheme, which appear in canonical order, these passages have been arranged in sequence to make an argument. The verse from Ephesians—"[remember [. . .] that you were [. . .]] alienated from the commonwealth of Israel"—sets out the bare fact of a covenantal and political distinction between Israel and the gentiles, the *status quo ante* of the Christian restructuring of that distinction.[63] The next passage, however,

---

[62] *DDC*, 307a: "hic paries intergerinus ille inter gentes nempe et Israelitas morte Christi tandem dirutus et solutus. Eph. 2. 14. ante hunc solutum gentes alienatae ab omni foedere fuere."

[63] *DDC*, 307a: "alienatae à re publica Israelis."

from Acts 14, begins to undermine any overly dichotomous reading of that past: "who [i.e., God] in ages past let all the nations proceed in their own ways. And yet he did not [allow] himself [to lack] witness, etc."[64] The last, from Acts 17, asserts a broader picture of God's salvific work: "[God [. . .] who out of one blood made the whole race of humankind [. . .]] so that they might seek the Lord, [to see] if perchance they might grope for and find [him]; although [indeed he is] not far away [from each one of us], etc. God, therefore, passing over the times of [that] ignorance, etc."[65] The collective effect of these passages is to argue that God's work always extended in some sense to Gentiles. At stake, then, is whether that work was coterminous with the Law of Moses. Milton answers in the negative, leaning on Acts 17 to hold that Gentiles could access God in ignorance of the Law, which therefore was not given "especially [*potissumum*]" to Israel, meaning that Gentiles could keep it from across the ethnic divide, but was rather given "only [*duntaxat*]" to Israel, meaning that it never had any claim on Gentiles.

The authority underpinning this marginal addition thus proves more assertive than that at work in the attendant changes to definition and heading. Milton is not simply attempting to write in harmony with external scripture and making the necessary adjustments; rather, he is shoring up his considered, revised position with argumentation. He does this in his own prose, but also by arranging passages of scripture to advantage (rhetorically, as opposed to the more neutral, logical practice of presenting them in canonical order). If the relationship between external and internal scripture operates on a spectrum, this confident move nudges the needle a few degrees toward the latter. The gesture is still relatively subdued in this case, but using scripture rather than responding to it marks a discernible shift because the agency is more clearly in Milton's hands.

The sixteen pages of I.27 under the heading "Throughout all nations" build on the changes to this eventful page in ways that demonstrate the broad formal range that the treatise's own words occupy, from relative submission, to external scripture, to full-throated speaking that claims the status of internal scripture. Notably, these pages seem to be a relatively late addition to (and expansion of) the manuscript; as this study continues, it will become increasingly apparent that the treatise's rhetorical excursions come materially

---

[64] *DDC*, 307a: "Qui praeteritis saeculis sivit omnes gentes incedere viis ipsarum, nec tamen se sine testimonio &c."

[65] *DDC*, 307a: "Ut quaererent Dominum si forte palparent invenirentque: quanquam non procul &c. tempora igitur ignorantiae praeteriens Deus &c."

60 MILTON'S THEOLOGICAL PROCESS

late in the stages of the treatise's composition, signaling that the turn toward rhetoric was an emergent feature of work on the treatise.[66]

In the "Throughout all nations" section, Milton engages his broader point in five waves: the usual heading and block of citations, to the end that the gospel extends to all nations (MS 317); some supplementary prose connecting this point to the abolition of the law, followed by further citations (MS 317–22); a seven-point argument for the law's abolition (MS 322–24); a prose argument that engages with exegesis along the way (MS 324–29); and, finally, a direct prose engagement with other theologians (MS 329–33). I have already discussed the formal features at work in the first two waves and so turn to the remaining three.

Both the seven-point argument and the section that follows share the form of an extended prose argument that engages in scriptural exegesis along the way, with scripture used to rhetorical ends. This kind of argument makes an even stronger claim for its own authoritative voice than the prose that makes an argument and arranges passages in support because now Milton is no longer presenting scriptural texts as effectively perspicuous but as in need of exegesis. Attention to only a portion of this extended section—one that bears directly on the question of internal scripture—will suffice to demonstrate the point. After insisting "that the whole Mosaic Law is abolished through the Gospel," Milton nevertheless avers: "And yet by this abolition of the law, in actual fact the law, that is, the summation of the law, is not indeed abrogated, but achieves its purpose in that love of God and one's neighbour which is born from faith through the spirit."[67] This idea that the law can be abolished without being abrogated grants Jesus's summation (quoting Deuteronomy and Leviticus) pride of place in the rule of faith, to the point that it becomes an expression of internal scripture that can drive interpretation of the external.

Milton develops this point in an ensuing paragraph that, in a confluence of form and content, uses internal scripture to engage in exegesis of the external by way of making an argument for internal scripture. Interpreting Romans 6:14–15, he writes:

So, as we said earlier, the summation of the law, obviously the love of God and one's neighbour, must by no means be thought to be abolished, but—only after its written surface has, as it were, been changed—to be etched on the hearts of

---

[66] On the additions to I.27, see the Appendix, pp. 260–62.

[67] *DDC*, 327: "totam legem Mosaicam per Evangelium aboleri. Et hac tamen legis abolitione, re quidem vera non abrogatur lex, id est, summa legis, sed finem suum assequitur in dilectione illa Dei et proximi, quae ex fide per spiritum nascitur." This passage evokes the "rule of charity" from the divorce tracts; see Chapter 5.

SCRIPTURE AND LITERARY FORM 61

the faithful with the spirit as writer, in such a way, however, that in particular commandments the spirit sometimes seems to disagree with the letter, if by not maintaining the letter we shall more rightly show regard for love of God and our neighbour. So Christ departed from the letter of the law, Mark 2:27, when he said that the sabbath was made for man's sake, not man for the sabbath's sake (if you should compare the fourth commandment). So [did] Paul when [he spoke] of marriage with an unbeliever as not for dissolution, which, on the other hand, is most sternly enjoined under the law. 1. Cor. 7:12: *I [say this], not the Lord.* For in interpreting each of those commandments, both that on the sabbath and that on marriage, the account taken of charity is preferred to all written law, just as it should also be preferred in [interpreting] all the rest.[68]

Whereas the method of headings and gathered passages allows Christ and Paul to speak for themselves, this method finds it necessary to speak for them—or at least to draw out the effects of their speaking as they did. Such human speaking becomes necessary because these are points where scripture is internally contradictory, as Milton observes by contrasting Jesus's statement with the fourth commandment. Rather than presuming scriptural harmony, or trying to preserve it, in these instances, the point is to highlight disharmony, albeit in service of an alternative harmony afforded by the internal-scriptural principle of charity. But this alternative harmony cannot become apparent by simply gathering scriptural passages under a heading; it requires human speech. Admittedly, scripture itself provides models of such speech, and it is to this end that Milton cites both Jesus and Paul. Elsewhere, in I.10, the sabbath and marriage are themselves directly at issue, but that is not the case here.[69] Instead, for some topics external scripture, here exemplified by the law of Moses, proves

[68] *DDC*, 328–29:

> Summa igitur legis, ut ante diximus, dilectio nimirum Dei et proximi, nequaquam existimanda est aboleri; sed veluti mutato solùm codice in cordibus fidelium, scriptore spiritu, exarari: ita tamen, ut in praeceptis particularib. aliud atque litera velle spiritus nonnunquam videatur, si literam non retinendo rectius dilectioni Dei et proximi consulemus. Sic Christus à legis litera discessit, Marc. 2. 27, cùm sabbathum propter hominem factum esse, non hominem propter sabbathum dixit, si quartum praeceptum conferas. sic Paulus de coniugio cum infideli non dissolvendo, quod contrà sub lege severissimè iniungitur. 1. Cor 7. 12. *ego, non Dominus*: in utrisque enim illis et de sabbatho et coniugio mandatis interpretandis, ratio habita charitatis omni scriptae legi praeponitur; quemadmodum et in reliquis omnibus praeponi debet.

[69] The topic of the Sabbath links the two instances of pages recopied by Skinner in the sequence of chapters where he otherwise let the Picard manuscript stand: MS 307a and MS 571–74, where, as Miller shows, a single verse (Colossians 2:17) led Milton to shift to a more radical form of anti-Sabbatarianism that understood the Sabbath as typologically abrogated under the Gospel; "Theological Typology," 232–48.

62 MILTON'S THEOLOGICAL PROCESS

inadequate, necessitating instead that one speak according to the internal scripture of charity. Jesus and Paul serve less as prooftexts than as exemplars.

The idea of Milton's interpretative practice as *imitatio Christi* will be developed further in Chapter 5; for now, it suffices to observe that Milton is claiming a remarkable kind of authority for his own words. Invoking the rule of charity hearkens back to the divorce tracts, which Annabel Patterson considered "exercises in how to make Scripture mean what you want it to mean."[70] Patterson's assessment succinctly captures the danger of an interpretative appeal to internal scripture; Milton might reply that Jesus and Paul are liable to the same charge and suggest that he could be in worse company than theirs. This hypothetical rejoinder has implications for Milton's ecclesiology, as will become clear in due course. That said, Patterson still has a point. Appeals to internal scripture unavoidably introduce subjectivity to interpretation, with predictably multifarious results. As in *Of True Religion*, commitment to process creates room for interpreters to err doctrinally without too much fear of eternal repercussions. Claiming to speak internal scripture simultaneously carries great authority and great potential for error. The two cannot be separated. All one can do is engage the process in good faith, trusting that God will pardon the inevitable unintended errors that arise along the way. Accordingly, one must speak internal scripture authoritatively, as though it will be vindicated in the end, but in the awareness that it might not be.

This kind of assertiveness characterizes the form at the far end of the spectrum I have been considering, which is prose that may allude to scripture but does not directly engage with it. In the case at hand, Milton engages instead with other Protestant theologians: Zanchius, Cameron, and Polanus. Milton does turn to scripture in his engagement with Polanus but not expressly with Zanchius, whom he quotes as holding, in his commentary on Ephesians 2, that "a very large part of theology depends" on the question of the law's total abolition.[71] Milton cites Zanchius as someone who shares his view, yet he offers

---

[70] Annabel Patterson, *Milton's Words* (Oxford: Oxford University Press, 2009), p. 116. See further, Theodore Long Huguelet, "Milton's Hermeneutics: A Study of Scriptural Interpretation in the Divorce Tracts and De Doctrina Christiana," PhD dissertation, University of North Carolina (1959), pp. 2–6.

[71] *DDC*, 330: "in huius quaestionis explicatione, non minimam partem Theologiae consistere." Milton slightly adjusts Zanchius's phrasing; the longer passage reads: "Credo, inquam, ex iis omnibus abundè liquere, propositae quaestionis solutionem: quomodo, *scil.* lex abrogata sit, & non abrogata: in cuius quaestionis explicatione, non minima pars Theologiae consistit." In context, Zanchius is writing about the bifurcation of the law along flesh/spirit lines:

> Aboleri enim lex dicitur per metonymiam, cum illis odium è cordibus nostris aboletur: & inscriptam in nobis amamus, quam extra nos positam, auersabamur: iuxta illud Apostoli, *Vbi Spiritus Domini, ibi libertas: &, si Spiritu ducimini, non estis sub lege*: Et, *Nihil damnationis est iis, qui non secundum carnem, sed secundum spiritum ambulant.*

Girolamo Zanchi, *Operum Theologicorum* (Geneva, 1619), Vol. II, tom. vi, 91.

SCRIPTURE AND LITERARY FORM   63

some correction: "And he proves his case accurately enough, but is not energetic enough in using what he has proved, getting entangled indecisively in many subsequent exceptions, which leave a slightly less attentive reader rather uncertain."[72] Milton seems to think that internal scripture ought to speak more directly than external, as though appealing to Christian liberty and the word written on believers' hearts by the spirit, as Zanchius does just prior to the quoted passage, ought to cut through the potential confusion occasioned by external scripture.[73] Perhaps this sensibility leads Milton down the reductive and narrowing path that the treatise so often takes, even as it also drives the material expansion of the treatise, seeing as the initial reference to Zanchius appears on the first page of a long (MS 320–27) insertion into the original fascicule.[74] For him, the internal scripture manifests as blunt assertion that bleeds occasionally into indignant eloquence—not as the kind of carefully qualified nuance exemplified by someone like Zanchius. In part, the difference is a matter of genre: the Ramist theological treatise embodies a formal drive toward reductive clarity that a work of scriptural commentary does not—especially not a work of commentary that uses more than 500 double-columned folio pages crammed with tiny print to discuss a brief epistle of 6 chapters.

Part of a long sentence in the paragraph following Milton's engagement with Zanchius shows internal scripture taking its place in Milton's revised rule of faith. Responding to the "believing Pharisees" who hold "that the law ought to be observed even under the gospel," he writes:

> one gets to know the will of God most correctly from the actual teaching of the gospel and the guidance of the promised spirit of truth, [and] finally from

---

[72] *DDC*, 330: "rémque satis accuratè probat; sed probatis non strenuè utitur; multis postea exceptionibus involutus ac fluctuans, quae lectorem paulò minus attentum, incertiorem dimittunt."

[73] See Zanchi, *Operum*, Vol. II, tom. vi, 90. He writes that "the [external] law is abolished through Christ, though not equally; for a certain kind of ceremony was abolished, such as cannot be revoked, but is rather negated by faith in Christ" (my trans.). This category covers animal sacrifice and so on. By contrast, the internal "is by no means abrogated: neither piety toward God, penitence and faith, the kernel of ceremonies, nor charity, peace, concord, justice, a civic spirit are taken up" (my trans.). Latin:

> lex per Christum abolita est, quanquam non aequaliter: caeremoniae enim quaedam ita fuerunt abolitae, vt reuocari non possint, quin fides in Christum negetur [...] Ad interna vero quod attinet, neutra abrogata est. cum neque pietas in Deum, poenitentia ac fides, nucleus caeremoniarum, neque mutua caritas, pax, concordia, iustitia, spiritus politicarum, sublatae sint.

Both theologians thus use the internal as a way of guaranteeing the continuation of the moral law into the gospel, but Milton disagrees with Zanchius that the abolition of the external law therefore extends only to the ceremonial, given his intentness on opposing external imposition generally, as in *A Treatise of Civil Power* (London, 1659). whose title page declares "That it is not lawfull for any power on earth to compell in matters of Religion." See further Kerr, "Shifting Perspectives," 132–37.

[74] The treatise's narrowing tendency appears in one of its distinctive keywords, *duntaxat*, which, as Campbell et al. write, "shows us the thrust of much of the work—to limit": *MMS*, 141.

64 MILTON'S THEOLOGICAL PROCESS

God's law written on the hearts of the faithful; but we acknowledge sin and are impelled to Christ's grace merely by knowing the law, not by carrying it out; for indeed we do not draw nearer to Christ by the works of the law, but stray further away from him, as scripture so often warns us.[75]

Milton articulates, in his own voice and with only indirect reference to scripture, how his version of the rule of faith works. Instead of combining the plain places of scripture with the teaching of the church, as Augustine does, Milton combines external and internal scripture. By acknowledging sin, however, he obliquely allows that claims to internal scripture can stray from Christ, which means that anyone who makes such claims is "impelled to Christ's grace." In this sense, Milton's rule of faith differs from Augustine's only in the ecclesiology it assumes: the "teaching of the church" becomes anything any believer says in good faith under the influence of the spirit, with an express reliance on grace to work the resulting cacophony toward harmony. Accepting such cacophony as the interim state of affairs, Milton has no compunction about speaking loudly: he expresses his position clearly and without apology or qualification even as the content implies the possibility that it could be the expression of sin and human confusion rather than the voicing of "God's law written on the hearts of the faithful." In his own way, by writing so forthrightly, Milton has embraced Luther's invitation to sin boldly.

Conclusion

Building on a discussion of Milton's concept of internal scripture, in relation to his practices of logic, rhetoric, and critical judgment, this chapter has mapped his theology of scripture along a continuum of literary forms. This map began with the Ramist scripture block, continued with matters of translating scripture (sometimes creatively), and moved into interpretative prose of various rhetorical kinds before culminating in prose where Milton argues with other theologians in ways that bear on scripture while addressing it only indirectly. I have offered relative deference to external scripture—the degree to which Milton is letting scripture change his mind rather than using it to try to change his readers' minds—as a heuristic framework for distributing the literary forms of internal scripture along this spectrum. This framework provides a useful way

---

[75] *DDC*, 330–31: "deinde, voluntas Dei ex ipsa doctrina evangelii et promisso spiritu veritatis duce, Dei lege denique cordibus fidelium inscripta rectissimè cognoscitur: peccatum autem agnoscimus, et ad gratiam Christi impellimur, legem duntaxat cognoscendo, non praestando; siquidem operibus legis non propius ad Christum accedimus, sed longius à Christo aberramus; ut scriptura toties monet."

of reading the treatise, but it also suggests that learning to read *De Doctrina Christiana* will require making sense of its position on two interrelated theological questions. The first, the question of the human capacity to understand and interpret scripture, is the subject of Chapter 2. The second, the question of how the relationship between scriptural and human authority plays out on the level of ecclesiology, is the subject of Chapter 3.

2

Human Capacity and Scriptural Interpretation

Chapter 1 examined the relationship between logic and rhetoric in Milton's engagement with scripture in *De Doctrina Christiana*, and it documented a range of literary forms in which the treatise's relationship to external scripture becomes increasingly subordinated to human rhetorical authority. This chapter turns to the theological underpinnings of human rhetorical authority as it works in the treatise. In taking up this matter, the chapter inevitably butts up against a familiar Protestant polemic that pits the authority of scripture against "merely human" interpretation, the latter often associated with the Roman magisterium's claims to authority. Milton is no stranger to this polemic; in the epistle, he compares the enforcement of human interpretation to violent enslavement: "our slavery endures still; not as previously to divine law, but what is most wretched of all, to human law; or, to speak more accurately, we must be slaves to *in*human tyranny."[1] As this wordplay suggests, however, Milton's position on human activity in religious matters is not reductively negative: the antithesis of inhuman tyranny would seem to be a liberty at once Christian and human even as human law remains a potentially problematic category. The status of rhetoric begins to come into view when *De Doctrina Christiana* takes up the question of human interpretative capacity in I.17 ("On Renewal, and also on Calling"), which considers the time and manner of that capacity's renewal from its lapsarian decay.

Here, a paradox begins to emerge, however, which is that Milton's eventual embrace of human argumentation in theology emerged from (and not in spite of) his deep commitment to scripture as the foundation of theology. The theological foundations of human interpretative activity emerge, in other words, as a product of Milton's insisting that scripture can speak for itself: he uses the relatively intuitive reasoning of Ramist logic and subtle forays into

---

[1] *DDC*, 4: "servitus adhuc durat; non legi, ut olim, divinae, sed, quod miserrimum est, humanae; vel, verius ut dicam, inhumanae tyrannidi servienda."

Milton's Theological Process. Jason A. Kerr, Oxford University Press. © Jason A. Kerr (2023).
DOI: 10.1093/oso/9780198875086.003.0003

rhetoric to argue for a human evaluative capacity geared explicitly toward the rhetorical delivery of the Word via preaching.[2] To be sure, in the chapter on Holy Scripture (I.30), Milton names interpretative difficulties that emerge from the biblical scholarship of his time: issues of corrupt textual transmission and so on.[3] These concerns—which would drive the development of modern biblical criticism in the hands of Thomas Hobbes, Baruch de Spinoza, Richard Simon, and others—certainly came to destabilize the notion of biblical authority, and they participated in the rise of religious rationalism in the last half of the seventeenth century. The transformation of Milton's perspective on the place of human activity in theological work, however, owes more to the painstaking effort required by his own methodology—the hard work of invention—than to the grand sweep of historical change. That work, on the thorny topic of the relationship between the human capacity to understand scripture and the larger economy of salvation, occurred at a very particular intersection of biblical texts, which Milton was reading alongside his usual interlocutors, Wolleb and Ames. The perceived inadequacies of these interlocutors seem to have provoked questions that challenged not only their own methodologies but also Milton's by bringing his logic to bear on matters of rhetorical concern in ways that trouble the ostensibly clear distinction between logic and rhetoric.

This focus on Milton's methodology complicates two common and unhelpfully binary ways of reading him and his work. One is the habit of debating whether he is "orthodox" or a "heretic." The other is the habit of treating the relationship between scripture and Milton's own words as a zero-sum contest of authority, as when scholars claim that Milton makes scripture mean whatever he wants it to mean.[4] I am arguing instead that Milton's heresies emerge organically from his orthodoxy and that he hopes to speak with the authority of scripture nowhere so fervently as when he is speaking in what appear to be his own words. Accordingly, Milton's anti-Calvinist theological claim that humans have a pivotal part to play in their own renewal—the view that underwrites his sense of a church characterized by a constant churn of human activity—nevertheless depends profoundly on a broadly Reformed insistence

---

[2] The use of reason to evaluate preaching informs Milton's argument in *Areopagitica*, 12:

> For those actions which enter into a man, rather then issue out of him, and therefore defile not, God uses not to captivat under a perpetuall childhood of prescription, but trusts him with the gift of reason to be his own chooser; there were but little work left for preaching, if law and compulsion should grow so fast upon those things which hertofore were govern'd only by exhortation.

[3] *DDC*, 395–98.
[4] See the discussion in Chapter 1, pp. 62–63.

68 MILTON'S THEOLOGICAL PROCESS

that God alone is the efficient cause of human spiritual transformation and salvation. Milton's theology remains in deep harmony with Calvin's even as he advances (in I.17) a position against which Calvin specifically inveighed.[5] Similarly, the manuscript shows Milton working assiduously to bring his theology of human capacity into consonance with scripture even as that theology eventually worked to undermine the very scripture-centric literary form out of which it emerged.

These contradictions only appear as such, however, when viewed from a relatively high altitude and with a long time-frame. Closer to the ground, where manuscript revisions enable us to trace parts of Milton's theological process one step at a time, these developments are much more organic, and the labels that we often use to classify theological positions ("Calvinist," "Arminian," etc.) become obstacles rather than aids to understanding. In the chapter laying out his treatise's methodology, Milton claims that "In this work nothing new is being taught" while also appealing to Jesus's parable of the householder in Matthew 13:52: "every scribe who has been instructed in the kingdom of the heavens is like some head of a household who brings out things old and new from his treasury."[6] As David Urban observes, Milton's appeal to this parable empowers him to pursue orthodoxy precisely by challenging it.[7] Understanding Milton's theology requires abandoning any attempt to pin down his allegiance to externally determined theological positions, at least temporarily, and instead tracking his thought through its own complex processes of development. The best way to ascertain Milton's views on the interpretation of scripture is to pay very close attention to his concrete practice—his own ways of reading.

The manuscript provides a useful window into Milton's shifting views because the relevant chapters—I.17 ("On Renewal, and also on Calling") and I.18 ("On Regeneration")—survive in a material form that preserves multiple layers of revision. Accordingly, tracking his change of mind involves engaging in depth with the ways of reading outlined in the introduction: close reading of scripture blocks alongside Wolleb and Ames, accounting for accrued layers of manuscript revision, and attention to forms of internal scripture like those identified in Chapter 1. In Milton's I.17–18, that means tracing how his reliance on scripture led him to revise the distinction between their topics from

---

[5] John Calvin, *Institutio Christianae Religionis* (Geneva, 1559), p. 282; Calvin, *Institutes of the Christian Religion*, ed. John T. McNeill; trans. Ford Lewis Battles (Louisville, KY: Westminster John Knox Press, 1960; repr. 2006), pp. 785–86 (III.xiv.19).

[6] *DDC*, 8: "Hic autem non novum quicquam docetur [...] Mat. 13. 52. *omnis scriba edoctus in regno caelorum, similis est cuipiam patri familias, qui profert è thesauro suo nova et vetera.*"

[7] David V. Urban, *Milton and the Parables of Jesus: Self-Representation and the Bible in John Milton's Writings* (University Park, PA: Pennsylvania State University Press, 2018), p. 200.

external/internal renewal to natural/supernatural renewal. Far from a merely semantic shift, this change in language facilitates an expansive understanding of what humans in their unsaved, "natural" state can do. Ultimately, in I.17 Milton argues that God, by grace, has renewed all humans in their natural state such that they are able to understand and evaluate scripture, which enables them to consent (or not) to the further act of grace that would begin to renew them in a saving way (the topic of I.18). With this complex view of human freedom, Milton develops a theological foundation for the rhetorical deployment of "internal scripture" that proves key for understanding the treatise's formal departures from the norms laid out in the epistle.

This chapter, then, undertakes two interrelated tasks: to demonstrate Milton's reliance on scripture as he revises his theological frameworks and to articulate the theology of human interpretative capacity that he develops through that work of revision. Separating the topics might have lent clarity, but ironically, I cannot separate what Milton joined together.

Theological Context

Given the Reformed context in which Milton was writing, the question of human capacity to understand and interpret scripture necessarily involves the question of how that capacity gets renewed from the damage it incurred in the Fall. As the title of I.17 ("On Renewal, and also on Calling") suggests, Milton connects renewal with calling, or the act by which God calls humans out of their sinful state and into the life of faith.[8] By bringing these topics together, Milton lays the foundation for his theology of human capacity, but in doing so, he parts ways with Wolleb and Ames and therefore sets himself the challenge of countering their positions on exegetical grounds. This counter-argument remains mostly obscured behind the literary form of the scripture block, however—or it would lie mostly obscured were it not for manuscript revisions that show Milton struggling to put his theology into scriptural language. Writing a theology that tries to let scripture speak for itself turns out to require significant human effort behind the scenes, with processes of invention lurking behind even the treatise's most intuitive and logical literary forms. In I.17, though, this effort results in a theology that opens the door for making such labors more

---

[8] Barbara K. Lewalski's influential "Protestant Paradigm of Salvation" involves, sequentially: election, calling, justification, adoption, sanctification, and glorification. Milton's "renewal" is not on this list, suggesting the need for a more detailed account of the theological landscape: *Protestant Poetics and the Seventeenth-Century Religious Lyric* (Princeton, NJ: Princeton University Press, 1979), pp. 13–27.

70 MILTON'S THEOLOGICAL PROCESS

overt in the text, in the rhetorical manner most prominently on display in I.5, the chapter on the Son of God. Understanding this theological basis for the treatise's unabashedly human speech thus requires tracing Milton's exegetical labors through the winding paths of the revisions to I.17–18.

Before turning to the material dimension of the revisions that enables us to see Milton's theological thought process, a bit of a terminological road map is in order. Just as a small helm turns a large ship, significant theological differences often hinge on details that can seem almost infinitesimal. Because Milton's argument can be quite dense—including the extremely compact literary form of the scripture block—the reading of his argument that follows is necessarily technical, even if it is more diffuse. My hope is that lingering briefly on some major terminological matters will aid readers in navigating a theological land-scape where a high level of abstraction does not, by any means, imply low stakes, either for the theology at hand or for understanding Milton's broader project in *De Doctrina Christiana*.

The place to begin is with the two terms that Milton anomalously links in the title of I.17: renewal and calling (or *vocation*, here used synonymously).[9] Given the complexity at hand, the definitions I offer should not be taken as com-prehensive but rather as foundations to be built upon as the chapter unfolds. Briefly, then, the theological significance of *renewal* proceeds from the damage incurred to human capacities in the Fall. The kind of renewal required neces-sarily depends on how a particular theologian understands human capacities in their pre- and postlapsarian states. Debates about renewal therefore often signal disagreements about these other logically prior issues—disagreements in which the topic of human will frequently takes center stage. In popular understand-ing, the difference is between a Lutheran/Calvinist insistence on the bondage of the will and an Arminian/Semipelagian insistence that the will, in some sense, remains free. This understanding is not without merit, but it is too simplis-tic for present purposes because theologians on all sides of the debate insist on freedom as an immutable quality of the will, understood in relation to the other core human faculty, the intellect. By this, they mean that the will, even after the Fall, operates free from coercion of any kind: the will either freely enacts the judgments of the intellect (intellectualism) or freely overrides them (voluntarism).[10]

It is in this insistence on the freedom of the will as a faculty that theologians on the Lutheran/Calvinist side of the debate seek to evade the charge, levied

---

[9] Milton's Latin for "calling" is invariably a form of *vocatio*.

[10] More precisely, Scotus's voluntarism contests the idea that the intellect judging the good affords an adequate foundation for ethical or moral life.

by theologians on the other side, that their view makes God the author of sin.[11] Humans are freely choosing the bad, not being compelled to do so by God's eternal decree. It was always a possibility, albeit unactualized, for such humans to choose otherwise.[12] The bondage of the will involves not the faculty (*voluntas*, will), but its function (*arbitrium*, choice).[13] Luther's famous book on this subject thus bears the title *De Servo Arbitrio*, not *De Servo Voluntate*. The will still chooses freely; it has just become incapacitated from choosing the good. The debate hinges on the how and why of this incapacitation. Alrick George Headley argues that Arminius remains intellectualist: the problem is that the intellect incorrectly judges the good, and the will freely acts on these faulty judgments. In these terms, renewal means restoring the intellect's capacity of judgment. Calvin, by contrast, understands fallen humanity in voluntarist terms, which is to say that the will can now overpower the judgment of the intellect, with bad results. In these terms, renewal means restoring the proper priority of the intellect over the will.[14]

A corollary to this difference between Arminius and Calvin—one with direct relevance to Milton, as we will see—involves the question of nature. Part of the problem is that the parties to the debate mean subtly different things by this term. At the risk of being reductive (because there is such a thing as Calvinist natural theology in the sense that the book of nature does meaningfully complement the book of scripture as a witness to God), the Calvinist view is that *natural*, applied to humans, means "unaided by grace."[15] Arminius seems to agree with this definition, but as will be discussed below, he denies that there is any such thing as a fully natural human, utterly bereft of the supernatural gifts that come with being created in the image of God. The fall damages that image

---

[11] For Milton's explanation of this view, see *The Doctrine and Discipline of Divorce*, 2nd edn (London, 1644), p. 39.

[12] For recent debates about contingency, see Willem J. van Asselt, Martin Bac, and Roelf T. te Velde, eds, *Reformed Thought on Freedom* (Grand Rapids, MI: Baker Academic, 2010); Richard A. Muller, *Divine Will and Human Choice: Freedom, Contingency, and Necessity in Early Modern Reformed Thought* (Grand Rapids, MI: Baker Academic, 2017); Paul Helm, *Reforming Free Will: A Conversation on the History of Reformed Views on Compatibilism (1500–1800)* (Fearn: Mentor, 2020).

[13] Alrick George Headley, *The Nature of the Will in the Writings of Calvin and Arminius: A Comparative Study* (Eugene, OR: Wipf and Stock, 2017), p. 16.

[14] Headley, *The Nature of the Will*, ch. 2. Calvin's remains an intellectualist understanding of voluntarism.

[15] For instance, "The natural order was that the frame of the universe should be the school in which we were to learn piety, and from it pass over to eternal life and perfect felicity. But after man's rebellion, our eyes—wherever they turn—encounter God's curse. [Erat quide[m] hic genuinus ordo vt mundi fabrica nobis schola esset ad pietatem discendam: vnde ad aeternam vitam & perfectam foelicitatem fieret transitus. sed post defectionem quocunque vertamus oculos, sursum & deorsum occurrit Dei maledictio.]": Calvin, *Institutio*, 113; *Institutes*, 341 (II.vi.1). See also the use of natural theology in Randall C. Zachman, "The Christology of John Calvin," in *The Oxford Handbook of Christology*, ed. Francesca Aran Murphy and Troy A. Stefano (Oxford: Oxford University Press, 2015), pp. 284–85.

72 MILTON'S THEOLOGICAL PROCESS

in humanity and the attendant gifts, but it does not eradicate them. In polemic, Calvinists accuse Arminians of being Pelagians—of claiming that humans are, if only in theory, naturally capable of the obedience that salvation requires. A brief passage from the Synod of Dort expresses this polemical understanding while emphasizing nature:

> And such as man was after his fall, such children he begat, namely a corrupt issue from a corrupt father, this corruption being by the just judgement of God derived from Adam to all his posterity (Christ only excepted) and that not by imitation (as of old the Pelagians would have it) but by the propagation of nature with her infection.[16]

Consequently, Calvinist renewal involves the purgation of original sin, whereas Arminian renewal involves the restoration of supernatural faculties that, even in the fallen state, retained some of their function, albeit not enough to accomplish salvation without the intervention of grace (this latter is a key point overlooked by the Calvinist polemic at Dort).

These different understandings of renewal lead to different understandings of the process by which God redeems humans from the fall. The usual terms are *justification* and *sanctification*, understood as part of a sequence of unfolding salvation, or *ordo salutis*—a sequence in which *calling* also plays an important part. As indicated above, Milton's decision to link renewal and calling is controversial, but what makes it so? Usually, *justification* refers to the process of being made righteous before God in Christ. Following received readings of Paul, the righteousness in question pertains to Christ, not to the person being justified, who will still need to undergo a transformative process of *sanctification* in which the righteousness of participation in Christ becomes personal righteousness. In most Reformed theologies, calling and justification are closely linked. Because, for Calvin, humans cannot resist God's call (they are freely but irresistibly drawn to God by it), calling all but immediately produces justification and inaugurates the process of sanctification. This calling is a matter of God's election, and in the supralapsarian model favored by Calvin and Beza, God decrees from eternity (i.e., before the Fall) whom he will call and whom he will not or, as the idea of double predestination comes to receive clearer articulation, whom he will elect to damnation. In these terms, the call goes out only to those whom God has elected to save.

As noted above, to Arminius and likeminded theologians, this supralapsarian scheme made God the author of sin. They responded by asserting that God calls

---

[16] Synod of Dort, *The Ivdgement of the Synode Holden at Dort* (London, 1619), p. 32.

everyone, but that only the elect will respond to it. In this model, calling and justification are still closely linked. The sticking point upon which subsequent debate turned is the idea that humans need to respond to the call, which means that they somehow have the capacity to do it. This is where Calvinist accusations of Pelagianism come in because, from their perspective, the Arminian view means that humans are capable of choosing to be saved or not, with the matter of election in their hands rather than in God's. Arminians, however, still understand God as the agent and cause of salvation. The issue for them was not free choice but clearing God from being the author of sin. Their aim was not to say that humans can save themselves but that humans ultimately bear the responsibility for their own damnation. As we will see, Milton shares this concern for making the reprobate (i.e., the unsaved) responsible, but he is also interested in the issue of free choice in the sense that humans need capacities to respond to the call as it appears in scripture and in preaching. This response, he insists, is not enough to produce justification (or, more accurately for his theological system, salvific renewal), but it still has a necessary part to play in an *ordo salutis* that attempts to combine a powerful interest in divine sovereignty with a degree of human moral responsibility.

This chapter traces Milton's process of thinking through how to accomplish this theological desideratum through revisions found in the manuscript pages of *De Doctrina Christiana* I.17–18. Of the two, I.18 is materially the less complicated. Prior to the revisions that appear on its pages, it represents a single stratum, meaning that all its pages (comprising a single folio) were recopied at the same time. I.17, by contrast, contains three strata, signaled by changes in paper size, watermark, and catchword evidence (see Figure 2.1): the chapter's first section (MS 221–28) is its newest, followed by MS 225–28, with MS 229–35 as the oldest stratum.[17] All these strata were, however, already in place when the revisions at issue in this chapter occurred. These revisions, in the hand of Amanuensis "A," are present in all three sections of I.17 and in I.18. Noticing the strata matters because it offers glimpses of the trail of composition and revision prior to the point at which we can begin following it in detail. In particular, the stretch of rhetorical prose on MS 225–26 suggests that Milton had already begun implementing the kind of human speech whose theological authorization this chapter will track—a reminder that changes of mind are rarely reducible to a single moment or event, but often unfold recursively over time.

[17] See the Appendix, p. 257.

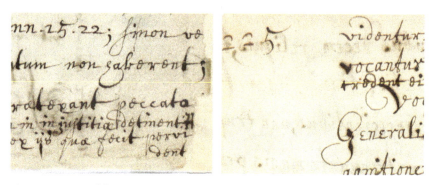

Figure 2.1 Detail from *DDC*, 224–25, where a mismatched catchword indicates a folio recopied to align with already existing material

Milton's Starting Point

On its largest scale, the change here under consideration involves the way that Milton frames the Ramist division between I.17 and I.18. Both address kinds of renewal, but Milton revised the distinction from one between external and internal renewal to one between natural and supernatural renewal. Theologically, this change matters because it helps Milton work toward a clearer articulation of what capacities for understanding and interpreting scripture exist in unsaved humans. From the perspective of learning how to read *De Doctrina Christiana*, it matters for the insight it gives into Milton as a reader of scripture, in conversation with Wolleb and Ames, among others. For readers of Milton more generally, it matters for the unparalleled window it offers into his process of thinking through a complex theological problem.

Some of the complexity arises from Milton's decision to consider calling and renewal in tandem, unlike his interlocutors. Wolleb considers calling in two chapters (I.20 on common vocation and I.28 on special vocation), while treating renewal in I.32, on sanctification, with justification appearing in I.31. Ames, similarly, treats calling in his I.26, justification in I.27, and sanctification in I.29 (the intervening chapter is on adoption). For Wolleb, both "renewal" and "regeneration" serve as synonyms for "sanctification," and, as the chapter sequence suggests, renewal comes several steps down the causal and logical chain from calling.[18] *De Doctrina Christiana*, by contrast, puts renewal and calling together in I.17, then treats regeneration as a separate topic in I.18, saves justification for I.22, and does not have a chapter on sanctification per se.

---

[18] Wolleb, 211 [180]: "*Appellatur* Regeneratio, Renovatio, Conversio, Poenitentia, Resipiscentia, & Glorificatio."

HUMAN CAPACITY AND SCRIPTURAL INTERPRETATION   75

Consequently, the treatise presents a different understanding of salvation than Wolleb does, with renewal happening in connection with calling, and these and regeneration all preceding justification, whereas for Wolleb, calling leads to justification, with renewal and regeneration following as effects.

Milton may complexly part ways with Wolleb and Ames, but he begins by taking up their traditional language of external and internal, for which Luther affords an important antecedent. The question is how much capacity to understand scripture resides in unregenerate humanity, or humanity in its "natural" state, unrenewed by the effects of grace. For Luther, the answer to this question was "none":

> To put it briefly, there are two kinds of clarity in Scripture, just as there are also two kinds of obscurity: one external and pertaining to the ministry of the Word, the other located in the understanding of the heart. If you speak of the internal clarity, no man perceives one iota of what is in the Scriptures unless he has the Spirit of God. All men have a darkened heart, so that even if they can recite everything in scripture, and know how to quote it, yet they apprehend and truly understand nothing of it [...] For the Spirit is required for the understanding of Scripture, both as a whole and in any part of it.[19]

Even though, on its surface, this passage is about the clarity of scripture, it bears directly on the interrelated issues of calling and election because of its implications for human capacities. Luther insists that scripture itself is externally or objectively clear in matters pertaining to salvation, but he adamantly denies that humans naturally possess any capacity to understand it unless and until the Spirit acts upon them and renews their capacities. He applies the terms "external" and "internal" grammatically to scripture, but in context, the reference point for these spatial terms is the human person. Internal clarity, "located in the understanding of the heart," refers to the human capacity for understanding, which is possible only when the spirit operates within a person. External clarity is so called because it involves actions like preaching that occur outside a person. This distinction involves some tension. Luther insists on the efficacy

---

[19] E. Gordon Rupp and Philip S. Watson, eds, *Luther and Erasmus: Free Will and Salvation* (Philadelphia, PA: Westminster John Knox, 1969), p. 112 [Martin Luther, *De Servo Arbitrio* (Wittenberg, 1525), fols B2r.-v]:

> Et ut breuiter dicam, Duplex est claritas scripturae, sicut & duplex obscuritas, Vna externa in uerbi ministerio posita, altera in cordis cognitione sita, Si de interna claritate dixeris, nullus homo unum iota in scripturis uidet, nisi qui spiritum Dei habet, omnes habent obscuratum cor, ita, ut si etiam dicant et norint proferre omnia scripturae, nihil tamen horum sentiant aut uere cognoscant.... Spiritus enim requiritur ad totam scripturam & ad quamlibet eius partem intelligendam.

76 MILTON'S THEOLOGICAL PROCESS

of preaching, saying of the external clarity that "nothing at all is left obscure or ambiguous, but everything there is in the Scriptures has been brought out by the Word into the most definite light, and published to all the world."[20] Meanwhile, however, the question remains of how people are to understand this preaching without first having been endowed with the spirit. The external call as offered in preaching may be clear, but only the internal call of the spirit can be efficacious.

When Milton takes up the dilemma of preaching, Ames proves especially influential. Unlike Wolleb, he does not place general and special calling in separate chapters but has only a single chapter on calling that uses a distinction between external and internal instead of general and special to discuss the "offer of Christ" (understood as the first part of calling, with receiving Christ as the second).[21] For Ames, "the outward is a propounding, or preaching of the Gospell or of the promises of Christ," while "the inward offer is a spirituall enlightning, whereby those promises are propounded to the hearts of men, as it were by an inward word."[22] The difference with the view that Milton will advance arises from the relationship among the external call, election, and the human capacity to receive preaching:

Those promises as touching the outward promulgation, are propounded to all without difference, together with a command to believe them, but as touching the propriety of the things promised, which depends upon the intention of him that promiseth, they belong only to the elect, who are therefore called the sonnes and heires of the promise. *Rom.* 9.8.[23]

Ames makes preaching available to all, but he insists that it is efficacious only for the elect, meaning that neither preacher nor hearer has anything to do with whether preaching has any effect. Milton agrees that the efficacy of salvation ultimately depends on God, but he also thinks that the human capacity to evaluate and respond to preaching matters. His challenge in I.17 is to find the right way of articulating the relationship between these two theological

---

[20] Rupp and Watson, *Luther and Erasmus*, 112 [Luther, *De Servo Arbitrio*, fol. B2v]: "Si de externa dixeris, Nihil prorsus relictum est obscurum aut ambiguum, sed omnia sunt per uerbum in lucem producta certissimam, & declarata toto orbi quaecunq; sunt in scripturis."

[21] Ames, 124 [132]. "Vocationes partes duae sunt: *oblatio* Christi, & ejusdem receptio."

[22] Ames, 125 [132–33]: "Externa est Evangelij, vel promissionum de Christo propositio aut praedicatio [. . .] Interna oblatio est spiritualis quaedam illuminatio, qua cordibus hominum proponuntur illae promissiones quasi per verbum internum."

[23] Ames, 125 [133]: "Promissiones istae, quoad promulgationem externam, sine discrimine proponuntur omnibus, una cum credendi mandato, sed quoad proprietatem rerum promissarum, quae ex intentione promittentis pendet, pertinent solummodo ad electos, qui idcirco vocantur *filij & haeredes promissionis.* Rom. 9. 8."

commitments, and he starts by taking up Ames' language of external and internal before finding it unsatisfactory and undertaking a series of revisions that implement a way of thinking about the problem that he finds more consonant with the language of scripture.

Prior to those revisions, Milton articulates the division between I.17 and I.18 as follows: "I term 'external' the renewal which reaches its limit in the external and natural man. And this comprises calling and the change which follows it in the external and natural man."[24] I.18, then, begins in its initial state by addressing "the manner of internal renewal, and this is **regeneration** and **ingrafting in Christ**."[25] In this configuration, a kind of non-regenerative, external renewal is possible in the "natural man," whereas regenerative renewal is purely internal and brings about a kind of union with Christ. For Milton, God's call extends to all people and carries with it a sufficient degree of renewal to enable a response—enough renewal, for instance, that a sermon calling one to repentance might have the desired effect—but not the degree of renewal that only results from God's work of redemption. Both Wolleb and Ames hint at the possibility of external renewal in these terms, but in their view, it suffices only to leave people without excuse and therefore meriting God's just condemnation; renewal per se only really comes with redemption.

In a passage that Milton ultimately deleted (see Figure 2.2), the manuscript offers limited insight into the process that led Milton to address renewal and calling together, but it also shows him wrestling with the implementation of this decision and the viability of his inherited framework:

> **External manner.** The theologians, indeed, are wont to divide vocation into external and internal: but that which they term internal not only properly speaking seems to be the vocation but also the election of believers; or rather

Figure 2.2 Detail from *DDC*, 222–23: the deleted passage

---

[24] *DDC*, 222: "Externa quae in exteriore et naturali homine terminatur. Estque vocatio, eámque sequens in exteriore et naturali homine alteratio."
[25] *DDC*, 236: "Interna renovationis ratio estque **regeneratio et insitio in Christum**."

78 MILTON'S THEOLOGICAL PROCESS

their regeneration, but is truly their election: Rom. 8: 28–30: [*those who have been*] *called as a result of his* [i.e., God's] *plan*; 1 Cor. 1: 26: *you discern your calling, brothers* [. . .] *God chose the things of the world that are foolish*; 2 Tim. 1: 9: [*God who* [. . .] *called us*] *with a holy calling* [. . .] *as a result of his purpose and grace.* And so, just as the vocation of a whole nation is sometimes in common parlance termed election, Deut. 7:6: *you* [i.e., Israel] *are a people holy to Jehovah* [*your God*]*; Jehovah* [*your God*] *has picked you out*; so election is sometimes called vocation, because it seems to be a sort of actual election, as they call it, if you refer it solely to the elect ones; or, in the common description, it is the same as regeneration; hence it has no place here.[26]

This passage begins by noting that the theologians seem to be making claims about the election or regeneration of believers when they divide vocation or calling into external and internal. Calling, meanwhile, only "sometimes [*nonnunquam*]" coincides with election, the conflation having more to do with sloppy speech habits than theological truth. Some calling, directed to the elect, does indeed coincide with regeneration such that the topic of election must be saved for later: "hence it has no place here." This confluence of topics does not, however, exhaust the concept of calling so that aspects of the topic remain pertinent to I.17.

Scripture plays a key role in the theological process on display in this passage. The language of the scriptural quotations themselves shows how closely Milton is engaging with Wolleb and Ames—"the theologians"—as he works out the distinction between calling and sanctification. Milton follows Wolleb in quoting 2 Timothy 1:9 using the word *proposito* instead of Beza's *praestituto* (even though Milton uses the latter in his quotation from Romans), and Milton and Ames both use the unusual *cernitis* instead of the forms of *videre* that tend to appear in Latin renderings of 1 Corinthians 1:26.[27] So, Milton's phrasing of

---

[26] *DDC*, 222–23 [Oxford, 556, Latin note i and Translation note i]:

> **Externa ratio**. Solent quidem theolog[i] vocationem distribuere in externam et internam: sed quam illi internam vocant, non solùm proprie vocatio verum etiam electio iam credentium; vel potius regeneratio videtur esse sed revera electio est; Rom. 8. 28. 29. 30.; *ex praestituto ipsius vocati.* 1 Cor. 1. 26; *cernitis vocationem vestram fratres—, quae stulta sunt mundi elegit Deu*[s.] 2 Tim. 1. 9; *vocatione sancta, ex suo proposito et grati*[a.] Itaque ut vocatio universae nationis communi more loquendi dicitur nonnunquam; Deut. 7. 6; *populus sanctus es Iehovae, te selegit Iehova—,* ita electio nonnunquam dicitur vocatio: eo quod actualis quaedam electio, ut loquuntur, videatur esse, si ad electos solos referas; aut, ut vulgò describitur, idem cum regeneratione est; proinde locum hic non habet.

[27] Milton quotes 2 Tim. 1:9 as "vocatione sancta, ex suo proposito et grati[a]"; Wolleb, 193 [164], quotes it as "Qui servavit nos, & vocavit, vocatione sancta; non ex operibus nostris, sed ex proposito & gratia, quae datae est nobis in Christo Jesu, ante te[m]pora secularia"; Beza (1598) reads, "Qui seruauit nos, & vocauit vocatione sancta: non ex operibus nostris, sed ex suo praestituto, & gratia, quae data quidem est nobis in Christo Iesu ante tempora seculorum." Beza's note offers *proposito* as a synonym

the scriptural passages in and of itself suggests that he is reading Wolleb and Ames.

Milton diverges with Wolleb and Ames in his thinking about divine agency and human capacities. Quoting Romans 8:30 in his chapter on calling (I.26), Ames emphasizes divine agency in a way that links election and calling: "Whom he predestinated, them also he called."[28] Wolleb quotes similarly, with only a slight difference.[29] Milton, meanwhile, quotes Romans 8:28 in a way that potentially uncouples calling and election even as he also cites (but does not quote) verses 29 and 30: "[those who have been] called as a result of his [i.e., God's] plan."[30] 1 Corinthians 1:26 has a similarly divergent potential. Ames, after defining calling as "a gathering of men together to Christ, that they may be united with him," specifies that "this therefore is that first thing which pertaines to the application of redemption" and quotes the passage from 1 Corinthians after quoting Ephesians 1:7–9.[31] The action of discernment implied by *cernitis* does not seem operative here; Ames's translator simply uses "see." Indeed, immediately following the quotation, Ames insists that "the Calling of men doth not in any sort depend upon [. . .] any indeavour of the called, but upon election and predestination of God only."[32] Meanwhile, the prospect of external renewal independent of regeneration that Milton is exploring in this sequence suggests the possibility that human discernment, aided by limited renewal, could mark the difference between election and reprobation. In Milton's hands, Ames's unusual word takes on greater significance. As for 2 Timothy 1:9, Wolleb quotes it in support of the proposition that "The principal efficient cause of vocation, is God; the impulsive is, his free mercy; the instrumental, the Ministery of the Word."[33] Tellingly, Wolleb quotes and Milton omits the part of the verse insisting that the attendant salvation is "not according to our works [*non ex operibus*

---

for *praestituto*, so either both Milton and Wolleb are following the note or Milton is simply quoting (selectively) from the verse as presented in Wolleb. With 1 Corinthians 1:26, most Latin Bibles—the Vulgate, various editions of Beza, all of the translations in Brian Walton's *Biblia Sacra Polyglotta* (London, 1657)—use forms of *videre* to render the Greek βλέπετε, but Milton, Ames (124 [131]), and both the 1623 Hanau and 1630 Geneva editions of Beza use *cernitis* instead, rendering their selection from verse 26 as "cernitis vocationem vestram." The first edition of Ames appeared at Franeker in 1623, the same year as the Hanau edition of Beza. Milton quotes verse 27 slightly differently ("quae stulta sunt") than Ames or Beza 1598/1623/1630 ("quae sunt infirma"), but the unusual *cernitis* is sufficiently uncanny as to warrant further consideration. (Thanks to John Hale for consulting Beza 1623 in the Dunedin Public Library on my behalf.) On these two editions of the JTB, see Chapter 1, n. 46.

[28] Ames, 124 [132]: "Quos praedestinavit, eos etiam vocavit."

[29] Wolleb, 193 [163–64]: "Quos enim praedestinavit vocavit."

[30] *DDC*, 222: "ex praestituto ipsius vocati."

[31] Ames, 124 [131]: "*Vocatio* enim est aggregatio hominum ad Christum, ut uniantur cum ipso [. . .] Hoc igitur primum illud est, quod pertinet ad applicationem redemptionis."

[32] Ames, 124 [132]: "Hinc vocatio hominum nullo modo ex [. . .] conatu aliquo vocandorum pendet, sed electione et praedestinatione Dei tantum."

[33] Wolleb, 193 [164]: "Caussa efficiens princeps vocationis, est Deus; impulsiva, gratuita ejus Misericordia; instrumentalis, Verbi Ministerium."

nostris]." Milton will, in due course, resolve the question of agency in God's favor but not at the expense of human action in the natural person in the way that Wolleb does. The language of scripture—*cernitis*—obliges him to strike a balance. Perhaps the preaching of the Word can be an instrumental cause of outworking God's will even if human discernment (aided by partial renewal) plays a part.

Revisions to the prose immediately preceding these passages show Milton grappling with their divergent potentialities. Initially, the text read: "but that which they call internal, is not properly calling, but is truly election."[34] Picard then revises as follows: "but that which they call internal not only seems to be vocation but also election," with a further insertion specifying that the election in question pertains to believers.[35] These revisions, and especially the change from "is" to "seems," show Milton's understanding of his interlocutors' framework growing more precise even as his doubt about its accuracy increases: they make calling *seem* like it pertains exclusively to the election of believers. At issue here is the nature of God's plan [*praestituto ipsius*], but Milton is still puzzling through the details of how exactly calling and election fit together in that plan.

Milton eventually concludes that the natural/supernatural framework makes better theological sense of the scriptural evidence than the external/internal one does. This change prompts the deletion of this passage, but even prior to its deletion, it shows that the logical scheme connecting I.17 and I.18 began as a kind of hunch or hypothesis whose veracity and implications still needed to be worked out. An element of dogmatism does remain in that Milton seems to have a prior commitment to the idea that some human capacity for discernment and reason can operate independently of regeneration, and he wants to connect this capacity with calling so that humans are able to respond to the call. The very capacity in which Milton dogmatically believes, however, also keeps him from being too dogmatic about believing it. The deleted passage's reference to "the theologians" shows him engaging with writers who do not share the view he seeks to articulate, and this engagement goes beyond merely framing his argument in opposition to theirs: rather, he is using the difference of opinion as a kind of productive resistance in the process of sorting out his eventual position. In this process, scripture affords a kind of common ground, a shared commitment that goes deeper than the different conclusions that might be drawn from it.[36]

---

[34] *DDC*, 222: "sed quam illi internam vocant, non proprie vocatio, sed revera electio est."
[35] *DDC*, 222: "sed quam illi internam vocant, non solùm vocatio verum etiam electio vel potius regeneratio videtur esse," with "jam credentium" inserted after "electio."
[36] Compare Milton, *Of True Religion* (London, 1673), p. 6.

HUMAN CAPACITY AND SCRIPTURAL INTERPRETATION 81

Reading Milton Reading Scripture with Wolleb and Ames

Scripture—and its uses by Wolleb and Ames—remains in the foreground as Milton works out the relationship between renewal and calling, which comes into focus in a block of scriptural citations at the beginning of I.17. These follow an initial definition of renewal as "that by which [man] is brought away from a state of being accursed and [an object] of divine wrath to a state of grace"— a definition that addresses renewal as a whole, prior to the external/internal subdivision that initially distinguished I.17 from I.18.[37] Eight passages comprise the sequence, which Milton presents out of canonical order even though it participates in the Ramist structure:

> Eph. 2: 3, 5, etc.: *we were by nature sons of wrath: you have been saved by grace*; and ch. 1: 3, 5: *who has blessed us with every spiritual blessing in the heavens in Christ*; Col. 3: 10: *and putting on that new* [man] *who is being renewed into acknowledgment according to the image of him who created him*; Eph. 4: 23–4: *but* [rather you were taught] *to be renewed in the spirit of your mind, and to put on that new man who has been created according to God for righteousness and true holiness*; 2 Cor. 4: 16: *yet the inner* [man] *is being renewed daily*; Titus 3: 5: [he saved us] *through the washing of regeneration and of renewal effected by the holy spirit*; Rom. 12: 2: [transform yourselves] *through the renewal of your mind for this purpose, that you may test what God's will is* [...]; Heb. 6: 4, 6: *for it cannot happen that they who once* [have been enlightened ...]; *if they should fall down, should again be renewed.*[38]

All these passages also appear in the relevant chapters of Wolleb and Ames, albeit in an interesting pattern. The two passages from Ephesians (2:3, 5 and 1: 3, 5) appear in their chapters on calling (special calling, in Wolleb's case), and the next three passages (Colossians 3:10, Ephesians 4:23–24, and 2 Corinthians 4:16) appear in their chapters on sanctification. Then comes a verse (Titus 3:5) that appears in Ames's chapter on calling, but Wolleb's chapters on justification

---

[37] *DDC*, 221: "Hominis renovatio est qua is ab statu maledictionis atque irae divinae ad statum gratiae deducitur."

[38] *DDC*, 221:

> Eph. 2. 3. 5 &c *eramus natura filii irae. gratia estis servati.* et cap. 1. 3. 5; *qui benedixit nobis omni benedictione spirituali in coelis in Christo.* Col. 3. 10; *et induentes novum illum qui renovatur in agnitionem secundum imaginem eius qui creavit illum.* Eph. 4. 23. 24; *renovari verò spiritu mentis vestrae, et induere novum illum hominem, qui secundum Deum conditus est ad iustitiam et sanctimoniam veram.* 2. Cor. 4. 16; *internus tamen renovatur indies.* Tit. 3. 5; *per lavacrum regenerationis et renovationis spiritus sancti.* Rom. 12. 2; *per renovationem mentis vestrae ad hoc, ut probetis quae sit voluntas Dei*—. Heb. 6. 4. 6; *nam fieri non potest ut qui semel*—: *si prolabantur, denuò renoventur.*

82 MILTON'S THEOLOGICAL PROCESS

and sanctification, followed by another verse (Romans 12:2) that appears in both of their chapters on sanctification. Finally, Hebrews 6:4, 6 appears in both of their chapters on (special) calling, as well as in Wolleb's chapter on perseverance.[39]

Milton's gathering in one place passages that appear disparately in his interlocutors indicates a logical disagreement involving both *inventio* and *dispositio*. Logical invention is the process of searching the commonplaces for apt arguments. If Milton was indeed reading Wolleb and Ames while composing I.17, as seems at least plausible, the very shape of his path through their texts as he considered which scriptural passages proved apt to his own case already suggests the nature of the disagreement, which will manifest as a divergent disposition (or arrangement) of those texts. This logical disagreement verges (if only slightly) into the territory of rhetoric when Milton presents the texts out of canonical sequence to argue that his *dispositio* is more plausible than his interlocutors'. These passages develop a distinct perspective on calling and renewal that puts a logical distinction in Wolleb and Ames (between external and internal renewal) to different use by insisting on the possibility of some renewal in the "external" or natural person—a relationship that proves pivotal for the subsequent revisions to the chapter.

To draw out the rhetorical work that Milton's arrangement of these verses performs, I begin, out of sequence, with Titus 3:5, a verse whose divergent uses by Wolleb and Ames give it a pivotal place in the scriptural trajectory that Milton is framing. Beza renders the verse thus: "Non ex operibus iustis quae fecerimus nos, sed ex sua misericordia seruauit nos per lauacrum regenerationis, & renouationis Spiritus sancti [KJV: Not by workes of righteousnes which we have done, but according to his mercy he saved us, by the washing of regeneration, and renewing of the holy Ghost]." By linking regeneration and renewal to being saved, the second half of the verse invites questions about the relationship between the topics that occupy I.17–18: renewal emerges as an act of the Spirit, while regeneration entails a salvific cleansing. The first half of the verse, meanwhile, connects these questions to the foundational debates about human and divine agency: salvation comes by God's mercy, not human works of righteousness.

Both Wolleb and Ames use Titus 3:5 in tandem with the external/internal distinction in ways that end up working against the possibility of "external renewal." For Wolleb, special vocation (the topic of his I.28, addressing a calling that "belongs only to the Elect," to be distinguished from I.20, "Of the Common Vocation to the State of Grace") happens in two ways: "outwardly

---

[39] Citations follow.

HUMAN CAPACITY AND SCRIPTURAL INTERPRETATION   83

[*extrinsecus*] by the Word of the Gospel; but inwardly [*intrinsecus*], by illuminating the minde and changing the heart, to be partakers of the grace of Salvation."[40] Wolleb notes that regeneration [*regeneratio*] is among the scriptural names for special calling, presumably in both its internal and external manifestations, which collapse to the degree that both apply only to the elect.[41] He does not, however, connect Titus 3:5 to calling, but rather to sanctification, where it appears in support of the claim that "The internal impulsive cause [of sanctification], is Gods free bounty."[42] For Wolleb, this verse refers only to the internal cause of sanctification; "The external impulsive cause, is Christ with his merit and efficacie," shored up by Ephesians 5:25.[43] This division between internal and external thus occurs within the internal aspect of the prior distinction, namely, the internal renewal associated with the special calling directed to the elect and issuing in sanctification. Wolleb acknowledges the possibility that people who have not (yet) been saved, including the reprobate (those whose damnation God has decreed), can experience a degree of internal renewal, but everything in his broader handling of the external/internal distinction weighs against allowing that this possibility might be actualized in any meaningful way.[44]

Similarly, Ames invokes the external and the internal to connect calling and regeneration on the basis of an election that arises solely from God's will.[45] He quotes part of Titus 3:5—"Not by works of righteousness, but by his own mercy"—in support of this proposition: "Hence the Calling of men doth not in any sort depend upon the dignity, honesty, industry, or any indeavour of the called, but upon election and predestination of God only."[46] Independent of their own works, the elect enter into union with Christ through calling's internal

[40] Wolleb, 192 [163]: "Sic fuit Vocatio electis & reprobis communis. Nunc specialis sequitur, quae solis Electis contingit. Est autem haec Vocatio, qua Deus electos, in se adhuc miseros & corruptos, extrinsecus Verbo Evangelii, intrinsecus autem mentis illuminatione & cordis mutatione vocat, ad participandam salutis gratiam." On Milton's larger engagement with the ideas of special and common vocation, see Stephen M. Fallon, *Milton's Peculiar Grace: Self-Representation and Authority* (Ithaca, NY: Cornell University Press, 2007), esp. ch. 2.

[41] Wolleb, 192 [163]: "*Appellatur in Scripturis* Nova Creatio, (*a*) Regeneratio, (*b*) Tractio, (*c*) Institutio divina, (*d*) & Resuscitatio. (*e*)."

[42] Wolleb, 212 [181]: "Caussa ejus impulsiva interna, est gratuita Dei benevolentia."

[43] Wolleb, 212 [181]: "Caussa Προκαταρκτικὴ, est Christus cum merito suo & efficacia."

[44] On the decree to reprobation, see Wolleb, 33 [25]. Wolleb attributes reprobation to God's will, not to the sin of the reprobate: "Absolutum est respectu causae efficientis impulsivae, quae nec in eligendis, est fides; nec in reprobandis, peccatum; sed liberrima Dei voluntas."

[45] For Ames, predestination "depends upon no cause, reason or outward condition, but it doth purely proceed from the will of him that predestinateth [Hinc etiam à nulla causa, ratione vel conditione externe pendet, sed purè proficiscitur à praedestinantis voluntate]": Ames, 117–18 [124]. Ames uses Romans 9:18 to locate election both to salvation and to damnation in God's will.

[46] Ames, 124 [132]: "Hinc vocatio hominum nullo modo ex dignitate, probitate, industria, vel conatu aliquo vocandorum pendet, sed electione & praedestinatione Dei tantum [...] Tit. 3. 5. *Non ex operibus justis, sed ex sua misericordia.*"

84 MILTON'S THEOLOGICAL PROCESS

efficacy.[47] For Ames, the external/internal distinction has to do with the "offer of Christ [*Oblatio Christi*]": "the outward is a propounding, or preaching of the Gospell or of the promises of Christ," while the "inward offer is a spirituall enlightning, whereby those promises are propounded to the hearts of men, as it were by an inward word."[48] This external call is "propounded to all without difference, together with a command to believe [the promises]," but only the elect, in fact, receive the promises.[49] Consequently, the universality of the call works primarily to bring about the "inexcusablenesse and humiliation of the sinner," from which only the elect will be saved, although at this point, Ames also admits that the non-elect can experience a measure, however insufficient, of this internal enlightenment.[50]

Putting the uses of Titus 3:5 by Wolleb and Ames together, the emphasis on an internal renewal achieved independently of human means threatens to undermine the distinction between calling and sanctification, which would render superfluous the "external" works of preaching or engaging with scripture. The initial definition of calling in Milton's I.17, however, explicitly takes up the possibility of renewal in the non-elect that serves to keep the distinction intact and preaching meaningful:

Calling is the external manner of renewal by which **God the father, in Christ, invites fallen humankind to knowledge of how his godhead is to be placated and worshipped; inviting believers indeed out of gratuitous kindness for the purpose of salvation, [but] non-believers for the purpose of removing their every excuse.**[51]

Here, the treatise equates calling with precisely the kind of external renewal at which Wolleb and Ames hinted, while implicitly distinguishing it from the kind of renewal associated with regeneration. Notably, this passage and the sequence of texts that follows it appear on a page in the chapter's latest stratum, suggesting that significant processes of revision already precede their current state.

---

[47] Ames, 124 [131]: "This Union is wrought by calling [Efficitur haec unio per vocationem]."

[48] Ames, 125 [132–33]: "Externa est Evangelij, vel promissionum de Christo propositio aut praedicatio [. . .] Interna oblatio est spiritualis quaedam illuminatio, qua cordibus hominum proponuntur illae promissiones quasi per verbum internum."

[49] Ames, 125 [133]: "Promissiones istae, quoad promulgationem externam, sine discrimine proponuntur omnibus, una cum credendi mandato, sed quoad proprietatem rerum promissarum, quae ex intentione promittentis pendet, pertinent solummodo ad electos, qui idcirco vocantur *filij & haeredes promissionis*. Rom. 9.8."

[50] Ames, 125 [132–33]: "Vt praeparentur tamen homines ad promissiones recipiendas, legis applicatio ordinariè praecedit ad peccati detectionem, & peccatoris ἀναπολογίαν, & humiliationem."

[51] *DDC*, 222: "Vocatio est externa renovationis ratio qua **Deus pater in Christo, ad agnitionem numinis placandi et colendi, lapsos homines invitat, et credentes quidem ex gratuitia benignitate ad salutem, non credentes ad tollendam omnem eorum excusationem.**"

HUMAN CAPACITY AND SCRIPTURAL INTERPRETATION   85

The chapter does go on to distinguish between general and special calling, but unlike in Wolleb and Ames, it dissociates the latter from election. General calling, for Milton, is universal: "General calling is that by which **God** in some way—and certainly to a sufficient extent—invites all to knowledge of his true godhead."[52] Special calling is selective, but Milton emphatically does not limit it to the elect: "**Special calling** is that **by which God whensoever he wishes invites these rather than those, whether they are** so-called 'chosen ones' or 'reprobates,' [and does so] more clearly and more often."[53] The call to the reprobate is not the decree of their damnation, but rather (as Milton makes clear under the relevant heading on the next page) so that they might be left without excuse as a testimony to others (Matthew 10:18). Indeed, Milton insists, via a quotation of Acts 13:46, that they pronounce themselves unworthy of eternal life.[54] They, not God, have decreed [*decernitis*] their damnation by repulsing God's call.

Read alongside Wolleb and Ames in like manner, the sequence as a whole maps a process of scriptural thought that culminates in this theology of renewal. The citations from Ephesians frame the rest of the sequence by highlighting the course of renewal in a way that invites attention to calling, as reading alongside Wolleb and Ames suggests. Complexly, although Milton's citations overlap with citations in Wolleb and Ames, Milton and his interlocutors opt to quote different, non-overlapping selections from the cited passages. Reading the parts that Milton quotes alongside Hieronymus Zanchius's commentary on Ephesians—which Milton references elsewhere in the treatise—helps to illuminate the theological difference that the treatise is drawing from its more overt interlocutors.[55]

Milton quotes from Ephesians 2: 3, 5 in a way that charts the arc of redemption: "we were by nature sons of wrath: you have been saved by grace."[56] Ames, meanwhile quotes only one word from verse 5: *vivificavit*, "he hath

---

[52] *DDC*, 225: "Generalis est qua **Deus** omnes aliquo modo ad agnitionem veri numinis, et quantum satis sit quidem invitat."

[53] *DDC*, 226: "**Vocatio specialis** est **qua Deus hos quàm illos, sive electos** quos vocant **sive reprobos, clarius ac saepius, quandocunque vult invitat.**" The phrase "quos vocant" has been inserted by "B." The large hand in this definition contrasts with its lack in the definition of general calling, which appears on the recto of the same leaf. The difference is puzzling.

[54] *DDC*, 227: "Act [...] 13. 46. *postquam illum repellitis, et indignos vos ipsos decernitis—.*"

[55] Jeffrey Alan Miller, "Milton, Zanchius, and the Rhetoric of Belated Reading," *Milton Quarterly* 47, 4 (2013): 199–219. Zanchius is Girolamo Zanchi (1516–90), a key figure in Reformed theology after Calvin's death.

[56] Compare KJV:

Among whom also wee all had our conversation in times past, in the lusts of our flesh, fulfilling the desires of the flesh, and of the minde, and were by nature the children of wrath, even as others: [...] Even when wee were dead in sinnes, [God] hath quickened us together with Christ, (by grace ye are saved).

Milton uses Eph. 2:3 to describe the children of unhappy marriages in *The Doctrine and Discipline of Divorce*, 17.

86 MILTON'S THEOLOGICAL PROCESS

quickened."[57] If this word seems in keeping with the arc suggested in *De Doctrina*, the context in Ames marks a crucial difference that will become increasingly apparent as the sequence of citations progresses: he quotes the verse to support the claim that "Passive receiving of Christ is that whereby a spirituall principle of grace is begotten in the will of man."[58] Here (appropriately for a man who made his name arguing against Remonstrant theology), Ames makes the renewal of human will an effect of irresistible grace; even the "active receiving" of Christ is "indeed drawn out and exercised by man freely, but certainly unavoydably, and unchangeably."[59] For Ames, the grammar of *vivificavit* suffices to make the point: God is the subject of the verb and humans the object, even when human will is, in some measure, at play.

Milton does not quote *vivificavit*, but Zanchius's commentary on Ephesians shows how the words he does quote might work to further a Calvinist theology like that espoused by Ames, while putting particular pressure on the concept of nature. From Ephesians 2:3, Milton draws the phrase *eramus natura filii irae*, "we were by nature children of wrath." For Zanchius, being the children of God's wrath means that "all humans, both Jews and Gentiles, have been dead through sin; they are both conceived and born in it, and they all walk in it." This death is a spiritual or eternal death, and "that is what the name 'children of wrath' means."[60] In these terms, spiritual death describes the natural human state, which Zanchius characterizes as having internal and external dimensions so as to encompass the entire person:

---

[57] Calvin, following Melanchthon, understands vivification as the second part of repentance, "the consolation that arises out of faith [*consolationem quae ex fide nascitur*]": *Institutio*, 210; *Institutes*, 594 (III.iii.3). English theologians like Ames, however, often use the term to refer to sanctification, either in whole or in part. Thanks to Brice Peterson for discussing this issue with me.

[58] Ames, 126 [134]: "Passiva receptio Christi est, qua spirituale principium gratiae ingeneratur hominis voluntati."

[59] Ames, 127 [135]: "Ab homine quidem liberè, sed certo, indeclinabiliter, aut invariabiliter elicitur & exercetur." Ames's key anti-Remonstrant work is *Coronis ad Collationem Hagiensem* (Leiden, 1618). On Ames's activities prior to the Synod of Dort, see Keith L. Sprunger, *The Learned Doctor William Ames: Dutch Backgrounds of English and American Puritanism* (Urbana, IL: University of Illinois Press, 1972), pp. 46–51.

[60] Girolamo Zanchius, *Operum Theologicorum*, Vol. II, tom. vi (Geneva, 1619), p. 53:

> Ad summam verò quod attinet horum trium versuum, abundè & perspicuè probauit Apostolus, *omnes homines tam Iudaeos, quàm Gentiles, mortuos fuisse per peccata, tum in quibus concepti & nati sunt, tum in quibus omnes ambularunt.* Mortuos inquam primùm spirituali morte, deinde aeterna, quia illius facti sunt rei, id quod significant nomine filiorum ir[ae]: vt jam taceamus de morte corporis.

All translations from Zanchius are mine. Zanchius echoes Beza, who holds that human nature is "not damaged, but dead through sin [*Neque enim naturam dicit laesam, sed mortuam per peccatum*]"; Beza, *New Testament* (Geneva, 1559), p. 637. Beza subsequently read this verse as evidence of the predestination of the damned: these "wrathful humans are passively judged by God as objects of eternal death [*passiuè homines irati Dei iudicio reos aeternae mortis*]": Beza, *New Testament* (Geneva, 1598), p. 267.

HUMAN CAPACITY AND SCRIPTURAL INTERPRETATION 87

Therefore, this corruption of the whole nature, which he in another place calls "concupiscence," here the Apostle names "nature," namely the beginning of all bad actions and motions, both internal and external. And consequently, because it [i.e., nature] is without law, it makes us children of wrath.[61]

For Zanchius, the natural human state is one of total depravity, and the internal/external distinction serves to drive the point of that totality home rather than to mark any meaningful difference. He does specify internal and external causes of sin: the internal include innate concupiscence (*concupiscentia innata*, with reference to verse 3) and human will (*voluntas nostra*), while the external include various invitations to sin and evil spirits (κακοδαίμονες).[62] But the purpose of this exposition is to "demonstrate the knowledge of our evil and most miserable state, in which we came to be through First Adam, so that we might more sweetly perceive the kindness of Christ."[63] In Zanchius's theological scheme, humans contribute nothing to salvation, Christ contributes everything, and the internal/external distinction only paints this radical difference more starkly.

Milton may not be engaging directly with Zanchius, but comparing their exegesis of Ephesians 2 illuminates Milton's eventual decision to abandon the external/internal distinction for a direct claim about nature and the supernatural. The phrase "children of wrath" invites a reading through the framework of double predestination (emphasized by *maledictionis* in the definition and *benedixit* and *benedictione* in the ensuing quotation from Ephesians 1), setting the stage for a scriptural re-evaluation of this theology to follow. Milton does not abandon the concept that humans begin in a state of being subject to divine wrath—the definition affirms as much—but rather puts it into conversation with other passages in ways that delimit the concept. Ephesians 2 leads the sequence because, as quoted, it succinctly captures the renewal at issue, from being children of wrath to being saved by grace. The rest of the sequence will work out what precisely that means.

The citation from Ephesians 1 builds on *gratia estis servati* by introducing the concept of benediction, which implicitly brings the issue of calling into play. Milton cites verses 3 and 5, but only quotes from verse 3. Wolleb, meanwhile,

---

[61] Zanchius, *Operum Theologicorum*, Vol. II, tom. vi, 53: "Hanc igitur naturae totius corruptionum, quam alibi quoque vocat concupiscentiam hîc appellat, Apostolus naturam, principium scilicet omnium malarum actionum & motuum, tam internorum quàm externorum. Ac proinde cùm sit ἀνομία, efficit nos filios irae."

[62] Zanchius, like Calvin, takes a voluntarist view of human nature in its fallen state; see Headley, *The Nature of the Will*, 39–52.

[63] Zanchius, *Operum Theologicorum*, Vol. II, tom. vi, 54: "Vt probè agnito malo nostro, statúque miserrimo, in quo eramus per Adamum primum, eò meliùs percipiamus etiam beneficium Christi."

88 MILTON'S THEOLOGICAL PROCESS

in his chapter on special calling, cites verse 5 but, in fact, quotes verse 6: "To the praise of the glory of his grace, wherein he hath made us accepted in the beloved."[64] He offers this quotation in support of the proposition that "The *Pelagians* absurdly teach, that by the grace of Vocation, we are to understand our natural abilities."[65] For Wolleb, humans can only become acceptable before God through the action of divine grace, not through any actions pertaining to their natural capacities. In a similar vein, with reference to verse 3, Zanchius associates benediction with "eternal predestination" as "prepared before the foundation of the world in Christ" and insists, via the incarnation, that the fruits are manifest "truly not in our persons, but in Christ."[66] On this account, calling—God's speaking of the benediction or good word—is inseparably connected to predestination from eternity, independent of any human action, and the ensuing goodness likewise belongs to Christ rather than to the elect per se. In this way, both Wolleb and Zanchius mark a firm boundary between the divine and the natural.

Milton departs from this view, as the sequence's organization suggests. Passages that Wolleb and Ames connect to sanctification interrupt the passages on calling, returning to that topic only with the concluding citation from Hebrews 6. Both Wolleb and Ames use that passage to acknowledge the possibility of some renewal occurring in the reprobate. Both raise this possibility only to dismiss it as not productive of salvation, but Milton instead sees in their suggestion that not only two kinds of calling (external and internal) but also two kinds of renewal are at issue. The intervening scriptures on sanctification work to sharpen this interpretative difference between Milton and his interlocutors. The sequence shows Milton rethinking the theological territory laid out by Wolleb and Ames while wondering on what basis to distinguish the two kinds of renewal.

The chapters on sanctification in Wolleb and Ames address renewal as it happens in the elect; by situating verses quoted in these chapters—the next four passages in the sequence—among verses about calling, Milton expands the scope of the renewal that they address. Significantly, Ames groups three of them

---

[64] Wolleb, 197 [166]: "Ad laudem gloriosae suae gratiae, qua nos gratis efficit sibi gratos in illo dilecto."
[65] Wolleb, 196 [166]: "Absurde Pelagiani per gratiam Vocationis naturales vires intelligi docent."
[66] Zanchius, *Operum Theologicorum*, Vol. II, tom. vi, 7:

> Primùm, in ipsa aeterna praedestinatione, quatenus nobis fuerant praeparatae ante mundi constitutionem in Christo. Secundò, quatenus re ipsa fuerint praestitae, nobisque exhibitae, verùm non in nostris (vt ita loquar) personis, sed in Christo tanquam in capite. In ipsius etiam persona, assumpta carne, perfecta fuit redemptio, expiata peccata, firmata vera iustitia, omnes denique thesauri & benedictiones positae, vitáque aeterna.

(Colossians 3:10, Ephesians 4:24, and Romans 12:2) together under one heading: "Vivification is the second part of sanctification wherby the Image or life of God is restored in man."[67] Wolleb similarly cites Colossians 3:9–10 under a heading referring to the "vivification of the new man."[68] Milton quotes the verse differently than Ames does because he finds the Vulgate closer than Beza's translation to the Greek, but the emphasis is the same: a new life, characterized by the renewal of God's image in humanity.[69] Ames uses an earlier citation of Ephesians 4:24 to make the point about transformation clear: "Sanctification is a reall change of a man from the filthinesse of sin, to the purity of Gods Image."[70] From these texts, Ames argues that the elect undergo a thoroughgoing spiritual transformation, entirely leaving their former state behind for a new one.

The remaining "sanctification" verses introduce some complications for the external/internal framework that Milton's chapter initially uses to distinguish between the two kinds of renewal while also showing that scripture shapes his revision of that framework. Scripture proves determinative, in the way that the portion of 2 Corinthians 4:16 that Milton quotes—"internus tamen renovatur indies"—sits uneasily with that distinction. On the one hand, linking renewal and calling means that some renewal occurs even before regeneration (the subject of I.18), so the idea that "the inner [man] is being renewed daily" helps his cause. Indeed, Ames uses an identical citation to support this point: "Because [the change] does not consist in relation and respect, but in really effecting [something], it therefore admits various degrees: of beginning, development, and perfection."[71] Milton uses this idea of gradual change to structure the division between chapters, but the verse's insistence that the *inner* person is transformed runs counter to the logical distinction that Milton wants to make between a kind of external renewal that precedes regeneration and the internal renewal that follows it. Connected to his logical scheme, the verse suggests that renewal accompanies regeneration, and that won't do. Milton could resolve the issue by reducing his already selective quotation even further, to "renovatur indies," but instead, he allows the scripture to drive revision of the logical

---

[67] Ames, 144 [153]: "Vivificatio est secunda pars sanctificationis, qua imago aut vita Dei in homine restituitur."

[68] Wolleb, 213 [182]: "Forma duobus actibus exprimitur, aversione à malo, & conversione ad bonum, (a): illa *mortificatio veteris*, haec *vivificatio novi hominis*, (b) illa *crucifixio & sepultura*, haec *resurrectio* nominatur. (c)." Wolleb uses (b) to reference "Coloss. 3, 9, 10."

[69] The Greek does not have the subjunctive implied by Beza's *sitis*.

[70] Ames, 140 [149]: "Sanctificatio est realis commutatio hominis à turpitudine peccati in puritatem imaginis Dei."

[71] Ames, *Medulla S. S. Theologiae* (London, 1629), p. 149: "Quia vero non in relatione & ratione consistit, sed in effectione reali; idcirco gradus varios admittit, inchoationis, progressus, & perfectionis." My translation; compare William Ames, *The Marrow of Sacred Divinity* (London, 1642), p. 140.

90 MILTON'S THEOLOGICAL PROCESS

scheme. Meanwhile, Romans 12:2 crucially explains why Milton is invested in pre-regeneration renewal in the first place: renewal is, as the verse says, "for the purpose of trying what is the will of God." Notably, Milton quotes the part of the verse containing this purpose clause (*ut probetis*), whereas Ames only draws attention to the fact of transformation itself. Ames associates this verse with "the second part of sanctification wherby the Image or life of God is restored in man," whereas Milton finds it compatible with an earlier stage of renewal.[72] By this means, the treatise presents as scriptural the idea that even the unregenerate can have the capacity to participate in the process of "probing every doctrine" described in the epistle.[73]

The passage from Hebrews 6 cements the distinction between two kinds of renewal that grounds the division between I.17 and I.18. Both Wolleb and Ames cite this verse in their chapters on calling to argue that reprobates can experience some limited kind of renewal, albeit not of the sort that leads to full regeneration and sanctification. Wolleb, distinguishing between general and special calling, writes that the former "is oftentimes outward onely," while the latter "is inward," with this caveat: "though sometimes it be internal in Reprobates; yet the light of salvation which it affords to the minde is but weak, and the joy with which it affects the heart is but momentary." Internal calling to the elect, meanwhile, "irradiates the mind with a ful light, and seasoneth the heart, not with a bare rellish, but with a true sense of spiritual gifts, and fils it with true and constant joy: that [to the reprobate] may be lost, but the gifts and graces of this [to the elect] can never be lost."[74] Wolleb maintains that salvation comes through divine action alone while nevertheless acknowledging that humans in their natural state can absorb some degree of the renewal that attends calling, although only the elect enjoy that renewal to its full extent. Similarly, Ames admits the possibility of some limited renewal occurring in the reprobate: "If any one oppose himselfe out of malice to this illumination, he commits a sin against the Holy Ghost, which is called unpardonable, or unto death. *Hebr.* 6. 6.

---

[72] Ames, 144 [153]: "Vivificatio est secunda pars sanctificationis, qua imago aut vita Dei in homine restituitur." As discussed in Chapter 1, pp. 52–56, Romans 12:2 often appears in contexts where Milton is interested in the human capacity to act.

[73] *DDC*, 4: "excutiendae ... cuiusque doctrinae."

[74] Wolleb, 197 [167]:

> Patet ex his, quae differentia sit Vocationis communis & specialis. Illa saepe tantum externa est: haec interna exsistit. Illa si maxime intrinsecus quoque in reprobis operetur, radio saltem cognitionis salutis mentem illustrat, & gaudio cor, non nisi momentaneo, afficit: haec vero mentem plena luce irradiat, & cor non gustu tantum, sed vero sensu quoque donorum spiritualium, adeoque vero & constanti gaudio perfundit. Illa amitti potest: hujus vero dona & gratia amitti nequeunt.

HUMAN CAPACITY AND SCRIPTURAL INTERPRETATION   91

& 10. 29."[75] The vehicle for this renewal is an "inward [*internum*] word" that the reprobate apparently cannot sufficiently internalize, although Ames does not clarify the precise nature of their failure.[76] The internal enlightenment experienced by the non-elect proves a chimera, proffered only to be rejected. At stake is the possibility of internal scripture as Milton understands it: who has access to it, and who does not?

Milton thus traces a challenging trajectory through this block of citations, from the notion in Ephesians 2 that humans are children of wrath to the idea in Hebrews 6 that even children of wrath might experience some degree of renewal. Both Wolleb and Ames separate calling from renewal, associating the latter with sanctification, a process of increasing human capacity that follows justification. Milton, however, holds that justification requires some exercise of the human capacity to try every doctrine, which means that said capacities need to be recovered from their fallen state but without resulting in full justification or the accompanying regeneration. These pressures all come to a head in the quotation from Titus, which Wolleb treats under sanctification and Ames under calling. Both writers make a point of assigning causality to God: for Ames, neither "office, probity, industry, nor any endeavor" brings about calling "but only the election and predestination of God," while Wolleb holds that "the internal impulsive cause [of sanctification] is God's gratuitous good will."[77] Only Ames allows for the slight possibility of the renewed human capacity the treatise affirms, and even then, he admits it only in the case of the damned. Milton goes beyond Ames by averring that the possibility of falling from grace articulated in Hebrews implies that remaining in grace likewise requires the exercise of some limited human capacity sufficient to respond to the call but not to produce justification. Selective quoting helps some—Ames focuses on the part of the verse denying the efficacy of works, while Milton opts for the part that talks about washing and renewal. Even that leaves Milton in a quandary, however, because the verse seems to link regeneration and renewal ("regenerationis et renovationis").

[75] Ames, 126 [133]: "Huic illuminationi si quis ex malitia se opponat, peccatum admittit in Spiritum Sanctum, quod irremissibile dicitur, vel *ad mortem. Hebr. 6. 6. & 10. 29.*"

[76] Ames, 125 [132–33]: "Oblatio Christi est externa, vel interna [. . .] Interna oblatio est spiritualis quaedam illuminatio, qua cordibus hominum proponuntur illae promissiones quasi per verbum internum."

[77] Ames, *Medulla*, 132: "Hinc vocatio hominum nullo modo ex dignitate, probitate, industria, vel conatu aliquo vocandorum pendet, sed electione & praedestinatione Dei tantum." Johannes Wolleb, *Compendium Theologiae Christianae* (Cambridge, 1642), p. 181: "Caussa ejus impulsiva interna, est gratuita Dei benevolentia." My translations: compare Ames, *Marrow*, 124; Johannes Wolleb, *The Abridgment of Christian Divinitie*, trans. Alexander Ross (London, 1650), p. 203.

92 MILTON'S THEOLOGICAL PROCESS

Collectively, then, these verses raise questions about the relationship between renewal and calling, in connection with the external/internal framework used by Wolleb and Ames. The scripture block addresses renewal in a way that covers both I.17 and I.18; the external/internal distinction that separates them first appears two sentences later. Nevertheless, the language of "nature" from Ephesians 2:3, together with the sense from 2 Corinthians 4:16 that even this lesser renewal happens internally, puts pressure on the distinction in ways that play out as the chapter undertakes to develop its most controversial component: the idea that some external renewal is possible independent of regeneration, or the internal renewal that accompanies sanctification. In keeping with Romans 12:2, this external renewal enables people to "test what God's will is" en route to the more thoroughgoing renewal of sanctification. Consequently, the verse sequencing involves rhetoric on two levels. Most obviously, it sets out to argue (albeit via relatively intuitive means) that Milton's *dispositio* is correct and those of Wolleb and Ames less so. More profoundly, this sequencing engages the very human capacity it defends, the capacity to understand and judge claims about ultimate matters, as present, for instance, in preaching.

Working through Uncertainty

Milton's methodological intention that his own words should "arise from the weaving together of the passages" where possible points to the next challenge on evidence in the revisions, which is figuring out how to implement scriptural language in the Ramist structure of argumentation—the question of logical definition.[78] Two passages in particular from the first sequence give rise to this challenge: "we were by nature sons of wrath" in Ephesians 2:3 and "yet the inner [man] is being renewed daily" in 2 Corinthians 4:16.[79] Together, these verses present "nature" and "internal" as opposites, suggesting an identification of the external with nature. So, which term should Milton use? Logical consistency suggests "external," but fidelity to scriptural language suggests "natural." The manuscript shows Milton thinking through the question, and tracing his process of thought shows him working out how exactly he understands the human capacity of judgment that the revisions show him exercising.

---

[78] *DDC*, 4: "ex ipso licet contextu scripturarum natis."
[79] *DDC*, 221: "Eph. 2. 3. 5 &c *eramus natura filii irae. gratia estis servati* [...] 2. Cor. 4. 16; *internus tamen renovatur indies.*"

The chapter proceeds in a way that indicates some uncertainty on Milton's part. An early instance appears on MS 222, where Milton argues that external renewal "reaches its limit in the exterior and natural man" and locates the ensuing change "in the exterior and natural man."[80] Here, the connection is conjunctive: *exteriore et naturali.* The connection becomes potentially disjunctive, however, when it next appears, on MS 228: "The change which follows calling is that by which the external or natural [*exterioris sive naturalis*] man's mind is divinely moved towards knowledge of **God**, and for the time being at least are changed for the better."[81] This subtle shift from "and" to "or" (even if an inclusive "or") suggests that Milton is beginning to think of "exterior" and "natural" not as complementary terms but alternative ones. This is merely a hint that Milton never carries through in the (multi-layered) fair copy that lies beneath the revisions. In the final paragraph of the chapter, on MS 234–35, Milton makes a summary of vocation in which "natural man" and "external manner of renewal" continue to coexist: "Calling, therefore, and the change which follows it in natural man, since they stem from a merely *external* [*externa*] manner of renewal, fall short of regeneration and do not confer salvation."[82]

Though Milton does not dispense with "external," we find him probing *naturalis* further on MS 229, in tacit conversation with Wolleb:

This change, insofar as it is by way of being an effect, has two parts: penitence; and, answering to that, faith. Each of these may be not only a true beginning [*inchoata*] but also either [merely] natural [*naturalis*] or [plain] fictitious; and as the penitence stands to [lasting] repentance, so faith of this sort stands to salvific faith.[83]

The word *inchoata* hearkens to Wolleb's treatment of justification, where he writes:

Justice of the person, is either begun [*inchoata*], or it is perfected [*perfecta*] [. . .] Begun justice, is that which the Holy Ghost begins in the faithful in this life, and perfects it in the other. The perfect righteousnesse of

---

[80] *DDC*, 222: "Externa quae in exteriore et naturali homine terminatur. Estque vocatio, eámq; sequens in exteriore et naturali homine alteratio."

[81] *DDC*, 228: "Vocationem sequens alteratio est qua exterior sive naturalis hominis mens ad agnitionem **Dei** divinitus movetur, et ad tempus saltem in melius convertitur."

[82] *DDC*, 234–35: "Vocatio itaque eámque sequens in naturali homine alteratio cùm de externa tantum ratione renovationis sint, citra regenerationem non conferunt salutem."

[83] *DDC*, 229: "Alterationis huius, quatenus effecti rationem habet, partes duae sunt: poenitentia, eíque respondens, fides: utraque non solum vere inchoata, sed etiam vel naturalis vel fictitia esse potest: útque poenitentia ad resipiscentiam, ita fides huiusmodi se habet ad fidem salvificam."

94   MILTON'S THEOLOGICAL PROCESS

Christ, then, is the gift of Justification; but that which is begun, is the gift of Sanctification.[84]

The distinction of external and internal that Milton has taken from Wolleb's discussion of vocation does not map neatly onto this new one of begun and perfected. Thus, he equates inchoate beginnings with the natural, implying (but not saying outright) that completed penance equates to the supernatural, as the revisions will eventually have it.[85] Whichever choice he makes, scripture does not explicitly provide language for both sides of the distinction.

Milton's use of the scriptural "natural" gains momentum on MS 232, where a further discussion of penitential faith contains two more references in Picard's fair copy: "The faith which answers to penitence is an assent—also natural [*naturalis*]—to the divine call, given with a confidence which is likewise natural [*naturali*] and often false."[86] These emphases on the natural in the context of a discussion of penitence enable Milton to assign even unsaved humans a degree of moral responsibility. As he notes in the definition on MS 222, the call goes out to "non-believers for the purpose of removing their every excuse."[87] The definition of special vocation on MS 226 similarly includes reprobates, if God so wills, the difference from common vocation simply being frequency ("more clearly and more often").[88] Finally, on MS 231, he observes that "Penitence is common to both the regenerate and the unregenerate. Instances of the unregenerate are Cain, Esau, Pharaoh, Saul, Ahab, and Judas, and very many others, in whom both contrition and confession and other marks of penitence are discerned."[89] The point is that even such notable reprobates as these—"by nature sons of wrath," as in Ephesians 2:3—possess the moral capacity to recognize sin in themselves as the product of a renewal that manifestly did not carry them on to sanctification. Granting this capacity proves necessary to their being found without excuse, as the treatise makes clear in its discussion

[84] Wolleb, 202 [171–72]: "Caussae justitia est, qua homo, alioquin peccator, in certo aliquo negotio innocens aut justus dicitur. Personae justitia est perfecta, vel inchoata [. . .] Inchoata est, quam Spiritus sanctus in fidelibus in hac vita inchoat, in altera vero perficit. Justitia igitur Christi perfecta, Justificationis; inchoata vero, Sanctificationis est donum."

[85] Milton aligns with Franciscus Junius, who holds that inchoate grace (unlike perfected grace) can operate in nature: *De Theologia Vera* (Leiden, 1594), p. 142. See also *PRRD*, I.264–69.

[86] *DDC*, 232: "Fides, quae poenitentiae respondet, est assensus etiam naturalis divinae vocationi perhibitus cum fiducia itidem naturali et saepe falsa."

[87] *DDC*, 222: "**non credentes ad tollendam omnem eorum excusationem.**"

[88] *DDC*, 226: "**Vocatio specialis est qua Deus hos quàm illos, sive electos** quos vocant **sive reprobos, clarius ac saepius, quandocunque vult invitat.**"

[89] *DDC*, 231: "Poenitentia et regenitis et non regenitis communis est. Exempla non regenitorum sunt Cain, Esauus, Pharao, Saul, Achabus, et Iudas, aliíque permulti; in quibus et contritio et confessio aliáque poenitentiae signa cernuntur."

under that heading: "Those, therefore, who are not being called are not inexcusable."[90] Moral capacity and unsaved status turn out to be separate matters. The question only remains as to which logical framework best captures that capacity's place in the treatise's larger theological scheme, in keeping with both the language and tenor of scripture.

By engaging with the concept of nature, Milton is at least implicitly in conversation with broader Reformed debates about natural theology, meaning the possibility that some knowledge of God is manifest in nature even if that knowledge is not saving.[91] This possibility has a scriptural foundation in Psalm 19, where the heavens manifest God's glory, but it also raises the question of what, exactly, *nature* means in the language of theology. Richard Muller explains the lay of the theological land in terms of Reformed opposition to Arminianism and Socinianism:

> The former [Arminians] argued that the light of nature was in fact a preparation for the light of grace and that the truths of natural theology could provide a basis on which a superstructure of revealed truth might be built; the latter [Socinians] argued that a "great tradition" of rational or natural truth extended back to Adam, supplemented by truths of revelation given throughout history.[92]

Milton's position is nearer to the Arminian view, influentially articulated in a 1597 epistolary debate between Jacobus Arminius and Franciscus Junius, whose chair in the Leiden theological faculty Arminius filled on Junius's death in 1602. The particulars of this debate are especially relevant to the present discussion because, whereas Zanchius (who died in 1590) had used language of external and internal, Arminius and Junius take up the language of natural and supernatural that Milton eventually adopts in its place.[93] Although scripture— specifically 2 Corinthians 4:16—seems to be the primary engine of Milton's revisions, as with the earlier comparisons to Luther and Zanchius, the debate between Arminius and Junius helps to illuminate the theological stakes.

---

[90] *DDC*, 225: "Qui igitur non vocantur, inexcusabiles non sunt." Poole, "Theology," 477, observes that making the wicked reject God on the basis of free will "was a seemingly unique move in contemporary systematic theology."

[91] See *PRRD*, IV.412–14.

[92] *PRRD*, I.279.

[93] Carl Bangs, *Arminius: A Study in the Dutch Reformation*, 2nd edn (Grand Rapids, MI: Francis Asbury, 1985), pp. 199–203; Mark A. Ellis, *Simon Episcopius's Doctrine of Original Sin* (New York: Peter Lang, 2006), p. 31; Keith D. Stanglin and Thomas H. McCall, *Jacob Arminius: Theologian of Grace* (Oxford: Oxford University Press, 2012), pp. 122–23. On "nature" in Arminius, see Headley, *The Nature of the Will*, 26–36.

96 MILTON'S THEOLOGICAL PROCESS

The debate turns, in part, on which aspects of the human nature manifest the image of God, before and after the Fall. Insisting that "no man was ever created by God in a merely natural state," Arminius argues:

For the creation of the first man, and, in him, of all men, was in the image of God, which image of God in man is not nature, but supernatural grace, having reference not to natural felicity, but to supernatural life. It is evident, from the description of the image of God, that supernatural grace in man is that divine image.[94]

For Junius, Arminius's view collapses the supernatural into the natural and makes grace common rather than peculiar.[95] Rather, argues Junius, "God contemplated man, in a merely natural state, and determined in his own decree to bestow upon him supernatural endowments."[96] Consequently, creation of the so-called natural man and the granting of supernatural gifts arise from distinct acts of the divine will.[97] Arminius argues in response that God created Adam and Eve with the supernatural qualities of knowledge, righteousness, and holiness, understanding these moral virtues as "accidental" qualities lost in the Fall and thus in need of soteriological renewal. Undamaged by the Fall, however, are what Arminius calls the essential faculties of the soul: "the intellect, and will, and freedom of the will, and other affections, actions, and passions, which necessarily result from them."[98] Arminius retains freedom of the will while allowing its bondage to sin via a Thomist argument whereby the intellect misapprehends

[94] Jacobus Arminius, *The Writings of James Arminius*, trans. James Nicholls and William R. Bagnall (Auburn and Buffalo, NY, 1853; repr. Grand Rapids, MI: Baker, 1956), III.100–101; Arminius, *Amica cum D. Francisco Junio de Praedestinatione* (Leiden, 1613), p. 99:

> quia homo nullus unquam in puris naturalibus à Deo est conditus [. . .] Conditus enim est primus homo, & in eo omnes homines ad imaginem Dei: quae imago Dei non est natura in homine, sed supernaturalis gratia; non habens respectum ad faelicitatem naturalem, sed supernaturalem vitam. Esse autem imaginem Dei in homine supernaturalem gratiam, ex imaginis Dei descriptione patet.

Milton references the *imago Dei* three times: once to argue that God is content for humans to apprehend him by recourse to a glorified concept of human form (*DDC*, 11–12) and once to argue that God creates human souls and bodies at the same time (*DDC*, 121). In neither case does Milton use this concept to advance something like Arminius's argument. I discuss the third case shortly.

[95] Arminius, *Writings*, III.102; *Amica*, 101.

[96] Arminius, *Writings*, III.103; *Amica*, 102: "hominem Deus in puris naturalibus contemplatus est, cui supernaturalia conferret decreto suo."

[97] This view partly retreats from Beza's supralapsarianism, which posits humans prior to creation as the objects of divine election; Bangs, *Arminius*, 200–201. Junius refers to creation as "the principle of nature, or its first term [*creatio sit principiu[m] naturae, vel primus terminus illius*]," distinct from supernatural grace: Arminius, *Writings*, III.112; *Amica*, 112.

[98] Arminius, *Writings*, III.121; *Amica*, 121: "Essentialia voco animam inque ea intellectum, & voluntatem voluntatisque libertatem, & reliquas affectiones, actiones, passionesque quae ex ijs necessariò fluunt. Accidentaria appello tum morales virtutes, tum agnitionem Dei, justitiam & sanctimoniam veritatis."

the good. Consequently, he understands grace as unfolding in two ways with respect to nature: in the pure and abstract sense of nature, grace "signifies the progress of goodness towards supernatural good, to be imparted to a creature naturally capable of it"; in the guilty and corrupt sense of nature, grace "signifies the ulterior progress toward supernatural good to be communicated to man," that is, mercy.[99] Unlike Junius, Arminius holds that humans in their natural state are capable of supernatural good even though they can only attain the fulness of supernatural good through grace.

Milton's view closely resembles Arminius's, albeit with subtle changes arising from a different theological context. Arminius's argument was more about election than human capacity: he thought that supralapsarianism made God the author of sin, so he was keen to argue that already sinful humans were the object of election, not humans as either envisioned in God's mind prior to creation (Beza) or humans at the time of creation (Junius). Milton, however, is thinking about the capacity of humans in their natural, fallen state to respond to the divine call, resting his understanding of *nature* on Ephesians 2:3 ("we were by nature sons of wrath"). Instead of referring to different means for coming to knowledge of God in different roles (the natural attesting to Christ as Creator and the supernatural to Christ as redeemer), for Milton, these words refer to different degrees of human capacity. In his usage, "natural" means humans in their unsaved state ("sons of wrath"), albeit sufficiently renewed to discern the need for, and assent to, the saving kind of renewal that Milton at first terms "internal" and later revises to "supernatural." In I.10, Milton argues that "man, made after God's image, had the whole law of nature born with him and implanted in him in such a way that he needed no directive towards it," with another reference to Ephesians 2:3 in I.11 indicating the radical shift in human nature that the Fall brought about and that the process of salvation works to renew.[100] The consonance between Milton's *imago Dei* theology and Arminius's extends into renewal such that Milton's understanding of renewed human capacity is akin to the Arminians' "light of nature" because it is an effect of grace, and for the same reason it is not the Socinians' rational truth.[101]

---

[99] Arminius, *Writings*, III.134; *Amica*, 134–35: "Illo modo accepta significat bonitatis progressum ad bonum supernaturale creaturae eius à natura capaci impertiendum: hoc modo, bonitatis ulteriorem progressum ad bonum supernaturale communicandum cum homine reo & corrupto, quae misericordiae etiam nomine in Scripturis appellatur."

[100] *DDC*, 142–43: "Quoniam autem homo ad imaginem Dei factus, totam naturae legem ita secum natam, et in sese insitam habuit, ut nullo ad eam praecepto indigeret." In I.11, see MS 166.

[101] On MS 306, Milton articulates a view more thoroughly in keeping with the Arminian position: "The unwritten law is that law of nature given to the first man, of which remnants and a certain gleam have persisted in the hearts of all mortals; in the regenerate, however, it is daily renewed in the direction of its pristine perfection by the working of the holy spirit [Non scripta est naturalis illa primo homini

98 MILTON'S THEOLOGICAL PROCESS

But neither still does this capacity arise from the efficacious grace of Reformed renewal. For Milton, grace enters the economy of salvation as a consequence of God's decreeing the freedom of second causes because if God had determined second causes (including the Fall), "then assuredly it was not the concern of God's grace but of his justice to restore one who fell by a necessary fall."[102] In terms of God's decree, this grace is limited to the foreknown mission of Christ, none of whose effects in individual persons is a matter of decree: "Without Christ's having been foreknown, therefore, no reconciliation of God with men who would fall—no grace—was decreed."[103] This view distinguishes Milton from Calvin's argument that predestination involves "God's eternal decree, by which he compacted with himself what he willed to become of each man," independent of the contingency of second causes—meaning that Milton holds a position that Calvin's successor, Beza, would call "Semipelagian."[104] Milton thus joins with Arminius (who also identifies the Fall with the contingency of second causes) in arguing that predestination to damnation is incompatible with God's grace, as manifest in the creation of rational creatures and in Christ's salvific mission.[105] Milton does align with Reformed theologians like Zanchius in finding the natural sufficient to leave people without excuse, but in his view, this outcome requires (what they would perceive as) his unorthodox position on renewal. At stake here is the capacity of scripture—and, by extension, preaching—either to lead people to salvation or to leave them without excuse, in their natural state, and this capacity only becomes efficacious, in Milton's view, if people have some meaningful capacity to test scripture, discern its truths, and respond to them.

---

data, cuius reliquiae et quoddam lumen omnium mortalium cordibus permansit; in regeneratis verò spiritus sancti opera indies ad perfectionem primaevam renovatur]." This page appears (next to its heavily revised neighbor, 307a) in a section that finds Milton rethinking his view on the Gentiles' access to the law of Moses. The temporal relationship between these changes and those in I.17–18 remains unclear. Arminius similarly holds that "Adam was able, with the aid of God, to fulfill the law by those powers which he had received in creation [potuit enim Adam ijs viribus, quas in creatione acceperat, Legem praestare, cum auxilio Dei]": *Works*, III.540; Jacobus Arminius, *Disputationes Publicae & Privatae* (Leiden, 1610), p. 130 [XIII.iii]. Arminius distinguishes the law given to Adam from that given to Moses; see Raymond A. Blacketer, "Arminius's Concept of Covenant in Its Historical Context," *Nederlands Archief voor Kerkgeschiedenis/Dutch Review of Church History* 80, 2 (2000): 216.

[102] *DDC*, 28: "profectò iam non ad gratiam, sed ad iustitium Dei pertinuit necessario lapsu lapsum restituere."

[103] *DDC*, 28: "Sine Christo igitur praecognito, nulla cum hominibus lapsuris reconciliatio Dei, nulla gratia decreta est."

[104] Calvin, *Institutio*, 337; *Institutes*, 926 (III.xxi.5): "Praedestinationem vocamus aeternum Dei decretum, quo apud se constitutum habuit quid de vnoquoque homine fieri vellet." On Beza, see Irena Backus and Aza Goudriaan, "'Semipelagianism': The Origins of the Term and its Passage into the History of Heresy," *Journal of Ecclesiastical History* 65, 1 (2014): 44.

[105] See Jacobus Arminius, *Examen Thesium D. Francisci Gomari de Praedestinatione* (N.p., 1645), pp. 10–32. On contingency in Reformed theology, see n 12 above.

This is to say that the possibility of theology itself, as Milton understands it, is at stake. For the Reformed, only supernatural theology is theology in the sense of setting out the path whereby humans can, through the process of salvation, come to knowledge of God in Christ. This is the *theologia viatorum*, or pilgrims' theology, and Milton departs from the Reformed by extending this theology into the natural human world, comprised of people universally, if only partially, renewed and thus tasked with exercising their newfound capacity faithfully because failure to receive and exercise the gift will incur God's just judgment.[106] But for Milton the theologian, the challenge remains of defining this capacity and articulating its place in Christian teaching. While he struggles to do this, as manifest in the manuscript revisions to I.17–18, scripture remains decidedly in the driver's seat of Milton's theology, even though keeping it there requires considerable effort on the part of Milton and his scribes. Consequently, a tension persists between the presumed unity of scripture and the multifarious beliefs derived from it. In the block of citations considered in the last section, this tension shows most clearly in 2 Corinthians 4:16 and Titus 3:5. Inconveniently for Milton's initial plans, the verse from 2 Corinthians speaks of internal renewal, and the verse from Titus brings together renewal and regeneration, not to mention the theological minefield of grace and works. The trouble is that Milton has begun to understand the internal renewal from 2 Corinthians in a way that extends into the external renewal discussed in I.17. In the contest between scriptural language and the Ramist framework borrowed from the theologians, scripture will prevail.

Revising the Distinction

Ultimately, the verses from Titus and 2 Corinthians put scriptural pressure on the external/internal framework that it could not sustain, leading Milton (through a series of revisions by Amanuensis "A") to replace the external/internal distinction with a natural/supernatural one. So now, the initial Ramist division in I.17 reads, "The manner of renewal is either natural or supernatural."[107] Accordingly, the uses of *externa* or *exteriore* in the ensuing lines all become variants on *naturalis*: "I term 'natural' [the renewal] which reaches its limit in the natural man. And this comprises calling and the change

---

[106] On supernatural theology and the *theologia viatorum*, see PRRD, I.255–69 (and ch. 5 more generally).

[107] DDC, 221: "Renovationis ratio est vel naturalis vel Supernaturalis."

100 MILTON'S THEOLOGICAL PROCESS

which follows it in the natural man."[108] Similarly, the definition changes: "Calling is that natural manner of renewal."[109] The entire passage under the heading **External manner** gets crossed out (as noted above; see Figure 1.1). In conjunction with this deletion, Picard takes the phrase "as a result of his plan [*ex praestituto ipsius*]" from the deleted passage and adds it interlinearly to the definition on MS 222. He also introduces it as a new headword via a marginal addition on MS 223, incorporating the two relevant scriptural passages (Romans 8:28, 29, 30 and 2 Timothy 1:9) from the deleted passage that were the source of this language (see Figure 2.3). The passage from Deuteronomy about the election of particular nations disappears, perhaps because the treatise takes that question up elsewhere.[110] *Exteriore sive* gets crossed out from the passage on MS 228, leaving only *naturalis* behind. At the end of I.17, a final *externa* gets crossed out and replaced with *naturali*.[111]

These revisions prompt further theological developments in the chapter as the effects of responsiveness to scriptural language ripple outward. Because the theology in question focuses on the capacity of humans in their natural state to engage with scripture, it bears on the very process that led to its articulation. On MS 228, in addition to deleting *Exteriore sive*, "A" also expands the passage in question via a marginal insertion. The initial passage held that the human mind is divinely moved toward knowledge of God, to which "A" adds that not only the mind but also "the will [is] to some extent renewed."[112] This revision thus takes the idea of trying God's will found in Romans 12:2 and develops it to include a capacity to assent to God's saving work (if not therefore the capacity to choose salvation outright). I.17, then, offers a case of Milton's theological process rein-forcing itself, as careful engagement with scripture drives further articulation of the capacities that make such engagement possible. Milton, here, is working out the theology that makes human *theologia in via* (or at least its beginnings) possible not just for highly educated amateur theologians like himself but for every human, saved or not. People in their natural state, his thinking goes, need some measure of freedom if a greater freedom is to become possible for them.

Milton speaks to this freedom in a (possibly earlier) insertion by Picard on MS 229 (see Figure 2.4) that conveys the complex relationship between

---

[108] *DDC*, 222: "Naturalem voco, quae in naturali homine terminatur. Estque vocatio, eámque sequens in naturali homine alteratio."

[109] *DDC*, 222: "Vocatio est naturalis illa renovationis ratio."

[110] The issue of national election drives the changes on MS 307–307a from *Israelitis potissimum* to *Israelitis duntaxat*, along with the ensuing discussion of the law's abrogation in I.27. See Chapter 1, pp. 56–59.

[111] *DDC*, 235.

[112] *DDC*, 228: "et voluntas aliqua ex parte renovata."

Figure 2.3 Detail from *DDC*, 223 showing the marginal insertion of a headword

102 MILTON'S THEOLOGICAL PROCESS

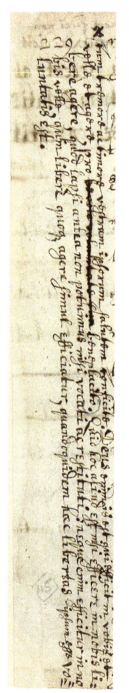

Figure 2.4 Detail from *DDC*, 229 showing a marginal insertion

HUMAN CAPACITY AND SCRIPTURAL INTERPRETATION   103

renewal and will both human and divine at work in the chapter. Here, too, scripture takes the driver's seat as the insertion begins by quoting Philippians 2:12–13: "With trembling and fear bring about your own salvation. For it is God who accomplishes in you both the [actual] willing and the [actual] doing, according to his good pleasure."[113] In keeping with the high stakes around questions of divine will, the treatise wrestles visibly with the wording of this passage, following *pro* with (perhaps) Beza's *benevolo* and then trying *voluntate sua* before crossing them both out together and settling on *beneplacito*—emphasizing God's good pleasure over too firm an insistence on will.[114] Wolleb, tellingly, lists this verse as grounding a possible objection to the doctrine of perseverance: "It is temerity, say they, to boast of the certainty of Faith, whereas our salvation should be wrought out with fear and trembling, *Phil.* 2.12." The elect, however, avoid this charge "because they ascribe not to their own strength the certainty of salvation, by which they may a thousand times fall off, without Gods grace."[115] Milton stands up as one of Wolleb's objectors:

> What else is this but God's accomplishing in us [the power] to act freely, which as fallen people we have previously been unable to do unless called and restored? For indeed *willing* is not brought about in us without the power to act freely being simultaneously brought about too, since this freedom is *the very essence* of the will.[116]

On this account, people owe the power to act freely—their liberation from the bondage of the will—to God, and yet the fruits of that free action still matter. When Milton claims that freedom is the very essence of the will, he is making an ontological point with which few, if any, Reformed theologians would disagree—even those who affirm that human will is utterly incapable of choosing the good in matters of salvation. Milton's soteriological claim about the

---

[113] *DDC*, 229: "cum tremore ac timore vestram ipsorum salutem conficite. Deus enim is est qui efficit in vobis et velle et agere, pro beneplacito."

[114] Oxford finds the word before *voluntate sua* illegible. It resembles *benevolo* enough to make that a plausible reading. The Vulgate in this place has *pro bona voluntate*. Alternatively, it could be two false starts (*be-* and then *vole-*). In any case, Picard crossed it all out, apparently in a single stroke.

[115] Wolleb 217 [185]: "Temeritatis esse, de fidei certitudine gloriari, cum salus potius cum timore & tremore sit operanda. Phil. 2.12 [. . .] quia salutis certitudinem non suis viribus adscribunt, per quas millies Dei gratia excidere possent." Ross's translation, "*without* Gods grace" responds to an awkwardness in Wolleb's Latin syntax that makes it seem as though God's grace enables the possibility of falling thousands of times.

[116] *DDC*, 229: "Quid hoc aliud est nisi efficere in nobis liberè agere, quod lapsi antea non potuimus nisi vocati ac restituti? neque enim efficitur in nobis *velle*, quin liberè quoque agere simul efficiatur, quandoquidem haec libertas *ipsum esse* voluntatis est."

104   MILTON'S THEOLOGICAL PROCESS

renewal of the will such that it can assent to the call is Arminian, but his claim about the freedom of the will as a faculty is not (speaking of the faculty, *voluntas*, as distinct from the function, *arbitrium*).[117]

Milton's scriptural argument for freedom thus extends the internal renewal addressed in 2 Corinthians 4:16 into the bounds of the natural (no longer the "external"), which prompts revisions to the beginning of I.18. There, Amanuensis "A" crosses out "the internal manner of renewal [*interna renovationis ratio*]" and replaces it with this extended explanation:

> The manner of supernatural renewal not only restores man's natural faculties—obviously, those of understanding rightly and willing freely—more fully than before, but also, outstandingly, creates the inward man anew as it were, and further yet it infuses the minds of the renewed by divine means with new supernatural faculties.[118]

Here, the old category of "the inward man" assumes its place within the revised framework. Instead of I.17 discussing external and I.18 discussing internal renewal, now the difference is between a partial renewal in the natural man (I.17) and the inward man being created anew (I.18). 2 Corinthians 4, rather than posing a problem to the framework with its language of internal change, now can refer to change across the spectrum running from natural to supernatural as the day-by-day process of transformation unfolds. In this way, the treatise has attempted to resolve the tension between renewal and calling that ran through the first group of citations.

Extending this internal renewal into the "natural" human state matters to Milton because it gives all people the capacity to respond to the exhortations of preaching and scripture, which both Wolleb and Ames associate with the external aspect of the call. The connection becomes clear in a marginal insertion on MS 231 by Amanuensis "M" during the discussion of penitence that showed how its marks can be found even among the unregenerate. To the assertion that the Bible contains frequent exhortations to penitence, "M" adds: "But all exhortation would be addressed in vain unless to people who were to some degree affected by at least this natural renewal, that is, to people

---

[117] See n. 12 above and Headley, *The Nature of the Will*, esp. ch. 2.

[118] *DDC*, 236: "Supernaturalis renovationis ratio, non solum naturales hominis facultates rectè nimirum intelligendi liberèque volendi plenius adhuc restituit, sed etiam internum praesertim hominem quasi novum creat, novasque etiam facultates supernaturales renovatorum mentibus divinitus infundit."

endowed with some mental judgment and freedom of the will."[119] Notably, this insertion adopts the logical framework of natural/supernatural introduced through the revisions by "A," suggesting its importance to developing the implications of that change. The emphasis on mental judgment and freedom of the will contrasts with the account of agency informing Wolleb's discussion of preaching: "The instrumental cause by which Faith is given to us, is ordinarily the Word of God, in those that are of years [. . .] Therefore the bare preaching of the Gospel is not the cause of Faith, but as it is joyned with the power of Gods Spirit."[120] In keeping with his larger theological perspective, Wolleb is careful, here, to make God the agent of salvation, with preaching as one of the means. The gap between his position and Milton's narrows somewhat on the next page, however, when he allows that the form of faith has three parts (knowledge, assent, and confidence), with the first two associated with both historical and saving faith but confidence alone identified with saving faith.[121] Like Milton, then, Wolleb is acknowledging that some aspects of faith can be possible in the unregenerate; the difference is that Milton emphasizes the specific pre-regeneration renewal of the capacities of reason and will that these aspects entail with an eye to the possibility for hearers to evaluate preaching and discern the presence of the Word in it.[122]

Conclusion

The process of revision to I.17–18 has shown Milton wrestling in an extended way with the language of internal renewal he encountered in 2 Corinthians 4:16, reshaping the treatise as he considers that verse's theological ramifications at length. These labors thus find him highly responsive to scripture, at some odds with his reputation for bending scripture to suit his own ends. They also find him (like Arminius before him) pursuing orthodox means to

---

[119] *DDC*, 231: "Hortatio autem omnis frustra adhiberetur, nisi hominibus naturali saltem hac renovatione aliquem in modum affectis, i. e. aliquo mentis iudicio atque arbitrii libertate praeditis."

[120] Wolleb, 199 [169]: "Caussa instrumentalis, qua nobis fides datur, in adultis ordinarie est, Dei Verbum. [...] Non igitur sola Evangelii praedicatio est caussa fidei, sed quatenus conjuncta est cum efficacia Spiritus sancti."

[121] Wolleb, 200 [169–70]: "Forma fidei docendi caussa tribus partibus describi solet, notitia, assensu, & fiducia [...] Notitia & assensus fidei historicae cum salvifica communis est; fiducia vero huic propria exsistit."

[122] Milton, like Arminius, takes an intellectualist view of postlapsarian humanity in which some intellectual activity (however imperfectly) informs the action of the will. See Headley, *The Nature of the Will*, ch. 2.

106 MILTON'S THEOLOGICAL PROCESS

heterodox ends, as his scripturally driven revisions have resulted in more powerful articulations of his initial sense that scriptural interpretation requires the exercise of human freedom. Milton will go to great lengths to defer to external scripture, but his deference cannot, in the end, be absolute. Wolleb and Ames hesitated to allow some renewal to the unregenerate because it risked a kind of Arminianism whereby human choice plays some role in salvation at the perceived expense of God's will. Milton's solution, especially the "supernatural" renewal associated with regeneration, responds to this concern even as it insists that preaching requires some degree of receptivity and cognitive response from its auditors to fill the important place granted it by Wolleb and Ames. Human engagement proves necessary not as an end in itself but as an occasion for the Holy Spirit's work. In the end, the "nature" by which humans were "sons of wrath" can remain such while nevertheless admitting some degree of internal renewal, in keeping with Arminius's view that the "natural" contains an element of the "supernatural." Such renewal is sufficient to the kind of testing suggested by Romans 12:2, all without risking the Pelagianism of claiming that humans in their natural state, however partially renewed, could—by their own efforts—arrive at regeneration. Even as he sides with Arminius, Milton is not therefore rejecting Wolleb and Ames as much as he is refining them, in light of scripture—just as he promised in the epistle but with ramifications for the human practice of scriptural interpretation that they never considered.

On the level of literary form, I.17 finds Milton departing from the bare style of scripture blocks, definitions, and headings promised in the first chapter. As noted above, even prior to the revisions discussed in the present chapter, Milton had already inserted a section of prose argumentation on MS 225–26 that necessitated the recopying of the chapter's middle section. In that passage, Milton argues that calling can extend even to people who do not know Christ—an argument that supports his thesis that even the unregenerate experience the degree of renewal that attends God's universal call. This prose passage interrupts the flow of the Ramist structure: the preceding paragraph defines general calling, and the one that follows takes up special calling. Milton's prose appears in support of his argument about general calling while bringing additional scriptural cases to bear, some with citations and some without. In a similar vein, the chapter's clearest articulation of what renewal accomplishes comes in the marginal insertion on MS 229, where Milton follows up his quotation of Philippians 2:12–13 with two interpretative sentences of his own. These formal departures show Milton putting into practice the "natural" activity of discerning and testing for which the chapter's theology argues. If anything, though, such passages require more discernment and testing than scripture because, as human speech (and especially as potentially unregenerate human speech), the potential for error is much higher. That potential for error invites inquiry into the problem of authority raised both by Milton's willingness to attempt "internal scripture" and by the need to discern and test the degree of his success. To that problem, Chapter 3 turns.

3

Theology and the Church

The preceding chapters have drawn attention to the forms of argumentative prose that depart from Milton's stated intention to let scripture crowd out his own words. This practice finds theological justification in his account of calling and renewal, which holds that all humans in their "natural," unregenerate state possess some capacity for understanding and interpreting scripture. This capacity equips people to hear and evaluate preaching so that they can assent to the "supernatural" renewal necessary for salvation. It also equips people—all the called, regenerate and unregenerate alike—to speak in ways that require such evaluation from others. This connection among calling, speaking, and evaluating is perforce ecclesial, meaning "of the church," from the Greek ἐκκλησία, deriving from the verb ἐκκαλεῖν, which means "to call out."[1] Working out the practicalities of that connection therefore requires that Milton develop an ecclesiology, a theology of the church.[2] I say "ecclesial" rather than "ecclesiastical" because Milton's interest is less in churches as formal institutions than in a broader concept of "church" that it will be this chapter's task to define.[3]

Milton's broad construction of calling and the need for ecclesiology to which it gives rise provoke a methodological crisis of sorts for the treatise, centered on questions of authority. The method of gathering scriptural passages under Ramist logical headings that largely derived from them was supposed to produce a systematic theology whose authority rested firmly in the words of scripture, but sections of prose argument threaten to unsettle that scriptural foundation by introducing the very human, rhetorical speech that the treatise's methodology set out to minimize. An influential interpretative principle from Augustine helps to name the problem. Called the rule of faith, it proposes to interpret difficult passages of scripture by reference to "the plainer

---

[1] *Oxford English Dictionary*, "ecclesia," n.

[2] The best previous account of the treatise's ecclesiology is Stephen R. Honeygosky, *Milton's House of God: The Invisible and Visible Church* (Columbia, SC: University of Missouri Press, 1993), esp. chs 2–3. Honeygosky sought to demonstrate the contiguity of Milton's ecclesiology with what he terms the Radical Reformed tradition. I consider, instead, how ecclesiology and literary form shape each other in *De Doctrina Christiana*.

[3] Compare Honeygosky, *Milton's House of God*, 31.

Milton's Theological Process. Jason A. Kerr, Oxford University Press. © Jason A. Kerr (2023).
DOI: 10.1093/oso/9780198875086.003.0004

passages of the scriptures and the authority of the church."[4] This rule of faith appeals to the proportion that governs the doctrinal structure of scripture, enabling the Bible to be self-interpreting on the assumption that something on a topic in one part of the Bible ultimately coheres with what other parts say, complex though the results may be.[5] This assumption, which finds scriptural warrant in Paul's injunction in Romans 12:6 to prophesy "κατὰ τὴν ἀναλογίαν τῆς πίστεως [according to the analogy (KJV: proportion) of faith]," gave Augustine's rule of faith (*regula fidei*) its common alternate name as the analogy of faith (*analogia fidei*). The proportionate place of each passage in the Bible's doctrinal structure might come more clearly into view, the thinking went, if these dispersed passages were brought together under pertinent headings.[6] Milton's initial methodology of gathering scriptural passages and organizing them under definitions and headings thus appeals to the first aspect of Augustine's principle, while his skepticism of exegetical tradition attempts to jettison the second. This method privileges what Milton calls "external scripture."

Ultimately, however, Milton privileges "internal scripture" as the rule of faith, arguing that "the spirit, rather than scripture, has been offered to us as the surer guide whom we ought to follow."[7] These claims seem entirely at odds with Augustine's appeal to "the authority of the church," and in crucial respects they are, but the section of Milton's chapter on Holy Scripture (I.30) where Milton describes this rule of faith—notably, in the latest stratum of the chapter's manuscript—nevertheless teems with ecclesiological argument.[8] Indeed, immediately after speaking of "the surer guide," Milton turns to the church:

For this is also certain, that the visible church has not always since Christ's ascension stood forth as the "pillar and bulwark of the truth," but [rather]

---

[4] Augustine, *De Doctrina Christiana*, trans. R. P. H. Green, (Oxford: Oxford University Press, 1995), III.3: "consulat regulam fidei, quam de scripturarum planioribus locis et ecclesiae auctoritate percepit."

[5] Rachel Trubowitz notes an affinity between Galileo's geometry and Milton's thinking about the proportional body of scripture: "The Fall and Galileo's Law of Falling Bodies: Geometrization vs. Observation and Describing Things in *Paradise Lost*," in *Milton and the New Scientific Age: Poetry, Science, Fiction*, ed. Catherine Gimelli Martin (New York and London: Routledge, 2019), p. 87.

[6] On Reformation use of the *locus* method, see *PRRD*, I.59, 96–108. On the Renaissance practice, see Mary Thomas Crane, *Framing Authority: Sayings, Self, and Society in Sixteenth-Century England* (Princeton, NJ: Princeton University Press, 1993).

[7] *DDC*, 397: "certiorem nobis propositum ducem spiritum quàm scripturam, quem sequi debeamus."

[8] *DDC*, 394 begins a new material segment of the chapter, marked by less embellished script and doctrinal departures from the more familiarly Protestant theology of scripture in the first three folios. See the Appendix.

110   MILTON'S THEOLOGICAL PROCESS

the hearts of the faithful [have stood forth]—which are properly speaking the "household and church of the living God," 1 Tim. 3:15.[9]

This pivot toward ecclesiology serves two functions. In the immediate context, this passage disqualifies the visible church as the arbiter of the text of external scripture, a role that Milton assigns instead to the codices themselves. More broadly, however, it works to redefine the church as "the hearts of the faithful," distinguishing the church as he understands it from any formal ecclesiastical body—an ecclesial arbiter, not an ecclesiastical one. Milton drives the point home in the chapter's conclusion, where he objects to the term "mother church," "unless we mean solely the mystical and heavenly Church, Gal. 4:26: *but that Jerusalem which is above is free,* [she] *who is the mother of us all.*"[10] This redefinition sets up an extended discussion of how belief in such a church is to function. Building on the distinction between external and internal scripture, Milton grounds belief in the scriptures in "the authority of the whole of scripture compared with itself" and in "the spirit itself which inwardly persuades each one of the faithful."[11] He concludes by privileging the latter: "all things are in the end to be referred to the spirit and the *unwritten* word."[12]

Milton aims in *De Doctrina Christiana* to express this unwritten word, using external scripture where possible and internal scripture where necessary. Such appeals to internal scripture require a church grounded in the spiritual liberty needed to ensure that they undergo rigorous evaluation, no matter who made them. Condemning "anyone [...] who imposes any sanctions and dogmas of his own on the faithful—each one of whom is ruled by God's spirit—against their will" as "imposing a yoke not only on human beings but also on the holy spirit itself," Milton gestures toward a church in which the spirit can work unimpeded on believers, freed from every external imposition.[13] These spiritual workings, however, seem not to reach perfection in any actual visible church; citing Acts 15:10, Milton argues that if even an ancient council of apostles refused to

---

[9] *DDC*, 397: "Hoc enim constat etiam, ecclesiam visibilem non semper ab ascensu Christi columnam aut stabilimentum veritatis extitisse, sed corda fidelium; quae proprie sunt domus et ecclesia Dei vivi, 1 Tim. 3. 15."

[10] *DDC*, 401: "Immo ne matris quidem ecclesiae venerando nomini attribuere nimium debemus [...] nisi mysticam duntaxat Ecclesiam intelligimus et coelestem Gal. 4.2[6] *illa verò quae sursum est Hierusalem libera est, quae est mater omnium nostrum.*"

[11] *DDC*, 398: "propter authoritatem totius scripturae secum collatae; [...] propter ipsum spiritum unicuique fidelium intus persuadentem."

[12] *DDC*, 398: "Sic omnia demum ad spiritum atque verbum non scriptum, scriptura ipsa teste referenda sunt."

[13] *DDC*, 399: "Qui igitur fidelibus, quorum unusquisque Dei spiritu regitur, sanctiones quascunque suas et dogmata [...] imposuerit, is non hominibus tantum, verùm etiam ipsi sancto spiritui iugum imponit."

THEOLOGY AND THE CHURCH   111

impose divine law on believers, "much less will any modern church, which cannot arrogate to itself the absolutely sure presence of the spirit, be able [to do so]."[14] Explicitly, the things that cannot be commanded in this way "are either not found in scripture, or are squeezed out by merely human reasonings that carry no conviction!"[15] Milton hopes that his words will not turn out to be such "merely human reasonings" but that the spirit will convey a conviction of their truth into his readers' hearts.[16] The realization of this hope depends, however, on the judgment of the spiritually liberated church that he envisions.

Because Milton's attempts to articulate internal scripture presume this ecclesial process of testing, ecclesiology necessarily informs the ways of reading that the treatise's "internal scriptural" literary forms invite. This chapter aims, therefore, to give an account of Milton's ecclesiology in *De Doctrina Christiana* and then to integrate that account with the discussion of internal scripture's literary forms from Chapter 1. There, relative deference to external scripture served as a heuristic device for placing Milton's prose in the treatise on a spectrum from least to most at risk of being adjudged "merely human reasonings." The ecclesial context leaves this spectrum intact, but it allows for a more nuanced approach to thinking about the kinds of authority that operate in such speech. By venturing farther from the relatively secure foothold of external scripture, Milton increases the risk that his words will amount to no more than the crabbed opinion of John Milton, the scrivener's son. But in the event that Milton's wilderness utterances turn out to be true, as revealed through the collective spiritual discernment of believers, they will no longer be merely his, but will become a truth common to all. Milton risks speaking for himself, but he hopes to speak scripture.

De Doctrina Christiana and Ecclesial Process

The church at issue in Milton's ecclesial process is not of the brick-and-mortar sort, or even of the gathered-in-someone's-home sort (hence my calling that process "ecclesial" rather than "ecclesiastical"). Although the treatise's chapters

---

[14] *DDC*, 399: "multo minus poterit ecclesia ulla hodierna quae praesentiam spiritus certissimam arrogare sibi non potest."
[15] *DDC*, 399: "quae in scriptura vel non reperiuntur, vel humanis duntaxat rationibus, quae fidem non faciunt, exprimuntur."
[16] Milton anticipates the critique of Eisenring, who finds that *De Doctrina Christiana* is "based almost exclusively on mere personal experience as the last and deepest source, while the objective sources and resources of faith and true common sense have been utterly lost": Albert J. Th. Eisenring, *Milton's De Doctrina Christiana: An Historical Introduction and Critical Analysis* (Fribourg: Society of St Paul, 1946), p. 153.

112   MILTON'S THEOLOGICAL PROCESS

"On the Visible Church" (I.29), "On Particular Churches" (I.31), and "On Church Discipline" (I.32) speak, in their way, to these kinds of churches, my concern lies less with what the treatise has to say about the practicalities of church life, important as they may be, than with its deeper ruminations about the concept of "church" itself, especially as these inform Milton's practice of internal scripture.

De Doctrina Christiana first frames its approach to the concept of church in the epistle, a brief letter introducing the treatise's work before it properly begins. This part of the treatise differs markedly from the rest, so a few words about its status as evidence are in order. Anthony Grafton notes that prefaces, while seemingly a logical place to discuss method, are inadequate to that end because they are epistolary by nature, and the "rhetorical conventions of the art of letter-writing [. . .] forbade too much discussion of technical problems as boring or inelegant." Furthermore, prefaces "tended to omit any reference to those predecessors to whom [the author] was most indebted," with the result that "prefaces often mislead the student who wishes to establish the background and aims of a philological work." Consequently, "no history that relies on prefaces alone can possibly be adequate."[17] Milton was quite gifted in the art of Latin epistolary, and the epistle to *De Doctrina Christiana* bears the nearest stylistic resemblance to his other Latin output.[18] Read with Grafton in mind, it is unsurprising that the epistle does not name Wolleb or Ames and that it describes the treatise's methodological departures from their work only in general terms. More pointedly, the epistle's ecclesial orientation owes explicitly to its epistolary genre, which occasions its opening address "**To all the churches of Christ**, and also to all who profess the Christian faith anywhere among the peoples."[19] This mode of address creates the difficulty of discerning between ecclesiology and epistolary convention, given that prefatory epistles of this kind expressly work to generate and define a community of readers.

In response to these concerns, this chapter does not rely on the epistle alone for its account of Milton's ecclesiology, but instead aims to establish connections between the epistle and the explicitly ecclesial chapters at the end of Book I. Here, another difficulty presents itself: chronology. I have been arguing that Milton's increasing reliance on internal scripture brought with it a generic

---

[17] Anthony Grafton, *Joseph Scaliger: A Study in the History of Classical Scholarship*, Vol. 1 (Oxford: Clarendon, 1983), p. 6.
[18] *MMS*, 76. See also Estelle Haan, ed., *John Milton: Epistolarum Familiarum Liber Unus and Uncollected Letters* (Leuven: Leuven University Press, 2019).
[19] *DDC*, 1: "**Universis Christi Ecclesiis,** nec non omnibus Fidem Christianam ubicunque Gentium profitentibus."

transformation of the treatise as it moved away from its initial methodological assumptions. In tandem with this argument, I have suggested that the move toward internal scripture places pressure on Milton's notion of the church: instead of a community united in its commitment to scripture, the church becomes a community that functions to test and try its members' internal scriptural utterances. But because the epistle, as an epistle, stands outside the genre of the rest of *De Doctrina Christiana*, its chronological placement in this transformation is not discernible by the methods used in the preceding chapters. Furthermore, because it is part of the section of the manuscript recopied by Daniel Skinner, its material state obscures any revisions that may have been present in earlier strata.

The problem of chronology recedes, however, in the face of the consonance between the epistle's ecclesial vision and that on evidence in Milton's earlier writings, notably *Areopagitica* (1644), where he imagines the church as a conversation, "not without dust and heat," joined with the aim of gathering scattered truth.[20] Whatever the epistle's placement in the chronological process of the treatise's composition, it articulates the tension between *sola scriptura* and human speech that increased as work on the treatise proceeded—between the desire to crowd out its own words with scripture, on the one hand, and its evocation of a church characterized by robust human discussion on the other.

More than a mere Pauline flourish or epistolary convention, the epistle's mode of address establishes the treatise's intended audience as ecclesial. Notably, it addresses itself to multiple churches rather than one; the criterion of professing the Christian faith seems more important to its intentions than does membership in any particular church.[21] Given that Milton is about to spend 745 manuscript pages professing the Christian faith, it seems important to ask what he understands that action as entailing. The epistle addresses this question at length as it details Milton's process of arriving at the project of writing a theological treatise. The process began with studying the Bible in its original languages, then proceeded to reading "some of the shorter Systems of theologians, and, following their practice, to distinguish appropriate topic-headings, under each of which I would classify whatever passages of the Bible presented themselves for extracting, so that I could recover and use them when I needed

---

[20] John Milton, *Areopagitica* (London, 1644), 12, 29–33.

[21] John K. Hale and J. Donald Cullington note that Milton's "nec non" "extends, corroborates, or pushes the speaker's emphasis from the first ['all the churches of Christ'] onto the second part of the connection ['all who profess the Christian faith']": "Universis Christi Ecclesiis: *Milton's Epistle for* De Doctrina Christiana," *Milton Studies* 53 (2012): 4–5.

114   MILTON'S THEOLOGICAL PROCESS

to."[22] These efforts produced a theological commonplace book, likely the lost *Index Theologicus*.[23]

Dissatisfied, however, with what he found in the work of the theologians he had been reading, Milton undertook his own systematic theology, distinct from the theological commonplace book. This work began with a strongly individualistic bent, but an ecclesial dimension is nevertheless present:

> Accordingly, because I judged that I could not in conscience entrust to these guides the whole authority for my faith or my hope of salvation, but yet that I absolutely must possess some systematic arrangement of Christian teaching or at any rate some disquisition upon it which could help my faith or my memory or both, the safest and wisest thing for me seemed to be to start again from the beginning and compile such a treatise for myself, by labour and lucubration of my own, to keep ready beside me—taken out of the word of God itself alone, and with complete fidelity too, if I did not want to be unfaithful to myself.[24]

This passage finds Milton taking responsibility for his individual faith, but it also shows him recognizing that this responsibility unfolds in a communal context. That context appears first in the theologians' understanding of themselves as "guides [*ducibus*]." The Protestant framework privileges the individual conscience, but it also includes considerable investment in structures intended to set individuals on the right path. Even as Milton found the theologians' treatises inadequate to his ends, he did not abandon them in composing *De Doctrina Christiana*, which (as I have already argued) engages with them extensively on scales both large and small. Milton's decision to compile a systematic theology involved an inward turn, to be sure, but he never ceased to participate in a larger conversation.

---

[22] *DDC*, 2: "tum Theologorum Systemata aliquot breviora sedulo percurrere: ad eorum deinde exemplum, locos communes digerere, ad quos omnia quae in scripturis haurienda occurrissent, expromenda cum opus esset, referrem."

[23] See Gordon Campbell, "Milton's *Index Theologicus* and Bellarmine's *Disputationes De Controversiis Christianae Fidei Adversus Huius Temporis Haereticos*," *Milton Quarterly* 11, 1 (1977): 12–16; Jeffrey Alan Miller, "Reconstructing Milton's Lost *Index Theologicus*: The Genesis and Usage of an Anti-Bellarmine, Theological Commonplace Book," *Milton Studies* 52 (2011): 187–219; and William Poole, ed., *Manuscript Writings*, Vol. XI, in *The Complete Works of John Milton* (Oxford: Oxford University Press, 2019), pp. 83–92.

[24] *DDC*, 2:

> Cum itaque his ducibus neque summam fidei, neque spem salutis posse me recte committere arbitrarer, et tamen aliquam doctrinae Christianae methodicam institutionem, aut saltem disquisitionem, quae subvenire vel fidei, vel memoriae, vel utrique possit, apprimè esse necessarium, nihil mihi tutius neque consultius visum est, quam ut ipse aliquid huiusmodi quod ad manum mihi esset, labore et lucubratione propriâ ex ipso adeoque solo Dei verbo, et fidelissimè quidem, nisi mihimet fortè infidus esse volebam, de integro componerem.

THEOLOGY AND THE CHURCH   115

Much as he had done earlier in *Areopagitica*, in *De Doctrina Christiana*, Milton frames that conversation as itself constituting a kind of church. Milton is often understood as having constituted a "church of one," "a Congregationalist without a congregation."[25] I am suggesting that neither of these formulations quite captures Milton's perspective on the church, but his stated desire not to be unfaithful to himself nevertheless invites reflection on what it means to be in a church with oneself. The passage above describes the process of compiling the treatise as one of "labour" and "lucubration," the latter word indicating work by candlelight. The treatise is not, in other words, simply a straightforward expression of the contents of Milton's mind or conscience. Rather, it is the product of a laborious extended dialogue between scripture, his mind, and his conscience. Even a church of one is constituted by conversation, not in the manner of a Coleridgean "oneversation" but rather in a complex interplay of accountability between scripture and the individual reader.[26] Much of this book is devoted to working out the shifting dynamics of that interplay of accountability as they unfold through the treatise's processes of revision.

Milton makes this idea of conversation-as-church explicit when he marks a transition between thinking of *De Doctrina Christiana* as a private document compiled for his own ends and a public document for the use of others. Declaring that he now "make[s] this account public," he anticipates that some opposition will arise because "I shall seem to have brought to light many things which will at once be discovered to conflict with some received opinions."[27] He responds to this probability by arguing for an ecclesiology that can not only handle such disagreement but also thrive on it:

> I beg and beseech all who do not hate the truth not to start shouting that the church is being thrown into confusion by this liberty of speech and enquiry, which after all is granted to the schools and so should certainly be denied to no believer; for we are enjoined to "investigate all things," and by the daily increase

---

[25] Michael Fixler, "Ecclesiology," in *A Milton Encyclopedia*, ed. William B. Hunter, Jr (Lewisburg, PA: Bucknell University Press, 1978), II.190–203; Tobias Gregory, *Milton's Strenuous Liberty* (forthcoming). Milton espouses a kind of Congregationalism in I.31.

[26] Samuel Taylor Coleridge speaks of his "*Oneversazioni*" in a letter of 5 May 1829 to Thomas Allson: *Samuel Taylor Coleridge: Letters of Samuel Taylor Coleridge*, ed. Earl Leslie Griggs (Oxford: Clarendon, 1956–71), IV.790. See also Bill Evans, *Conversations with Myself* (Verve, 1963), a "solo" album in which Evans overdubs three piano parts in unfolding dialogue with the standard tunes he is playing and what his earlier selves had played; Gregory Clark, *Civic Jazz: American Music and Kenneth Burke on the Art of Getting Along* (Chicago, IL: University of Chicago Press, 2015), p. 23.

[27] *DDC*, 3: "Haec si omnibus palam facio [...] tametsi multa in lucem protulisse videbor quae ab receptis quibusdam opinionibus discrepare statim reperientur."

116 MILTON'S THEOLOGICAL PROCESS

of the light of truth the Church is much more illuminated and upbuilt than it is confused.[28]

The Restoration likely put an end to Milton's hopes of publishing *De Doctrina Christiana*, and the state of the manuscript (in particular, Skinner's sense that many chapters required recopying) suggests that it was not entirely ready for the press, but the epistle nevertheless registers an intention to issue the treatise publicly. As this passage makes clear, Milton understands his reading public as "the Church [*Ecclesia*]." In context, this word can hardly refer to a particular church, given the epistle's address "to the Universal Churches of Christ." Rather, these plural churches together constitute "the Church" in which the process of debating and discussing matters of Christian doctrine conduces (Milton hopes) to "the daily increase of the light of truth."

A church that does not allow for robust exploration of doctrine and debate about the results is, to Milton, no church at all. He describes the freedom of debating doctrine as crucial:

> I intend to make everyone understand [...] just how crucial it is for the Christian religion that the freedom be granted not simply of probing every doctrine, and of winnowing it in public, but also of thinking and indeed writing about it, in accordance with each person's firm belief. Without that liberty, there is no religion, no Gospel; violence alone prevails.[29]

Too often, he argues, accusations of heresy amount to overhasty reactions that circumvent this vital process of discussion and discernment: "certain unjust and irrational people calumniously condemn whatever they judge to deviate from the traditional doctrine, without comparing the biblical evidence, and instead forging onto it some invidious name such as 'heretic' or 'heresy.'"[30] Milton shares these readers' interest in avoiding heresy, but he objects to

---

[28] *DDC*, 3: "Illud oro atque obtestor omnes, quibus veritas odio non est, ne libertate hac disserendi ac disquirendi quae scholis conceditur, nullis certè credentibus non concedenda, turbari ecclesiam clamitent, cum explorare omnia iubeamur, et veritatis luce indies aucta, illustretur atque aedificetur longè magis Ecclesia quàm turbetur."

[29] *DDC*, 4: "Id denique ago [...] intelligere omnes possint, quanti intersit religionis Christianae, concedi libertatem non excutiendae solum cuiusque doctrinae, palamque ventilandae, sed etiam de ea, prout cuique fide persuasum est, sentiendi atque etiam scribendi. sine qua libertate, religio nulla, Evangelium nullum est; sola vis viget."

[30] *DDC*, 4: "iniquorum quorundam hominum et rationis expertium, quicquid abhorrere à doctrina vulgo tradita iudicaverint, id non scripturae testimoniis collatis, sed invidioso quolibet nomine vel haeretici vel haeresos impacto, per calumniam damnent."

the undue and careless haste with which they arrive at judgment.[31] Absent discussion and debate, the church proves more bound to tradition than truth.

In keeping with his insistence on the necessity of trial by debate, Milton concludes the epistle by submitting his treatise to the judgment of this collective church: "For the rest, my brothers, cultivate the truth with charity; judge of this writing according to the spirit of God guiding you; use it with me, or indeed do not use it, unless I have persuaded you with full conviction by the clarity of the Bible."[32] This gesture places the power of determining the authoritative status of the treatise's conclusions in a community of readers. Milton participates in the community, to be sure, but he cannot control its judgment. He hopes to have contributed to the process of arriving at the truth, but this last sentence of the epistle to *De Doctrina Christiana* leaves room for doubt about the ultimate utility of his contribution, especially in his frank invitation not to use the treatise if its appeals to the Bible have proven unpersuasive. Milton anticipates that in the public process of winnowing doctrine, the wind will carry some of his words away as chaff.

When Milton writes about particular churches in I.31, practical concerns moderate the highflying abstraction of the epistle's ecclesiology. The key consideration here is size: Milton writes that "whatever pertains to making a church a church, can all be done duly and in order in a particular church, within private walls, in a not so large assembly of the faithful."[33] He argues further that "a church, having grown unjustifiably numerous, [...] largely disqualifies itself from the fruit of assemblage"—a condition the tithes-averse Milton attributes to "the avarice of its pastors."[34] A church "small enough to need no more than a private home for its worship" renders the prospect of a theological conversation that works its way slowly toward a kind of doctrinal consensus significantly more plausible than when the church is imagined in the epistle's sweeping and universal terms.[35] Practically, then, Milton imagines this conversation unfolding among a relatively small group of people, ideally "well-versed in every

---

[31] On slow, collective deliberation as a feature of parliamentary resistance to Charles I, see Todd Butler, *Literature and Political Intellection in Early Stuart England* (Oxford: Oxford University Press, 2019), ch. 4.

[32] *DDC*, 5: "De caetero, fratres, veritatem colite cum charitate; de his, prout Dei spiritus vobis praeiverit, ita iudicate: his mecum utimini, vel ne utimini quidem, nisi fide non dubia scripturarumque claritate persuasi."

[33] *DDC*, 416: "quicquid denique ad constituendam ecclesiam pertinet, id omne potest in ecclesia particulari intra privatos parietes in coetu fidelium non ita magno rectè atque ordine fieri."

[34] *DDC*, 416: "Immò eiusmodi ecclesia iusto numerosior dum pastorum avaritiae consulit, fructu conveniendi magna ex parte ipsa sese frustratur." Milton devotes pp. 406–13 to arguing against the compulsory financial support of ministers.

[35] Fixler, "Ecclesiology," 201.

118   MILTON'S THEOLOGICAL PROCESS

gospel doctrine and in testing, by means of the scriptures and the spirit, any teacher whatever, or even all teachers at once, even if these tout themselves by the [exclusive] name of 'the church.'"[36] "Any teacher whatever" surely includes Milton himself. There is no historical record of Milton's participating in the kind of house-church that he envisions in this chapter, and yet its practical ecclesiology usefully brings the epistle's grand statements nearer to the earth.

Internal Scripture and the Foundations of Theology

Milton incorporates this ecclesial process of adjudicating human speech into his account of the foundations of theology, in contrast to Wolleb and Ames. As the literary genre of systematic theology developed among the medieval scholastics, arguments about method led to discussions of prolegomena becoming part of the genre.[37] "Prolegomena" refers to matters that must be addressed before the work of theology proper can commence, including questions of what constitutes theology and which methods are appropriate to it. *De Doctrina Christiana* is no exception to this pattern. It addresses matters of prolegomena in the epistle, as we have seen, and in I.1, "What Christian Doctrine is, and how many are its parts."[38] The chapter begins with a definition:

> **Christian doctrine** is that which Christ (though he was not known by that name from the beginning) imparted in all ages by divine communication concerning God and his worship, to promote the glory of God and the salvation of humankind.[39]

This definition introduces the headings that govern the chapter's content. The first two are "**Christ**" and "**By divine communication**."[40] The third sets out the distinction between "**faith,** or **the knowledge of God**, and **charity** or **the**

---

[36] *DDC*, 413: "ii sunt habendi, qui neque ullius doctrinae euangelicae neque cuiusvis doctoris per scripturas et per spiritum explorandi sunt rudes; ne doctorum quidem omnium simul, etsi ecclesiae se nomine venditabunt."

[37] *PRRD* I, ch. 2. By "literary genre of systematic theology," I refer to the late medieval development of philosophical theology alongside the formation of universities, as distinct from patristic literature, whose institutional contexts were more exclusively ecclesiastical, however philosophically engaged the writing. St. Anselm of Canterbury (*c.* 1033–1109) is a pivotal figure in this transition. Systematic theology (like poetry) encompasses multiple subgenres.

[38] *DDC*, 7: "Quid sit Doctrina Christiana, quótque eius partes."

[39] *DDC*, 7: "**Doctrina Christiana** est quam Christus (licet eo nomine non a principio cognitus) de Deo eiusque cultu ad gloriam Dei salutemque hominum seculis quibuscunque divinitus tradidit."

[40] *DDC*, 7: "**Christus** […] **Divinitus**."

worship of God" that separates the two books of *De Doctrina Christiana*, just as it does the similar two-part works of Wolleb and Ames.[41]

Milton's treatise may share its major principle of organization with Wolleb and Ames, but he handles the place of human activity in scriptural interpretation and theology differently, as the works' titles reveal. Wolleb's work is called *The Abridgment of Christian Divinitie: So exactly and Methodically compiled, that it leads us, as it were, by the hand To the Reading of the Holy Scriptures, Ordering of Common-Places, Understanding of Controversies, Cleering of some Cases of Conscience.*[42] Ames's is *The Marrow of Sacred Divinity, Drawne out of the holy Scriptures, and the Interpreters thereof, and brought into Method.*[43] Wolleb's title declares that his task is to bring Christian divinity into a compendious form for ease of use, to include not only the reading of scripture but also the *loci communes* (or commonplaces) that had, by this point, become a familiar feature of systematic theology and, beyond that, some controversies and cases of conscience. As Wolleb explains in his "Preface to the Reader," he undertook this task for the aid of both ordinary Christians and students of divinity, that is, theologians:

> For as it concerns every Christian to be skilled in the chief Catechistical Heads at least, that by their help and guide they may with the greater profit hear and read Gods word; so it becomes all Students in Divinity, before all things to imprint in their memories the *Anatomie* of the Body of *Theologie*; that in the Common Places, in the Definitions and Divisions of heavenly doctrine, they may be exact and perfect.[44]

The purpose, then, of his treatise is less the discovery of true doctrine than its anatomization for ease of use by others. Ames, more modestly, omits discussion of controversy and puts off cases of conscience for a later treatise, but his larger aim is the same, with the image of a *medulla* or marrow "drawn out of the holy scriptures" capturing even more vividly the sense of an anatomy that

---

[41] *DDC*, 8: **"Partes doctrinae Christianae duae sunt: Fides,** seu **Cognitio Dei,** et **charitas** seu **Dei cultus."**

[42] That is, *Compendium Theologiae Christianae Accurata methodo sic adornatum, Ut sit SS. Scripturas legendas, Ad Locos Communes digerendos, Ad Controversias intelligendas, Manuductio.*

[43] That is, *Medulla S.S. Theologiae, Ex Sacris literis, earumque, interpretibus, extracta, & methodicè disposita.*

[44] Wolleb, fol. A3r [A2r]: "Ut enim cujusque hominis Christiani interest, minimum praecipua capita catechetica tenere, quorum ductu Verbum Dei fructuosius audiat & legat; ita sacrarum quoq; Literarum studiosos, ante omnia corporis Theologici anatomen memoriae suae imprimere convenit, ut Locos Communes, Definitiones & Distributiones rerum Divinarum, in numerato habeant."

120 MILTON'S THEOLOGICAL PROCESS

cuts through externalities to present the living marrow.[45] In his own preface, he justifies this practice by saying

> that all have not so great leasure, or so vast a wit, as to hunt the Partrich in the Mountaines, and Woods: but that the condition of many doth rather require, that the nest it selfe, or the seat of the matter which they pursue, bee shewed without any more adoe.[46]

His aim is not to bring readers along as he pursues the hunt but rather to present them with the "nest it selfe," already found, gathered, and prepared for presentation.

The difference between these works and Milton's has to do with scripture. Scripture plays a key part in the systems of both Milton and his interlocutors. Wolleb intends his system to send his readers to scripture with greater profit than before, and Ames declares that his marrow is drawn out of scripture for his readers' benefit. Crucially, however, the systems themselves are at one remove from scripture, prompting the protest of Milton's title: *On Christian Doctrine sought out from the sacred writings alone.*[47] Much has been made of "alone [*duntaxat*]," and rightly so, because it signals Milton's refusal to operate at a remove: he prefers to deal directly with scripture. Kelley, in his introduction to the Yale edition, finds the claim disingenuous because the text of *De Doctrina Christiana* attests abundantly to Milton's knowledge of, and engagement with, other theologians.[48] I am arguing, however, that such engagement is not finally at odds with *duntaxat* for reasons having to do with what I have been describing as the treatise's aspiration to speak scripture, along with the ecclesial practice of adjudicating such aspirations. The title hints at these reasons in a word that has received less attention: *petita*, which Oxford translates as "sought out."[49] Whereas Ames offers a *Medulla S.S. Theologia, ex sacris literis* [. . .] *disposita*, Milton writes *De Doctrina Christiana ex sacris duntaxat libris petita.* Ames proposes to present the essence of scripture, extracted and prepared for presentation, while Milton proposes to seek Christian doctrine out of scripture. Ames's *methodicè disposita* is true of both works, but they differ in what they propose to arrange. Ames and Wolleb set out to arrange doctrine

---

[45] The later book is William Ames, *De Conscientia* (Amsterdam, 1631).

[46] Ames, fol. A4v [A4r–v]: "omnibus non esse vel otium tam pingue, vel ingenium tam vastum, ut perdicem in montibus & sylvis persequerentur; sed postulare potius multorum conditionem, ut nidus ipse, aut sedes rei quam sectantur sine ambagibus demonstretur."

[47] "**De Doctrina Christiana** ex sacris duntaxat libris petita."

[48] On *duntaxat*, see e.g., Yale, 106–08, and *MMS*, 139–41.

[49] Yale, less helpfully, has "drawn from," also used to translate Ames's *ex* in "Ex Sacris literis."

THEOLOGY AND THE CHURCH   121

methodically—anatomically—so that readers can have it in a compendious and accessible form. Milton, by contrast, sets out to arrange *scripture* methodically so that readers interested in doctrine might seek it more readily:

> In this work nothing new is being taught: rather, I seek only, for the sake of the [reader's] memory, to place at his fingertips things which are read in dispersal in the holy books, by bringing them together for convenience into a single body, so to speak, and by distributing them under definite headings.[50]

Unfortunately, scripture handles distinct doctrines in various places, so Milton offers to help himself and his readers by gathering salient passages under appropriate doctrinal heads.

Milton's eventual reliance on internal scripture and its attendant prose troubles this methodological insistence, however. The task now at hand, therefore, is to ascertain how the apparent formal aberrations of internal scripture came to be. In short, arranging scripture under doctrinal heads turns out to be much more difficult than initially appears and becomes ever more difficult the more detailed one wishes those heads to be. This difficulty, I suggest, lies behind the epistle's final acknowledgment that its conclusions are contestable but also, more profoundly, behind its assertion that the church is the forum in which such contestation ought to occur. Whereas Wolleb and Ames hope to present an anatomy of pure doctrine so that churches and their members might rest on a sure foundation, Milton understands the church as the means for seeking out pure doctrine through the tumult arising from the members' individual, good-faith, if inevitably flawed, interpretative efforts, what he in *Areopagitica* calls "brotherly dissimilitudes that are not vastly disproportionall."[51]

The first chapter, in its handling of prolegomena, argues for human interpretative activity by showing its ultimate compatibility with the title's *duntaxat*. The chapter does this when it sets out to defend, on scriptural grounds, its adoption of a Ramist approach to the commonplacing method: "Although this proceeding is easily defended on grounds of Christian prudence, let it nevertheless be seen rather to rely on divine admonition."[52] The treatise then adduces a series of scriptural passages in support of organizing doctrinal ideas systematically: Matthew 13:52, 2 Timothy 1:13, Hebrews 6:1–3, Romans 6:17, 2 Timothy

---

[50] *DDC*, 8: "Hic autem non novum quicquam docetur, sed memoriae tantummodo consulitur; ut quae sparsim sacris in libris leguntur, commodè velut in unum corpus redacta, perque certos digesta locos, ad manum sint."

[51] Milton, *Areopagitica*, 32.

[52] *DDC*, 8: "Quod factum, quanquam Christiana prudentia facile defenditur, divino tamen monitu niti potius videatur." On Ramism and commonplacing, see Crane, *Framing Authority*, 35–38.

122 MILTON'S THEOLOGICAL PROCESS

1:13 (again), Romans 2:20, and Acts 20:27. One of these —2 Timothy 1:13— Wolleb had used to begin his *Compendium* by way of putting the systematic enterprise on a biblical foundation. His aim is to enable "Students in Divinity, before all things to imprint in their memories the *Anatomie* of the Body of *Theologie*; that in the Common Places, in the Definitions and Divisions of heavenly doctrine, they may be exact and perfect."[53] He is explicit in his intent not to expand on work done by other theologians; his task is to anatomize doctrine, not develop it:

> Now in this kind divers eminent men, furnished with a far greater measure of Spiritual *Unction* then my self, have afforded such helps to young Students, that he who goes about to adde any thing to these, will seem to light a candle at noon tide, or to garnish the firmament with more stars.[54]

In Milton's hands, this scriptural defense of method defies the method it defends as it works to authorize departures from precedent as necessary. This section of the chapter follows after the heading "**By divine communication [Divinitus]**," but it is framed more as a response to that heading than as a part of it: "One must seek this doctrine, therefore, not from the schools of those who philosophize, nor from human laws, but solely from the sacred writings, with the holy spirit as guide."[55] "Therefore" is the key word here: the treatise is developing a conclusion that should follow from the passages in the preceding scripture block. The point of the two paragraphs that follow is to bolster the "divine" part of "By divine communication," provoking the question of why the gathered passages did not suffice to make this point but also the more interesting question of what this putative insufficiency says about the treatise's interpretative assumptions. In this overt discussion of the treatise's methodology, the treatise already departs from what it declares, invoking *sola scriptura* to defend the kind of active human speaking that this formal exception embodies. This departure also indicates the way that internal scripture often becomes necessary when the logical structure—*dispositio*—itself is at issue.

The paragraph about seeking doctrine "solely from the sacred writings" and not from the philosophical schools seems, on its face, an unlikely place to

---

[53] Wolleb, fol. A3r [A2r]: "ita sacrarum quoq; Literarum studiosos, ante omnia corporis Theologici anatomen memoriae suae imprimere convenit, ut Locos Communes, Definitiones & Distributiones rerum Divinarum, in numerato habeant." See Yale, 18, 128n.

[54] Wolleb, *Compendium*, fol. A3r [A2r]: "Atque hoc in genere, viri longe uberiore Spiritus sancti unctione instructi, talia studiosae Juventuti subministrarunt adminicula, ut, qui alia iis superaddere satagit, multis lucernam in meridie accendere, aut sidera caelo addere velle."

[55] *DDC*, 7: "Haec igitur doctrina, non ex philosophantium scholis, neque ex humanis legibus, sed ex sacris duntaxat literis, praeeunte sancto spiritu, petenda est."

find a defense of human activity, and yet the scriptures quoted after the initial sentence work to that end. Because they appear out of canonical order, they function as a logical sequence. The first passage, 2 Timothy 1:14 ("guard that excellent thing entrusted by the holy spirit who dwells in us"), calls the reader to action through the imperative *custodi*.[56] The "excellent thing [*praeclarum*]" exists independently of the person to whom it has been given in trust [*depositum*], and yet the trust itself requires some custodial action from the trustee. The relationship between such spiritual deposits and the people who hold them in trust does not therefore split cleanly between active and passive but is, instead, a dynamic relationship with giving and receiving on both sides. The next passage, Colossians 2:8, names a danger in this relationship: "[see] that there be no one who might carry you off as prey through philosophy."[57] Given the place for human activity designated in the previous passage, the danger here does not lie in the human per se but rather in the potential for the human to fall out of proportion (i.e., *analogia*) in the dynamic relationship with the spirit. The trouble with philosophy in this context is that it is too human, not that it is human at all. The remaining two passages explicitly avow the necessity of human speech and judgment, first in a political and then in a political-ecclesial context. Daniel 3:16 offers a defense of bold public speech before political rulers: "[Shadrach, Meshach, and Abed-nego said to the king,] We are not troubled about answering you [the king] on this subject."[58] Acts 4:19 then calls rulers themselves to "judge [for yourselves] whether it be righteous in God's sight to listen to you [i.e., the Sanhedrin] rather than to God."[59] Both instances imply human action informed by the spirit: reliance on the spirit does not silence the Hebrew children but spurs them on to untroubled boldness. Similarly, Peter and John call the Sanhedrin to a judgment determined by reliance on God. In both cases, these verses could be read as arguing for a reduction of the human to mere instrumentality, calls to get the human out of the way so that the spirit can work unimpeded. As the first text showed, however, even when the spirit puts a human capacity to use, the capacity is not merely passive; people endowed with the spirit must undertake some action of their own to accomplish its purposes.

The sequencing itself illustrates this principle by curating the texts, allowing the passage from 2 Timothy (as the chosen "plain place") to color the interpretation of what follows. The treatise is not speaking in its own words at this moment (it simply quotes the passages in question from its preferred Bibles),

---

[56] *DDC*, 7: "praeclarum illud depositum custodi per spiritum sanctum, qui inhabitat in nobis."
[57] *DDC*, 7: "ne quis sit qui vos depraedetur per philosophiam."
[58] *DDC*, 7: "ut respondeamus tibi de hac re, non sumus solliciti."
[59] *DDC*, 7–8: "an iustum in conspectu Dei vobis potius auscultare, quam Deo, judicate."

124 MILTON'S THEOLOGICAL PROCESS

but by arranging the passages as it has, the treatise subtly makes a case for the necessity of human action even in a moment devoted to disavowing reliance on philosophy and human law in favor of *sola scriptura*. Indeed, the act of curation in this sequenced passage points also to the similar act at work in selecting passages presented in canonical order. Even when the treatise is most transparently scriptural, the human element has not been reduced to passivity but rather operates with different gradations of activity, on the spectrum delineated in Chapter 1. The authority of the human interpreter is everywhere at stake. The treatise thus means to be quite ingenuous when it avows, "In this work nothing new is being taught."[60] Reliance on scripture serves as the guarantor of this claim, but not at the expense of human action. Rather, reliance on scripture subjects human action to a qualitative test: because human cannot be eliminated from the process, the question is whether or not it comports with—what, exactly?

Assessing the quality of human action invites its own hermeneutical questions. Richard Baxter's heuristic query—"Is the Scripture to be tryed by the Spirit, or the Spirit by the Scripture[?]"—offers one approach to such questions, as does Geoffrey Nuttall's use of it to think about the range of Puritan faith and experience.[61] In Milton's terms, though, Baxter's question becomes hermeneutical rather than heuristic. Instead of pinpointing the treatise's place on a spectrum of attitudes, the question names a dialectical process that interpreters engage. As Milton puts it, doctrine must be sought "solely from the sacred writings, with the holy spirit as a guide."[62] Just as Augustine's rule of faith depends on the interplay of scripture and tradition, Milton's depends on the interplay of scripture and spirit, with the human interpreter as the implied but necessary third element and therefore also as the authority whose trustworthiness needs examining. It bears saying that the rule of faith was a polemical affair from the start: Augustine defines it only to deploy it against an Arian reading of John 1:1.[63] Some amount of argument about which passages counted as the "plain places of scripture" and why was always part of the picture. The tradition of the church operates alongside the plain places of scripture precisely because arbitrating scripture's multifariousness requires some external intervention.

With the advent of Protestantism, this problem emerges as a sideways debate about what kinds of externality comport with scripture. Milton himself is of

---

[60] *DDC*, 8: "Hic autem non novum quicquam docetur."

[61] Richard Baxter, *A Christian Directory* (London, 1673), p. 910; Geoffrey F. Nuttall, *The Holy Spirit in Puritan Faith and Experience* (Chicago, IL: University of Chicago Press, 1992 [1946]), p. 23.

[62] *DDC*, 7: "ex sacris duntaxat literis, praeeunte sancto spiritu, petenda est."

[63] Augustine, *De Doctrina Christiana*, III.ii.3: "Iam nunc exempla considera. Illa haeretica distinctio, *in principio erat verbum, et verbum erat apud deum, et deus erat*, ut alius sit sensus: *verbum hoc erat in principio apud deum*, non vult deum verbum confiteri. Sed hoc regula fidei refellendum est."

two minds about the authority of tradition. In *Of Prelatical Episcopacy* (1641), he captures the tension in two sentences, directed against Tertullian: "Beleeve him now for a faithfull relater of tradition, who you see such an unfaithfull expounder of the Scripture. besides in his time all allowable tradition was now lost."[64] This statement carefully tries to have it both ways: tradition can be admissible if it truly comes from the apostolic period, but the test of whether or not the tradition has been preserved lies not in scriptural support per se but in whether the conveyors of the tradition are faithful interpreters. Scripture still has primacy here but not altogether at the expense of tradition. After all, *Of Prelatical Episcopacy* occupies itself with arguing about what constitutes the true tradition, consulting "as wee must needs in those stale, and uselesse records of either uncertaine, or unsound antiquity, which if we hold fast to the grounds of the reformed *Church*, can neither skill of us, nor we of it, (so oft as it would lead us to the broken reed of *tradition*."[65] This opening salvo defends the pamphlet's engagement in patristics as begrudging but necessary. In this sense, Stanley Fish is mistaken to argue that the tract "is determined to say nothing at all," insisting that, for Milton, "the scriptures themselves do not need anything, and most certainly they don't need us."[66] In contrast to the zero-sum relationship between scripture and everything else that Fish's analysis assumes, the tract does not argue for the rejection of all non-scriptural writing but rather insists that scripture is the rule against which such writing is to be measured. Tradition may, indeed, "bee of *Divine* constitution" if it passes the scriptural test, and Milton is simply arguing that much of tradition does not.[67] Accordingly, *De Doctrina Christiana* generally refuses such appeals to external authority but with the consequence that its own authority enters into the hazard. If the scriptural perspicuity undergirding the rule of faith turns out to be less accessible than assumed, what status accrues to the arguments that become necessary in the absence of available appeals to magisterial authority? That question turns

---

[64] John Milton, *Of Prelatical Episcopacy* (London, 1641), p. 17. Capitalization of second sentence *sic*. Tertullian is "unfaithfull" in arguing that "The Father is the whole substance, but the Son a derivation, and portion of the whole." On this point, Filippo Falcone has argued for a discontinuity between the antiprelatical tract and *De Doctrina Christiana*: "*Irreconcilable (Dis)Continuity*: De Doctrina Christiana *and Milton*," *Connotations* 27, (2018): 94; compare Filippo Falcone, "*More Challenges to Milton's Authorship of* De Doctrina Christiana," *ACME* 63, 10 (2010): 243. See the argument in Chapters 4 and 5.

[65] Milton, *Of Prelatical Episcopacy*, [1–2]. Punctuation *sic*. The tract is unpaginated until p. 9.

[66] Stanley Fish, "Wanting a Supplement: The Question of Interpretation in Milton's Early Prose," in *Politics, Poetics and Hermeneutics in Milton's Prose*, ed. David Loewenstein and James Grantham Turner (Cambridge: Cambridge University Press, 1990), p. 41.

[67] Milton, *Of Prelatical Episcopacy*, [2]. I likewise disagree with Honeygosky's assessment that Milton treats church externals as self-consuming; *Milton's House of God*, 68.

126   MILTON'S THEOLOGICAL PROCESS

out to be one for the church to handle, albeit hardly a church in the usual sense of the word.

Scripture and Ecclesiology

A commonplace of Milton criticism has it that the great poet ended his life as a "church of one."[68] The phrase seems to owe to Milton's early self-description as "Church-outed by the Prelats," abetted by John Toland's biographical assertion that "in the latter part of his Life, he was not a profest Member of any particular Sect among Christians, he frequented none of their Assemblies, nor made use of their peculiar Rites in his Family."[69] A passage from *De Doctrina Christiana* likewise seems to support this view:

> Although it is the duty of each of the faithful to join a correctly instituted church if that can be done, Heb. 10:25: *not forsaking our mutual joining together, as is a habit for some, but encouraging one another* [. . .], yet those who cannot do that conveniently or with a fully informed conscience are not for that reason excluded from or destitute of the blessing imparted to the churches.[70]

Assuming that Milton is here describing his own choices about ecclesiastical participation, this passage nevertheless affirms his ongoing participation in the universal church, comprised—as the definition immediately preceding has it—of "the entire multitude of the called who, all over the world in any place whatever, openly worship God the father in Christ either individually or together with others."[71] Pointing back to the theology of I.17, Milton defines the visible church (manifest both in the universal church and in particular

---

[68] See e.g., Fixler, "Ecclesiology" and the idea that Milton "consolidated Church, Scripture, and Sacrament into *the sacred individual believer as a single mythic form*" in Honeygosky, *Milton's House of God*, 16.

[69] John Milton, *The Reason of Church-Government* (London, 1641), p. 41; John Toland, *A Complete Collection of the Historical, Political, and Miscellaneous Works of John Milton* (Amsterdam, 1698), I.46. See further Geoffrey F. Nuttall, "Milton's Churchmanship in 1659: His Letter to John Labadie," *Milton Quarterly* 35, 4 (2001): 227–31.

[70] *DDC*, 375: "tametsi cuiusque est fidelium se ecclesiae rectè institutae, si fieri potest, aggregare, Heb. 10. 25, *non deserentes aggregationem nostri mutuam, sicuti mos est quibusdam, sed adhortantes alii alios*—, tamen qui id commodè aut informata plenè conscientia facere nequeunt, non idcirco benedictione ecclesiis impertita excluduntur aut expertes sunt."

[71] *DDC*, 374: "**Universalis** est **universa multitudo vocatorum toto orbe terrarum quovis loco vel separatim vel unà cum aliis Deum patrem in Christo palam colentium.**"

churches) as "the assembly of the called [. . .] whether they be regenerate or not."[72] Even if Milton in practice worships alone, he understands himself as a member of this larger body.[73]

Identifying the visible church as the multitude of the called (regenerate or not) puts scripture front and center in Milton's conception of the church. As discussed in Chapter 2, Milton combines calling and renewal in the way he does so that all humans have the capacity to read scripture, interpret it, and hear preaching while evaluating the results. This capacity for evaluation leaves those who do not assent to the further renewal of regeneration without excuse, making them, and not God, responsible for the outcome. Including all the called in the church means, however, that the resulting efforts of interpretation and evaluation will be both varied and imperfect. Considered through the lens of the rule of faith, then, Milton's ecclesiology points to a problem of authority grounded in scriptural truth. Protestant that he is, Milton accepts scripture as the basis of truth. Accessing that truth, though, turns out to be more difficult than it appears. The intrinsic doctrinal structure of scripture proves less than clearly discernible (or at minimum remains contestable), leaving the desired authoritative foundation in scripture frustratingly elusive. Milton does place great emphasis on the individual's duty to interpret scripture in concert with the Spirit, but the purpose of this emphasis is the establishment of truth—and, with that truth, authority.[74] With such authority in place, the rule of faith will finally be able to work as designed—including the authority of the church, albeit in modified form.

The treatise's modification of church authority centers on scripture, as becomes clear from the way that it places the chapter on scripture (I.30) in between the chapters on the visible church (I.29) and particular churches (I.31). These chapters are of interest for their content but also for their formal relationship to the treatise's Ramist scheme—or, rather, their lack of formal relationship to it. As Gordon Campbell has observed, the last five chapters of Book I bear a messy relationship to the preceding chapters and to each other. From Campbell's perspective, the organizational jumble suggests that Milton did not quite

---

[72] *DDC*, 366: "Vocatorum coetus est **visibilis ecclesia**. Vocatorum, inquam, in communi, sive regeniti sint sive non." Oxford translates *regeniti* as "reborn."

[73] On Milton's historical church participation, see Thomas N. Corns, "Milton's Churches," *in The Church and Literature*, ed. Peter Clarke and Charlotte Methuen (Woodbridge: Boydell, 2012), pp. 185–201. On the plurality of Milton's church, see Honeygosky, *Milton's House of God*, 73.

[74] See David Ainsworth, "Milton's Holy Spirit in *De Doctrina Christiana*," *Religion and Literature* 45, 1 (2013): 9–10.

128 MILTON'S THEOLOGICAL PROCESS

finish revising the treatise.[75] In light of the rule of faith, though, this organizational relationship bears on the question of prolegomena, or the foundational presuppositions of theology: what is the relationship between the church and the work of theology?

On this point, Milton differs from Wolleb and Ames. The heart of the matter is the relationship between ministers (both extraordinary and ordinary) and scripture. I.30, "On Holy Scripture," is key to this relationship. Campbell argues that this chapter's placement likely owes Ames, who places his chapter on scripture (34) between the chapters on extraordinary (33) and ordinary (35) ministers.[76] Milton's first chapter mentions scripture only to defer discussing it: "We not unfairly demand that Christians believe in **the scriptures**, from which we take these teachings. But we shall treat of their authority at the proper place."[77] This choice operates at some tension, however, with Milton's more usual interlocutor, Wolleb, whose *Compendium* addresses scripture in a section of "Praecognita" preceding the first chapter. The question here is where scripture belongs in its own intrinsic doctrinal structure: as the foundation of everything, or in connection with the specific question of the church.[78] Campbell connects the opening phrase of I.30 ("The name 'holy scripture' is given to the prophets', apostles', [and] evangelists' writings, as being divinely inspired") to the definition of extraordinary ministers in I.29 ("Such were the prophets, apostles, evangelists, and the like").[79] With regard to the church, however, I.29 goes on to argue that ordinary ministers—who can be "any faithful people whatever"—are capable of administering the church's liturgy, contingent only on their gifts and opportunity.[80] In due course, I.30 takes pains to argue that "no one is to be prohibited from the reading of scripture, but that on the contrary it is appropriate that the scriptures be either listened to or read through assiduously

---

[75] Gordon Campbell, "De Doctrina Christiana: Its Structural Principles and Its Unfinished State," *Milton Studies* 9 (1976): 243–60. Kelley offers a rejoinder that depends in part on relocating I.30; "On the State."

[76] Campbell, "*De Doctrina Christiana*," 254.

[77] *DDC*, 7: "**Scripturis,** unde haec hausimus, credi a Christianis haud iniquè postulamus; de earum verò autoritate suo loco tractabimus."

[78] Muller argues that "in the hands of the Protestant writers [. . .] Scripture is the *principium*, not merely a source of *principia*"; accordingly, the use of scripture as *principium* produces a logical conundrum of self-grounding akin to Russell's paradox (which involves a set of all sets that do not contain themselves as members), given that the theological task at some point requires *principia* about scripture. Is scripture in the set of *principia* derivable from scripture, or not? *PRRD*, I.202.

[79] Campbell, "*De Doctrina Christiana*," 254; *DDC*, 382, 378: "Scripta prophetarum, apostolorum, euangelistarum, utpote divinitus inspirata, *scriptura sacra* dicitur"; "Tales fuere prophetae, apostoli, evangelistae; et similes."

[80] *DDC*, 379: "Ordinarii ministri esse possunt quilibet fideles, donis modò instructi (quae eorum missio est) quoties opportunum erit."

THEOLOGY AND THE CHURCH   129

by people of every kind and rank."[81] Thus, scripture originates with extraordinary ministers, but its use in the church resides with ordinary ministers, that is, with any person possessing the requisite gifts. Connecting this distinction back into the larger question of Ramist organization, scripture originates outside the church, which enables it to function as the grounding of everything, while the actual use of scripture remains firmly within the church, under the purview of ordinary people trying to make good on whatever spiritual gifts they may possess.

In deciding where to place his treatment of scripture, Milton is therefore also deciding on the relationship between scripture and church that informs the rule of faith. If he chooses the strict Protestant approach of *sola scriptura*, scripture remains the province of the extraordinary ministers, delivered now to a church no longer in need of the divine prerogatives attending such ministrations. Such, indeed, is Wolleb's position. He argues that the testimony whereby Christians may know that scripture is divinely inspired has two facets: "The principal testimony is that of the Holy Spirit, outwardly in the Scripture it self, inwardly in the minds and hearts of the faithful, being illuminate by him speaking and perswading the divinity of the Scriptures. But the ministerial testimony is the testimony of the Church."[82] For Wolleb, the Spirit's testimony counters Catholic reliance on church authority: "The Romanists urge the Churches authority alone, which they have in such high esteem, that they will have the whole authority of Scriptures to have its dependence from the Church."[83] In this way, Wolleb divorces the authority of scripture from the authority of the church, as becomes clear when he addresses the testimony of the church itself:

although [the church's testimony] is to be received as from Gods minister, yet it is false that the Scriptures authority depends on it; For what can be more absurd, then to make the words of the Master to receive their authority from the Servant, [...] or that the Rule should have its dependence upon the thing ruled?[84]

---

[81] *DDC*, 386: "Haec omnia evincunt, lectione scripturae neminem esse prohibendum; immo potius ab omni hominum genere atque ordine scripturas assiduè vel audiri vel perlegi convenire."

[82] Wolleb, 4 [3]: "Principale est testimonium Spiritus sancti, foris, in ipsa Scriptura; intus vero in corde ac mente hominis fidelis ab ipso illuminati, loquentus, eique Scripturae divnitatem persuadentis. Ministeriale vero testimonium est testimonium Ecclesiae."

[83] Wolleb, 5 [3]: "Pontificii solius Ecclesiae testimonium urgent, tantique illud faciunt, ut omnem Scripturae autoritatem ab Ecclesia pendere contendant."

[84] Wolleb, 6 [4]: "Jam ad Ecclesiae testimonium quod attinet, tametsi illud tanquam à Dei Ministra, acceptandum sit, falso tamen statuitur, Scripturae autoritatem ab illo dependere; quid enim absurdius, quam Patrisfamilias verba à famulo, [...] regulamque à regulato dependere?"

130 MILTON'S THEOLOGICAL PROCESS

In order to make scripture the sure foundation for his theology, Wolleb establishes a firm hierarchical relationship between it and the church: scripture governs, the church is governed, and the rule of faith has no place for the church. Ecclesiologically, this argument is antipapal, bent on denying the need for any such authoritative ministry in a church endowed with scripture (although, in practice, Wolleb's "ordinary ministers"—pastors, doctors, presbyters, and deacons—have power to correct doctrinal error in their congregations).[85]

Milton shares this antipapalism, as evidenced by his calling "extraordinary" the kind of ministry capable of producing statements sufficiently authoritative to warrant classification as "scripture." But Milton expands the category of extraordinary ministers beyond the ancient apostles and evangelists: "**Extraordinary** ministers are those sent from and inspired by God to instruct or reform the church both by the living word and by their writings."[86] Here, he goes beyond Ames, who allows, in theory, that extraordinary ministers might be called "for the extraordinary restoring of a Church being fallen," but in practice holds that "*Wicliffe, Luther, Zwinglius*, and such like, that were the first restorers of the Gospell, were not to speak properly, extraordinary Ministers."[87] For Milton, by contrast, such ministers may reform the church as well as institute it, and "their writings [*scriptis*]" are not necessarily scripture in the canonical sense. Add to this the next chapter's insistence on "the spirit and the *un*written word" as the rule of faith and Milton imagines the church less as a vehicle for keeping the "fruit" of extraordinary ministers in "perpetuall use," as Ames sees it, and more as a place for continuing the reforming work that the extraordinary ministers put in motion. Indeed, in Milton's model the possibility remains open that anyone could become an extraordinary minister if they had the right gifts for the calling.

Similarly, whereas Wolleb retains some form of the lay/cleric distinction as a way of delimiting ecclesial authority, Milton, for all practical purposes, abolishes the distinction, with the effect of situating the question of ecclesial authority onto a body of "ordinary ministers" coterminous with the church itself:

> Every single one of the faithful has the right of interpreting the scriptures, of interpreting them for himself, I mean; for he has the spirit, the guide into

---

[85] Wolleb, 170–76 [142–48].

[86] *DDC*, 378: "Ministri **extraordinarii** sunt divinitus missi et inspirati ad ecclesiam et viva voce et scriptis vel instituendam vel reformandam."

[87] Ames, 165–66 [176–77]: "ad collapsae restitutionem extraordinarium [...] Wiclephus, Lutherus, Zwinglius & similes Euangelij restauratores primi, non fuerunt propriè loquendo extraordinarij ministri."

THEOLOGY AND THE CHURCH   131

truth; he has the mind of Christ; indeed no one else can fruitfully interpret [for him] unless he himself also make the same interpretation for himself and his conscience.[88]

Crucially, this move produces a different relationship between scripture and the church than that at work in Wolleb. For Milton, scripture ought to ground doctrine and theology, but that grounding is mediated through the individual interpreter working with the spirit to understand scriptural truth, which is mediated, in turn, by the ecclesial community of interpreters. Milton can look to Jesus and Paul as exemplary interpreters because "every single one of the faithful" includes them, too. Indeed, he avers that Jews granted Jesus the opportunity to teach in the synagogue "not as to the Christ but as to any suitably gifted individual."[89]

The authority of the church thus re-enters Milton's rule of faith in a way that explains the placement of I.30. Instead of eliminating the church from the rule, as Wolleb (halfway) did, Milton reconfigures the church as a body of interpreters, each attempting individually to "make the same interpretation for himself and his conscience." The "church of one" argument tends to concede that Milton sees himself as being part of the universal church to whom he addresses the treatise's epistle, but it also tends to understand that universal church in fairly abstract terms that render it negligible in practice. At stake in Milton's ecclesiology is the rhetorical authority (albeit grounded in the spirit) to interpret scripture such that others would independently arrive at the same conclusions, effectively imbuing such interpretations with the force of (internal) scripture.[90] The version of the rule of faith at work here allows the church—as a collective body (if, perhaps, in visible practice a small one), not a concentrated *magisterium*—a vital role in working out the sense of scripture, but the question remains as to what kind of authority this rule of faith imputes to individual interpreters.

---

[88] *DDC*, 390–91: "Ius interpretandi scripturas, sibimet inqua[m] interpretandi, habet unusquisque fidelium: habet enim spiritum, veritatis ducem; habet mentem Christi: immo alius nemo interpretari cum fruct[u] potest, nisi ipse quoque sibi conscientiaéque suae idem interpretetur."

[89] *DDC*, 424: "facta enim est Christo ista potestas ab Iudaeis non ut Christo, sed ut cuilibet donis praedito." Compare Honeygosky, *Milton's House of God*, 191.

[90] Ken Simpson uses Erasmus's translation of *logos* in John 1:1 as *sermo* (instead of *verbum*) to frame God's self-revelation in scripture as a rhetorical *speaking* that instantiates an interpretative community: *Spiritual Architecture and Paradise Regained: Milton's Literary Ecclesiology* (Pittsburgh, PA: Duquesne University Press, 2007), pp. 8–14. In my view, such speaking also characterizes the community itself, and rhetorical means are necessary but not sufficient to adjudicate whether the speaking is, in fact, divine.

132   MILTON'S THEOLOGICAL PROCESS

Redefining Individual Authority through the Church

Milton takes up the relationship between authority, scripture, and church in I.30, in a passage (again, from the latest stratum of the chapter) that evokes and reconfigures the rule of faith:

> All the same, one does indeed believe in the scriptures in a general and over-arching way, first because of the authority either of the visible church or of the handwritten codices; next, however, [one believes] in the church and the actual codices and their individual parts because of the authority of the whole of scripture compared with itself; and finally, [one believes] in the whole of scripture because of the spirit itself which inwardly persuades each one of the faithful [. . .] Thus, on scripture's own witness, all things are in the end to be referred to the spirit and the *un*written word.[91]

This passage does not reject the authority of the visible church but rather situates that authority as the beginning stage of a process. Believing scripture because the church says so is not so much bad as inadequate: the church is not bereft of authority altogether, but neither is it the final authority. Milton thus partly lays aside the Augustinian/Catholic rule of faith. He then raises the Protestant version ("the authority of the whole of scripture compared with itself") before qualifying that, too, and proceeding to the final stage in the process: the inward witness of the spirit to each of the faithful. In relation to scripture, this process begins with the rule of faith being manifest external to scripture, in the tradition of the church, after which it becomes manifest internally before becoming external again in the spirit's witness. Now, the rule of faith has become a harmonious truth that transcends the limitations of the scriptural text (variants in the codices, textual corruption, etc.).

At first blush, this trajectory toward locating authority in the spirit seems to support a "church-of-one" ecclesiology. Why does a person endowed with the spirit need other people? Immediately after making spiritual witness the final stage in accessing "scriptural" truth, though, the treatise places this claim in a

---

[91] *DDC*, 398:

> Utcunque scripturis generatim et universim quidem creditur, primo propter authoritatem sive ecclesiae visibilis sive codicum manuscriptorum; postea verò ecclesiae ipsísque codicibus eorúmque singulis partibus propter authoritatem totius scripturae secum collatae; toti denique scripturae propter ipsum spiritum unicuique fidelium intus persuadentem. . . . Sic omnia demum ad spiritum atque verbum non scriptum, scriptura ipsa teste referenda sunt.

THEOLOGY AND THE CHURCH   133

social and political context that both includes and constrains the exercise of human authority:

> Anyone, therefore, who imposes any sanctions and dogmas of his own on the faithful—each one of whom is ruled by God's spirit—against their will, [whether he does it] in the name of the church or in that of a Christian magistrate, is imposing a yoke not only on human beings but also on the holy spirit itself.[92]

Being "ruled by God's spirit" thus includes ethical obligations toward others, which this passage defines in primarily negative terms, a non-imposition that presents Christian liberty as *freedom from* rather than *freedom to*. Under a "church-of-one" reading, ecclesiology per se manifests as external imposition on internal conscience, the consequence of a practical need for order that vanishes once the pesky problem of other people—with their differing views about scriptural interpretation or religious practice—similarly dissolves into pure internality. The treatise does obliquely allow, however, that one's own sanctions and dogmas could be imposed on the faithful with their consent (although *imponere* might no longer be the right verb in that case). A "church of one" rests on the fantasy of a direct connection to God shorn of the complications attending human community, and I am arguing that *De Doctrina Christiana* decisively rejects this fantasy. Instead, an ecclesiology based on persuasion and the collective work of the spirit has replaced the direct relationship between the spirit and the individual believer as the venue in which scriptural or spiritual truth gets worked out.

This ecclesiology may be based on persuasion, but it is not altogether rhetorical because persuasion rests on shared access to the spirit as well as on deliberative reason. Indeed, the treatise insists that its *ecclesia* cannot be rhetorical as such but rather requires an alternative form of authority, arguing that neither apostles, councils, modern churches, nor magistrates ought "to command that the faithful must even believe only those things which are either not found in scripture, or are squeezed out by merely [*duntaxat*] human reasonings that carry no conviction!"[93] The holy spirit ultimately grounds the authority of the church, but at stake is how the human beings who constitute the visible church

---

[92] *DDC*, 399: "Qui igitur fidelibus, quorum unusquisque Dei spiritu regitur, sanctiones quascunque suas et dogmata sive ecclesiae, sive Christiani magistratus nomine inviti[s] imposuerit, is non hominibus tantum, verùm etiam ipsi sancto spiritui iugum imponit."

[93] *DDC*, 399: "credenda solum fidelibus imperare quae in scriptura vel non reperiuntur, vel humanis duntaxat rationibus, quae fidem non faciunt, exprimuntur."

134 MILTON'S THEOLOGICAL PROCESS

act in ways consonant with the spirit's authority with respect to the other people in the visible church. Beyond the negative ethic of non-imposition, Milton allows obliquely for the possibility that reason, if it is not *merely* human, may carry conviction (or build faith, as the Latin might also be translated). Much rides on this distinction between the human and the merely human: no modern church can "arrogate to itself the absolutely sure presence of the spirit" because of the probability that something merely human is squeezing out the spirit.[94] If the title's claim to draw Christian doctrine "from the sacred scriptures alone [*ex sacris libris duntaxat*]" does not, via the concept of internal scripture, necessarily preclude human interpretative activity, the "merely [*duntaxat*] human" here suggests that the opposition to a scriptural basis is not the human per se but the human that, unaided by the spirit, does not conform to the proportion [*analogia*] of faith.

If the apparently zero-sum relationship between the spirit and the merely human seems an unlikely foundation on which to build a theology of human scriptural interpretation, as a practical matter, investment in a shared sacred text makes human ecclesial activity unavoidable, which in turn, makes such a theology necessary. I have been arguing that the struggle to use the rule of faith as an interpretative tool similarly steered Milton into the practical necessity of such a theology, including in its ecclesiological dimension. In other words, if Milton is a church of one, it is not a condition he accepts so much as a problem he struggles against. No church can claim "the absolutely sure presence of the spirit," which means that, in practice, the spirit's work unfolds in other venues. Any hope of attaining truth requires the presence of others and not just in the abstract and isolating sense often conveyed in accounts of Milton's ecclesiology, even if the treatise's apparent lack of a contemporary readership bears it out.

In *De Doctrina Christiana*, then, the question of authoritative human scriptural interpretation turns on a kind of hermeneutic golden rule—one should be the kind of other interpreter that one wishes others to be, given one's own struggles and uncertainties—in keeping with the epistle's concluding invitation for readers to "use this writing with me."[95] This ethic of reciprocity amounts to a way of balancing the need to attempt authoritative speech (in the spirit of "as if") with the practical reality that authority (in the sense of a final ground and adjudicator of truth) remains deferred, leaving good-faith use, in the meanwhile, as an alternative to final determination. In addressing the treatise to "all

---

[94] *DDC*, 399: "multo minus poterit ecclesia ulla hodierna quae praesentiam spiritum certissimam arrogare sibi non potest."
[95] *DDC*, 5: "his mecum utimini

the churches of Christ [*Universis Christi Ecclesiis*]," Milton is not arrogating to himself "the absolutely sure presence of the spirit"; he is, rather, striving to speak in the way that he must if he hopes that the truth attending the full presence of the spirit might become manifest.[96] The merely human, imperfect and problematic as it may be, emerges as a practical necessity, and this necessity takes on a theological dimension as the treatise makes the resulting actions responsible in positive terms to scripture (both the external written word and the internal spiritual inscription on the heart) and in negative terms to "merely human reasonings that carry no conviction." The merely human must be rejected in the end, but accomplishing that end requires considerable human activity in the meantime.

Speaking Scripture

As I have been arguing, the treatise manifests its coming to terms with the need for such interim human activity in its methodological departures from the basic Ramist method of gathering scriptural passages under headings. These departures result in Milton redefining his rule of faith around the human speech of "internal scripture" and the ecclesial adjudication it requires. Consequently, human work participates with frank imperfection in a larger spiritual and ultimately ecclesial process that aims to compensate and correct for the merely human. Working out a robust theological system does not involve assuming a posture of reasoned distance or objectivity but rather risking—and inevitably making—errors that can then be winnowed in public.[97] The resulting rule of faith qualifies the Protestant ideal of *sola scriptura* on two points: it recognizes the necessity of human means to achieve that end, and it understands scripture in broad terms as "the *un*written word." For Milton, scripture alone does not suffice to produce a doctrinal structure that conforms to the intrinsic logic of scripture.[98] Even if gathering scriptural passages under doctrinal heads might be the ideal formal outcome of this process, it proves methodologically inadequate to producing that outcome. Different kinds of human intervention,

---

[96] For a reading of this address, see Hale and Cullington, "*Universis Christi Ecclesiis.*"

[97] Milton's estimation of the public is not always this optimistic; see Paul Hammond, *Milton and the People* (Oxford: Oxford University Press, 2014). Milton's views of the public occupy a spectrum, with statements like this marking out the idealistic end.

[98] Compare Muller's account of Spanheim, for whom theology departs from scripture by disclosing its own foundation (i.e., scripture as *principium*): *PRRD*, I.202–203, quoting Friedrich Spanheim, Sr, *Disputationum theologicarum syntagma, pars prima* (Geneva, 1652), I.xvi.

136   MILTON'S THEOLOGICAL PROCESS

including rhetorical efforts at persuasion, turn out to be necessary, and examining the methodological effects of these interventions shows that the treatise, in its human voice, aspires to speak scripture—albeit the internal scripture of the spirit rather than the external scripture found in the Bible.

Milton emphasizes the authority of internal scripture against the backdrop of editorial work on the Greek New Testament by Erasmus and Beza.[99] These editors

> weigh almost everything not by [the authority] of the visible church, but by the integrity and number of the manuscripts. If the integrity of these codices varies or wavers, it is inevitable that the editors themselves are also undecided and have nothing which they can follow or establish as the absolutely sure word of God and [its] uncorrupted text.[100]

Milton's interest in establishing a reliable biblical text is considerable, as evidenced by his attentiveness to the treatise's Latin renderings of scripture. Even so, this effort is not sufficient to the task of working out doctrinal truth, especially without recourse to ecclesiastical authority. More than the external word itself, the underlying proportion or *analogia fidei* is at issue; hence the need for internal scripture and the spirit even if, in the interim, internal scripture manifests still more diversity and variation than manuscript transmission does. The same kind of adjudication necessarily exists in either case, lending prospective legitimacy to human words that aspire to express spiritual truths.

The Preface to I.5 clarifies the spirit's role in Milton's understanding of human authority: "For indeed I have taken upon myself to refute, not the authority of scripture, which is inviolable, but human interpretations whenever refutation is needed, such being my right, no, rather my duty as a human being."[101] In this sentence, the paradoxical authority with which Milton speaks in the treatise receives its clearest articulation: his duty as a human being requires that he undertake the refutation of human opinions. The spirit serves as the field on which this contest of human duty against human interpretation plays out:

> If indeed I were conducting this controversy with people who could show forth to us that the doctrine which they uphold was directly unfolded from

---

[99] DDC, 396–97.

[100] DDC, 397–98: "Editores [. . .] novi testamenti Graeci, cuius prima authoritas est, non ecclesiae visibilis, sed manuscriptorum fide ac numero omnia ferè ponderare: quorum fides codicum si variat aut vacillat, ipsos quoque editores ambigere necesse est, nec habere quid pro certissimo Dei verbo textúque incorrupto sequantur aut statuant."

[101] DDC, 48–49: "Neque enim scripturae authoritatem, quae sacrosancta est, sed hominum interpretationes humano iure immo vero officio quoties ita facto est opus, suscepi redarguendas."

THEOLOGY AND THE CHURCH   137

heaven by a veritable voice divine, he would manifestly be impious who dared to murmur against them, let alone protest. But if my opponents are people who cannot lay claim to anything beyond human powers and the spirit we all share, what is fairer than that they should allow another person—who is investigating the truth by the same method and path as they are, and is equally desirous of benefiting others—to play his own individual part in diligent research and free discussion?[102]

Here, Milton admits a distinction between the certainty that would attend "a veritable voice divine" and "the spirit we all share." Indeed, the external seems to hold out the promise of some certitude, only to have it slip perpetually away. Milton presents the spirit as alternative, but this option also has its complications, in that many people of varying opinions share access to the same spirit. Deferring to the spirit produces rhetorical probabilities, not logical verities.

The internal, though, offers some hope that the external does not. Finding additional manuscripts of the Greek New Testament, for instance, would only add to the collection of textual variants without offering any final resolution to the problem that variants exist in the first place. Milton was certainly familiar with the ways that manuscript evidence could challenge the authenticity of scriptural passages, with the Johannine comma being the most notorious case.[103] Admittedly, once the internal scripture moves from a "church-of-one" framing to a collective vision grounded in "the spirit we all share," the risk similarly appears of endlessly proliferating opinions without hope of resolution—a risk ameliorated by the small size of Milton's ideal gathered church. Even so, by its very existence, the treatise bears witness to a hope that this messy process will eventually yield truth. Indeed, the hope manifests as the process, the gritty work of assembling and reassembling a text that aspires to be internal scripture, even in its use of the external.

Internal scripture thus becomes the name for the complex rule of faith that I have been arguing the treatise aims to articulate. Accordingly, this rule of faith has two parts—external scripture and the ecclesial work of human interpretation grounded in the shared spirit—each of which aims to express internal

---

[102] *DDC*, 49:

> Quod si cum iis controversia haec esset, qui voce ipsa divina explicatam sibi coelitus quam tuentur doctrinam praestare nobis possent, impius plane sit, qui contra vel mutire nedum obstrepere ausit: Sin ii sunt, qui supra vires humanas, communemque spiritum nihil vendicare sibi queant, Quid est aequius quàm ut permittant alteri eadem atque ipsi ratione ac via veritatem indaganti, et prodesse aliis aequè cupienti, suas quemque sedulò inquirendi, liberèque disserendi partes obtinere.

[103] See *DDC*, 59–60. On the Johannine comma, see Chapter 1, n. 56.

138 MILTON'S THEOLOGICAL PROCESS

scripture but only partly succeeds. This aspirational quality helps to explain the authority at work in the treatise's prose, which unfolds according to a dialectical process that moves back and forth between the two aspects of the rule of faith. The treatise aims, both in its assemblage of scriptural texts and in its own words, to give voice to internal scripture, and in doing so, it presents its own words as prospectively scriptural, albeit subject to revision in light of either external scripture or the spirit. The resulting authority thus combines supreme arrogance (Milton's hope that his words will be read as scripture) with striking humility (the possibility—and indeed probability—that even he might change his erstwhile scriptural mind). In its glaring acknowledgment of probable imperfection, manifest materially in the revisions that appear on most Picard pages, this authority is simultaneously merely human and hopeful that, through the spirit, it might transcend its human origins.

Conclusion: Authority and Ways of Reading *De Doctrina Christiana*

Since *De Doctrina Christiana* was discovered in 1823, readers have turned to it as a record of Milton's theological views—or, in the case of Thomas Burgess and his intellectual heirs, worked assiduously to deny that the theological views it expresses are indeed Milton's. This way of reading, however, inadequately accounts for the complexity of how the treatise authorizes its own speaking voice, which is at once Milton's and not Milton's, and thus circumvents the question of the treatise's authoritative status by recasting it as a question of authorship.[104] Bearing in mind Joseph Loewenstein's demonstration that Milton's indisputably canonical texts authorize themselves in a variety of ways, the larger issue here is the appropriateness of attaching Milton's name to the treatise not as a matter of historical provenance but as a matter of naming the authoritative voice with which the treatise aspires to speak.[105] Proposed ways of reading the treatise need to account for how it constructs its own rhetorical authority.

Several moments in the epistle invite readings of *De Doctrina Christiana* as expressions of Milton's personal theology, as when he writes that "God has opened the way of eternal salvation solely to each person's individual faith, and

---

[104] See, however, the acute reading in Regina M. Schwartz, "Citation, Authority, and *De Doctrina Christiana*," in Loewenstein and Turner, *Politics, Poetics and Hermeneutics*, pp. 227–40. See further Jason A. Kerr, "Milton and the Anonymous Authority of *De Doctrina Christiana*," *Milton Quarterly* 49, 1 (2015): 23–43.

[105] Joseph Loewenstein, *The Author's Due: Printing and the Prehistory of Copyright* (Chicago, IL: University of Chicago Press, 2002), ch. 7, esp. pp. 220–21.

demands from us that whoever wants to be saved must have a personal faith of their own."[106] On one reading of this sentence, the entire point of Milton's compiling the treatise is to work out his own personal faith such that the treatise itself stands as a document of that faith's content. In a historical sense, this is true: the treatise records Milton's theological conclusions at the time(s) of writing—taking account of the surviving manuscript as a record of multiple times and stages of Milton's thinking.[107] Historically accurate as this view may be, it depends on looking at the treatise in a manner external to its own rhetorical self-understanding. The treatise does not set out to be an articulation of John Milton's theology; its goal is to express "the way of salvation" as "opened" "to each person's individual faith," not to express the idiosyncratic contents of an individual faith—the difference between the accusative *viam* and the dative *fidei*. The distinction between what is revealed and to whom matters because if the treatise succeeds at its stated aim, it is claiming to speak something other than itself. Articulating "Milton's theology" is not at all the same thing as articulating "the way of eternal salvation," and the treatise's express goal is avowedly the latter, not the former. Thus, the phrase that John Carey mellifluously renders as "my dearest and best possession" invites too much attention on Milton as the possessor, whereas the Latin—haec, quibus melius aut pretiosius nihil habeo—puts the emphasis, instead, on the valuation of that which he is most fortunate to possess.[108] Milton aims, in the treatise, to give voice to something other than himself.

Putting Milton's name on the voice that speaks in the treatise gets the history right but the rhetoric wrong. The material evidence indicates that the treatise in all probability came from his desk, and the echoes of and even overt conversations with his other works seem unmistakable. But rhetorically, the treatise aspires to speak a truth independent of itself, authorized by scripture and the Spirit rather than by Milton. Should Milton succeed in giving voice to some universal truth, it ceases at that moment to be merely his but escheats, as it were, back to the church, in the broad sense of "church" laid out above. Returning to the epistle's last sentence, with its invitation to use the treatise's contents or not, the operative theory of church in that passage assumes that the parts of the treatise that are merely Milton's will ultimately land on the cutting-room floor, even if they prove temporarily useful to the larger project of discerning truth. As

---

[106] *DDC*, 1: "Verùm cùm aeternae salutis viam non nisi propriae cuiusque fidei Deus aperuerit, postuletque hoc à nobis, ut qui salvus esse vult, pro se quisque credat."

[107] See further Hale's treatment of Milton's personality in the treatise's Latin; *Milton's Scriptural Theology: Confronting* De Doctrina Christiana (Leeds: Arc Humanities Press, 2019), pp. x–xii and *passim*.

[108] *DDC*, 3; Yale, 121.

Chapter 1 argued, Milton's understanding of internal scripture invites readers (paradoxically) to see a correlation between the vehemence of his expression and how lightly it ought to be held, including by him. Milton undertook the inordinate labor of compiling the treatise not because he wanted to express his own theological views but because he wanted to contribute to the ecclesial process of discovering and giving voice to a truth larger than himself.

PART TWO
THE SON OF GOD

4

The Form of Book I Chapter 5, "On the Son of God"

A major question in debates about the authorship of *De Doctrina Christiana* has been when, if Milton wrote the treatise, he departed from the Trinitarianism evinced in his earlier writings, such as the celebration of "one *Tri-personall* GODHEAD!" in *Of Reformation* (1641).[1] The literary form of Milton's antitrinitarian chapter on the Son of God (I.5) provides a tantalizing series of clues that bear on this question. Readers of *De Doctrina Christiana* have long recognized I.5 as a formal outlier, rather unlike any other chapter in the treatise.[2] The usual Ramist literary form of definitions, headings, and scripture blocks appears unevenly in the chapter's fifty manuscript pages, concentrated primarily in the final ten pages. The remainder of the chapter engages extensively with scripture, albeit mostly in the kinds of prose argumentation that I have been classifying under Milton's category of "internal scripture." Indeed, I will argue that internal scripture has come to constitute the chapter's argumentative structure, rendering the Ramist structure vestigial. Although other chapters (like I.16 and I.27) include pages added later to accommodate stretches of prose argumentation, these processes of revision and expansion are likely minor by comparison with those required to produce I.5. Scholarly focus on the chapter's content has obscured the implications of its form. What the chapter says matters but so does the process by which it came to say it.

In brief, the form suggests that Milton's position on the Son of God evolved in the course of his work on the treatise.[3] The exact trajectory of that evolution

---

[1] John Milton, *Of Reformation* (London, 1641), p. 87. See also *MMS*, 91; and Filippo Falcone, "Irreconcilable (Dis)Continuity: *De Doctrina Christiana* and Milton," *Connotations* 27 (2018): 92–93.

[2] See e.g., John K. Hale, *Milton's Scriptural Theology: Confronting* De Doctrina Christiana (Leeds: Arc Humanities Press, 2019), ch. 9.

[3] Arthur Sewell argued that the treatise's anti-trinitarianism arose through "revisions of and additions to Jeremie Picard's version": *A Study in Milton's* Christian Doctrine (London: Oxford University Press, 1939), p. 29 (see further pp. 28–34, 92–108, and 162–70). In Maurice Kelley, *This Great Argument: A Study of Milton's* De Doctrina Christiana *as a Gloss upon* Paradise Lost (Princeton, NJ: Princeton University Press, 1941), ch. 3, Kelley critiques Sewell's argument that work on the treatise unfolded in three stages, with the third stage incomplete at Milton's death, along with his argument that some revisions to the treatise postdate *Paradise Lost*, correctly finding these views insufficiently grounded in evidence. Kelley does not, however, adequately account for the treatise's stratification, the way that pages were

---

Milton's Theological Process. Jason A. Kerr, Oxford University Press. © Jason A. Kerr (2023).
DOI: 10.1093/oso/9780198875086.003.0005

144   MILTON'S THEOLOGICAL PROCESS

is hard to parse out because when Daniel Skinner recopied the first fourteen chapters, he literally papered over the (probably abundant and messy) revisions on evidence in what was presumably the Picard (et al.) version of these pages. Even had those pages survived, the material state was likely even messier than that in a chapter like I.28, by far the most materially complex of the surviving Picard chapters. Of the seven folios comprising I.28, only the first and the last belong to the same stratum, and the middle folio (MS 350–53) serves as an awkward bridge between much-revised discussions of the Lord's Supper and baptism.[4] Skinner seems unlikely to have copied out the very long I.5 if it had existed in a condition approaching a clean, fair copy. Further evidence that I.5 represents an evolving position appears in its capacity to generate prose intrusions in other chapters—especially ones that Skinner found it necessary to recopy—like the extended prose discussion of Christology in I.14 (MS 188–94) or, possibly, the prose discussion of God's oneness in I.2 (MS 15–16).[5] These details suggest that I.5 in its current form results from revisions on a scale unparalleled elsewhere in the treatise, indicating that its topic proved more difficult than any other for Milton to get right—and to persuade his readers that he had got right.[6]

A firm answer to the question of when Milton changed his mind about the Trinity seems unlikely to emerge, given the state of the extant material evidence.[7] Nevertheless, the ways of reading developed in the preceding chapters make it possible to discern some aspects of how, and why, his mind changed. Milton's normative working method seems to have been collating scriptural evidence while also reading treatments of the topic at hand in other theologians, notably Wolleb and Ames, and considering the scriptural foundations of their positions. I will argue that this method proved pivotal for Milton as he

---

recopied and replaced or whole sections added in. He notes (pp. 44–45) the unusual pagination in I.25 and explains it as the result of Picard's recopying, but he does not note any other instances, seeming to view the Picard pages as a single fair copy. This chapter undertakes to read the material traces of stratification (and therefore revision) behind the Skinner pages.

[4] This awkwardness includes having the least dense page of the manuscript (MS 352) on the recto of a dense and messy verso (MS 353); see the Appendix, pp. 262–63.

[5] Kelley notices that a change in Milton's views about the Trinity seems to have occasioned revisions during what he calls the "second preliminary [i.e., pre-Picard] stage" in the treatise's composition; Yale, 18, 21. Attention to stratification suggests that the bulk of related revisions likely happened during the period of Picard's involvement with the treatise.

[6] Jeremy Specland argues that Milton's exegesis of Psalm 2 in I.5 fails to cohere; "Unfinished Exegesis: Scriptural Authority and Psalm 2 in the Miltonic Canon," *Milton Studies*, 62, 1 (2020): 57–63.

[7] Specland finds Milton exploring anti-trinitarian possibilities in his 1653 *terza rima* versification of Psalm 2: "Unfinished Exegesis," 63–67. The multiple strata in the Picard manuscript suggest a flurry of activity in the late 1650s, leading me to surmise that the treatise's anti-trinitarianism was a late development.

THE FORM OF BOOK I CHAPTER 5, "ON THE SON OF GOD" 145

read Psalm 2's reference to God begetting a Son in his preferred Latin Old Testament alongside the treatments of the Son's generation in Wolleb and Ames. The exegetical problems occasioned by this very particular collision of materials appear to have led to Milton concluding that his interlocutors' view that the Son was begotten from eternity failed the ecclesial test of discernment. Consequently, Milton seems to have found himself, contrary to expectation, needing to work out an alternative position on the Son.[8] Alongside the process of developing that position emerged the need to defend it in the face of what he knew would be entrenched opposition from the *ecclesia*, to which he had addressed the epistle and in which he claimed his own place in the Preface to I.5.

The chapter's highly rhetorical literary form attests to the immense labor that these tasks entailed, but it also indicates that the treatise's Ramist methodology and its attendant theology of scripture proved inadequate to the case at hand. Psalm 2:7 was a familiar (if controversial) proof text for the Trinity, so Milton could not simply quote it under a heading denying the Son's eternal generation and expect to persuade anyone. This topic made internal scripture necessary in a new way, which means that nothing challenged Milton's commitment to his intended methodology more than work that resulted from it. Furthermore, the way that the topic of the Son obliged Milton to turn to internal scripture also drove him to think in new ways about the church—traditionally understood as the Body of Christ, thanks to Paul in 1 Corinthians 12 and elsewhere—as the forum for expressing and discerning the truth of spirit-driven speech.

I.5's existence in a formally complex state while addressing a theological topic with significant bearing on the methodological implications of that form means that it represents a pivotal case for the question of how to read *De Doctrina Christiana*. Its importance to understanding the treatise's project and Milton's theology thus extends well beyond Milton's implication in the long and (in his time) resurgent heresy of anti-trinitarianism, which is not so much a position that the treatise expresses as a position that forced Milton to rethink how he did theology.[9] The present chapter undertakes to read I.5's formal evolution as well as the surviving evidence will permit, while Chapter 5 takes up the methodological and ecclesiological implications of the treatise's theology of the Son. Together, they argue that Milton's work on this topic fundamentally exposed,

---

[8] *Pace* Lehnhof's argument that Milton engages in "backward reading," or fitting biblical texts to predetermined conclusions: Kent R. Lehnhof, "Deity and Creation in the *Christian Doctrine*," *Milton Quarterly* 35, 4 (2001): 239–40.

[9] Michael Lieb finds Milton neither fully Arian nor fully Socinian but *sui generis* in his anti-trinitarianism; *Theological Milton: Deity, Discourse, and Heresy in the Miltonic Canon* (Pittsburgh, PA: Duquesne University Press, 2006), chs 7–8. Michael Bauman, *Milton's Arianism* (Frankfurt am main: P. Lang, 1987), nevertheless remains a significant treatment.

146 MILTON'S THEOLOGICAL PROCESS

on the level of literary form, the limits of *De Doctrina Christiana* to do the kinds of theological work that Milton needed it to do. The recognition of these limits vitally informs the relationship between the treatise and *Paradise Lost*, where a different literary form empowered Milton to embrace internal scripture in a new way.

Placing the Topics of the Son and the Holy Spirit

To understand how external scripture came to produce the eventual heterodoxy of I.5, it will first be useful to rehearse the theological stakes, which center on the issue of generation and its relationship to divine decree, which is how God's will becomes manifest, both internal to Godself and externally in things like pre-destination and creation.[10] The Son is, per biblical passages like John 3:16, the Father's "Only Begotten," and the question is what that means. The Westminster Confession offers a Reformed orthodox view:

> In the Unity of the God-head there be Three Persons, of one substance, power, and eternity; God the Father, God the Son, and God the Holy Ghost. The Father is of none, neither begotten, nor proceeding: The Son is eternally begotten of the Father: the Holy Ghost eternally proceeding from the Father and the Son.[11]

The Westminster Divines emphasize the eternity of all three persons. From this perspective, begetting and proceeding do not name the origins of the Son and the Spirit but refer, rather, to modes of relationship among the divine persons, both immanent and economic, such that the persons themselves are coeternal.[12]

Milton's departure from this position is evident on the level of Ramist structure. For Milton's Trinitarian interlocutors, like Wolleb and Ames, all this begetting and proceeding comes logically prior to any divine decree, which issues from the Triune God rather than any one of the persons. Wolleb, for instance, discusses the "Persons of the Deity" in his I.2 before going on to address divine decree in I.3. There, he distinguishes between the internal and external works of God, including "the Generation of the Sonne" and "the Production of the Holy Ghost" among the internal, while the external includes "Predestination,

---

[10] On the anti-trinitarianism of *De Doctrina Christiana* in Reformed context, see *PRRD*, IV.96–99, 210–11.

[11] Westminster Assembly of Divines, *Articles of Christian Religion* (London, 1648), II.iii (p. 8).

[12] "Immanent" refers to the relationships of the persons internal to the Trinity and "economic" to the manner of their cooperation in human salvation.

THE FORM OF BOOK I CHAPTER 5, "ON THE SON OF GOD" 147

Creation, and the like, which have relation to the Creatures as objects without God."[13] Wolleb subsequently takes up predestination in I.4 and creation in I.5. For Ames, likewise, several chapters on God (I.4–6) precede the chapters on decree (I.7), creation (I.8), providence (I.9), and governance (I.10).

De Doctrina Christiana, by contrast, affirms "that the Son of God was begotten by a decree of the Father," specifying that the decree in question is special instead of general and therefore not from eternity.[14] Consequently, *De Doctrina Christiana* follows the chapter on God (I.2) with two chapters on God's internal efficiency (I.3 on Divine Decree and I.4 on Predestination) before proceeding to matters of external efficiency with the chapters on the Son of God (I.5) and the Holy Spirit (I.6). Only then does *De Doctrina Christiana* turn to creation (I.7) and questions of providence and special and general governance (I.8–10). On this account, then, the Son and the Spirit do not participate in the work internal to God but are, rather, themselves external products of God's work, like creation but logically prior to it.

These are scandalous conclusions from the perspective of Trinitarian orthodoxy, but the fact of their scandal has got in the way of considering what the treatise can tell us about how Milton arrived at them. I.5 and I.6 both bear scant resemblance to the Ramist method articulated in the epistle and I.1, which suggests the possibility that they did not, in their earliest instantiation, espouse the views for which they have since become notorious. So, how did they come to be what they are? The first clues to understanding I.5's journey to its final form lie, in fact, in I.6, "On the Holy Spirit."[15] Measured against the formal expectations laid out in the epistle and I.1, I.6 stands out as very odd indeed. Rather than present a definition and then break down that definition into various headings driven by the scriptural witnesses, the chapter, instead, dwells on the problem of definition itself, considering first the relevant Old Testament passages (MS 99–100) and then the New Testament ones (MS 100–103). Next follows a section of prose argument (MS 103–105) addressing a series of passages from both testaments taken by others to hold that the Holy Spirit is God. Then follows

---

[13] Wolleb, 26 [20]: "Opus Dei ad intra est, quod non ad terminum extra Deum refertur: Velut Intellectio, qua Deus intelligit se ipsum; Generatio Filii, Productio Spiritus Sancti. Opus Dei ad extra est, quod ad terminum extra SS. Trinitatem refertur. Talia sunt Praedestinatio, Creatio, & similia, quae creaturas, tanquam terminu[m] extra Deum respiciunt."

[14] *DDC*, 24: "**Decretum Dei speciale** [. . .] Ex his cunctis locis apparet, Filium Dei decreto Patris fuisse genitum." The definition of general decrees appears earlier in the chapter, MS 18: "Generale est quo **Deus omnia ab aeterno quae quidem volebat aut facturus ipse erat, liberrimè, sapientissimè, sanctissimèque decrevit.**"

[15] Kelley does not mention the chapter's unusual literary form; *This Great Argument*, 106–18. Lehnhof finds its rhetorical argument a mirror image of that in I.5: "Deity and Creation in the *Christian Doctrine*," 242.

148   MILTON'S THEOLOGICAL PROCESS

a discussion of divine attributes (MS 105–108) devoted, as in I.5, to arguing that the Father alone is God. Finally, the chapter concludes with a discussion (MS 108–10) of what can be said about the Spirit's nature and role. Although some large-hand headings do appear early in the chapter, they are not preceded by a definition, and if short scripture blocks do follow, so also does plenty of prose. Accordingly, the chapter looks, for the most part, like exploratory work near the beginning of Milton's process as he compares biblical places in hopes of ascertaining the tenor of scripture on this topic. Skinner's recopying partly obscures whether the moments that display a clear kinship with I.5 are products of that initial work or later additions, or whether the chapter represents new exploratory work undertaken in the wake of I.5.

The opening sentences of I.6 set the stage for these formal oddities by leaving the chapter's precise place in the Ramist scheme unclear—and, surprisingly, drawing attention to the fact. The first sentence identifies a structure clearly enough: "**After the Father** and **the Son** our next task is to discuss **the Holy Spirit**, since it is called the spirit of the father and the son."[16] As noted above, however, the chapters on Son and Spirit do not, in fact, immediately follow the chapter on God (now understood as the Father alone), although the recursive quality of Ramist structure makes the claim defensible. Even so, the sentence is silent on the matter of whether the topic pertains to the internal works of God (the orthodox view) or to the external (Milton's eventual view). The opening sentence of I.6 thus leaves this crucial organizational matter ambiguous, and the next sentence pointedly refuses to clarify the issue: "But as to its nature, scripture is silent on how it has its being or why it came into being: thus we are warned not to be rash."[17] The final sentence of the opening paragraph explicitly refrains from settling the question: "Since therefore the spirit is not said to be generated, nor created, nor may agreement be reached from scripture as to any other mode of its existing, in the face of so great a silence of sacred authorities it is necessary that our method leave the matter open."[18] The treatise is treading carefully on territory of considerable theological import, but the method cannot leave the matter entirely open because the chapter has to go somewhere in the Ramist scheme. The professed uncertainty on this point, weighed against the fact of the chapter's placement, suggests that its language gives us an unusual

---

[16] *DDC*, 98: "**A Patre** et **Filio** proximum est ut de **Sancto Spiritu** dicamus; quando et patris et filii spiritus appellatur."

[17] *DDC*, 98: "Quod autem ad naturam eius attinet, quo modo existat, quòve extiterit, scriptura tacet: unde nos temerarii ne simus, admonemur."

[18] *DDC*, 99: "Cùm itaque spiritus nec generari dicatur, neque creari, neque quo alio existat modo ex scriptura constet, in tanto sacrorum authorum silentio dehiscat methodus necesse est."

THE FORM OF BOOK I CHAPTER 5, "ON THE SON OF GOD"   149

glimpse into Milton's second-order thinking about the treatise's structure (as opposed to the theological content itself).

So, why is I.6 where it is? The Oxford edition's chart of the treatise's Ramist structure groups I.5–6 together under "generation," as a subcategory of the external efficiency of God's decrees.[19] Oxford bases this determination on two pivotal passages from I.5. The first opens the preface to that chapter by jointly announcing "the **Son of God and the Holy Spirit**" as the topics about to be discussed.[20] The second opens I.5 proper by announcing a transition from the internal efficiency of God's decrees to the external efficiency, declaring that external efficiency "is either **generation** or **creation** or **governance of all things**."[21] This subdivision corresponds to the sequence of chapters following I.5–6: the treatise handles creation in I.7 and various forms of governance in I.8–10. Thus, by implication and the mere fact of sequence (but not by any explicit statement at the beginning of the chapter), I.6 and the topic of the Holy Spirit fall under the heading of generation, understood as an aspect of God's external decree, even as the second sentence of the chapter itself urges caution on this very question and the last sentence of the first paragraph explicitly denies that the chapter belongs under this heading. Milton seems to be invoking multiple perspectives at once, to dizzying effect.

In the event, the concluding paragraph of I.6 also bears out the chapter's placement in Oxford's diagram. There, Milton insists that

> the holy spirit, as it is a minister to God, and accordingly not uncreated, had been created, that is, produced, from God's substance not by a necessity of nature but by the free will of the agent, before the world's foundations were laid, as one may believe, after the Son, and far inferior to the son.[22]

This conclusion manifestly makes the Son and the Spirit distinct products of similar processes of generation, aligned clearly with the external working out of God's decrees—as is also evident in I.5, which explicitly uses the qualities of flowing out, issuing, proceeding, and so on to ground the Spirit in God's external efficiency.[23] Even so, the structure of I.6 presents its statement to this effect

---

[19] Oxford, lxvii. Compare Gordon Campbell, "*De Doctrina Christiana*: Its Structural Principles and Its Unfinished State," *Milton Studies* 9 (1976): 247.

[20] *DDC*, 48: "**De Filio Dei Sanctoque Spiritu**."

[21] *DDC*, 49: "Estque vel **generatio** vel **creatio** vel **rerum omnium gubernatio**."

[22] *DDC*, 110: "spiritum sanctum, cum sit Deo minister, ac proinde non increatus, ex substantia Dei, non necessitate naturae, sed libera voluntate agentis creatum, id est, productum fuisse ante iacta, ut credibile est, mundi fundamenta, post Filium, filioque longe inferiorem."

[23] *DDC*, 49: "emanare tamen et egredi et procedere et spirari a Patre, quae omnia externam efficientiam testantur."

150 MILTON'S THEOLOGICAL PROCESS

as the reasoned outcome of an exegetical process rather than as a dogmatic statement of scriptural doctrine in the Ramist manner of most other chapters.

I have been arguing that reading *De Doctrina Christiana* entails trying to discern the processes of thought and intertextual engagement behind the definitions, scripture blocks, and various forms of prose argumentation. By leaving its method open, as the first paragraph declares, I.6 puts these processes nearer the surface than in any other chapter. The relative visibility of Milton's theological process in I.6 makes the ambiguity of the chapter's opening sentences all the more interesting because they declare that the Holy Spirit's place in the treatise's Ramist scheme was anything but a foregone conclusion, a tentativeness apparently still on evidence in the chapter's final pre-Skinner state. In this light, it is possible (if not demonstrable) that the treatise began, at least by default, with a Trinitarian Ramist structure on the model of Wolleb and Ames. I.6 begins by questioning such a structure, not by rejecting it outright. As Milton's work on other topics indicates, such questioning was critical to his theological process, even when he aimed to shore up the position under consideration. The intervening sentences of the first paragraph—between the ambiguous opening and the concluding statement of irresolution—take aim at the traditional doctrine of procession, grounded in John 15:26, concluding that "This solitary expression [ἐκπορεύεται] [. . .] signifies the sending, not the nature, of the spirit; in which sense the son too is quite often said ἐξελθεῖν—whether one chose to translate that as *to go out* or *to issue* [*procedere*]—from the father; so far as we can see, the meaning is the same."[24] This reading leans unmistakably against *homoousios*, the idea that the Spirit (along with the Son) is "of one being" with the Father, and under Skinner's recopying, we cannot tell where it might fit in the treatise's process of revision. Whatever the case, the final sentence leaves the question of the spirit's origins—and the place of this *locus* in the Ramist structure—open, indicating that the Trinitarian possibility has not yet been decisively rejected or, at minimum, that the precise details of a theological alternative have not yet been fully worked out. Theologically, the final state of I.6 reveals a Milton who was still very much in the process of ascertaining and articulating his position.

---

[24] *DDC*, 99: "quod solum verbum [. . .] missionem spiritus, non naturam significat; quo sensu etiam filius ἐξελθεῖν sive *egredi* sive *procedere* à patre id malit quisquam interpretari, quod, quantum nobis liquet, idem valet, saepius dicitur."

The Disruptive Force of Scripture

If the treatise did not begin with a clear, already developed anti-trinitarian position on the Holy Spirit, such also appears to have been the case with the Son. The roots of the matter lie in I.3, "On Divine Decree," and unfold in conversation with Wolleb and Ames, with scripture once again driving the treatise's departure from its usual interlocutors. Whereas the Theologians push their scriptural citations off into the margin, Milton aspires to a theology centered on scripture, to the point of drowning out his own words.[25] This difference suggests the following method: Milton reads the Theologians on a given topic, notes the biblical passages they have referenced, considers what other passages might be relevant, then gathers all of these passages together, upon which he works to formulate a definition that captures their doctrinal import.

Psalm 2 lies at the heart of Milton's disagreement with the Theologians. Verse 7 references the begetting of a Son, so its importance is obvious, but the complexity of the exegetical difficulties unfolds against the backdrop of the whole psalm. The poem's occasion is the rage of heathen kings who set themselves against the Lord and his anointed, referring to the Davidic king (v. 1–2). The Lord responds by laughing (v. 4) and by reasserting the position of his "King upon [his] holy hill of Sion" (v. 6), declaring that the king is his begotten son (v. 7) and empowering him to crush the heathen kings like a potter's vessel with his iron rod (v. 9). The psalm then concludes by advising the heathen kings to be wise (v. 10), which means serving the Lord (v. 11) and kissing the Son-king to avert his rage (v. 12). On a historical level, this poem participates in familiar tropes of the Ancient Near East: framing wars between peoples as wars between their gods, asserting the secondary divinity of the vanquishing king, and using this royal divinity to urge on other nations a vassalage both political and religious. This historical sense lends itself to reading a link between the anointed son-king and the messianic son of God, but the divine assertion of this king via a "decree" issued on "this day" (v. 7), central to the poem's response to the heathen kings' impending threat, poses theological obstacles to reading it as a Trinitarian account of the relationship between the Father and the Son.

Reading Wolleb and Ames together with scripture brings these theological obstacles into view. Wolleb, for instance, twice articulates the doctrine of the Son's eternal generation without offering any scriptural support whatsoever: "The Son is the second Person, begotten of the Father from eternity" (in I.2, "On

---

[25] Wolleb and Ames do not, in fact, push their citations into the margins, but their citational style is much more spare than Milton's.

152 MILTON'S THEOLOGICAL PROCESS

the Divine Persons") and "There be two generations of the Son: the one eternal, to wit of the Father; the other temporal, namely of the Virgin his mother" (in I.16, "Of the Person of Christ God and Man").[26] Ames, meanwhile, notes in his I.5 ("Of the Subsistence of God") that "The relative property of the Father is to beget," citing Psalm 2:7, John 3:16 ("only-begotten Son"), and Hebrews 1:6 ("the first begotten"). Ames quotes only what he takes to be the most pertinent part of Psalm 2:7, in the Latin of the 1585 Junius–Tremellius translation (JTB): "Filius meus es, ego hodiè genui te," omitting the beginning of the verse, with its reference to the decree: "Narrabo ex decreto."[27] Neither Wolleb nor Ames associates this begetting with divine decree because both of them understand such decrees as issuing from the united Trinity.[28]

Nevertheless, Psalm 2:7 contains a reference to the decree or something like it concerning the Son's begetting, presenting complications for a Trinitarian exegesis.[29] The heading for Psalm 2 in the 1585 JTB illustrates the complexity, referring jointly to the "reign of David and Christ [*regnum Davidis & Christi*]." The connection between these two figures comes through the concept of "the anointed one" (Masoretic Text מְשִׁיחֹו [*māšîaḥ*]), which JTB renders, via Greek, as *Christum* in verse 2. A note explains that the more usual Latin word would be *unctum*, "either David the type or Christ, who is the truth of types."[30] *Christum*, while narrowly permissible on etymological technicalities, nevertheless risks collapsing the historical sense (having to do with the Davidic monarchy) and the typological reference to Jesus as the fulfillment of the Davidic kingship. In verse 7, meanwhile, the JTB note works to dissociate *decreto* from eternal decree, reading it instead as signifying, generically, "adoption into the calling and administration of God's reign, which ought to be accommodated typically to David and perfectly to Christ."[31] As for the word *hodie*—"today"—that places

---

[26] Wolleb, 19 [15], 102 [83]: "Filius est secunda persona, à Patre ab aeterno genita"; "Duae sunt Filii generationes: aeterna una, qua genuit eum Pater; temporalis altera, qua natus est ex Virgine."

[27] Ames, 17-18 [18]: "Patris relativa proprietas est *gignere*. Psal. 2. 7. *Filius meus es, ego hodiè genui te*. Ioh. 3.16. *Vnigenitus filius*, Heb. 1. 6. *Primogenitus*." Ames's quotation of Psalm 2 mirrors the 1585 JTB (STC 2059); the Vulgate differs by one word: "filius meus es *tu* ego hodie genui te" (my emphasis).

[28] Neither addresses the decree (I.3 in Wolleb and I.7 in Ames) until he has finished discussing the Trinity, unlike Milton, who discusses the Son (I.5) after the decree (I.3).

[29] Compare Muller: "The exegetical debate among the Reformed rendered the text of Psalm 2:7 a less than adequate proof of a doctrine on which all agreed and a point for difficult debate with the Socinians, who declared it a reference to David alone and irrelevant to the doctrine of the Trinity": *PRRD*, IV.261. Milton's exegesis puts him at odds with both the Reformed and the Socinians. For the Socinian view, see Valentin Smalcius, *The Racovian Catechism* (Amsterdam, 1652), p. 34 [Samuel Przpkowski, *Catechesis Ecclesiarum quae in Regno Poloniae* [. . .] *Affirmant* (Racovia [i.e., London], 1651), pp. 47–48].

[30] 1585 JTB, VT, tom. III, 39: "*Christum*] id est, unctum; sive Davidem typum, sive Christum qui est typorum veritas" (my trans).

[31] 1585 JTB, VT, tom. III, 40: "Heb. *ad decretum*. *Filius meus*] id est, adoptatus in vocationem & administrationem regni Dei; quod & typicè ad Davidem, & perfectè ad Christum accommodari debet; ut Act. 13.33. Heb. 1.5. & 5.5" (my trans).

THE FORM OF BOOK I CHAPTER 5, "ON THE SON OF GOD"   153

the decree in time rather than eternity, the JTB roots it solely in a double historical sense: "when David was anointed by Samuel [. . .] and when Christ the first-begotten was brought into the earth [*in orbem terrarum*]."[32] This reading of the begetting as referring to Christ's mortal birth draws on Hebrews 1:6, another verse cited by Ames, which, following the quotation of Psalm 2:7 in verse 5, uses the phrase "firstborn in the earth [*primogenitum in orbem terrarum*]." All this careful exegesis works to decouple Psalm 2:7 from the eternal decree even as this edition of the Bible evinces some commitment to the doctrine of the Trinity.[33]

This exegesis puts Ames, as an expounder of Trinitarianism, in something of a double bind. The Son's earthly begetting suffices to establish begetting as a core quality of the Father, so Ames's quotation of Psalm 2:7 in that place need not reference the eternal begetting at all. The next paragraph complicates this possibility, however:

> The relative property of the Sonne is to be begotten, that is, so to proceede from the Father, that he is partaker of the same Essence, and doth perfectly resemble his nature: and hence, he is the second in order, *Heb.* 1.3. The brightnesse of his glory, and the Character of his Person.[34]

The language is Trinitarian, and the talk of procession and partaking of the same essence necessarily implies the eternal begetting.[35] The verse from Hebrews certainly supports a high Christology (i.e., one emphasizing Christ's divinity more than his humanity), but it does not talk of begetting. That must wait until verse 5, which quotes Psalm 2 without reference to the Davidic context. There, the 1585 JTB note on *hodie* abandons the historical reading it had used for the

---

[32] 1585 JTB, VT, tom. III, 40: "*Hodie*] cùm a Schemuele David unctus est, I. Schemu. 16.14, & cùm Christus primogenitus in orbem terrarum inductus est, Heb. 1.6."

[33] See e.g., the note on Genesis 1:3, 1585 JTB, VT, tom. I, 1. The edition does not, however, print the Johannine comma; NT, 406.

[34] Ames, 18 [18]: "Filij est *gigni*, id est, à patre ita procedere, ut ejusdem essentiae sit particeps, & naturam ejus perfectè referat, & hinc ordine secundus est. *Heb.* 1.3. *Effulgentia gloriae, & character personae illius.*"

[35] In the Niceno-Constantinopolitan creed, "proceed" refers to the Spirit's *relatio personalis*, or the incommunicable property distinguishing it from the other divine persons. Ames's "proceed" refers, instead, to the *processio intellectualis aut naturalis* by which the Father generates the Word, with the Spirit's procession understood as an activity of the divine will, a *processio per voluntatem* emerging from both Father and Son [*filioque*]. These processions do not entail ontological derivation from or subordination to their points of origin; all three persons share in the same divine essence. See Richard A. Muller, *A Dictionary of Latin and Greek Theological Terms*, 2nd edn (Grand Rapids, MI: Baker Academic, 2017), s.v. "relatio personalis" and "processio intellectualis."

154   MILTON'S THEOLOGICAL PROCESS

Psalm: "The Son was begotten from eternity by the Father, but the eternal generation was represented by worldly time, so it adds *hodie*."[36] This note admits that the scriptural language speaks of "worldly time," while insisting that this language cannot mean what it says. Hebrews does use Psalm 2:7 in a manner more congenial to eternal generation than the original verse itself, and yet *hodie* remains to complicate the verse's transition to its new theological context.

The point is not to accuse Ames of any subterfuge or sleight of hand but rather to observe that the exegetical foundations for the principle of the Son's eternal generation are not especially firm. They are, as it turns out, particularly ill suited to holding up under the pressure exerted by Milton's normal method of proceeding in the treatise, especially given the contingent circumstance of the Psalm translation he had ready to hand in his preferred Latin Old Testament, either the 1624 Hanau or the 1630 Geneva edition of Junius–Tremellius. Milton first quotes Psalm 2:7 (following this version) in I.3, "On Divine Decree": "I am going to explain the decree: Jehovah said to me, 'You are my son: I have today begotten you.'"[37] Unlike other versions of the Bible available to Milton, these later editions of the JTB foreground the decree not only by translating the Hebrew חֹק [*ḥōq*] as "decretum" instead of as "statutum," "pactum," or "praeceptum," as several versions in Walton's polyglot Bible have it, but also (unlike the 1585 edition) by putting the relevant word first: "decretum enarraturus sum."[38] Milton's 1653 versification of the psalm similarly foregrounds the decree—"A firm decree/I will declare; the Lord to me hath say'd/Thou art my Son I have begotten thee/This day"—with enjambment emphasizing both the decree and the troublesome *hodie*, perhaps suggesting that Milton had earlier noticed the peculiarities of this JTB rendering.[39] The connection is not inevitable. For instance, the Vulgate includes the relevant phrase with the preceding verse, which associates the "precept" with the constituting of a king, not the begetting of a son: "Ego autem constitutus sum rex ab eo super Sion montem sanctum ejus, praedicans praeceptum ejus." In tandem with *hodie*, the emphasis on decree in the verse as Milton quotes it has two radical theological consequences: it suggests that the Son's existence results from a decree for which there was a before and an after (even if these were before the foundation of the world

---

[36] 1585 JTB, NT, 365: "Filius à Patre ab aeterno genitus est, sed aeterna illa generatio, suo tempore mundo representata fuit, ideò addidit (hodie.)"

[37] *DDC*, 24: "decretum enarraturus sum; Iehova dixit mihi, Filius meus es, ego hodiè genui te."

[38] 1585 JTB, VT, tom. III, 39–40; Brian Walton, ed., *Biblia Sacra Polyglotta* (London, 1657), III.88–89. Thanks to Donald Cullington for consulting the 1623/24 JTB on my behalf. On 1623/24 Hanau versus 1630 Geneva, see Chapter 1, n 46.

[39] Milton, *Poems* (London, 1673), p. 131. See also Specland, "Unfinished Exegesis," 63–67.

THE FORM OF BOOK I CHAPTER 5, "ON THE SON OF GOD" 155

and the beginning of time per se).[40] In this way, the rendering of Psalm 2:7 in Milton's go-to Old Testament seems to have disrupted the Trinitarian exegesis that let this verse support the Son's eternal generation without making it a product of divine decree. From its small beginnings, this exegetical disruption radically reshaped the treatise and lit a fuse under its reception history from the nineteenth century to the present.

The Literary Form of I.5

The disruption wrought by Psalm 2:7 appears primarily in the literary form that I.5 takes as it abandons Ramism for an organization grounded in internal scripture. I have been calling the Ramist moments that remain in the chapter "vestiges" because they point to the influence of Wolleb and Ames on what would seem to be its earliest form—assuming that it began, as the other chapters appear to have done, with Milton reading Wolleb and Ames alongside a stack of Bibles. Wolleb gives Milton some of his structural divisions when he sets out to "prove the Divinity of the Son and Holy Ghost. 1. From their Names. 2. From their Properties. 3. From their Works. 4. From their Divine Honours."[41] Ames, likewise, provides language that the treatise will take up by speaking of attributes (*attributa*, rather than properties, *proprietates*) such as "Omnipotency, Immensity, Eternity, and such like."[42] The story of this chapter's literary form hinges on how these lists of attributes, which might have structured the chapter in Ramist fashion, instead end up being subsumed in a larger, internal-scriptural project that turns them negative, that is, saying that these attributes do *not* pertain to the Son in his own person.

These systematic approaches leave their clear traces on I.5. The chapter's first large-hand word (after working through the initial Ramist subdivisions, down to "generation") is "**Pater [Father]**," on MS 49. The next—"**Attributa [Attributes]**"—does not appear until MS 63, where it sets up a list of other large-hand headings: "**Omniscientiam [Omniscience]**" and "**Supremum [...]** imperium [**Supreme** dominion]" (MS 63), followed by "**Bonitatem summam [Supreme goodness]**" and "**Gloriam summam [Supreme glory]**" (MS 65). Two further headings follow, seemingly on the same organizational level as

---

[40] To be clear, the anti-trinitarian reading resides in Milton; these editions' wording is merely the occasion.

[41] Wolleb, 21 [16]: "probationes divinitatis Filii & Spiritus S. 1. à nominibus. 2. à proprietatibus. 3. ab operibus. 4. ab honoribus divinis."

[42] Ames, 13 [13]: "omnipotentia, immensitas, aeternitas & similia." See further the discussion on 19–21 [20–22]. On Reformed treatment of the divine attributes, see *PRRD*, III.

156   MILTON'S THEOLOGICAL PROCESS

Attributes: "**Opera** [Works]" and "**Honorem Divinum** [Divine honour]" (MS 65–66). Large hand next appears on MS 77, in a case ("**Palmarius** locus [the prize passage]") that is not a heading and again in like manner ("**Placaeo Salmuriensi**," "**Junius**," and "**Placaeus**," which are proper names) on MS 80, 82, and 84; it does not indicate headings again until MS 84: "The Apostles after him [i.e., the son] also attest this same debt, namely of his **very identity**, his **very life, attributes, works**, and, finally, **divine honour**."[43] This list, approximately, covers the rest of the chapter, with fairly predictable subheadings keeping the organization more or less clear.[44]

The chapter's repetition of this basic list, in tandem with the initial "**Father**," suggests a bipartite structure. The first time through, the list works to connect these attributes to the Father: "That the divine **attributes** also belong to the Father alone is taught by the Son, to the exclusion even of himself."[45] The second time, the list structures an argument that these attributes, when associated with the Son, in fact indicate the Son's debt to the Father: "That the son himself gives the father credit not only for the name of God and Jehovah but also for whatever else he possesses."[46] Viewed through this rough lens, the chapter's first thirty-five pages treat the Father, while the ensuing fourteen treat the Son (albeit negatively, by arguing that his apparent attributes are, in fact, the Father's). Granted, much more happens in those first thirty-five pages—and especially the fourteen between "**Pater**" and "**Attributa**"—than this attention to the Ramist skeleton lets on. Nevertheless, the skeleton points at minimum to the vestiges of an argumentative structure according to the method laid out in the epistle and I.1.

This structure, notably, comports with the first sentence of I.6: "**After the Father** and **the Son** our next task is to discuss **the Holy Spirit**, since it is called the spirit of the father and the son."[47] In Wolleb, the Spirit's deity is proved by way of a similar list to the Son's, with the first item being "From his name God."[48] I.6. likewise begins by taking up, under its first large-hand heading,

---

[43] *DDC*, 84: "quod idem etiam post eum testantur Apostoli, **ipsum** videlicet **esse id quod est, vitam ipsam, attributa, opera, honorem** denique **divinum**." The shift in large-hand practice from indicating Ramist divisions to emphasizing proper names suggests the presence of different strata underneath Skinner's copy, as in I.27, where the usage of large hand for proper names—and, indeed, the use of proper names at all—appears in the multi-folio insertion of an extended prose argument: Appendix, pp. 260–62.

[44] Minor instances of logical fuzziness in the execution need not detain us.

[45] *DDC*, 63: "**Attributa** etiam divina solius esse Patris docet Filius, excluso etiam seipso."

[46] *DDC*, 84: "Ipsum filium, non nomen Dei et Iehovae solum, verùm etiam quicquid praeterea habet, patri acceptum referre."

[47] *DDC*, 98: "**A Patre** et **Filio** proximum est ut de **Sancto Spiritu** dicamus; quando et patris et filii spiritus appellatur."

[48] Wolleb, 22 [17]: "Nomen, Deus."

THE FORM OF BOOK I CHAPTER 5, "ON THE SON OF GOD"   157

"**The name of spirit.**"[49] This discussion ensues for several pages before "the divine properties assigned to the spirit are adduced."[50] The properties in question are omniscience (MS 105), omnipresence (MS 106), divine works (MS 106), and divine honors (MS 107). In parallel to I.5, under this last category, the chapter takes up instances when the spirit is invoked.

Taken together, these observations suggest that, underneath everything else that these two chapters became, they began with a clear debt to Wolleb's logical structure, considering first the properties of God per se (as Wolleb does in his first chapter) before proceeding to discuss the properties of Son and Spirit in roughly parallel fashion (as Wolleb does in his second chapter). Wolleb's chapter divisions leave him with little to say about the Father per se—one sentence, in fact: "The Father is the first Person of the Deity, existing from himself, begetting the Son from eternity, and with him producing the Holy Ghost."[51] (Part of a sentence later in the chapter adds that "the Father is from himself, not onely by reason of his essence, but also of his personality.")[52] The first chapter does not speak of the Father's properties but of God's, taken to mean the Trinity as a whole, insisting that "The Divine Properties are neither separable from the essence, nor from each other."[53] Milton, taking the Father alone to be God, will, in the event, agree with this point.

On the matter of the Son, then, Milton's debt to Wolleb includes significant pressure on two related points. The first involves the suggestion of a tripartite logical structure, discussing the attributes of the three divine persons in turn but with an apparent gap on the *locus* of the Father. Probing the gap by reading Wolleb and Ames together makes generation one of the Father's primary attributes, a point left underdeveloped by Wolleb but connected with Psalm 2:7 and Hebrews 1:6 by Ames. The pivotal verse from Psalm 2, with its *decretum* and *hodie* in the Hanau and Geneva editions of the JTB (also reflected in Milton's 1653 versification), only adds to the pressure by driving a potential wedge between the Father's attributes and the Son's. From whom, exactly, does divine decree issue if the existence of one Trinitarian person depends on it? Can the Son participate in the decree of his own begetting? Where does all of this leave the Holy Spirit? Reading Wolleb and Ames alongside the Bible, just

[49] *DDC*, 99: "**Nomen spiritus.**"
[50] *DDC*, 105: "Tum proprietates divinae attributae spiritui afferuntur." The use of *proprietates* rather than *attributa* may suggest a debt to Wolleb rather than Ames.
[51] Wolleb, 19 [15]: "Pater est prima Deitatis persona, à seipso exsistens, Filium ab aeterno gignens, & cum eodem Spiritum s. producens."
[52] Wolleb, 24 [18]: "Pater non essentiae tantum, sed & personae ratione est à seipso, Filius à Patre, Spiritus s. à Patre & Filio."
[53] Wolleb, 14 [10]: "Proprietates divinae, nec ab essentia, nec à se invicem separabiles sunt."

158 MILTON'S THEOLOGICAL PROCESS

as Milton said he was going to do in the epistle, put him on a collision course with these questions, whether he came into that reading an anti-trinitarian or not.

Internal Scripture and the Son

I have argued that the treatise's formal departures from the bare method of Ramist logic—rhetorical prose of various sorts and uses of scripture not bound to the Ramist structure—aspire to the status of scripture, subject to the grand ecclesial process of winnowing and sifting. By this standard, I.5 contains far more "internal scripture" than any other part of *De Doctrina Christiana*. Internal scripture comes into play when external scripture (i.e., the Bible) proves inadequate on its own, either to make a doctrinal point or, more frequently, to justify a topic's placement in the theological framework. When such justification is required, internal scripture often becomes explicitly rhetorical, as occurs on a grand scale with I.5. On the topic of the Son, Milton and his Trinitarian interlocutors arrive at radically different conclusions even though they both turn to Psalm 2 and its appropriations in Hebrews. But whereas internal scripture usually amounts to a bit of prose argumentation under a given subheading, in I.5 it takes over the chapter, driven first by Milton's own (apparently) changing mind and second by the need to justify his emerging position. Accordingly, I argue that I.5 became more internal-scriptural and rhetorical in form through a process of revision to what appears to have been an initially tripartite Ramist structure addressing each member of the Godhead in turn. Such a tripartite structure need not, of course, imply a commitment to *homoousios*, the sharing of a single divine essence by three distinct persons.[54] Even so, as I began to argue in the previous section, the evidence suggests that the chapter did not necessarily start out by rejecting *homoousios* either. Milton's theological process obliged him to test that doctrine against the scriptural witness, whatever his prior commitment to it may have been.

Attending to internal scripture gives a different sense of the chapter's organization than that afforded by its Ramist skeleton. The roadmap provided by the Oxford editors proves useful:

---

[54] *Homoousios* ("same being"), as distinct from *homoiousios* ("similar being")—a concept put forth in the fourth century as an alternative to the emerging orthodoxy, giving extraordinary theological weight to a single letter.

THE FORM OF BOOK I CHAPTER 5, "ON THE SON OF GOD"   159

The chapter consists of: Preface (MS 48–9); then Ramist distinctions, leading to an account of Generation (MS 49–57); and refutation of opposing views (MS 58–end of chapter). This lengthy refutation starts with analysis of the only two relevant biblical passages (MS 58–60), then proceeds by way of further rebuttals (MS 60) to the start (MS 61) of an extended tripartite discussion, virtually a fresh essay, refuting opponents' arguments rather than analysing passages. Its *partitio* is announced at MS 61i: it will be shown, first (**primum** = Part I), that the name, attributes, and works of God, and the divine office itself, are attributed by the Son and his apostles only to one God, the Father; next (**deinde** = Part II), that whenever scripture attributes them to the Son they are easily attributable in their primary and proper sense to the Father alone, and— in an interior sub-division (Part II.b) of this section—that the Son admits this and the apostles attest it; and that accordingly (**proinde** = Part III) the Son and his apostles acknowledge the Father's universal superiority to the Son. Part I occupies MS 61–8, Part II MS 68–95 (including II.b, MS 84–95), and Part III MS 95–8.[55]

The editors admit some uncertainty, occasioned by the messiness of the material and the "intermittency of composition"; nevertheless, their guide offers insight into the structure of the chapter as we now have it.

Considering the Oxford roadmap alongside the account of the Ramist structure in the previous section suggests that, following the initial account of generation, even the Ramist structure itself has been subordinated, formally, to a rhetorical argument that aims to express internal scripture. The initial discussion of divine attributes (the first instance of the list adapted from Wolleb) thus begins on MS 60–61, amidst a response to opponents, not on MS 63, with the word **Attributa**. Similarly, the second instance of the list roughly aligns with what Oxford identifies as Part II.b, with the discussion thus beginning some sixteen pages earlier than its first Ramist large-hand subheading. The *partitio* occurs not in a Ramist definition but in a passage of argumentative prose that takes its own structural cues from other argumentative prose—in this case, the preceding discussion of the two major New Testament passages held to support the Trinity, John 10:30 and 1 John 5:7.

The practice on evidence in the Picard pages of the treatise suggests that these internal scriptural elements likely represent the accretion of revisions on the Ramist frame to the point that the Ramist frame no longer serves as the chapter's central structural support. Just as recopied Picard pages can carry

---

[55] Oxford, 233 n. i.

160   MILTON'S THEOLOGICAL PROCESS

discernible traces of preceding strata of revision, so too with the Skinner pages. Some small evidence for this survives. The manuscript of I.5 contains myriad minor corrections but also three marginal insertions, on MS 50, 71, and 82. On MS 50, the insertion adds Paul's interpretation of Psalm 2:7 in Acts 13:32–33, a usage well in line with marginal insertions in the Picard pages. The insertion on MS 71 (see Figure 4.1) consists of a biting prose statement ("Only a superexcessively credulous person [... Credulus plus nimio...]"), about which Oxford opines: "The addition may have been an explosive afterthought when, having heard his main argumentation read back, Milton strengthened it with introductory ridicule."[56] On MS 82, the insertion includes argumentative prose and engagement with several passages of scripture, with Oxford characterizing it as "An authorial afterthought, like that on MS 307A/308, which DS missed at first. His keying sigla vary: some are his own, some those of his copy."[57] I join Oxford as reading these insertions as products of Skinner's working with heavily revised Picard pages that make inadvertent omissions easy. Presumably, the density and complexity of revision in these pages is what rendered recopying necessary in the first place, in keeping with the evidence of MS 307A, where Skinner's transcription also proved unsurprisingly fallible.[58]

Given such practices elsewhere, I.5 is therefore striking in the literary forms that its anti-trinitarian argument employs: extended and explicitly rhetorical prose argumentation, to include passages of in-depth exegesis and even scripture-blocks subordinated to the prose, not the series of Ramist definitions, subheadings, and scripture blocks that would be in keeping with the treatise's announced method. True, the Ramist skeleton does, in the chapter's extant version, work vehemently in support of the anti-trinitarian position. But if the treatise began with that position, why not proceed according to the stated method? The revisions to I.17–18 show that the Ramist structure itself can be adapted to arguing positions at odds with the orthodoxy espoused by Wolleb and Ames—even if there, too, some crucial prose enters via the margin to drive the point home.[59]

The formal difference between I.5 and I.17 turns on the rule (or analogy/proportion) of faith. I have argued that the presence of internal scripture indicates pressure points in the structure of the rule of faith itself such that

---

[56] Oxford, 170 n. 139.

[57] Oxford, 192 n. 198. MS 308 (Skinner's recopy of 307a) contains an interlinear insertion (incipit: *huius*), keyed with a small x, of a passage that had also been interlinearly inserted on the extraordinarily messy Picard original.

[58] See Oxford, 686–97 n. i.

[59] See the discussion in Chapter 2 (pp. 100–104) of the marginal insertion on MS 229.

THE FORM OF BOOK I CHAPTER 5, "ON THE SON OF GOD"   161

Figure 4.1 Detail from *DDC*, 71 showing Skinner's marginal insertion

Ramist method no longer suffices and arguments justifying a particular concept's proportionate place in that structure become necessary. Indeed, the chapter turns rhetorical immediately after the initial Ramist *divisio* as it argues that "generation must be external efficiency," seeking to demonstrate that

162   MILTON'S THEOLOGICAL PROCESS

Milton's placement of the topic is more plausible than the Theologians'.[60] It is at these moments that Milton's wrestle with the rule of faith—the nature of Christian doctrine itself—comes most clearly into view. Accordingly, such moments are of interest for what they reveal about Milton's processes of thought and the stakes of the problems he is working through, perhaps more so than for the conclusions at which he arrives. In I.5, then, we get to see Milton grapple with why exactly the Son matters for Christian doctrine. The wrestle does involve the usual categories of *essentia, substantia, hypostasis,* and so on but not, I submit, for the usual reasons, like striking (or upsetting) the balance between modalism and tritheism or between the Son's two natures.[61] Rather, I argue that Milton's insistence on the Son's essential distinction from the Father has primarily to do with the rule of faith per se. As Milton rethinks the part of the rule of faith touching the tradition of the church (i.e., the collective process of discerning truth through practices of internal scripture), the Son's free unity with the Father serves both as a model for the church and a guarantor of its possibility in ways that *homoousios,* with what Milton takes as its implied necessity, cannot.

Indeed, the rule of faith provides the key to understanding the interaction of the several variables at play in giving I.5 its final form, both aesthetic and theological. The heart of the issue is, I think, the question of what to do with Psalm 2:7 in relation to the Son's origin, given the not-altogether-satisfactory treatment of this question in Wolleb and Ames (or Polanus, for that matter, who quotes the *hodie* but does not attempt to reconcile it with the claim, immediately following, that the Father begot the Son from eternity).[62] Milton emphasizes this verse at several points early in the chapter. I quote one of particular importance:

> From all the previously cited passages, when they have been compared—especially with the whole second Psalm—and most carefully appraised, it is readily apparent that it is not by a necessity of nature, as is customarily claimed,

---

[60] *DDC*, 49: "Externam autem esse efficientiam generationem necesse est."

[61] On the historical development of the Trinity, see Declan Marmion and Rik Van Nieuwenhove, *An Introduction to the Trinity* (Cambridge: Cambridge University Press, 2011), esp. ch. 3. As a likely influence on Milton, Gordon Campbell and Thomas N. Corns cite Tremellius's translation of the Syriac *qnoma* (the rough analogue to the Greek *hypostasis*) with the Latin *essentia*: "De Doctrina Christiana: An England That Might Have Been," in *The Oxford Handbook of Milton*, ed. Nicholas McDowell and Nigel Smith (Oxford: Oxford University Press, 2009), p. 430.

[62] Amandus Polanus, *Syntagma Theologiae Christianae* (Hanover, 1609), p. 1290 (III.iv). For an attempt, in the 1680s, to counter the argument that *hodie* refers to a moment in time, see Petrus van Mastricht, *Theoretico-Practica Theologia* (Amsterdam, 1682), p. 404 (II.xxvi). Mastricht treats *hodie* as easily dismissible, not raising the issue again even in the chapter's arguments against Remonstrants and Socinians, p. 410.

THE FORM OF BOOK I CHAPTER 5, "ON THE SON OF GOD" 163

but by the Father's decree and will that the Son had been in whatever way begotten, just as much as he had been appointed high priest and king, and raised from the dead.[63]

This passage presents its conclusions as a methodological product of the rule of faith (*analogia fidei*) through the comparison of passages (*analogia scripturae*), while singling out Psalm 2 as the foundational "plain place" on this topic, to which Milton must bend the other, more obscure places. Consequently, it points back to the Son's origin as a product of divine decree, which has the effect of justifying I.5's placement in the Ramist scheme among the topics pertaining to God's external rather than internal efficiency. Finally, and vitally for Milton's larger theological project, it frees the existence of the Son from necessity. Milton writes, in I.3, that "God did not decree anything absolutely which he left in the power of free agents: the whole course of scripture shows this," and he devotes the bulk of the chapter to arguing (mostly in prose) that God's decrees and foreknowledge are compatible with creaturely freedom.[64] Just as necessity requires only that God be God, it requires only that the Son, as a creature, be free.

Necessity, here, means two things: external constraint on the will but also a logical freedom from self-contradiction. When Milton writes, "Indeed I do not even concede any necessity in God to act, but only that he is necessarily God," he denies (in keeping with the Reformed tradition) that God's will operates under any constraint, while also arguing that God cannot will things that would entail his ceasing to be God, closing the door on such self-contradictions as the infamous rock too heavy for God to lift.[65] Parting ways with the Reformed, Milton rejects *homoousios* and co-eternality because they would impose this second kind of necessity on the Son so that the Son's union with the Father might be the more remarkable for having the alternate possibility clearly on the table.[66] The Reformed understand the Son as being free in the sense of technically being able to will otherwise because he participates in the divine essence. By understanding the Son as not sharing the divine essence, however, Milton makes willing

---

[63] *DDC*, 51: "Ex omnibus autem superius citatis locis praesertim cum toto Psalmo 2.do collatis et diligentissime animadversis facilè apparet, non necessitate naturae, quod contendi solet, sed decreto et voluntate Patris tam fuisse Filium quocunque modo genitum quam pontificem et regem constitutum atque ex mortuis suscitatem."

[64] *DDC*, 19: "Nihil itaque Deus decrevisse absolutè censendus est quod in potestate liberè agentium reliquit: id quod scripturae totius series ostendit."

[65] *DDC*, 21: "Verum nec in Deo necessitatem agendi ullam concedimus: sed esse quidem necessariò Deum." On the principle of non-contradiction, see *PRRD*, III.443–56.

[66] The Reformed insist that the Son is able to choose otherwise: Richard A. Muller, *Divine Will and Human Choice: Freedom, Contingency, and Necessity in Early Modern Reformed Thought* (Grand Rapids, MI: Baker Academic, 2017), esp. Part III. By contrast, Milton seems to see ontological unity as foreclosing the possibility of the Son's union with the Father being truly free.

164   MILTON'S THEOLOGICAL PROCESS

otherwise the norm rather than the exception because most things outside God voluntarily incline to disunion with the divine. Consequently, the Son's union stands out.

Much of the rest of the chapter continues the justificatory work grounded on Psalm 2 in the opening pages. Indeed, it is striking just how much of the chapter is devoted to arguing what the Son is *not*, to the point that even the Ramist skeleton gets co-opted to this end. Every element of the structure outlined by the Oxford editors serves this negative purpose until Part III asserts the Son's subordination. Oddly, given its title, the chapter makes more positive claims about the Father than it does about the Son. Overwhelmingly, its work is to show that the *locus* of the Son does not belong in its traditional position (i.e., alongside that of the Father as an immanent participant in Deity) because the import of Psalm 2 for the Son's (metaphorical) generation will not permit it. This view operates in tandem with an orthodox(!) view of the incommunicability of divine attributes; thus Ames: "[T]hose attributes, which in their formall respect, i[n]clude something proper to the Divine *Essence*, are altogether incommunicable: as Omnipotency, Immensity, Eternity, and such like."[67] Together, these positions drive the chapter's argument, identifying the divine attributes with the Father alone, denying that they in any way pertain directly to the Son, and concluding, finally, that the Son, as witnessed by Father, Son, and apostles, is subordinate to the Father.

This Christological conclusion has an ambiguous relationship with the treatise's Ramist structure. On the one hand, the conclusion serves to justify the topic's placement in the treatise's logical structure. On the other hand, the treatise seems unable to carry out this justification using Ramist tools, turning instead to rhetoric as it attempts to persuade readers that its placement is more plausible than the traditional Reformed one. In this ambiguity, the chapter tacitly acknowledges the limits of logic's aspiration to closure (and here I recall the familiar habit of contrasting the "closed" treatise with the "open" *Paradise Lost*), but, as Kurt Gödel demonstrated in the twentieth century, logical systems

---

[67] Ames, 13 [13]: "Ista attributa, quae in suo formali includunt aliquid essentiae divinae proprium, sunt planè incommunicabilia: ut omnipotentia, immensitas, aeternitas & similia." If the Father and Son share the same essence, as Ames holds, then the attributes are communicated necessarily between them (in what is known as the *communicatio idiomatum*) even as they remain incommunicable outside the divine essence. By making the Son distinct in essence from the Father, his participation in the attributes becomes free, rather than necessary, even as the attributes themselves pertain only to the Father. The Son's is simply a persuasive *imitatio Patris*, bolstered by the power attending divine commissions like the one to create the world.

THE FORM OF BOOK I CHAPTER 5, "ON THE SON OF GOD"   165

may aspire to closure, but they cannot achieve it.[68] Gödel showed that eliminating self-reference from logic proves impossible and that the fact of self-reference indicates the existence of some element beyond the logical system. I.5 represents just such a moment of self-reference for the Ramist logic that governs most of *De Doctrina Christiana*, a moment when the treatise reflects self-consciously on its own Ramist structure. For such work, that structure proves inadequate, and rhetoric enters the picture.

Rhetoric is, by its nature, probabilistic, but its unexpected use in a treatise explicitly devoted to unfolding Christian doctrine logically perhaps explains why it nevertheless drives so insistently toward closure, as if embarrassed by the exigency of resorting to rhetoric. The treatise thus exhibits a doubleness ably captured by John Creaser, a "division of impulses" such that even though "the whole enterprise speaks to his openness of mind, [. . .] the urge to say the last word and close off debate is frequently apparent."[69] Even so, the rhetorical meta-level remains present as a reflection on the rule of faith rather than a methodical implementation of it, manifest as the chapter adopts probabilistic language at odds with its own drive toward closure. Examples abound already in the first paragraph following the Ramist *divisio*, in language like "must be [*necesse est*]" (which amounts to a kind of special pleading), "will be more clearly evident [*quod clarius* [. . .] *apparebit*]" (which promises persuasive evidence), "the other passages adduced indicate only figurative generation [*caetera quae afferentur loca metaphoricam tantum generationem indicant*]" (which introduces a long sequence of quotations interspersed with interpretative prose, like the rhetorical question "What name, pray, but that of Son? [*Quod autem nomen nisi Filii?*]").[70] In the name of affirming, such passages, in fact, argue and undertake to persuade. Other moments are explicitly argumentative, as when Milton takes on Ambrose's reading of Greek definite articles in prose that rises to unexpected heights, given the topic:

And surely trust, especially in a principal article of faith, is such that it ought not to be squeezed out and, as it were, torn out of passages dealing with another point—sometimes doubtful ones, too, because of a variant reading and meaning—it ought not to be chased after with some bird-trap out of articles and particles; it ought not to be dug out of ambiguities, or else

---

[68] For an accessible discussion, see Ernest Nagel and James Newman, *Gödel's Proof*, ed. Douglas R. Hofstadter (New York: New York University Press, 2008).
[69] John Creaser, "'Fear of Change': Closed Minds and Open Forms in Milton," *Milton Quarterly* 42, 3 (2008): 173, citing similar conclusions drawn by John K. Hale.
[70] *DDC*, 49–50.

166   MILTON'S THEOLOGICAL PROCESS

obscurities—like the Delphic oracle's answers—but quaffed by the mouthful out of the clearest springs.[71]

This passage explicitly works to render implausible a particular approach to reading, not just mounting attacks on several fronts but doing so in a syntactically complex sentence that builds toward its climactic promise of a better option. The Oxford editors note that Milton's passionate rhetoric in this place echoes and responds to Beza's similarly passionate annotation on the scriptural passage in question.[72] Milton meets argument with argument, not with the promised quaff from clearer, logical waters, and his vehement language paradoxically participates in the very sort of discussion it is trying to close down.

In such passages, rhetoric all but explicitly emerges from the inadequacy of logic. Ascertaining the Son's proper place in relation to God is the same work as ascertaining the Son's place within the proportional structure of the *analogia fidei*. The chapter's form, consisting more of "internal scriptural" prose than of Ramist headings and so on, indicates that Milton's argument about the Son is incidental to a larger argument about the Son's place in the *analogia fidei*. In my view, therefore, the chapter's justificatory, rhetorical thrust represents Milton's own process of thinking about the Son's place in the structure of theology at least as much as it represents a polemic against his "opponents."[73] Psalm 2:7, particularly as rendered in the Hanau or Geneva edition of the JTB, seems to have been determinative in obliging Milton to associate the Son's begetting with divine decree, obliging him to rethink what may have been a tripartite discussion of the attributes pertaining to each divine person in a manner inspired by Wolleb. It is possible, though not finally demonstrable, that an earlier state of the treatise placed the chapter(s) on the Son and the Spirit *before* the chapter on divine decree, just as Wolleb had done. Be that as it may, the current state of I.5 seems more readily explicable as the product of a theological process that does not take its unorthodox logical positioning of (or position on) this topic as given. Certainly, the chapter's controversial views need defending, given the theological environment, and the chapter engages in plenty of it. Even so, the

---

[71] *DDC,* 75:

> Et fides certè ea est, in re praesertim cum primis credenda, quae non ex locis aliud agentibus, lectione etiam nonnunquam varia atque sensu dubiis, unde exprimi et quasi extorqueri, non ex articulis aut particulis aucupio quodam captari, non ex ambiguis aut obscuris quasi pythia responsa erui, sed ex clarissimus fontibus pleno ore hauriri debeat.

[72] Oxford, 237–38 n. lxvii.
[73] See the discussion in Chapter 2 (pp. 77–80) of the deleted passage on MS 222–23.

THE FORM OF BOOK I CHAPTER 5, "ON THE SON OF GOD"   167

radical formal departure from Ramism suggests that the need for defense was not an intrinsic part of the chapter at its instantiation but rather emerged along the way. But if the treatise's arguments about the Son overwhelmingly take the form of internal scripture, I submit that it is because the very tenability of internal scripture as a concept in Milton's theology rests on the Son, as Chapter 5 will argue.

Conclusion

One reflection on the literary form of I.5 yet remains. I have been arguing that the chapter takes the form of internal scripture because it is primarily devoted to justifying its place in the Ramist system. But if, as I argued earlier, most uses of internal scripture in the treatise at least aspire to supplement external scripture rather than supplant it, something more like supplanting has happened, with the consequence that I.5 calls the assumptions governing the Ramist approach into question. The Oxford outline shows that Milton eventually gave the chapter an organizational structure that is not Ramist. Although we can only speculate about the thought processes behind this decision, the question remains why, after arriving at his heterodox view of the Son, Milton did not present that view using the Ramist method of headings and scripture blocks. I suspect that the answer is because the passages in question are all so controversial that they would require extensive prose exegesis and argument. In other words, the chapter's internal-scriptural form might not simply be the result of inertia stemming from the sunk costs in the massive effort of revision but might rather be the deliberate result of a judgment that revising the results into Ramist form would be to little effect. Rhetoric had become all but necessary. Indeed, the chapter's form suggests that on this pivotal question of Christian doctrine, Milton no longer found external scripture sufficient to decide the issue. Instead, every position—even the orthodox one—turned out to depend for its demonstration on a kind of internal scripture. Faced with this situation, he did the best he could to argue the case that he felt external scripture warranted, but he turned frankly to internal scripture to argue it. If the resulting prose does sometimes rise to an energetic rhetorical pitch in which Milton's voice shines through, it more frequently produces what John Hale describes as "a priori or arbitrary or warped reasoning" that finally "manhandles scripture in a theology grounded solely on scripture."[74] Although the literary form of I.5 shows that Milton no

---

[74] Hale, *Milton's Scriptural Theology*, 119.

longer finds tenable the theology of scripture that first animated the project of *De Doctrina Christiana*, the internal scripture on evidence in the chapter seems hampered in its possibilities by still remaining tied to the form of a treatise. To explore the fuller potentialities afforded by the concept of internal scripture, Milton was going to need a different literary form.

5

The Son of God and Milton's Church

Chapter 4 argued that the topic of the Son tested the limits of Milton's theological method to the breaking point such that the argumentative, rhetorical prose associated with internal scripture came to overwhelm the Ramist method centered on external scripture. This degree of reliance on internal scripture hints at an ecclesial problem because Milton expects that the church will be hostile to what he has become persuaded is a doctrinal truth. The chapter's extensive argumentation thus indicates a worry that the ecclesial process of discernment might arrive at the wrong conclusion—an outcome hardly conducive to the faith that Milton has invested in that process. As such, I.5 finds Milton once again grappling with the question of what constitutes a reliable rule of faith.

The present chapter argues that Milton's heterodox theology of the Son emerges in part as a response to this question. Where Augustine had posited the plain places of scripture and the authority of the church as the rule of faith, Milton's initial method appealed to the presumed internal coherence of the Bible itself ("external scripture"), as he hoped to represent that coherence by gathering passages under topical headings and then using the assembled passages to frame doctrinal definitions in Ramist fashion. Milton hoped that direct appeal to the Bible would persuade both himself and the church that he had arrived at correct doctrinal conclusions. As he came up against the limits of this approach, occasioned by his sense that tradition had misread the Bible, Milton instead presented "the spirit and the *un*written word" (i.e., "internal scripture") as the rule of faith, replacing Augustine's appeal to the authority of the church with a conception of the church as a forum in which all believers participate in the collective process of discerning doctrinal truth.[1] The literary form of I.5, however, draws attention to the church's fallibility as a problem in need of resolution: the very contentiousness of Milton's argumentation reflects his sense that, in the church as he imagines it, what he takes to be the truth might not prevail.

The problem of human fallibility raises the hotly contested question of Milton's atonement theology. Milton enters a field framed by multiple competing

---

[1] *DDC*, 398: "Sic omnia demum ad spiritum atque verbum non scriptum, scriptura ipsa teste referenda sunt."

Milton's Theological Process. Jason A. Kerr, Oxford University Press. © Jason A. Kerr (2023).
DOI: 10.1093/oso/9780198875086.003.0006

170   MILTON'S THEOLOGICAL PROCESS

options, broadly understood as pitting Anselm's satisfaction theory and its subsequent transformation into Reformed penal substitution theory against Peter
Abelard's moral exemplar (or moral influence) theory and its sixteenth-and-
seventeenth-century Socinian cousin.[2] In these terms, Anselm (c. 1033–1109)
understood atonement as satisfying the debt to God's justice incurred by human
sin, with the Reformed version of the theory holding that Jesus substitutes
for humans in suffering the punishment for sin that God's justice requires.
Meanwhile, Abelard (1079–1142) held that a just God would not require the
murder of his Son, arguing instead that Christ's passion kindled the flame of
love in human hearts, inspiring them to follow the saving example of Christ's
life. Socinians likewise emphasized the example of Christ's life, understanding humans as having been created with reason that equips them to follow in
Jesus's footsteps once his example has given them the necessary knowledge.
Such is the received picture, although close engagement with the primary texts
and recent scholarship indicates some need for adjustment. For instance, the
idea that Anselm's atonement theology operates primarily within a feudal context that centers law and vengeance rather than grace is no longer tenable and
neither is the idea that Abelard's theory of atonement is purely exemplary and
contains no objective dimension in which Christ meaningfully effects salvation
rather than merely pointing the way to it.[3]

Scholars have debated whether Milton favors exemplary or satisfactory
atonement, but these theologies prove inadequate as resolutions to the problem of ecclesial fallibility as Milton presents it. In its Reformed instantiation,
penal substitution locates the agency behind redemption entirely with God.
Humans can, and should, perform good works, but they possess the capacity
to do so only because God has first acted on them via irresistible grace. Milton's
account of renewal in I.17, discussed in Chapter 2, finds him rejecting this view,
locating some (grace-given) capacity for discernment even in unregenerate
humanity. The renewal that created this capacity comes through unmerited
grace, but the further grace required for regeneration comes only when
humans assent to it after having been persuaded to do so by encounters with

---

[2] On Anselm's atonement theology and Reformation developments, see Heather Hirschfeld, *The End
of Satisfaction: Drama and Repentance in the Age of Shakespeare* (Ithaca, NY: Cornell University Press,
2014), pp. 19–27.

[3] The feudal reading of Anselm is owed to Jasper Hopkins, *A Companion to the Study of St. Anselm*
(Minneapolis, MN: University of Minnesota Press, 1972), p. 197, reiterated in "God's Sacrifice of Him-
self as a Man: Anselm of Canterbury's *Cur Deus Homo*," in *Human Sacrifice in Jewish and Christian
Tradition*, ed. Karin Finsterbusch, Armin Lange, and K. F. Diethard Römheld (Leiden: Brill, 2007), p.
256; for more recent perspectives, see David S. Hogg, "Christology: The *Cur Deus Homo*," in *The Oxford
Handbook of Christology*, ed. Francesca Aran Murphy and Troy A. Stefano (Oxford: Oxford University
Press, 2015), pp.199–201.

the Word, either directly in the Bible or through preaching. Moral exemplar atonement theology, at least in the Semipelagian form popularly imputed to it, takes insufficient account of the persistent human fallibility that lies behind Milton's insistence on the need for the kind of renewal discussed in I.17. A church comprised of people who are told to follow the Son while lacking the capacity to do so could hardly prove an effective means of discerning doctrinal truth.

On my reading, *De Doctrina Christiana* presents a two-stage atonement theology in which penal substitution enables a renewal of human capacities that makes it possible for people to look to Christ as an exemplar they might strive to follow. Vitally for Milton's rule of faith, Christ's example also has an ecclesial dimension, one made possible precisely by the treatise's heterodox view of the Son. If shifting the balance of the rule of faith toward internal scripture seems to portend a church characterized by the proliferation of irresolvably diverse views all offered, frustratingly, in search of a tantalizing truth, the Son as Milton conceives him holds out the possibility of a being who is essentially distinct from the Father but who, nevertheless, proves capable of speaking in harmony with the Father's otherwise inaccessible truth. For Milton, the Son anchors the possibility of internal scripture while extending hope that the ecclesial process of truth discovery might prove fruitful instead of merely cacophonous. In this sense, the Son serves as the organizing principle of the church, the being who simultaneously demonstrates and makes possible (by renewing human capacities) the kind of work that God has called the church to do.

The Son described in I.5 provides hope that internal scripture might lead to doctrinal truth without, however, resolving the problem of foundations and definition intrinsic to the practice of internal scripture. He enacts the possibility of freely speaking in harmony with God without showing what exactly that harmony looks like—a shift that marks Milton's firm departure from the Socinian emphasis on revealed knowledge as the central function of Christ's example. This uncertainty results in part from the same problem of necessity and free will that contributed to Milton's theological insistence on the Son's essential distinction from the Father: the church's union with the Son must be no less free than the Son's with the Father, and that means refusing the bondage that a too-certain articulation of the truth might risk imposing. The shift toward internal scripture in Milton's rule of faith thus includes a shift in his notion of slavery to God (as expressed in the chapter on Christian liberty, I.27), where anything that might resemble actual slavery drops away. *De Doctrina Christiana* does not fully take up the complex problem of freedom that emerges from this shift,

172   MILTON'S THEOLOGICAL PROCESS

however; that work remains for *Paradise Lost*, the subject of this book's next chapter.

Atonement and the Process of Christian Doctrine

The question of why the Son matters to the project of *De Doctrina Christiana* necessitates making sense of the treatise's atonement theology. As suggested above, I argue that Milton associates Christ's satisfaction with the renewal discussed in I.17 and that renewal enables people to look to the Son as an exemplar: renewal enables humans to attempt speaking scripture in imitation of the Son.[4] This view puts me somewhat at odds with both sides of the scholarship on Milton and the atonement. One side, perhaps with deeper roots, finds Milton affirming penal substitution in keeping with Reformed orthodoxy. Exponents of this view include C. S. Lewis and C. A. Patrides in the mid-twentieth century and, more recently, Russell M. Hillier and Samuel Smith.[5] The other side, which has gained more purchase in recent years, looks to the incomplete state of Milton's poem "The Passion" and, finding that Milton generally shies away from the bloodier aspects of atonement imagery, argues that he had a perennial discomfort with penal substitution and preferred a moral exemplar atonement theory.[6] Exponents of this view include, among others, Denis Saurat, John Rogers, and Gregory Chaplin.[7] A third view, in John Leonard's terms, is William Empson's acknowledgement

[4] On liberation through *imitatio Christi*, see Jason A. Kerr, "*De Doctrina Christiana* and Milton's Theology of Liberation," *Studies in Philology* 111, 2 (2014): 346–74.

[5] C. S. Lewis, *A Preface to* Paradise Lost (Oxford: Oxford University Press, 1960), pp. 90–91; C. A. Patrides, *Milton and the Christian Tradition* (Oxford: Clarendon Press, 1966), ch. 5; Russell M. Hillier, *Milton's Messiah: The Son of God in the Works of John Milton* (Oxford: Oxford University Press, 2011), ch. 1; Samuel Smith, "Milton's Theology of the Cross: Substitution and Satisfaction in Christ's Atonement," *Christianity and Literature* 63, 1 (2013): 5–25. William Poole roots Milton's commitment to satisfaction in Independent defenses of the regicide; "Theology," in *Milton in Context*, ed. Stephen B. Dobranski (Cambridge: Cambridge University Press, 2010), pp. 479–80.

[6] On the paucity of English Calvinist passion narratives, see Debora Shuger, *The Renaissance Bible: Scholarship, Sacrifice, and Subjectivity* (Berkeley, CA: University of California Press, 1993), ch. 3. See, however, the bloody emphasis in the Latin title (*Salus electorum, sanguis Jesu*) of John Owen's *The Death of Death in the Death of Christ* (London, 1648).

[7] Denis Saurat, *Milton: Man and Thinker* (New York: Dial Press, 1925), ch. 4; Gregory Chaplin, "Beyond Sacrifice: Milton and the Atonement," *Publications of the Modern Language Association of America* 125, 2 (2010): 354–69. John Rogers argues that Milton espouses penal substitution in *De Doctrina Christiana* and *Paradise Lost* but rejects it in *Samson Agonistes*: "Delivering Redemption in Samson Agonistes," in *Altering Eyes: New Perspectives on* Samson Agonistes, ed. Mark R. Kelley and Joseph Wittreich (Newark, DE: University of Delaware Press, 2002), pp. 72–97. Chaplin has since argued that Milton is effectively Pelagian: "Milton's Beautiful Body," in *Immortality and the Body in the Age of Milton*, ed. John Rumrich and Stephen M. Fallon (Cambridge: Cambridge University Press, 2017), pp. 91–106.

THE SON OF GOD AND MILTON'S CHURCH 173

that Milton's God requires satisfaction, followed with an argument that Milton would have readers reject that God along with his appalling atonement theology.[8]

Cutting across these views, though, is the question of Milton's anti-trinitarianism. Most of the critics discussed above, with the partial exception of Lewis and the fuller one of Patrides, accept that Milton denied the orthodox Trinity.[9] The rest agree that Milton takes an unorthodox view of the Godhead, although Hillier is the most vociferous in challenging the aptness of "Arian" as a label for Milton's position.[10] In his broadside against the notion that either *De Doctrina Christiana* or *Paradise Lost* espouses an orthodox position on the Godhead, Michael Bauman includes atonement in his description of Arian theological positions but does not explicitly argue that Milton espouses an Arian atonement theology—although he does argue that Milton's view of the Son's mediatorial work depends on an Arian reading of the Son.[11] Going beyond Bauman, Chaplin argues that Milton holds Arian views of both the Son and atonement, grounded in the ontological continuity between humans, angels, and the Son.[12] Andrew Barnaby, in turn, develops a kenotic approach to *imitatio Christi* whereby humans paradoxically contribute to their own exaltation through humble obedience.[13] Smith, by contrast, and with him David Urban, argues that Milton rests an orthodox atonement theology on an Arian Son.[14] In a similar vein, Hillier argues for penal substitution while arguing that Milton's

---

[8] John Leonard, *Faithful Labourers: A Reception History of* Paradise Lost, *1667–1970* (Oxford: Oxford University Press, 2013), pp. 477–78; cf. William Empson, *Milton's God*, rev. edn (Cambridge: Cambridge University Press, 1981), chs 3, 7.

[9] Lewis, *Preface*, 86–87 acknowledges the unorthodoxy of *De Doctrina Christiana* but argues that readers of *Paradise Lost* would not "have discovered the poet's Arianism without the aid of external evidence." Patrides, *Milton and the Christian Tradition*, 15–16, already subscribes to the orthodox-but-subordinationist reading of the Son soon to appear in William B. Hunter Jr, C. A. Patrides, and J. H. Adamson, *Bright Essence* (Salt Lake City, UT: University of Utah Press, 1971) (and based on already published work by himself and his *Bright Essence* coauthors, Hunter and Adamson).

[10] "Arian" refers to the view, espoused in the third and fourth centuries by the presbyter Arius and his followers, that the Father's begetting of the Son happened in time, meaning that the Son is not coeternal with the Father and therefore also not God from all eternity. For a fuller definition, see Michael Bauman, *Milton's Arianism* (Frankfurt am Main: P. Lang, 1987).

[11] See Bauman, *Milton's Arianism*, 44–46 for the discussion of Arian atonement theology, and pp. 112–20 for an argument that Milton's atonement theology requires a Son subject to change, in contravention of orthodoxy.

[12] Chaplin, "Beyond Sacrifice," 359.

[13] Andrew Barnaby, "'The Form of a Servant': At(-)onement by Kenosis in *Paradise Lost*," *Milton Quarterly* 52, 1 (2018): 1–19. On Milton and *imitatio Christi*, see further Daniel Shore, *Milton and the Art of Rhetoric* (Cambridge: Cambridge University Press, 2012), ch. 6. *Kenosis* refers to Christ's self-emptying, described in Philippians 2:7: "But made himself of no reputation (ἐκένωσεν), and took upon him the forme of a servant, and was made in the likenesse of men" (KJV).

[14] Smith, "Milton's Theology of the Cross"; David V. Urban, "John Milton, Paradox, and the Atonement: Heresy, Orthodoxy, and the Son's Whole-Life Obedience," Studies in Philology 112, 4 (2015): 817–36.

174   MILTON'S THEOLOGICAL PROCESS

anti-trinitarian Son cannot be Arian because he is consubstantial (although not coessential) with the Father.[15] Somehow, anti-trinitarian views of the Son are able to underwrite both views of atonement, the substitutionary and the exemplary.

Part of the tension emerges from the tendency to treat these two models of atonement as distinct and opposed—a tendency dating to contemporary critiques of Abelard by Bernard of Clairvaux and William of St Thierry and, more recently, to Hastings Rashdall in the early twentieth century.[16] The reading of Abelard as exemplarist owes to passages like the following, from his *Commentary on the Epistle to the Romans*:

> Nevertheless it seems to us that in this we are justified in the blood of Christ and reconciled to God, that it was through this matchless grace shown to us that his Son received our nature, and in that nature, teaching us both by word and by example, persevered to the death and bound us to himself even more through love, so that when we have been kindled by so great a benefit of divine grace, true charity might fear to endure nothing for his sake.[17]

Witnessing Christ's example should kindle in humans the desire to do likewise—a perspective that, read in isolation, seems to make Christ's role in effecting human salvation indirect at best. Other passages, however, counter the notion that Abelard understood humans as capable of obedience without divine aid, as when he makes God's love (central to the passage just quoted) the means of human obedience: "Therefore, our redemption is that supreme love in us through the Passion of Christ, which not only frees us from slavery to sin, but gains for us the true liberty of the sons of God, so that we may complete all

---

[15] Hillier, *Milton's Messiah*, 21.

[16] Hastings Rashdall, *The Idea of the Atonement in Christian Theology* (London: Macmillan, 1919), pp. 357–64.

[17] Peter Abelard, *Commentary on the Epistle to the Romans*, trans. Steven Cartwright (Washington, DC: Catholic University of America Press, 2011), pp. 167–68; Commentaria in Epistolam Pauli ad Romanos, in Petra Abaelardi Opera Theologica, Vol. I, ed. Eloi Marie Buytaert, OFM, Corpvs Christanorvm Continvatio Mediaevalis, Vol. XI (Turnhout: Brepols, 1969), pp. 117–18 (iii.26):

> Nobis autem uidetur quod in hoc iustificati sumus in sanguine Christi et Deo reconciliati, quod per hanc singularem gratiam nobis exhibitam quod Filius suus nostram susceperit naturam et in ipsa nos tam uerbo quam exemplo instituendo usque ad mortem perstitit, nos sibi amplius per amorem adstrixit, ut tanto diuinae gratiae accensi beneficio, nihil iam tolerare propter ipsum uera reformidet caritas.

THE SON OF GOD AND MILTON'S CHURCH   175

things by his love rather than by fear."[18] In several places, Abelard even explicitly states that Christ bore punishment in humans' stead, as in his comment on Romans 4:25:

> He is said to have died **on account of our transgressions** in two ways: at one time because we transgressed, on account of which he died, and we committed sin, the penalty of which he bore; at another, that he might take away our sins by dying, that is, he swept away the penalty for our sins by the price of his death, leading us into paradise, and through the demonstration of so much grace— by which, as he says, "No one has greater love"—he drew back our souls from the will to sin and kindled the highest love of himself.[19]

The discussion of kindling love in humans explicitly links this objective, substitutionary dimension of Abelard's atonement theology to its more infamous exemplarist dimension. Thus, Abelard does grant high theological significance to following Christ's example, but he understands that humans' ability to do so depends utterly on the workings of a grace made possible by Christ's passion, which he even understands as involving a kind of penal substitution.[20]

In the seventeenth century, however, Socinianism affords a more plausible source than Abelard for a moral exemplar theology of atonement.[21] Unlike Milton and the Socinians, Abelard was Trinitarian (albeit still unorthodox), and this further confluence makes the Socinians more likely interlocutors for Milton, who infamously licensed the *Racovian Catechism* for publication.[22] Unlike Abelard, however, Socinians do not affirm an objective dimension of

---

[18] Abelard, *Commentary*, 167–68; *Commentaria*, 117–18 (iii.26): "Redemptio itaque nostra est illa summa in nobis per passionem Christi dilectio quae nos solum a seruitute peccati liberat, sed ueram nobis filiorum Dei liberatem acquirit, ut amore eius potius quam timore cuncta impleamus."

[19] Abelard, *Commentary*, 204; *Commentaria*, 153:

> Duobus modis PROPTER DELICTA NOSTRA mortuus dicitur, tum quia nos deliquimus propter quod ille moreretur et peccatum commisimus cuius ille poenam sustinuit, tum etiam ut peccata nostra moriendo tolleret, id est poenam peccatorum, introducens nos in paradisum, pretio suae mortis auferret et per exhibitionem tantae gratiae, quia ut ipse ait *maiorem dilectionem nemo habet*, animos nostros a uoluntate peccandi retraheret et in summam sui dilectionem incenderet.

[20] See Thomas Williams, "Sin, Grace, and Redemption," in *The Cambridge Companion to Abelard*, ed. Jeffrey E. Brower and Kevin Guilfoy (Cambridge: Cambridge University Press, 2004), pp. 261–63; and Cartwright, in Abelard, *Commentary*, 43–51.

[21] In brief, the Socinian view is that "Christ saved men through his teaching and example, not by atoning for their sins on the cross": Sarah Mortimer, *Reason and Religion in the English Revolution: The Challenge of Socinianism* (Cambridge: Cambridge University Press, 2010), p. 15.

[22] Abelard's first work on the Trinity, *Theologia Summi Boni*, was condemned at the Council of Soissons in 1121. See Jeffrey E. Brower, "Trinity," in Brower and Guilfoy, *The Cambridge Companion to Abelard*, pp. 223–57. On Milton and the *Racovian Catechism*, see Gordon Campbell and Thomas N. Corns, *John Milton: Life, Work, and Thought* (Oxford: Oxford University Press, 2008), pp. 244–48.

176   MILTON'S THEOLOGICAL PROCESS

atonement: "Christ [. . .] saveth the Faithfull in a two-fold way; for first, by his example, he moveth them to persist in the way of Salvation that they have entred into. Next, he standeth by them in every combate of temptations, afflictions, and troubles, and at length delivereth them from Eternall Death."[23] Christ is an example and support, but he is not a redeemer. Satisfaction, the *Catechism* argues, is repugnant to the scriptural witness of God's free forgiveness, and keeping forgiveness free means banishing any objective notion of atonement.[24] Deliverance is not the same as redemption because the latter implies a transaction while the former remains a free act of God.[25] Indeed, the "Bloud, or Death of Christ" functions only to "confirm the Divine will" to humanity, and the *Catechism* goes on to call "fallacious, erroneous, and very pernicious" the idea "that Christ by his death merited Salvation for us, and fully satisfied for our sins."[26] God freely forgives humans, and Christ's role is to restore by his example (especially in the resurrection) the knowledge that humans need if they are to live faithfully.[27]

As we will see, Milton explicitly rejects Socinian atonement theology in *De Doctrina Christiana*. Instead, he advances something like an Abelardian theology that incorporates both satisfactory and exemplary dimensions in a much more systematic way than Abelard's commentary permitted, albeit radically re-inflected by anti-trinitarianism. The Ramist structure of *De Doctrina Christiana* shows the integration of objective and subjective atonement, beginning in I.14, "On Man's restoration, and Christ as redeemer," which subdivides human restoration into redemption and renewal.[28] The topic of redemption occupies I.14–16, while renewal picks up with I.17 and occupies the rest of Book I. Those who argue that Milton espouses penal substitution do so on the basis primarily of I.16 ("On the Pursuance of Redemption") and its recapitulation in I.22 ("On Justification") without fully recognizing its place in the larger project of restoration, which necessitates particular attention to the account of renewal in

---

[23] Valentin Smalcius, *The Racovian Catechism* (Amsterdam, 1652), pp. 122–23 [Samuel Przpkowski, *Catechesis Ecclesiarum quae in Regno Poloniae [. . .] Affirmant* (Racovia [i.e., London], 1651), p. 172]: "Duae ejus rei extitere causae, quemadmodum duplici ratione Christus etiam suos servat. Primùm enim exemplo suo, ut in salutis viâ, quam sunt ingressi, persistant, suos movet: deinde iisdem in omni tentationum, laborum & periculorum certamine adest, opitulatur, & tandem ab ipsâ aeternâ morte liberat."

[24] Smalcius, *Racovian Catechism*, 127 [Przpkowski, *Catechesis Ecclesiarus*, 178].

[25] Smalcius, *Racovian Catechism*, 135 [Przpkowski, *Catechesis Ecclesiarus*, 185–86].

[26] Smalcius, *Racovian Catechism*, 124, 126 [Przpkowski, *Catechesis Ecclesiarus*, 174, 177]: "Quî verò sanguis aut mors Christi nobis voluntatem Dei confirmavit? [. . .] Etsi nunc vulgò Christiani sentiunt, Christum morte suâ nobis salutem meruisse, & pro peccatis nostris plenariè satisfecisse, quae sententia fallax est, & erronea, & admodum perniciosa."

[27] On knowledge and the "way of salvation," see Smalcius, *Racovian Catechism*, 10–13 [Przpkowski, *Catechesis Ecclesiarum*, 14–20].

[28] *DDC*, 183: **"Partes eius sunt redemptio et renovatio."**

THE SON OF GOD AND MILTON'S CHURCH   177

I.17. Understanding Milton's atonement theology (gathered under the heading of "restoration") requires considering redemption and renewal together. At the seam between these two halves of atonement lies the discussion of satisfaction in I.16, which occupies a section (MS 209–16) that was recopied and tipped into the fascicle before receiving its own copious revisions—signs that Milton labored considerably over this topic.[29] At the heart of this added section is a long paragraph, spanning MS 210–15, under the heading "**On behalf of all** [**Pro omnibus**]," that would seem to have been the impetus for the recopying, and it is this section that primarily sets the stage for I.17.

Before that paragraph, however, is one under the heading "**Price on behalf of** [**Pretium pro**]" where Milton explicitly espouses penal substitution while also rejecting aspects of both Reformed and Socinian positions.[30] Quoting the relevant words (forms of λύω, often in conjunction with the preposition or prefix ἀντί), Milton argues that "The Greek [words] plainly signify 'through the substitution of one person for another,'" which shows, on his reading, that external scripture effectively mandates an understanding of atonement by penal substitution.[31] Milton drives this point home by concluding the paragraph (in Picard's fair re-copy, before any additional revisions) with a sentence against Socinian atonement theology: "Those who maintain that Christ faced death not in our place for the purpose of redemption but only for our good and by way of example are vainly trying to evade the evidence of these [scriptural] passages."[32] The paragraph's position on Socinianism becomes more complex, however, when Milton has Amanuensis "B" add the following sentence to the end of the paragraph, via the margin: "At the same time I do admit not seeing how those who claim that the son is of the same essence as the Father can adequately explain either his incarnation or his satisfaction."[33] With this addition, Milton joins the Socinians (among others) in rejecting the Trinity while doing so in service of an atonement theology that Socinians rejected.

Milton does not elaborate in this place on why satisfaction, as he understands it, requires an anti-trinitarian theology of the Son; instead, the explanation appears in a section of I.5 where the Son's work of reconciliation and his

---

[29] See the Appendix, pp. 256–57.

[30] *Pretium* enters this heading through a series of revisions by Amanuensis "B," who adds interlinear citations of 1 Corinthians 6:20 and Romans 5:10 that prompt the change. On Milton's soteriology as Arminian rather than Reformed or Socinian, see Esther van Raamsdonk, *Milton, Marvell, and the Dutch Republic* (London: Routledge, 2020), ch. 5.

[31] *DDC*, 210: "Graeca autem per mutationem unius loco alterius planè significant."

[32] *DDC*, 210: "Quorum locorum evidentiam frustra eludere conantur, qui Christum non nostro loco redemptionis causa, sed nostro tantum bono et velut exempli gratia mortem oppetisse contendunt."

[33] *DDC*, 210: "hoc tamen fateor, me non videre quo pacto qui filium eiusdem cum Patre essentiae esse volunt, eius vel incarnationem, vel satisfactionem possint satis expedire."

178 MILTON'S THEOLOGICAL PROCESS

relationship to the church are recurring themes. There, Milton writes: "[The Son] could not have been a mediator, he could not have been sent by and obedient to the Father, unless he were by nature lesser than God the Father."[34] The relationships of being sent and being obedient both imply the Son's relative and nonreciprocal passivity to the Father. The orthodox might call this an economic subordination resulting from the Father's begetting of the Son, which Milton confuses with an ontological subordination. For Milton, though, satisfaction cannot happen without incarnation, which also creates (in his view) an ontological distinction between the Father and the Son because, as Bauman explains, both incarnation and the death required for satisfaction "separate [the Son] from the Father's immutable *essentia*."[35] To make satisfaction, the Son needed to undergo change and could not therefore be the unchangeable God.[36]

Milton further distinguishes the Son in his redemptive capacity from the Father when he takes up Acts 20:28: "God's church, which he purchased through his own blood." He makes two related points. The first is to dissociate "blood" from "God," using two readings to suggest that the Son is meant instead of the Father: "For that is 'through his own son,' as elsewhere: God does not have blood of his own, and what term is more frequently substituted for 'offspring' than 'blood'?"[37] The Father has blood only metaphorically, in the form of the incarnate Son, with his literal blood. The second point involves using textual criticism to change the referent of "God" from the Father to the Son: "The Syriac version, however, writes not 'God's' but 'Christ's church,' as our recent version writes *the Lord's church*."[38] Cumulatively, Milton uses these variants to

---

[34] *DDC*, 73–74: "At inquam mediator esse non potuit, mitti et obsequi non potuit, nisi natura minor Deo et Patre." See Urban, "John Milton, Paradox, and the Atonement," 835; Bauman, *Milton's Arianism*, 112–20.

[35] Bauman, *Milton's Arianism*, 117. On the Reformed view that the entire Trinity acted in the incarnation, even though the Son alone took on human nature, see *PRRD*, IV.255–74. Milton asserts God's changelessness on MS 14.

[36] On the shifting early modern English understanding of "satisfaction," see Hirschfeld, *The End of Satisfaction*, ch. 1.

[37] See Charles F. DeVine, "The 'Blood of God' in Acts 20:28," *Catholic Bible Quarterly* 9, 4 (1947): 381–408. Thanks to Carl Griffin for pointing me to this source.

[38] *DDC*, 73: "*ecclesiam Dei, quam per proprium sanguinem acquisivit*. Nam id est, per proprium filium, ut alibi: Deus enim propriè sanguinem non habet. et quid frequentius quàm sanguis pro sobole dicitur. verum Syriaca versio non Dei, sed Christi ecclesiam scribit; ut nostra recens *Domini ecclesiam*." Discussion of *nostra recens* begins with Sumner, 114 n. 2. Burgess proposed that "nostra recens" refers to Jeremias Felbinger's *Das Neue Testament* (Amsterdam, 1660), which renders the relevant phrase "di gemeine dess Hern" (corrected from Burgess's quotation; see Felbinger, *Das Neue* Testament, 387), arguing, "Nor has *any* [other] Version of the seventeenth century been yet discovered that has the meaning which is ascribed to it in the Latin Treatise": Thomas Burgess, *Milton Not the Author of the Lately-Discovered Arian Work De Doctrina Christiana* (London, 1829), pp. 30–31. Burgess, p. 57, notes further that the Latin translation of the Syriac in Walton's *Biblia Sacra Polyglotta* ("ecclesiam illam Domino") could be a source for the phrase—a suggestion later repeated by Harris Francis Fletcher, *The Use of the Bible in Milton's Prose* (Urbana, IL: University of Illinois Press, 1929), pp. 86–88 and already current in Burgess's time; see H. J. Todd, *Some Account of the Life and Writings of John Milton* (London,

THE SON OF GOD AND MILTON'S CHURCH   179

associate the church with the incarnate Son rather than the Father, while also allowing that the Son is, on some occasions, the proper referent for the word "God."

This connection between the Son and the church will prove critical for understanding the exemplary dimension of atonement. The long paragraph under the heading "**On behalf of all**" establishes the prospective basis for the church by articulating something akin to Amyraut's hypothetical universalism.[39] A sentence early in the paragraph (partly added via the margin) conveys the thrust of its argument. Drawing on Romans 5:18 ("[through one justification] blessing [has flowed] onto all humankind") and 2 Corinthians 5:14 ([for we determined that] if one man died in behalf of all, then surely all had died"), Milton concludes: "If this follows in logic, then so does its converse, that if all died because Christ died for all, then he also died for all who died, that is, for all universally."[40] Milton is arguing that Christ's penal substitution is at least hypothetically universal in its reach. The limitation on the extent of that act's efficacy comes through calling, as Milton writes in anticipation of his next chapter's arguments:

Certainly, those whom he will judge, he calls to penitence; but he will also judge all individually; therefore he also calls all individually to penitence. But he could not have deemed anyone worthy of the grace of this call if Christ had not interposed his satisfaction, one not only sufficient in itself but also efficacious (so far as this depends on God's will) in relation to all—if indeed his call is a serious one! But the call and the gift are God's province; their acceptance

1826), p. 360. Burgess, however, rejects this suggestion on the grounds that the Latin translation was not recent work but indebted either to Immanuel Tremellius or Gabriel Sionita. Campbell and Brock observe that the references to Syriac in *De Doctrina Christiana* are invariably to Tremellius's translation, which does, indeed, read *ecclesiam Christi* in this place, translating "'i(d)teh damšiḥā [Church of Christ]." They observe the likelihood that Milton's amanuenses, unlike Milton himself, could not read Syriac and were thus dependent on translations. Possibly, then, Milton's scribes mistook the Latin translation in Walton's Polyglot for evidence of a variant reading from the Syriac, leaving the Polyglot as a viable candidate for *nostra recens*: Gordon Campbell and Sebastian P. Brock, "Milton's Syriac," *Milton Quarterly* 27, 2 (1993): 76–77. Thanks to Carl Griffin and Kristian Heal for help with the Syriac and for discussion of this verse from a text-critical perspective.

[39] Seeking an alternative to Miltonic authorship, Paul Sellin finds resonances between the treatise and Amyraut's theology in I.3–4: "'If Not Milton, Who Did Write the *DDC*?': The Amyraldian Connection," in *Living Texts: Interpreting Milton*, ed. Kristin A. Pruitt and Charles W. Durham (Selinsgrove, PA: Susquehanna University Press, 2000), pp. 237–63. The treatise cites Saumur theologians John Cameron (Amyraut's teacher), Josue de la Place (Placaeus), and Louis Cappel (Ludovicus Cappellus) by name; on the treatise's named interlocutors, see John K. Hale, *Milton's Scriptural Theology: Confronting* De Doctrina Christiana (Leeds: Arc Humanities Press, 2019), ch. 5.

[40] *DDC*, 210: "Rom. 5.18. *beneficium in omnes homines.* 2 Cor. 5:15. *si unus pro omnib. mortuus fuit, nempe omnes fuisse mortuos.* id si sequitur, etiam vice versa sequitur, si omnes mortui sunt quia Christus mortuus est pro omnibus, etiam pro omnib. mortuum esse qui mortui sunt; i. e. pro universis." The insertion begins with the citation from 2 Corinthians and continues through an additional citation of Ephesians 1:10.

180 MILTON'S THEOLOGICAL PROCESS

is faith's province; [and] if faith be wanting to the efficacy of the satisfaction, it does not follow that the satisfaction was not given efficaciously but that it was not accepted.[41]

Departing both from Arminianism (which avers double predestination) and Amyraldism (which teaches the predestination only of the elect, who alone accept the universally offered satisfaction), Milton makes the efficacy of satisfaction contingent on a human choice to accept the call.[42]

For Milton, however, the human capacity to choose is itself affected by Christ's satisfaction. Responding to the argument, grounded in Titus 2:14, that salvation applies only to a "special people" and not to all humankind, Milton argues that "'to redeem' is not the same as 'to purify': he has indeed redeemed all transgressors universally, but purifies only those who are desirous of good works, that is, believers; for without faith no works are good."[43] Christ's penal substitution thus brings about redemption for all, with redemption now indicating the renewal in the natural human state that attends the call, as I.17 goes on to argue. But redemption is not the same as purification—the supernatural renewal that is the subject of I.18. In this way, Christ's penal substitution is what makes it possible for humans to engage in the process of sifting and winnowing doctrine that responding to the call entails. Indeed, Milton argues that "without that fullest satisfaction not even the smallest measure of grace could in any way be imparted"—to include the "smallest measure of grace" that renews humans enough to respond to the call but not enough to be purified outright.[44]

Purification, then, relies on a process other than penal substitution, necessary though that is as the foundation for the larger process of restoration. Here,

---

[41] *DDC*, 213:

> Certè quos iudicabit, eos ad poenitentiam vocat; omnes autem et singulos iudicabit; omnes ergo et singulos ad poenitentiam vocat; vocationis autem gratia dignari neminem potuisset, nisi interposita Christi satisfactione, non in se solùm sufficienti verùm etiam ad omnes, quantum in voluntate Dei situm est, efficaci, siquidem seriò vocat. Verùm vocatio et donatio est Dei; acceptio est fidei: quae si satisfactionis efficaciae desit, non idcirco satisfactio efficaciter non est data, sed non accepta.

[42] Amyraut may admit the possibility of double predestination when he allows that scripture gives no other reason than God's free will why the non-elect are left to their condition even as he broadly emphasizes God's choice of the elect amidst the charity of extending grace (hypothetically) to all. "Ni l'Escriture ne nous apprend autre raison de ce chois que Dieu a fait des uns pour leur eslargir le salutaire don de la foy, & de ce qu'il a laissé les autres hommes en arriere en leur condition, que la libre volonté de Dieu": Moyse Amyraut, *Brief Traitté de la Predestination* (Saumur, 1634), p. 111. Amyraut's chapter IX resists taking this point to its double-predestinarian conclusion.

[43] *DDC*, 214: "Respondeo, redimere non est idem ac purificare: redemit universos quidem transgressores; purificat non nisi studiosos bonorum operum, i. e. credentes: sine fide enim nulla opera sunt bona."

[44] *DDC*, 212: "cùm sine ille plenissima satisfactione gratia ne minima quidem ullo modo possit impertiri."

THE SON OF GOD AND MILTON'S CHURCH   181

Milton's stated rejection of Socinian atonement theology—"Those who maintain that Christ faced death not in our place for the purpose of redemption but only for our good and by way of example are vainly trying to evade the evidence of these [scriptural] passages"—comes into perspective.[45] Milton is not denying Christ's exemplary power so much as he is denying that it alone suffices as a model of atonement. Rather, Milton holds that Christ's example can be efficacious in human lives only on the prior basis of penal substitution. If penal substitution brings about redemption, a version of moral exemplar atonement facilitates purification.

Each atonement theology has its place in Milton's structure of salvation [*ordo salutis*], as he makes clear near the end of I.16. Emphasizing the need for a human practice of kenotic (i.e., self-emptying) *imitatio Christi*, Milton argues that "Man's restoration, therefore if we should bear in mind Christ's satisfaction and his moulding us to conform with his emptying out, derives from desert," citing a series of New Testament passages "which proclaim a system of remuneration and reward."[46] The concept of Christ's "moulding us to conform" rescues this theology from Pelagianism, however:

Nor need we fear lest by this reasoning we bring in a doctrine of human merits: for by that moulding of ourselves to him no more is added to Christ's fullest satisfaction than is added by our good works to [our] faith: for faith justifies, yet it is a faith not without works. And if we deserve anything, if we are in any way worthy, it is God who has made us worthy in Christ.[47]

Satisfaction and an attendant monergism make the subsequent *imitatio Christi* possible; the only difference between this view and orthodox Calvinism is Milton's insistence that the *imitatio* becomes possible prior to justification.[48] Thus,

---

[45] *DDC*, 210: "Quorum locorum evidentiam frustra eludere conantur, qui Christum non nostro loco redemptionis causa, sed nostro tantum bono et velut exempli gratia mortem oppetisse contendunt."

[46] *DDC*, 218: "Restitutio itaque hominis, si Christi satisfactionem respiciamus, nostrámque cum eo exinanito conformationem, ex merito est: quo pacto illa intelligenda sunt quae remunerationis et praemii reddendi rationem prae se ferunt." On kenosis, see n. 13 above.

[47] *DDC*, 219:

Nec verendum est, ne hac ratione meritorum nostrorum doctrinam inducamus: ista enim conformatione nostra nihilo plus accedit ad satisfactionem Christi plenissimam, quàm nostris operib. ad fidem: fides enim iustificat, ea tamen fides quae sine operib. non est: et si quid meremur, si qua ratione digni sumus, Deus dignos nos fecit in Christo.

[48] On Milton's monergism (the view that God alone effects human salvation), see further I.22 ("On Justification"): "Nor meanwhile is Christ's satisfaction at all downgraded, both since our faith is imperfect and [since], accordingly, the works of faith can in no other way please God except insofar as they depend on God's mercy and Christ's righteousness, and sustain themselves by that alone [Nec satisfactioni interim Christi quicquam derogatur, cùm et fides nostra imperfecta sit, et proinde opera fidei non

182 MILTON'S THEOLOGICAL PROCESS

he can affirm that "man's restoration derives from pure grace," while also insisting, as Calvin himself did, on the necessity of good works (made possible by the prior action of divine grace) to human moral perfection.[49] Considered apart from what Milton says about satisfaction, his emphasis on *imitatio Christi* might look Socinian, but, read together, his perspectives on satisfaction and *imitatio Christi* instead produce a *sui generis*, quasi-Abelardian cousin of the Reformed theological tradition to which he is responding. A pithier label would be convenient, but part of the point is that pithy labels often prove obstacles rather than aids to understanding theological arguments.

The treatise helps to clarify the part that satisfaction plays in this process of new life and growth. Later in I.21, Milton subdivides growth into "absolute (internal) or relative (external)."[50] Relative or external growth is justification, as the opening sentence of I.22 explains.[51] This subdivision corresponds to that which originally governed the distinction between I.17 (external renewal revised to natural) and I.18 (internal renewal revised to supernatural). This arrangement suggests that satisfaction—a topic that connects I.16 and I.22— serves as the mechanism for the renewal in the natural human state that I.17 establishes as the foundation of the human capacity to accept the offer of salvation or be found without excuse. The internal thus refers to the developmental growth that continues through life as people develop their spiritual gifts. This growth, Milton affirms, derives from God the Father through the Son but requires human cooperation: "Spiritual growth, unlike what happens in physical growth, appears to be partly within the power of the regenerate themselves."[52] Satisfaction makes this growth possible in the first place by giving humans the required capacity, but satisfaction does not eliminate the need for humans to exercise that capacity. Milton had long espoused a human need for such spiritual exercise, from the statement in *An Apology* (1642) that "not only the body, & the mind, but also the improvement of Gods Spirit is quickn'd

---

alia ratione Deo placere queant, nisi quatenus misericordia Dei iustitiáque Christi nituntur, eáque sola se sustinent]." *DDC*, 278–79.

[49] *DDC*, 219: "restitutio hominis est ex mera gratia." Calvin addresses the need for human works (while distinguishing them from the cause of salvation) in John Calvin, *Institutes of the Christian Religion*, ed. John T. McNeill; trans. Ford Lewis Battles (Louisville, KY: Westminster John Knox Press, 1960), Book III.

[50] *DDC*, 264: "Estque ea vel absoluta sive interna vel relata sive externa."

[51] *DDC*, 268: "Fuit auctio regenerati hominis absoluta sive interna: sequitur relata sive externa."

[52] *DDC*, 265: "Spiritualis auctio, contra atque fit in auctione physica aliqua ex parte penes ipsos regeneratos esse videtur." Milton discusses the Father and Son in the two preceding paragraphs.

THE SON OF GOD AND MILTON'S CHURCH   183

by using" such that "overmuch leaning" on liturgy could lead people to "loose even the legs of their devotion" to his inability, in *Areopagitica* (1644), to praise a virtue that is "cloister'd," "unexercis'd," and, in a spiritually resonant word, "unbreath'd."[53]

Using satisfaction to renew human capacities makes it possible for humans to attempt speaking scripture in imitation of Christ. Absent such renewal, any prospective scripture would be merely human and therefore fail to prove scriptural. But neither is renewal so complete as to guarantee that any human's words will become scripture. Rather, renewal opens up a domain of human freedom in which people are capacitated to undertake speaking scripture in imitation of Christ's own freedom. Enabled by satisfaction, humans can begin the process of choosing union with God—of which the ability to speak scripture is one sign—in the same way that Christ himself chooses it.

Human Christ, Divine Power

For Christ's freedom to be meaningfully exemplary for humans, it needs to be a condition of his human as well as his divine nature. Milton argues this position on several fronts, first by holding that both Christ and humans operate outside the sphere of God's absolute decrees, which is to say, in a condition of freedom.[54] He strengthens his case further in his insistence that Christ fully and freely enters into the condition of humanity while retaining his divine nature—a matter that he takes up in I.14, "On Man's restoration, and Christ as redeemer."[55] Christ's exemplary potential depends on his humanity, and his participation in the divine nature raises the crucial issue of divine attributes that occupies Milton at such great length in I.5. He expresses the difficulty of articulating the relationship between the two natures by referencing, in I.14, the Theologians' declaration that the incarnation is "far the greatest mystery of our religion after

---

[53] John Milton, *An Apology against a Pamphlet* (London, 1642), p. 48; *Areopagitica* (London, 1642), p. 12.

[54] On human freedom and the decree, see Benjamin Myers, *Milton's Theology of Freedom* (Berlin: Walter de Gruyter, 2006), pp. 47–52. Michael Bryson discusses *imitatio Christi* in *The Tyranny of Heaven: Milton's Rejection of God as King* (Newark, DE: University of Delaware Press, 2004), ch. 5, but insufficient attention to the gap between renewed human capacities and the capacities of the human Son renders his reading of *imitatio Christi* too Pelagian.

[55] *DDC*, 183: "De Hominis restitutione et Christo redemptore." On the two natures, see, briefly, Arthur Sewell, A Study in Milton's Christian Doctrine (London: Oxford University Press, 1939), pp. 121–22. My argument requires a closer engagement than Sewell's.

184   MILTON'S THEOLOGICAL PROCESS

[the mystery] of the three persons [existing] in a single essence of God."[56] He goes on, however, to insist that only the incarnation can be held as a mystery on scriptural grounds: "But concerning the mystery of the trinity absolutely no word exists in sacred scripture: meanwhile this incarnation *is* quite often [in Scripture] called a mystery," citing 1 Timothy 3:16 and several other places.[57] Milton follows the scriptural citations with a florid paragraph warning against affirming anything about the incarnation too rashly: for example, "How many enormous tomes of Theologasters shall we throw out from God's temple like pollutants and dust-heaps!".[58] By his own admission, Milton can only affirm, but not fully explain, how the theological pieces fit together, how exactly the humanity that makes Christ imitable by humans comports with the divinity that unites him with God (if not essentially), or how exactly Christ's human imitability (even if facilitated by satisfaction-driven renewal) translates into the possibility of humans attaining the kind of union with God that might enable them to speak scripture. The mystery of the incarnation is the gravitational center of Milton's approach to Christian doctrine, the black hole around which his theological galaxy orbits.

Fools rush in where Milton fears to tread. Nevertheless, he does say enough about the two natures to show how this doctrine serves as a bridge connecting Christ's free union with the Father to the prospect of humans freely finding union with the Father in Christ—the prospect residing in the possibility of speaking scripture. Crucially, Milton insists that the mystery must include Christ's becoming fully human. He responds with mockery to Zanchius's remarks that "Properly speaking, he took upon him human nature, not man"

---

[56] *DDC*, 187–88: "Incarnationem autem hanc Christi, qua is, Deus cùm esset, humanam naturam assumpsit, caroque factus est, nec tamen unus numero Christus idcirco esse desinit, mysterium religionis nostrae longè maximum esse, post illud trium personarum in una Dei essentia, statuunt Theologi." As the source behind "the Theologians," Yale, 420 n. 19, cites *Leiden Synopsis*, XXV, 2, citing, in turn, Heinrich Heppe, *Reformed Dogmatics*, a.k.a. Schriften zur reformirten Theologie (Elberfield: R. L. Friderichs, 1860). Here is the Latin:

> Hoc mysterium, post illud de S. S. Trinitate, trium scilicet in una essentia personarum, quo tres personae realiter inter se distinctae unam eandemque essentiam habent, & in una numero essentia uniuntur, summum est: quo quidem duae perfectae naturae in una persona Filii Dei uniuntur: unde Apostolus hoc mysterium, *quod Deus manifestatus est in carne, magnum pietatis mysterium* appellat, 1 *ad Timotheum* 3.16.

Johannes Poliandrus, Andreas Rivetus, Antonius Walaeus, and Antonius Thysius, *Synopsis Purioris Theologiae*, 3rd edn (Leiden, 1642), p. 294. On the limitations of Heppe as a source for a reliable historical understanding of Reformed theology, see *PRRD*, I.130–31. *Ad fontes*, as the saying goes.

[57] *DDC*, 188: "Verùm de mysterio triadis verbum in scriptura sacra extat omninò nullum: incarnatio haec interim haud rarò mysterium nominatur."

[58] *DDC*, 188: "quot immensa volumina Theologastorum ex Dei templo velut inquinamenta ac rudera eiiciemus!"

THE SON OF GOD AND MILTON'S CHURCH   185

and that "the Logos, when existing in the virgin's womb, took human nature for itself":

> I omit the fact that these secrets exist nowhere in scripture, and yet they are no less boldly handed down than if he who dares to hand them down on his own assurance had himself been present in Mary's womb at this mystery— as if indeed someone who takes on human nature would not also take on man![59]

Milton has no patience for the view that understanding Christ as fully human might somehow derogate from or prove incompatible with his being also fully divine.[60] The mystery is that these two things cohere—and Milton also has no patience for the metaphysical terminology ("subsistence," "persona") often used to explain it, although he will use "hypostatic union" (no doubt due to the fact that the Greek word ὑπόστασις appears several times in the New Testament).[61] Rather than probe too nearly into how that union works, Milton firmly holds that a fully human Christ can also participate in the divine nature, maintaining the compatibility of his view with the hypostatic union against Zanchius's association of it with the Nestorian belief in two distinct natures.[62] Echoing the prologue to John, he concludes: "How much better it is, therefore, to know only this: that our Mediator, the son of God, was made flesh; that he is called, and is, both God and man, he whom for that reason the Greeks in a single word most aptly call Θεάνθρωπον."[63] The mystery lies less in how God could become human than in how a human could also be God. Incarnational

---

[59] *DDC*, 189:

> *Assumpsit humanam naturam*, inquit, *non hominem proprie loquendo. Nam λόγος in utero virginis existens, humanam naturam sibi ipse* [. . .] *assumpsit* [. . .] Mitto quod haec arcana nusquam in scriptura, nec minus tamen audacter sunt tradita quàm si in utero Mariae ipse huic mysterio interfuisset qui haec sua fide tradere audeat: Quasi verò qui naturam humanam assumit, non hominem quoque assumat.

[60] Milton disagrees with the Socinian rejection of a divine nature in Christ as "repugnant not onely to sound Reason, but also to the holy Scriptures [Nam id non solùm rationi sanae, verùm etiam divinis literis repugnat]." Smalcius, *Racovian Catechism*, 28 [Przpkowski, *Catechesis Ecclesiarum*, 40].

[61] See 2 Corinthians 9:4, 11:17; Hebrews 1:3, 3:14, and 11:1. For the Christological usage, the most relevant of these by far is Hebrews 1:3, which describes the Son as "χαρακτὴρ τῆς ὑποστάσεως αὐτῶ" (KJV: "the expresse image of his [i.e., God's] person"). Theodore Beza [*New Testament*] (Geneva, 1598) renders this phrase as "character personae illius." Milton cites this verse in support of his own definition: *DDC*, 13.

[62] Just prior to the passage that Milton quotes, Girolamo Zanchi writes, "Hoc autem haereticum est dicere, est enim haeresis Nestorij": *Operum Theologicorum* (Geneva, 1619), Vol. I, p. 416 (tom. I, Part 2, l. 2, c. vii).

[63] *DDC*, 192: "Quanto satius est igitur scire hoc tantum, Mediatorem nostrum Dei filium carnem esse factum, Deum atque hominem et dici et esse, quem idcirco Graeci uno verbo aptissimè Θεάνθρωπον

186 MILTON'S THEOLOGICAL PROCESS

theology tends, understandably, to assume a hierarchical relationship between God and humans such that the bridge across the gap begins on God's side, in keeping with the account of *kenosis* in Philippians 2.[64] If the Father's begetting means anything at all, that mystery remains operative, and yet Milton's removing the Son from coessentiality with God means that the incarnation also includes beginning the bridge from the human side—a counterintuitive proposition, given both the Neoplatonic hierarchy itself and the Reformed tendency toward Augustinian assumptions that the chasm, from the human side, is unbridgeably vast. Hence the mystery.

For Milton, the doctrine of Christ's two natures also means that Christ must be one with the Father in a way other than essence, and this fact has ramifications for how Christ carries out his role as mediator. If the Son's essence were the same as the Father's, Milton writes, "it could not coalesce into one person with man without the Father also being contained in the same union— without man, too, becoming one person with the Father, just as with the son, which is impossible."[65] By this logic, essential unity with the Father would prevent Christ from being a mediator because his hypostatic union with humanity would bring humanity into essential union with the Father. Instead of combining three persons (or more if humanity gets included) into one essence (which is impossible, as Milton insists at great length in I.5), two essences combine in one person through the incarnation, "by which although he was God he took on human nature and was made flesh, and yet does not for that reason cease to remain numerically one."[66] Milton has posited a Christ who is essentially distinct from God and yet participates in the divine nature, even as he is human. Reading Colossians 2:9 ("in him dwells all the fullness of Deity corporeally"), Milton avers, "in which passage I would understand, not Christ's divine nature, but the comprehensive power of the father, [and understand] that the full completion (rather than 'fullness') of his promises dwells in Christ as man, [but]

---

vocant." I have substituted the Greek in the translation for Oxford's transliteration and translation, "God-man."

[64] Athanasius grounds the ontological distance on the doctrine of creation *ex nihilo*: *On the Incarnation*, trans. John Behr (Yonkers, NY: St Vladimir's Seminary Press, 2011), ch. 5 and *passim*. Cyril of Alexandria quotes Philippians 2 relentlessly in *On the Unity of Christ*, trans. John Anthony McGuckin (Yonkers, NY: St Vladimir's Seminary Press, 1995), pp. 55 and *passim*.

[65] *DDC*, 192: "eadem si esset, in unam personam cum homine coalescere non posset, quin pater etiam eadem unione contineretur, quin homo quoque eadem persona cum Patre haud secus atque cum filio fieret, quod impossibile est."

[66] *DDC*, 187: "Incarnationem autem hanc Christi, qua is, Deus cùm esset, humanam naturam assumpsit, caroque factus est, nec tamen unus numero Christus idcirco esse desinit."

THE SON OF GOD AND MILTON'S CHURCH   187

is not, as people say, 'hypostatically joined to him as man.'"[67] Christ possesses "the comprehensive [*omnimodam*] power of the Father" while also being fully human.

United in Love and Speaking

Milton's insistence in Christ's full humanity enables Christ to serve as the model for human ecclesial activity, in which humans attempt to speak divine truths. The mystery of incarnation consists in how exactly Christ possesses divine power as a human—in I.5, Milton writes that "religion's supreme mystery is not Christ, but God the father in Christ"—and this mystery involves a complex interplay of freedom between the Father and the Son.[68] That interplay, in turn, informs the human freedom that makes speaking scripture possible. The Son's participation in the divine nature involves both his being sent by God and his obedience, as Milton argued in I.5 by way of insisting on his subordination: "he could not have been a mediator, he could not have been sent by and obedient to the Father, unless he were by nature lesser than God the Father."[69] The sending locates agency with the Father: Christ did not commission himself. Writing in I.14 of the accomplishment entailed in redemption, Milton avers "that these things can be done by him to whom God granted them; that is, by God's beloved son, with whom God has declared himself well pleased."[70] Christ could not perform redemption by his own merits because only God could do that, but God granted him the power, and he freely performed as requested. This arrangement preserves God's supremacy and free will by making redemptive power originate in the Father alone.

Christ, meanwhile, freely and obediently performs what God has empowered and commissioned him to do, and the power of his example for humanity consists in this combination of freedom and obedience. Christ's obedience matters not because it merits the trust that the Father has placed in the Son but because the Father is "well pleased" when people put his gifts to good use. Neither is this obedience purely a product of the divine nature: "If, finally, he is *blessed*, he received even blessing and divine honour as a man no less than

---

[67] *DDC*, 187: "Col. 2. 9. *in eo inhabitat omnis plenitudo Deitatis corporaliter*, hoc loco, non divinam Christi naturam, sed omnimodam virtutem patris, omnem impletionem potius quàm plenitudinem promissorum eius habitare, non hypostaticè uniri, quod aiunt, Christo homini."

[68] *DDC*, 74: "summum enim pietatis mysterium non est Christus, sed Deus pater in Christo."

[69] *DDC*, 73–74: "At inquam mediator esse non potuit, mitti et obsequi non potuit, nisi natura minor Deo et Patre."

[70] *DDC*, 193: "ab eo cui Deus haec dedit posse; id est, à Deo filio dilecto, in quo complacuisse sibi testatus est."

188 MILTON'S THEOLOGICAL PROCESS

as God: Rev. 5:12: *worthy is that slain lamb to receive power and riches and strength and honour and glory and blessing.*"[71] The full participation of Christ's human nature ensures his freedom for if the divine nature, having been given from God, acted alone, Christ would be a mere vessel, and God would be pleased in himself, not in Christ. Much like humans receive divine renewal that creates an opportunity to obey or not, Christ's divine commission demands his own free response. Christ does not, of course, stand in need of an atoning satisfaction in the same way that humans do, but even in Christ's case, Milton refuses the Pelagian (or Socinian) option of an innate capacity for self-elevation.[72] The sinless Christ still required divine power and a divine commission to become the Redeemer, and even in those elevated tasks, his human obedience had a part to play.

This careful balancing of divine and human wills, both in Christ's mediatorial work and in the human response to it, opens the way to understanding how Milton articulates the relationship between obedience and unity with God. In Christ, Milton posits a being who is fully human and yet possessed of the divine nature to the point of being one with the Father (just not in essence). In this being resides the possibility of humans themselves entering into union with the Father, mediated by Christ and his act of penal substitution, which Milton succinctly expresses in I.16: "The effect and end-purpose of the whole mediatorial pursuance [of redemption] is the satisfaction of divine justice on behalf of all, and the moulding of the faithful to the image of Christ."[73] As discussed above, this "moulding of the faithful to the image of Christ" suggests that Christ's unity with the Father provides an analogy for the possibility of human unity with God along the lines promised in John 17—only analogy because human obedience requires Christ's mediation, whereas Christ receives empowerment to obey directly from God.

For both Christ and humans, unity with God can only come through free obedience, not through any kind of divinely imposed necessity. Milton's concept of free obedience draws on the paradoxical notion of "slaves to God" in Romans 6, which presents a picture of union so thoroughgoing that it might appear like slavish following while yet being utterly free, the product of liberation from bondage to sin. For the Son, this freedom is less from the bondage

---

[71] *DDC*, 74: "*benedictus* denique si est, benedictionem etiam tam ut homo quàm ut Deus, divinumque honorem accepit: Apoc. 5. 12. *dignus est agnus ille mactatus, qui accipiat potestatem et divitias et vires et honorem et gloriam et benedictionem.*"

[72] On Socinian theological anthropology, see Mortimer, *Reason and Religion*, 15–19 and *passim*.

[73] *DDC*, 209: "Effectum et finis totius administrationis mediatoriae est divinae iustitiae pro omnibus satisfactio, et fidelium ad imaginem Christi conformatio."

THE SON OF GOD AND MILTON'S CHURCH   189

to sin than from the bondage to necessity, and Milton effects this liberation with his theology of the decree. Indeed, Milton is at some pains to reconcile the concept of divine decree with freedom. He begins with God the Father: "God's general decree is that by which **God decreed from eternity, with absolute freedom and wisdom and holiness, all things which he willed, or else which he was going to do.**"[74] Building on Ephesians 1:11 ("who does all things according to the purpose of his own will"), Milton argues that God is "not compelled, not driven by any necessity, but just as he willed," indicating independence from the influence of any other will.[75] God's investment in the freedom of others, in turn, requires a (freely chosen) limitation on the extent of such absolute decrees: "We must therefore conclude that God did not decree anything absolutely which he left in the power of free agents: the whole course of scripture shows this."[76] Milton's phrase "the whole course of scripture" indicates that he understands a strict separation between God's absolute decrees and the power of free agents as a core component of the rule of faith. In these terms, although the Hanau/Geneva JTB rendering of Psalm 2:7 might have provided the impulsive cause for moving the Son outside the realm of God's absolute, eternal decree, that verse might also simply have been the means of developing what Milton saw as a much broader pattern of scriptural teaching to its conclusions. In any case, the Son's relationship to the Father's absolute decree puts him alongside humanity in the world of things "which [God] left in the power of free agents," his freely performed redemption operating alongside a purification that comes to humans only "willingly and through faith."[77]

Unlike humans, however, the Son experiences unity with God to such a degree that the divine attributes are manifest in him, if not attributable in any way to him, as Milton argues at length in I.5.[78] In this way, I.5 maintains the Father's freedom (his independence from any other will), while not having much to say about the Son's freedom. Even so, the pattern established in the discussion of divine decree continues there as Milton draws on the Gospel accounts of the Son's limited knowledge (Matthew 24:26 and Mark 13:32) to

---

[74] *DDC*, 18: "Generale est quo **Deus omnia ab aeterno quae quidem volebat aut facturus ipse erat, liberrimè, sapientissimè, sanctissimèque decrevit.**"

[75] *DDC*, 18: "Eph. 1. 11. *qui agit omnia ex consilio voluntatis suae* [...] non coactus, nulla necessitate impulsus, sed prout voluit."

[76] *DDC*, 19: "Nihil itaque Deus decrevisse absolutè censendus est quod in potestate liberè agentium reliquit: id quod scripturae totius series ostendit."

[77] *DDC*, 214: "purificatus nemo nisi volens et per fidem."

[78] Compare Smith, "Milton's Theology of the Cross," 11.

190 MILTON'S THEOLOGICAL PROCESS

argue "that Father and Son do not in a numerical sense have the same intelligence or will."[79] From the Father's side, this position merely confirms Milton's earlier interpretation of the statement in Ephesians 1:11 that God "does all things according to the purpose of his own will" as "meaning certainly what he himself alone does, and wills, not what any others do, nor what he does along with those to whom he has granted the nature and power of free agency."[80] The Father's essential independence of will requires that the Son's will can make no claim on him. Indeed, Milton makes the point that even when any free agent (including the Son) acts alongside the Father, the apparent confluence neither implies any influence on the divine will nor any influence of the divine will on others. The Father's freedom and the freedom of "those to whom he left the nature and power of free will" at least have the potential to operate in mutually non-coercive parallel.

To the extent that I.5 does offer a positive theology of the Son, it is that he, both because he does not share the Father's essence and almost in spite of it, can freely operate in this kind of parallel with the Father. As such, the Son models the proper exercise of freedom for humans, having renewed the human capacity for freedom through his act of penal substitution and the subsequent call. This kind of parallel operation does not entail full participation in the attributes of the person being followed: just as the Son does not thereby acquire the Father's knowledge of "the day and the hour," so neither do humans presumably gain access to aspects of the Son like his mediatorial office. This exclusivity and freedom from encroachment by divine necessity is what it means for a being to be possessed of a distinct *ens* or being. Significantly, even humans are free from divine encroachment in this way:

> Accordingly, all necessity must be removed from our freedom, nor even must that shadowy and external necessity based on immutability or prescience be admitted to the discussion. If any necessity remains, then as I said earlier it either determines free agents to a single course of action or else compels them against their will or else assists them when willing or else does nothing.[81]

---

[79] *DDC*, 64: "At nec intellectum nec voluntatem numero eandem esse Patris et Filii, multis ex locis docetur."

[80] *DDC*, 18: "Eph. 1. 11. *qui agit omnia ex consilio voluntatis suae.* nimirum quae ipse quidem solus agit, et vult; non quae agunt caeteri omnes, aut ipse cum iis quibus liberè agendi naturam ac potestatem concessit." Sumner, Yale, and Oxford translate "cum iis" with variations on "in cooperation with." Milton's Latin in this clause is compressed, implying the verb, but "with those" does not necessarily imply a theology of cooperation per se.

[81] *DDC*, 21–22: "Omnis igitur a libertate necessitas removenda est; et ne illa quidem immutabilitatis aut praescientiae umbratica et externa admittenda. Si ulla manet necessitas, ut suprà dixi, aut liberos determinat ad hoc unum, aut nolentes cogit, aut volentes adiuvat, aut agit nihil."

THE SON OF GOD AND MILTON'S CHURCH   191

This refusal of divine encroachment protects humans from being "created with a propensity for sinning" and protects God from the consequence that humans will be "the cause of [their] sins only *per accidens*, God being the cause of the sins *per se*."[82] Milton's language for God's action concerning free agents suggests a kind of retreat or withdrawal: *concessit* on MS 18 and *reliquit* on MS 19. Freedom begins as *freedom from* and only gradually becomes *freedom to* under the influence of renewal, which develops the capacity for freedom without determining how people will use it. The Son, then, acting outside the pale of the divine essence, freely uses his capacities to live in such a way that others—in spite of his own protestations (at least per Milton)—might mistakenly arrive at the impression that he possesses the divine attributes in his own right instead of holding them as gifts from God.

Milton does not think that humans are able to reproduce the Son's whole-life obedience on their own. Renewal, regeneration, justification, and the rest would not be part of his theological system if he did. Indeed, the imperfections of human theological systems themselves arise from humanity's limited capacities. As such, the Son provides a bridge of sorts between the archetypal theology that God alone can know (capital-T Truth) and the ectypal theology that is the knowledge of divine things as accommodated to human capacities. In Milton's version of this traditional distinction (he does not use the words themselves), the Father alone has access to archetypal theology and the Son approximates it as well as any being who is essentially distinct from God could do.[83] Humans, who join the Son in the ectypal practice of *theologia viatorum*, are pilgrims whose renewed capacities enable them to grow in their understanding and practice of divine things, in the manner modeled by the Son, who represents the nearest that ectypal theology can approach to archetypal.

A model for how humans might approach divine truth thus appears in Milton's discussion of the Son's unity with the Father as he attends to a passage alleged on behalf of Trinitarianism: John 10:30, "I and the father are one."[84] Looking to the context of this verse, Milton argues for the Father's supremacy on the basis of verse 29 ("greater than all [*maior omnibus est*]"), alongside John 14:28 ("greater than I [*maior me est*]") before positing forms of unity besides

---

[82] *DDC*, 22: "quasi in propensione ad peccandum conditus: si nolentes cogit, reddetur homo sub illa decreti coactione causa peccatorum tantùm per accidens, Deus causa per se."

[83] Muller characterizes the Reformed orthodox view. "Ectypal theology *in se* is, thus, the ideal case of communicated theology, the accommodated form or mode of the archetype readied in the mind of God for communication to a particular kind of subject, namely, Christ, the blessed, or the redeemed on earth": *PRRD*, I.235. Milton puts greater emphasis on Christ as the medium whereby God communicates ectypal theology to rational creatures. Compare Amandus Polanus, *Syntagma Theologiae Christianae* (Hanover, 1609), pp. 9–14 (I.iii–iv).

[84] *DDC*, 58: "Ioan. 10. 30. *ego et pater unum sumus*."

192   MILTON'S THEOLOGICAL PROCESS

the essential. The first form is speaking "because they merely speak one thing, do one thing."[85] This, Milton claims, Jesus articulates in John 10:38, "believe the works, so that you may know and believe that the Father is in me, and I in him," along with 14:10: "do you not believe that I am in the Father and the Father in me? The words which I speak to you I do not speak of myself; but the Father who remains in me, he himself is performing the works."[86] From these passages, Milton concludes: "Here he evidently distinguishes the Father from his whole self, but says that the Father does indeed remain in him; which declares not that their essence is one, but merely that their communion is very close."[87] The form of this close communion is speaking the same words, and this, in practice, is what it means for the Father to remain in the Son. In these terms, doctrinal purity is itself a kind of communion with God as one bodily speaks words not one's own. Indeed, Jesus deflects the potential accrual of authority to himself in just this way by crediting the Father with the words that he speaks. This deflection might give the appearance of essential unity, but Milton insists that it is only an appearance, the effect of misreading Jesus's humility.

Milton's refusal of Jesus's essential unity with the Father enables it to become a model for human unity with both. Quoting John 14:20–21 and 17:21–23, Milton avers that Jesus "declares that he and the Father are one in the same way that we are one with him, and that is definitely not in essence, but in love, in communion, in agreement, in charity, in spirit, and finally in glory."[88] This sequence charts a process of attaining progressively greater degrees of unity. This sense of progress appears in the list's inclusion of two related terms: love [*dilectione*] and charity [*charitate*]. Milton's understanding of how these terms relate to each other appears in his discussion of Christian liberty in I.27. Arguing that "the whole Mosaic law is abolished through the Gospel," Milton asserts, however, that the law's "actual fact [*re vera*]" and "summation [*summa*]" is not abrogated "but achieves its purpose in that love [*dilectione*] of God and one's neighbour."[89] Shortly thereafter, Milton connects this *summa* to interpretation, saying that literal interpretation is not warranted "if by not maintaining the letter we shall

[85] DDC, 58: "quia unum loquuntur, unum agunt."

[86] DDC, 59: "v. 38. operibus credite, ut cognoscatis et credatis Patrem in me esse, et me in eo. Sic cap. 14. 10. non credis me in Patre et Patrem in me esse? verba quae ego loquor vobis, à meipso non loquor; sed Pater qui in me manet, ipse facit opera."

[87] DDC, 59: "hîc Patrem a seipso toto evidenter distinguit, sed Patrem in se manere quidem ait; quod non essentiam eorum unam sed communionem tantum arctissimam declarat."

[88] DDC, 59: "Secundò, declarat se et Patrem esse unum quo modo nos cum eo unum sumus: id utique non est essentia, sed dilectione, communione, consensu, charitate, animo, gloria denique."

[89] DDC, 327: "totam legem Mosaicam per Evangelium aboleri [. . .] sed finem suum assequitur in dilectione illa Dei et proximi."

THE SON OF GOD AND MILTON'S CHURCH   193

more rightly show regard for love [*dilectioni*] of God and our neighbour."[90] Milton then elevates this practice of consultation into a principle, which he calls the "account taken of charity [*ratio habita charitatis*]" that interpretation of commandments about the sabbath and marriage requires.[91] Love [*dilectio*] is the action that fulfills the law, and charity [*charitas*] is the name for the framework, encompassing both love and law, within which this fulfillment can be understood.

Communion and consensus function as steps in the progression from love (action) to charity (principle). Writing in I.24, "On Union and communion with Christ and his members," Milton quotes John 14:23 as his second reference developing the idea of "that union and communion": "if anyone loves me, he will keep my word, and my father will love him, and we shall come to him and dwell with him."[92] The starting-point is love, evidenced by two appearances of *diligo*. Later in this sequence of scriptures, Milton quotes 1 John 1:3, 6, and 7, which treats communion less as a state of being than a manner of action:

> *and may our communion be with the father and with his son Jesus Christ: if we should say that we have communion with him, and [yet] walk in darkness, we are lying and not acting honestly. But if we walk in the light, just as he is in the light, we have mutual communion with him[.]*[93]

The focus is on sincerity of action, manifest in a collective walk with Christ rather than orthodoxy of belief. Again, "just as [*sicut*]" denotes that human walking in light merely figures divine being in light: communion is not literal or essential union.

Milton's term for this collective walk with Christ is "consensus [*consensu*, rendered 'agreement' by Oxford]," which refers to a unity in the action of professing belief or testifying, not necessarily to a unity of testimonial substance. In the paragraph following the one where Milton lists the modes of divine unity, he attacks the infamous Johannine comma (1 John 5:7), a verse that offered perhaps the strongest biblical support for the Trinity but which

[90] *DDC*, 328: "si literam non retinendo rectius dilectioni Dei et proximi consulemus."

[91] *DDC*, 329. On Milton's "rule of charity" in relation to Augustine's, see James B. Potts, Jr, "Milton and Augustine: The Rule of Charity," *Explorations in Renaissance Culture* 16 (1990): 101–10.

[92] *DDC*, 287: "de Unione et communione cum Christo eiúsque membris"; "Unio ista et communio"; "*si quis diligit me, sermonem meum servabit, et pater meus diliget eum, et ad eum veniemus, et apud eum habitabimus.*"

[93] *DDC*, 287–88: "*et communio nostra sit cum patre et cum filio eius Iesu Christo: si dixerimus nos communionem habere cum eo, et in tenebris ambulamus mentimur, nec sincerè agimus. Quòd si in luce ambulamus, sicut ipse est in luce, communionem habemus cum eo mutuam.*" Milton's rendering accords with Beza. The Vulgate uses "societatem" throughout instead of "communionem," meaning that Milton's choice of Beza works to further his point.

194   MILTON'S THEOLOGICAL PROCESS

manuscript evidence revealed to be a late interpolation. He writes that this verse, even if it must be accepted, attests only to "unity of agreement [*consensûs*] and testimony" or, in other words, "one witnessing of three witnesses, one testimony."[94] The divine persons, therefore, are united through the activity of testifying, and people can be united with them in the same way. Communion, or dwelling in God through the activity of Christian profession, leads naturally to consensus or walking with God through collective action. In this context, "consensus" refers simply to this unity of action and need not extend to the content of the testimonies produced thereby. Indeed, this very possibility— that essential difference can nevertheless conduce to unified action—lies at the heart of Milton's thinking about the godhead and of his insistence that people can be united "just as" the divine persons are. This model of unity in the act of professing is the substance of Milton's addressing the treatise "**To all the churches of Christ**, and also to all who profess the Christian faith anywhere among the peoples."[95] Charity crowns Milton's list of the modes for bringing difference into a harmonious unity "in spirit and glory [*anima gloria denique*]."

If the Son attains a unity of professing with the Father, the prospect of human unity with Father and Son is ecclesial in nature. Christ's mediation enables the robust debate that characterizes Milton's concept of the church to develop towards a unity of profession. This mediation hinges on the interrelated principles of non-coercion and charity. In I.15 ("On the Mediatorial Office"), Milton insists that "**Christ, made king by God the father, rules and preserves the church gained by him, principally by internal law and spiritual power**," going on to emphasize that Christ's rule, unlike that of human magistrates, is non-coercive:

> seeing indeed that he rules not only bodies, as the civil magistrate does, but above all else mind and conscience; and that not by force and bodily arms but by those things which in the world's judgment are weakest. Wherefore also all external coercion must be absent from the kingdom of Christ, which is the church.[96]

---

[94] *DDC*, 59–60: "unitate consensûs et testmonii"; "una trium testium testificatio, unum testimonium." On Milton and the Johannine comma, see Grantley McDonald, *Biblical Criticism in Early Modern Europe: Erasmus, the Johannine Comma and Trinitarian Debate* (Cambridge: Cambridge University Press, 2016), pp. 134–36. See further Chapter 1 n. 56.

[95] *DDC*, 1: "**Universis Christi Ecclesiis**, nec non omnibus Fidem Christianam ubicunque Gentium profitentibus."

[96] *DDC*, 202–03:

> **Christus à Deo patre rex creatus acquisitam ab se ecclesiam interna potissimum lege ac spirituali potestate regit atque conservat** [. . .] quandoquidem non corpora solùm, ut

THE SON OF GOD AND MILTON'S CHURCH   195

Christ himself models this freedom from coercion in his assumption of the mediatorial office "**Willingly**," a point Milton establishes by quoting scriptural passages about love (*dilectione* or *charitate*): "John 15: 19: *just as the father has loved [dilexit] me, so too have I loved you*; Rom. 8: 35: *who shall separate us from the love [dilectione] of Christ? shall the sword, [. . .]?*; Eph. 3: 18–19: *that love [charitatem] of Christ's which towers above all knowledge.*"[97] In this vision of the church, unity comes about through practices of uncoerced love, with Christ as the chief exemplar. He does not become the mediator out of necessity born from ontological unity with God; rather, his union with God and the unity with and among humans that he hopes to effect both arise from his freely chosen love.[98]

In the context of Milton's social Trinitarianism, the ontological dimension of his attempts to speak scripture at last comes into view. The last sentence of the epistle admits of an uncertainty for which the rest of the treatise provides little or no evidence:

> For the rest, my brothers, cultivate the truth with charity; judge of this writing according to the spirit of God guiding you; use it with me, or indeed do not use it, unless I have persuaded you with full conviction by the clarity of the Bible; last of all, live and thrive in Christ our Saviour and Lord.[99]

Milton acknowledges that his strenuous efforts both to marshal the witness of external scripture and to give voice to the internal scripture might have been less than persuasive. He admits that he could be wrong, and he commits his writing to the collective judgment of the universal churches of Christ, with a call to "cultivate the truth with charity." This combination of an acknowledged potential for error and collective ecclesial charity undergirds the human hope for unity with God in Christ—and, in this sense, the final clause, with its call to live and thrive in Christ, is not mere quasi-Pauline boilerplate. For Milton,

---

magistratus civilis, sed animum maxime et conscientiam regit: idque non vi et armis corporeis sed iis rebus quae mundi iudicio infirmissimae sunt. quapropter et vis omnis externa ab regno Christi, quae est ecclesia, abesse debet.

[97] *DDC*, 198: "**Libens**. Ioann. 15. 9; *prout dilexit me pater, ita et ego dilexi vos*. Rom. 8. 35; *quis nos separabit à dilectione Christi? num gladius,—?* Eph. 3. 18. 19; *charitatem illam Christi omni notitia supereminemtiorem.*"

[98] Milton's definition of Christ's kingship concludes with "**[and] conquers and subdues his enemies**" but relegates this act to the eschaton (see the inserted "namely at the second coming" appended to his quotation of Psalm 2:9, "you will smash them with an iron rod"). *DDC*, 204: "**Hostes vincit atque debellat**. Psal. 2. 9. &c; *confringes istos virgâ ferreâ*. secundo nempe adventu."

[99] *DDC*, 5: "De caetero, fratres, veritatem colite cum charitate; de his, prout Dei spiritus vobis praeiverit, ita iudicate: his mecum utimini, vel ne utimini quidem, nisi fide non dubia scripturarumque claritate persuasi; in Christo denique Servatore ac Domino vivite ac valete."

imitatio Christi, and the unity with Christ to which it leads, is not ultimately an individual affair.

The practical question, though, is how individuals participate in this collective enterprise. For Milton, it means speaking the truth (at least as well has he can work it out) with supreme confidence, even bluster. But his well-documented ego is only half the picture, and this is where ontology comes in.[100] Humility plays an indispensable role in Milton's theology, but he outsources humility to the ecclesial structure in which he participates. A commitment to humility, in the sense of delivering his ideas to a collective judgment that might find them wanting, operates in tandem with a robust mode of expression that does not appear humble in the least. Consequently, Milton's practice can seem to convey a higher view of human capacities than a careful reading of his theology will support. The theology of renewal articulated in I.17 makes grace the cause of human capacity, but this theology also obliges him to exercise his particular gifts as robustly as possible and then commit the products to the churn of collective debate and discussion, out of which the truth will—he hopes—emerge. And when that truth emerges, then the church as a whole will participate in the Son's unity of profession with the Father.

This structural humility is why noting Milton's heresies, while factual in a sense, misses the mark. As Tobias Gregory has argued, Milton continues to hold a pejorative view of heresy even as he redefines the term, for example, in the "heretick in the truth" passage of *Areopagitica*.[101] Milton does not desire to be a heretic; he wants to espouse divine truth. Instead of opposing himself to heresy outright, though, he understands it instrumentally, not only as an inevitable byproduct of the human quest for truth but also as an occasion for that quest to inch one step closer to its goal. Milton can afford to be boldly wrong about theology because even his error can contribute to the collective ecclesial process of coming into closer harmony with God, in Christ. He places greater faith in the process than in his conclusions.

Milton's freedom to have faith in the process—a freedom from the intolerable burden of needing to discover truth on his own as a fallible human being—derives directly from his unorthodox insistence on a Son who can participate

---

[100] On the well-documented ego, see e.g., Richard Strier, "Milton against Humility," in *Religion and Culture in Renaissance England*, ed. Claire McEachern and Debora Shuger (Cambridge: Cambridge University Press, 1997), pp. 258–86; and Stephen M. Fallon, *Milton's Peculiar Grace: Self-Representation and Authority* (Ithaca, NY: Cornell University Press, 2007), pp. ix and *passim*.

[101] Tobias Gregory, "How Milton Defined Heresy and Why," *Religion & Literature* 45, 1 (2013): 148–60. Compare Janel Mueller, "Milton on Heresy," in *Milton and Heresy*, ed. Stephen B. Dobranski and John P. Rumrich (Cambridge: Cambridge University Press, 1998), pp. 21–38; Milton, *Areopagitica*, 26–27.

THE SON OF GOD AND MILTON'S CHURCH   197

fully in humanity while simultaneously participating in divine attributes that properly pertain only to the Father. Indeed, the belief that Christ, through the mysterious mediation of the incarnation, can redemptively put even Milton's errors into the service of divine truth sits at the very center of his faith in an atonement.

Conclusion: The Son and the Rule of Faith

The prospect of speaking scripture at the methodological heart of *De Doctrina Christiana* thus rests on Milton's heterodox theology of the Son even as that theology itself results from the messy process of attempting first to ground his account of Christian doctrine on scripture and then from the ensuing need to speak scripture.[102] In this way, Milton's most cantankerous and vehement expressions in the treatise owe an odd debt to his humility, his willingness to change his mind as he attempted to bring his theology into greater harmony with the unity of speaking that connects the Son to the Father. Milton the imperfect human strives to model his methodology on the sinless Son's mysterious incarnational union of the divine and the human.

But, as the last chapters have stressed, Milton's methodology is not finally about the strivings of one man, a "church of one" hoping to attain solitary communion with the Father through Christ. Rather, we are now in a position to see how his theology of the Son grounds the ecclesiological dimension of his methodology. In I.31, "On Particular Churches," he envisions a kind of "self-sufficient and complete church" that

> has neither any human being nor any assembly or conventicle [set] over it on earth to which it could lawfully be subjected, because—equally with any other human being or any order or synod outside itself—it can hope to possess the scriptures and the promises, the presence of Christ and the presiding of the spirit, and the grace of gifts which is to be gained by communal prayer.[103]

---

[102] Milton reworks the Reformed understanding of scripture as theology's *principium cognoscendi* and God as its *principium essendi*. Compare *PRRD*, III.159–64.

[103] *DDC*, 415:

> integra tamen in sese et perfe[c]ta ecclesia [...] neque mortalium quenquam neque coetum ullum aut conventum supra se habet in terris cui iure subiiciatur, cùm et scripturas et promissiones, praesentem Christum et praesidem spiritum et donorum gratiam apud se precibus impetra[n]dam, aeque ac alius extra se quivis mortalium, aut quaevis classis aut synodus, sperare sibi posset.

198 MILTON'S THEOLOGICAL PROCESS

Several features distinguish such a church. Eschewing the idolatry that Milton associates with papal church-government, this church subjects itself to the Father alone, in imitation of Christ's own unmediated and free submission to the Father.[104] Christ mediates this submission by effecting the satisfaction that makes *imitatio Christi* possible. Thus freely subjected to the Father through Christ (in the sense that no human coercion is involved), the church can "hope to possess the scriptures and the promises," which is to say that it can hope to possess at last the truth of Christian doctrine (along with the attendant promises) expressed in the scriptures—a truth hitherto kept out of grasp by the human imperfections both in the church members and in the scriptures themselves as textual artifacts. The hope of attaining this truth arises from the practice of prayer [*precibus*] and the resulting grace of gifts [*donorum gratiam*] in the church, which, by invoking the multiplicity of gifts in Paul's body of Christ (1 Corinthians 12), affords a more serene way of framing the robust and contentious debate that Milton described in the epistle. The goal, perhaps, is the kind of extempore collective prayer that Milton imagines for Adam and Eve in Book 5 of *Paradise Lost*.[105]

Rethinking robust debate and the practice of internal scripture through the notion of ecclesial prayer has consequences for how we understand what *De Doctrina Christiana* is. It is not a contribution to the history of (theological) ideas. Neither is it a dusty tome in which the poet of *Paradise Lost*, to everyone's embarrassment, tries his hand at being George Eliot's Casaubon. Rather, it is an offering, one of Milton's attempts to lend his voice (harmoniously, he hopes) to the church's sacred strain. The only embarrassing thing about it is the awkward sincerity of its vehemence—the way that the vehemence leaves Milton terribly exposed and vulnerable.

To be sure, Milton does list "any other human being" alongside "any order [*classis*] or synod" as an entity that might hope to possess the scriptures and the promises, so the "church-of-one" option is still on the table in the sense of a Congregationalist without a congregation.[106] Even so, such a church of

---

Oxford's "communal" seems to emerge from the context (the church as a whole is the grammatical subject) rather than directly from the Latin. The "prayer [precibus]" is communal by implication because the passage speaks of the church as a whole and not of the individuals that comprise it.

[104] Milton reads the "every knee shall bow" passages (Isaiah 45:12, 23; Romans 14:10–11; Philippians 2:9–11) as referencing submission to the Father, not the Son: *DDC*, 113.

[105] On the Morning Hymn (*Paradise Lost*, V.155–208) as an ideal model of worship, a form of communal prayer set against what Milton views as the corrupt alternatives, see Achsah Guibbory, *Ceremony and Community from Herbert to Milton: Literature, Religion, and Cultural Conflict in Seventeenth-Century England* (Cambridge: Cambridge University Press, 1998), pp. 204–205.

[106] Tobias Gregory, *Milton's Strenuous Liberty* (forthcoming).

one remains a particular member that participates in the universal church as it collectively strives to possess the scriptures and the promises. Milton describes that process in ways that tellingly echo his theology of the Godhead: "particular churches can consult together fraternally and harmoniously [*consensu*], and [can] for a common purpose do things which they believe will benefit the universal church."[107] The churches are to strive to be one with each other not in essence—visible churches can be distinct from each other without threatening the integrity of the universal whole—but in consensus, in the harmony of their witness. Perhaps Milton, as an organist and the son of a composer, might allow the possibility that this harmony could be polyphonic, with many independent voices beautifully interwoven. Perhaps the Son might do more than double the Father's part, just as Milton himself might call a tune other than that of Nicaea and Chalcedon and yet remain in the choir. Or perhaps, in Nicaea and Chalcedon he sees something more like the foreclosure of music itself.

Milton's Christology is therefore central to his redefined rule of faith. When Milton finds it necessary to step outside of the external scripture and venture his own internal scripture, he might seem to be appealing to a *homoousios* that binds the apparently irreconcilable parts of scripture into one Platonic whole, an implied unity of essence that connects the disparate biblical voices. The formal state of I.5, however, suggests something else entirely, resting as its final form does on the persuasive tools of rhetoric: the vision of scripture that Milton attempts to present as coherent is probable, not necessary. Certainty is the goal, but it remains elusive. I have argued that the process of revision that rendered the Ramist skeleton of the chapter more or less vestigial resulted from Milton changing his mind about the Son on the basis of scripture, but it also shows him changing his mind about scripture. If scripture supports his view of the godhead, as he insists at extraordinary length, why not recast this belated conclusion in Ramist form? Perhaps, as with the later chapters of Book I, he never got around to the revisions—which would be understandable, giving the daunting size of I.5. But, as the Oxford editors' outline suggests, the chapter does have a coherent logical structure, albeit not a Ramist one. Rather than a colossal failure to adhere to Ramist form, the chapter represents Milton's abandonment of Ramism, with its assumption that scripture's underlying essential unity is either knowable or representable by logical means alone. The

---

[107] *DDC*, 417: "Possunt tamen ecclesiae particulares inter se fraterno more atque consensu consilia communicare et in commune agere quae universae ecclesiae ex re fore crediderint."

work of theology turned out to require more freedom than Ramism allowed, and, in the treatise's greatest irony, the application of Ramist method and deep commitment to external scripture worked together with Psalm 2 to present Milton with a new internal-scriptural model of freedom in the Son of God. Unable to realize that freedom fully in the genre of the Ramist theological treatise, Milton began to seek it instead in the epic poem already taking shape as his work on the treatise came to an end.

PART THREE
PARADISE LOST

Interlude

On *De Doctrina Christiana* and *Paradise Lost*

Thus far, this book has set out to establish a method of reading *De Doctrina Christiana* without recourse to *Paradise Lost*, arguing that Milton's treatise takes as its point of departure the Reformed tradition by treating scripture as the cognitive foundation (*principium cognoscendi theologiae*) and the Son of God as the essential foundation (*principium essendi theologiae*). The treatise operates in continuity with these norms even as it reshapes them toward different doctrinal ends. Attention to the foundations of theology shows how the treatise's project evolved significantly over time, indicating that *De Doctrina Christiana* is an artifact of a theological process rather than a straightforward articulation of Milton's theological views, some of which (like his views of the Son and the Sabbath) seem to have changed radically in the course of his work on the treatise.[1]

This way of reading *De Doctrina Christiana* upsets the assumptions governing most accounts of the treatise's relationship to *Paradise Lost* over the past two centuries. The chapters of Maurice Kelley's influential *This Great Argument* (1941) that set out to adduce doctrinally parallel passages of the epic and the treatise, for instance, work from the assumptions that the treatise requires minimal interpretative reading—it says what it says—and that its use of scripture in most cases takes a distant back seat to Milton's own words. Such careful reading as the treatise merits tends to be intertextual and propositional, in efforts to identify its relationship to the doctrinal views expressed by other contemporary theologians in the broadly Reformed tradition. That is valuable work, and Kelley's theological notes may be the primary reason why the recent Oxford edition has not altogether superseded its Yale predecessor. Even so, such comparative work assumes that the manuscript records a clear, fixed expression of Milton's views, not allowing for the complex variability of the material artifact on that point. I am not arguing that we should treat *De Doctrina Christiana* as a vast pool of unvariegated incertitude or that we should dismiss it as a record of Milton's theological views; all I am saying is that getting at those views requires close, careful reading that attends rigorously to Milton's use of scripture, his

---

[1] Concerning the Sabbath, see Jeffrey Alan Miller, "Theological Typology, Milton and the Aftermath of Writing," DPhil thesis, University of Oxford, ch. 4.

204   MILTON'S THEOLOGICAL PROCESS

engagement with interlocutors like Wolleb and Ames, his recourse to rhetorical prose, and the ways that the manuscript points to variability great and small across all of these dimensions. The treatise is an artifact of Milton's thinking, not of his thought.

This book's proposed way of reading points beyond merely producing a clearer account of the treatise's propositional content, however—especially where the treatise's relationship to *Paradise Lost* is concerned. Readers like Balachandra Rajan are right to point to the generic differences between the theological treatise and the biblical epic as an interpretative gulf to be navigated and to argue that reducing *Paradise Lost* to its propositional theological content does it a disservice.[2] C. S. Lewis long ago (and David Urban more recently) have proposed jettisoning *De Doctrina Christiana* as an aid to interpreting a poem that was perfectly capable of standing theologically on its own prior to 1823. They accept the treatise as Milton's while denying that it need have any interpretative bearing on the epic.[3]

Urban, however, helpfully finds in I.5 "a Milton who was not codifying his final conclusions about the Son of God," which invites the question of how a theological treatise understood in more tentative terms might relate to the late poems.[4] The continued life of argument against Miltonic authorship of *De Doctrina Christiana*—the tradition inaugurated in the nineteenth century by Bishop Burgess and others—rests on two major points. The first is style; as Urban puts it, I.5 was written "by a Milton whose pedantic presentation of the Son's relation to the Father runs counter to the writings of one who demonstrates unmatched abilities to articulate theological concepts in artistic language."[5] I have addressed this kind of argument by drawing attention to the ways that *De Doctrina Christiana* is more rhetorical than accounts of its genre or style tend to allow. Rhetoric need not produce poetic results—to claim such is to accept the Ramist reduction of rhetoric to ornamentation—but rhetorical invention, with its creativity and expansiveness, comes nearer to poetry than does its more strictly logical cousin. That Milton turned such creative energy

---

[2] Balachandra Rajan, Paradise Lost *and the Seventeenth Century Reader* (London: Chatto & Windus, 1962), pp. 22–38.

[3] C. S. Lewis, *A Preface to* Paradise Lost (Oxford: Oxford University Press, 1960), pp.91–92; David V. Urban, "Revisiting the History of the *De Doctrina Christiana* Authorship Debate and Its Ramifications for Milton Scholarship: A Response to Falcone and Kerr," *Connotations* 29 (2020): 177–81. In more recent work, Urban clarifies that his position does not preclude engaging with *De Doctrina Christiana* while interpreting Milton's late poems but rather reflects an emphasis on working out those poems' Christologies on internal grounds: "The Increasing Distance between *De Doctrina Christiana* and Milton's Poetry: An Answer to John K. Hale," *Connotations* 32 (2023): 1–10.

[4] Urban, "Revisiting the History," 181.

[5] Urban, "Revisiting the History," 181.

toward cantankerous and confining ends may explain why *De Doctrina Christiana* proved unable to scratch the itch that initially motivated it. The episode with Alexander More bears unhappy witness to this side of Milton's personality, and one might hope that in moments of self-awareness he managed to resist it.[6]

The second and more significant point of resistance to Miltonic authorship is perceived doctrinal discrepancy. Urban notes the treatise's neglect of John 8:58, a text clearly alluded to in both *Paradise Lost* and *Paradise Regained*, and examples could be multiplied, but this one might stand in for the lot.[7] At this point, any assertion that treatise and epic are perfectly consonant in their theologies could only seem tendentious, even to those who accept that Milton wrote *De Doctrina Christiana*, in part because—like the Christological interpretation of Psalm 2—some of the relevant interpretative questions remain more or less permanently open to contestation.[8] The issue runs deeper, however, and it rests on a sense that *Paradise Lost* is a considerably more refined aesthetic object than *De Doctrina Christiana*. (The aspirationally materialist Milton of *Paradise Lost* might approve this criterion.) Accordingly, in the "rule of faith" that governs interpretation of Miltonic texts, the epic's airier substance ought (paradoxically) to carry greater weight than the treatise's crude matter such that in points of doctrinal discrepancy, *Paradise Lost* wins.[9] Urban writes in harmony with C. A. Patrides, who memorably described the treatise as a "singularly gross expedition into theology." By this, he meant several things: that it is "prosaic," lacking "the very essence of theological language"; that it is "rather seriously marred" by its views on the Godhead; and that it, like Milton's unfinished poem on "The Passion," found him taking up a subject "above the years he had" and then wisely abandoning it. Consequently, for Patrides, "Milton's *De Doctrina Christiana* is a theological labyrinth. *Paradise Lost* is a window to the sun."[10] The argument is that Milton's successes are so glorious and obvious that we have little cause to meddle with his failures, numbering *De Doctrina Christiana* clearly among the

---

[6] See Gordon Campbell and Thomas N. Corns, *John Milton: Life, Work, and Thought* (Oxford: Oxford University Press, 2008), pp. 260–65. Milton continued to attack More in scurrilous print even after being credibly and repeatedly informed that More was not the author of the treatise against which Milton was defending himself.

[7] Urban, "Revisiting the History," 180; see further the various essays by Falcone.

[8] Analogously, the concept of musical consonance remains elusive. Is it based on the pure ratios of the harmonic series—in which the sequences of fifths and octaves become increasingly misaligned—or on something like a system of equal temperament, in which fifths and octaves line up but at the expense of knowing what thirds actually sound like? Are we in the world of Bach's *Well-Tempered Clavier* or that of Harry Partch's invented instruments and Ben Johnston's string quartets? The answer, happily, is both.

[9] Compare *PL*, IV.977–1015.

[10] C. A. Patrides, "*Paradise Lost* and the Language of Theology," in William B. Hunter Jr, C. A. Patrides, and J. H. Adamson, *Bright Essence* (Salt Lake City, UT: University of Utah Press, 1971), pp. 168–69.

latter. Should not the treatise therefore be "downward purg'd," like the "black tartareous cold Infernal dregs/Adverse to life" described in Raphael's account of the creation (*PL*, VII.237–39)?

I have already suggested that Milton ultimately found the epic more amenable than the treatise for the theological work he set out to do, which brings us back to the question that began this book: why should anyone read *De Doctrina Christiana*? The answer for me is that, even if the treatise proved unable to do what Milton needed or wanted it to do, the road to that impasse is immensely illuminating. Patrides and Urban see the impasse but not the road. And the road did not end circa 1660, when Milton seems to have laid aside the treatise, with its perceived inadequacy as only one reason among many. That road does not point directly or inevitably toward *Paradise Lost* any more than Milton's incipient decision to attempt to work out his beliefs for himself on the basis of scripture pointed directly or inevitably toward things taking a serious detour thanks to Psalm 2. Chapter 6 shows how reading *De Doctrina Christiana* through its engagement with the foundations of theology illuminates Milton's similar engagement in *Paradise Lost*. One need not find the results of the treatise on this point either satisfying or finally compatible with the epic for the treatise to remain, on the level of methodological reflection, an intertext with significant insight to offer readers of the poem.

Chapter 6 turns to ecclesiology as a way of illuminating how *Paradise Lost*, like *De Doctrina Christiana*, wrestles with problems of theological method. The point, however, is not to privilege ecclesiology as the one true point of connection between *De Doctrina Christiana* and *Paradise Lost* but rather to illustrate that reading the treatise in terms of theological process invites new kinds of questions about the epic. Reading *Paradise Lost* alongside *De Doctrina Christiana* is not to make the epic a monument to a monument to dead ideas, a reduction of living verse into sepulchral prose.[11] Rather, the byways of Milton's thinking all belong to the same map, even though some of the roads are dead ends, while others curl confusedly back on themselves—even, I would argue, in the epic. To this end, the Conclusion reflects on the value in thinking with patience and care about things that Milton rejects or about places where his own projects went awry. In this way, just as the first two parts of this book have attended both to the project of *De Doctrina Christiana* and to Milton's wrestle with its limitations, this last part will attend to both theological process and its limitations in *Paradise Lost*. Doing with *Paradise Lost* what Milton

---

[11] On *Paradise Lost* as "a monument to dead ideas," see Sir Walter Alexander Raleigh, *Milton* (New York and London: G. P. Putnam's Sons, 1900), p. 85.

himself did with *De Doctrina Christiana* seems like a good way of honoring his avowed theological method, which means examining the parts of the epic that resist the larger theological argument that he shapes. Just as we ought not let just praise for the epic occlude these less assimilable aspects, excising *De Doctrina Christiana* from the map or relegating it to an appendix can only result in an incomplete and perhaps ultimately hagiographic *eikon* of a man who was, after all, only human, and *humani nihil a me alienum puto.*[12]

---

[12] In Terence, these words ("nothing human is alien to me") justify neighborly meddling, but decontextualization facilitates their later use as a humanist motto of sorts: Terence, *Heauton Timorumenon*, in *Terence: In Two Volumes*, ed. and trans. John Sargeaunt (Cambridge, MA: Harvard University Press, 1912), Act I line 77.

6

The Process of *Paradise Lost*

The preceding chapters have argued that ecclesiology lies at the heart of theological method in *De Doctrina Christiana*. Ecclesiology seems an unlikely point of continuity between the treatise and *Paradise Lost*, however, given the epic's relative silence about the concept of "church." This word appears only twice in the epic, in neither instance very felicitously. The first is in Book IV, where, after Satan's entrance into "Gods Fould," the epic offers this comparison: "So since into his Church lewd Hirelings climbe" (IV.192–93). This instance casts a portentous shadow on the second, in the Argument to Book XII, which promises to address "the state of the Church till his second Coming." The portent is borne out by the warning that, after the apostles' deaths, "Wolves shall succeed for teachers, grievous Wolves" (XII.508). Beyond this anticlericalism and the first parents' extempore morning hymn, the epic is more or less unconcerned with the kinds of ecclesiological questions that occupy the last part of *De Doctrina Christiana*, Book I. Accordingly, the major study of Milton's ecclesiology has almost nothing to say about *Paradise Lost*, focusing overwhelmingly on Milton's prose.[1] On the level of propositional claims about ordinary and extraordinary ministers, the marks of the church, and the like, treatise and epic scarcely lend themselves to comparison, let alone a substantive argument about continuity or otherwise. Kelley's list of parallels, covering four chapters of the treatise (summarized in just over a page), runs only to two additional pages.[2]

Nevertheless, as I have argued, the ecclesial dimension of Milton's thinking about the foundations of theology in *De Doctrina Christiana* extends beyond explicit discussions of ecclesiology and ecclesiastical institutions in a way that invites attention to the ecclesial dimensions of *Paradise Lost*. The point of continuity from which these explorations depart has to do with the practice of speaking internal scripture, the ecclesial process of vetting such utterances, and

[1] Stephen R. Honeygosky, *Milton's House of God: The Invisible and Visible Church* (Columbia, MO: University of Missouri Press, 1993), p. 253.
[2] Maurice Kelley, *This Great Argument: A Study of Milton's* De Doctrina Christiana *as a Gloss upon* Paradise Lost (Princeton, NJ: Princeton University Press, 1941), pp. 178–81.

Milton's Theological Process. Jason A. Kerr, Oxford University Press. © Jason A. Kerr (2023).
DOI: 10.1093/oso/9780198875086.003.0007

210   MILTON'S THEOLOGICAL PROCESS

the Son's role as a model for and theological foundation of the church.[3] These questions are deeply interwoven into the poem's reception history, whether in Matthew Poole's 1683 decision to treat *Paradise Lost* seriously as a work of biblical exegesis or in the sense, shared by many readers over the centuries, that the epic's achievement is doctrinal as well as aesthetic.[4] The interconnection between these matters of reception and the poem's Christology goes some way toward explaining why the appearance of *De Doctrina Christiana* occasioned such a shock. Nevertheless, in the epic as in the treatise, an unorthodox Christology proves vital to the attendant ecclesiology.

The poem's ecclesiological struggle—and ultimately its theodicy—centers on an unresolved tension between actuality and potentiality.[5] The heart of the struggle is the poem's anti-trinitarian account of the relationship between the Father and the Son, whose colloquies provide the poem with some of its primal church scenes, or scenes that dramatize an ecclesial process of speaking and testing, as described in *Areopagitica* and *De Doctrina Christiana*. The concept of "substance" connects Milton's anti-trinitarianism with his account of matter, both of which hinge on the potentiality of the many to become one while raising questions about which manners of oneness comport with free will. Milton understands substance as a principle of ontological commonality, while essence is a principle of individuation. If the theodicy involves clearing the Father from charges of tyranny, then it depends on freeing the Son's unity with the Father from necessity or coercion. The poem works to preserve the Son's freedom not by executing a free-will defense but through its thinking about substance, a concept that complexly links Milton's anti-trinitarianism with his account of *ex Deo* creation and the resulting view of matter.[6] Ultimately, Milton guarantees

---

[3] I begin where William Poole concluded: "If the Bible is God's property, so is *Paradise Lost*, though God might do well to survey this particular asset with ambivalence": *Milton and the Idea of the Fall* (Cambridge: Cambridge University Press, 2005), p. 194.

[4] On Matthew Poole, see Jason P. Rosenblatt, *Torah and Law* in Paradise Lost (Princeton, NJ: Princeton University Press, 1994), pp. 82–83.

[5] Rumrich finds these Aristotelian concepts foundational for Milton's thinking about matter: *Matter of Glory: A New Preface to* Paradise Lost (Pittsburgh, PA: University of Pittsburgh Press, 1987), ch. 4.

[6] On theodicy via free-will defense, see Dennis Richard Danielson, *Milton's Good God* (Cambridge: Cambridge University Press, 1982), responding to William Empson, *Milton's God*, rev. edn (Cambridge: Cambridge University Press, 1981). These books stand in for the competing critical traditions discussed by William Kolbrener, *Milton's Warring Angels* (Cambridge: Cambridge University Press, 1997). On Milton's materialism and anti-trinitarianism, see David Bentley Hart, "Matter, Monism, and Narrative: An Essay on the Metaphysics of *Paradise Lost*," *Milton Quarterly* 30, 1 (1996): 16–27; on monism's authoritarian potentialities, see Rachel J. Trubowitz, "Body Politics in *Paradise Lost*," *Publications of the Modern Language Association of America* 121, 2 (2006): 402.

THE PROCESS OF PARADISE LOST   211

the Son's freedom by insisting on the freedom of substance itself, once alienated from God and liberated from the necessity of "goodness," to determine whether and how it will enact union with the divine.[7] As a result, God—and God's goodness, the subject of theodicy—remains in some sense unactuated, still *in potentia*.[8] The poem's theodicy turns out to depend on matter's free, harmonious reunion with the God that sent it forth.

This plurality of liberated substance becomes the poem's model for the church (as the community of the called, *ecclesia*, not as a particular ecclesiastical institution or visible church), while providing an ontological framework for thinking about internal scripture in terms of potentiality and actualization. The colloquies between the Father and the Son show this relationship at work as the Son improvisationally speaks internal scripture that, because it realizes its potential to actuate God, becomes scripture for the community, an expression of a hitherto unknowable and unexpressed harmony. On this point, *Paradise Lost* picks up where *De Doctrina Christiana* left off as it uses the intertwined accounts of the Son and matter to think about the conditions under which internal scripture might move from singular statement to shared affirmation— or, conversely, might be rejected by the church and cosmically expelled.[9] The

---

[7] With Rogers, I read the poem against Milton's claim in the *Art of Logic* that matter is a passive principle: *The Matter of Revolution: Science, Poetry, and Politics in the Age of Milton* (Ithaca, NY: Cornell University Press, 1996), ch. 4; *AL*, 15. The terms "matter" and "substance" are not synonymous in the poem: "matter" remains mysterious and undefinable, while "substance" moves in degrees up and down the scale of being described by Raphael, with "body" and "spirit" acting as different degrees of substance; see Phillip J. Donnelly, "'Matter' versus Body: The Character of Milton's Monism," *Milton Quarterly* 33, 3 (1999): 79–85; N. K. Sugimura, "*Matter of Glorious Trial*": *Spiritual and Material Substance in Paradise Lost* (New Haven, CT: Yale University Press, 2009), ch. 2. Both are arguing against Stephen M. Fallon's argument for Milton's monism in *Milton among the Philosophers: Poetry and Materialism in Seventeenth-Century England* (Ithaca, NY: Cornell University Press, 1991), ch. 3; Fallon offers a revised view in "John Milton, Isaac Newton, and the Life of Matter," in Catherine Gimelli Martin, ed., *Milton and the New Scientific Age: Poetry, Science, Fiction* (New York and London: Routledge, 2019), pp. 211–37. On Milton's materialist angelology, see Jonathan Goldberg, *The Seeds of Things: Theorizing Sexuality and Materiality in Renaissance Representations* (New York: Fordham University Press, 2009), ch. 5; Joad Raymond, *Milton's Angels: The Early Modern Imagination* (Oxford: Oxford University Press, 2011), ch. 11; and Rebecca Buckham, "Milton's Strange Angels," in Kevin J. Donovan and Thomas Festa, eds, *Milton, Materialism, and Embodiment: "One First Matter All"* (Pittsburgh, PA: Duquesne University Press, 2017), pp. 111–36.

[8] Rumrich refuses to divorce God from the potentiality in Chaos, against, influentially, A. B. Chambers, "Chaos in *Paradise Lost*," *Journal of the History of Ideas* 24, 1 (1963): 55–84; Rumrich, *Matter of Glory*, ch. 4, esp. 61–63. What Rumrich writes of matter could be said of the church. "Substance for Milton is thus not a static condition of being even though it is the principle that underlies it. Instead, it implies a process, the working out of God's will in the stuff of existence": *Matter of Glory*, 68. Thomas Festa recasts theodicy as "the problem of the good," in an "effort to take into account the alienness of the good and the reality of our loves": "Eve and the Ironic Theodicy of the New Milton Criticism," in *The New Milton Criticism*, ed. Peter C. Herman and Elizabeth Sauer (Cambridge: Cambridge University Press, 2012), p. 187. God, matter, and theodicy all resist definition because all remain amenable to unactualized potentiality.

[9] Kenneth Borris links the incarnational theology of epic and treatise: "Milton's Heterodoxy of the Incarnation and Subjectivity in *De Doctrina Christiana and Paradise Lost*," in Kristin A. Pruitt and

212   MILTON'S THEOLOGICAL PROCESS

Son makes internal scripture work, but the church might not, and that possibility leaves the poem's theodicy unresolved. Making the realization of God's goodness contingent on the human church leaves the door wide open for the possibility that Milton's God is just as bad as the sordid side of Christian history might suggest. The success of Milton's theodicy, then, turns on the prospect of the church becoming, finally and improbably, good.

By placing his theodicy in the hands of the church, Milton is indulging an optimism that, given his own writings from *Lycidas* to *A Treatise of Civil Power*, also contains an unmistakable streak of tragedy because failure seems almost inevitable. An optimism unaware of its own tragic dimensions, though, is not tragedy but farce, and just such an awareness of failure's probability may explain the aptness of Milton's epic subject to his underlying theological aims. The stories of the Fall and the War in Heaven foreground theological error and thus put Milton in the position of having to think the church from a perspective that will brook little idealism. His choice of subject also raises the stakes of his internal scriptural practice by highlighting his own potential for error. Indeed, the probability of successfully conveying the complex web of truths entailed in his subject seems vanishingly small, to the point where the prospect of even knowing how to evaluate their correctness also recedes from view. The poem reflects on this problem by imagining the church in concert with the complex ontology of *ex Deo* creation and the ensuing movement of substance up and down the scale of being. God will be knowable (in some still partial sense) once the church brings the alienated divine substance back into harmony with God, but in the interim, the terms of that harmony remain difficult to grasp, with the consequence that the "obedience" of striving toward it has more to do with improvisation and the play of potentialities than with rote performance.[10]

If such internal-scriptural improvisation became necessary while working on *De Doctrina Christiana*, it is fundamental to the project of *Paradise Lost*. This improvisational quality makes it easy to see the epic as a tour de force, and certainly much about the invocations invites that impression—for example, "Things unattempted yet in Prose or Rhime" (I.16), where the prose in question might include *De Doctrina Christiana*. Yet the poem's ecclesial dimension also brings out its vulnerability—not only the vulnerability to possible error but also the vulnerability that makes its project possible in the first place. Understanding

---

Charles W. Durham, *Living Texts: Interpreting Milton* (London: Associated University Presses, 2000), pp. 264–82.

[10] See Jason A. Kerr, "Prophesying the Bible: The Improvisation of Scripture in Books 11 and 12 of *Paradise Lost*," *Milton Quarterly* 47, 1 (2013): 13–33.

Milton as a "church of one" reads him, incorrectly, as pursuing invulnerability and self-sufficiency, when his approach to the vulnerability that structures church life is much richer than hitherto appreciated.[11] Precisely because *Paradise Lost* privileges Milton's acts of internal scriptural creativity so highly, the resulting faults are no longer in scripture but in himself. The poem's theodicy is thus not a fait accompli but rather something toward which it vulnerably strives. This vulnerability lies in the way that the poem places the success of the enterprise, to a large degree, in other hands such that the theodicy only works if the non-coercive church that Milton imagines can come into being. Milton's God is not good by default; rather, the burden of proof rests on the church's collective capacity to actuate a God who is good—a task at which Milton himself may not have succeeded. In these terms, *Paradise Lost* enacts Milton's struggle to imagine—and to play his part in—the church on which his theodicy depends. The challenge—rendered more acute by the ontological account of God that it entails—is to enact the kind of freely chosen harmony with God that theodicy requires, a unity that preserves rather than obliterates difference.[12] As the preceding chapters have suggested, attending to the process of the struggle itself will illuminate more than a simple evaluation of (or argument for) its success.

God, Satan, and the Church

Milton's attempt at theodicy begins with the Son, who (in some sense like all matter) is the (potential) means of creation while also being a creature. The theodicy involves framing the Son's unity with the Father and attendant goodness as the products of freedom rather than essence and ontological necessity. For Milton, unlike the Nicene Fathers, "begotten" can only mean "made," as he explains in *De Doctrina Christiana*: "God by his own will created—that is, generated, or else brought forth—the Son as the first of all things, endowed with divine nature, just as in the fullness of time he wondrously engendered a human nature from the Virgin Mary[.]"[13] As a creature, the Son shares in

---

[11] "Repudiating vulnerability thus means repudiating the condition that makes possible our pursuits, even the misguided pursuit of invulnerability and self-sufficiency": Erinn Cunniff Gilson, "Vulnerability and Victimization: Rethinking Key Concepts in Feminist Discourses on Sexual Violence," *Signs: Journal of Women in Culture and Society* 42, 1 (2016): 76.

[12] On the importance of voluntary worship in the poem, see Achsah Guibbory, *Ceremony and Community from Herbert to Milton: Literature, Religion, and Cultural Conflict in Seventeenth-Century England* (Cambridge: Cambridge University Press, 1998), pp. 195–202.

[13] *DDC*, 52–53: "Deus Filium rerum omnium primum divina natura praeditum sua voluntate creavit sive generavit aut produxit; sicut in plenitudine temporis humanam naturam ex Maria virgine mirifice procreavit."

214   MILTON'S THEOLOGICAL PROCESS

the Father's substance but not his essence. On this point, the notorious terminological complexities involving the relationship between the Greek terms οὐσία and ὑπόστασις and the Latin terms *essentia, substantia, subsistantia*, and *persona* come into play.[14] Milton's approach stands in contrast to the mature orthodoxy of the early church, as established by Basil of Caesarea. For Basil,

> *Ousia* [οὐσία], the essence (or substance or nature) of God corresponds to the Latin *substantia* as that essential being which Father, Son, and Spirit have in common. *Hypostasis* [ὑπόστασις], on the other hand, refers to a Person of the Trinity and defines that which is circumscribed or limited (akin to the Latin *persona*).[15]

For Milton, however, "*hypostasis*, Heb. 1: 3, which others translate as either 'substance' or 'subsistence' or 'person,' is none other than that same most perfect essence whereby God's existence is from him, in him, and through him."[16] Milton identifies the limiting aspect of divine identity (*hypostasis*) with essence (οὐσία or *essentia*), whereas substance (*substantia* or *subsistantia*) refers to the shared common element of existence. As David Bentley Hart explains, Milton "sharply distinguishes between 'essence' and 'substance,' meaning by the former the unique and incommunicable Godhead of the Father, and by the latter that which the Father can impart to the Son in limited measure."[17] The Father shares "substance" with the Son and with all of creation, while "essence" individuates beings within this shared substance such that nothing is coessential with anything else but everything is (in a manner of speaking) consubstantial with everything else.

If Trinitarian theology affords one approach to the philosophical problem of the many and the one, Milton complexly alters the terms. Trinitarian orthodoxy as it emerged from the early councils emphasizes oneness—indicated by the centrality of *homoousios* to the controversy against Arianism or forms of tritheism—while also insisting on the distinction of the persons as a balance against Sabellian modalism, the view that Father, Son, and Spirit were "modes" of the one God rather than distinct persons. The unity of God (to include the full divinity of the Son) remains the key point, alongside the acknowledgment

---

[14] For an overview, see Yale, 140 n. 30; for greater depth, see Declan Marmion and Rik van Nieuwenhove, *An Introduction to the Trinity* (Cambridge: Cambridge University Press, 2011), ch. 3.

[15] Marmion and van Nieuwenhove, *An Introduction to the Trinity*, 72.

[16] DDC, 13: "hypostasin proinde illam Heb. 1. 3. quam alii vel substantiam vel subsistentiam, vel personam vertunt, nihil esse aliud quàm essentiam ipsam perfectissimam, qua Deus à se, in se, et per se est."

[17] Hart, "Matter, Monism, and Narrative," 23.

that oneness can (from the perspective of the orthodoxy established at the ecumenical councils) be taken too far, as in the Sabellian case. The many remains an operative category but within a governing framework of the one: divine simplicity admits of internal distinction.[18] This orthodoxy understands individuality as a property of the many (the three *hypostaseis* or *personae*), whereas Milton understands it as a property of the one, distinguished by an indivisible essence: "Hence it is understood that God's essence, since it is the simplest, allows nothing compound within it."[19] The maximal simplicity of the Father's individual essence distinguishes him from all other beings such that his singular identity becomes paramount. As Hart puts it, "abstract essence— 'whoness,' to resort again to a useful barbarism—is not dissoluble into a higher identity; there is no such thing as coessentiality."[20] In the case of Milton's Father, then, the governing framework of the one excludes the many and could not, he repeatedly argues, meaningfully be a framework of the one on any other terms.

Milton firmly insists on the essential differentiation of persons while nevertheless uniting them through a shared substance, understood as the same degree or quality of prime matter. This balance of differentiation and union is, in a nutshell, the problem of the church, where the shared project of truth discovery coincides uneasily with the individual vagaries of internal scripture and the chaotic variation that results. The Son's relationship with the Father thus affords a model for the church in the way that it shows the Son actuating God's goodness. Milton dramatizes this process of actuation through the divine colloquies in Books V and III, transitioning from a hypothetical unity of speaking [*consensus*] in *De Doctrina Christiana* to actual dialogue in *Paradise Lost* that shows the Son's process of coming into greater harmony with the Father. The change in genre matters: the treatise is not merely a doctrinal script for the characters in the poem to mum out, indecently "writhing and unboning their Clergie limmes" while the young Milton hisses.[21] Rather, the poem insists that the Son's words matter, that they do more than simply instantiate some previously articulated truth, that they constitute half of a genuine dialogue and not just the performance of already-rehearsed lines with nothing at stake. By presenting the Son's union with the Father as contingent on the Son's own actions, Milton makes their relationship into a model of the church, with their conversations as models of church life. The contingent nature

---

[18] On divine simplicity and internal distinction, see *PRRD*, III.33–46, 53–61, 70–82.
[19] *DDC*, 13: "Ex quo intelligitur, essentiam Dei, simplicissima cum sit, nihil compositi in se admittere."
[20] Hart, "Matter, Monism, and Narrative," 23.
[21] John Milton, *An Apology against a Pamphlet* (London, 1642), p. 14.

of the relationship means that Milton's theodicy—is God good, or is God a tyrant?—remains up in the air, while Milton's own poetic efforts show him in the process of trying to bring God's as yet undefined goodness into being.

The relational contingency of the theodicy draws attention to the political-theological dimension inherent in Milton's heterodox depiction of the Son, which some scholars have identified with republicanism or the politically subversive qualities of Arianism itself.[22] In these frameworks, politics informs ecclesiology, but, as with many other seventeenth-century figures, like Richard Baxter, Milton's ecclesiology drives his politics, not the other way around.[23] Lingering on the ecclesiological consequences of how he depicts the Son will allow us to go beyond merely arguing that the poem's Christology is, in fact, antitrinitarian (or politically radical) and work toward an understanding of how the poem's heterodox Christology is central to its project as a whole. The Son's narrative trajectory as a character has an ecclesial dimension in the way that his actions unfold in non-essential relation to the Father. With essential unity comes necessity, but, as Raphael tells Adam of God, "Our voluntarie service he requires,/Not our necessitated" (V.529–30). Only a union based on free obedience will do, and as for Father and Son, so also for the church.[24] The Son's dialogue with the Father thus models a progressive development of ecclesial unity that unfolds with his narrative arc.[25]

The Father's first elevation of the Son includes a command to the angels that establishes the basis of ecclesial union in the Son's reign via a complex system of analogy.

> Under his great Vice-gerent Reign abide
> United as one individual Soule
> For ever happie: him who disobeyes
> Mee disobeyes, breaks union, and that day
> Cast out from God and blessed vision, falls
> Into utter darkness, deep ingulft, his place
> Ordaind without redemption, without end.
>
> (V.609–15)

[22] David Loewenstein, "Rethinking Political Theology in Milton," *Journal for Early Modern Cultural Studies* 18, 2 (2018): 44–45, 47; John P. Rumrich, "Milton's Arianism: Why It Matters," in Stephen B. Dobranski and John P. Rumrich, *Milton and Heresy* (Cambridge : Cambridge University Press, 1998), pp. 86–89.

[23] As John P. Rumrich points out, Baxter and Milton agreed about little; nevertheless, they share a career trajectory of writing about ecclesiology before turning to politics; *Milton Unbound: Controversy and Reinterpretation* (Cambridge: Cambridge University Press, 1996), pp. 30–33.

[24] *De Doctrina Christiana* I.15 emphasizes that the Son assumes his mediatorial office (which includes kingship over the church) willingly and that he likewise exercises his office by noncoercive means. See Chapter 5.

[25] Bauman maintains (against Hunter) the Son's progression from state to state in the epic:

This passage suggests three distinct modes of union. The Son's status as "Vice-gerent" implies an administrative union with the Father such that the Son's actions accurately represent what the Father commissioned him to do. The union of the angels under his reign "as one individual Soule" proves trick-ier to understand, especially given Trinitarian uses of "individual" to mean "one in substance or essence" or, similarly troubling from Milton's perspective, "numerically one."[26] Milton's use of simile—"*as* one individual Soule"—rescues him from these implications, however, and in any event, the metaphorical soul proves divisible, for a disobedient angel "breaks union" and is "Cast out from God" in a manner more like the "dregs/Adverse to life" (VII.238–39) than like the expropriated matter that became Chaos.[27] Unity among the angels there-fore derives from obedience to the Son's reign, whence the third sort of unity, that which the church enjoys with God through the Son. The angels' relation-ship with God is mediated by the Son's vicegerent rule, and yet the fact that the disobedient are "cast out from God" suggests that the three kinds of unity at play in the passage are themselves become "as one individual Soule," with voluntary obedience as the bond.

At this level of abstraction, where union operates by analogy, beings that are unequal can nevertheless conform to the same proportion. In a narra-tive poem, however, Milton cannot avoid the difficult practicalities attending unequal union for long, and Satan's rebellion brings them to the fore, as when Satan asks his followers:

> Who can in reason then or right assume
> Monarchie over such as live by right
> His equals, if in power and splendor less,
> In freedome equal?
>
> (V.794–98)

Satan, bent on retaining his own perceived pre-eminence, has nevertheless just finished voicing the counterargument: "for Orders and Degrees/Jarr not with

---

[26] *OED*, "individual," adj., 1, 4.

[27] A complex middle case is the expulsion from Eden, which Milton frames in material terms: "Those pure immortal Elements that know/No gross, no unharmoneous mixture foule,/Eject him tainted now" (XI.50–52); see Poole, *Milton and the Idea of the Fall*, 188. Such passages find Milton grappling, however indirectly, with the mathematical question of whether infinity (God's, in this case) admits of subtrac-tion. On Milton's engagement with infinity and Galilean mathematics, see Rachel J. Trubowitz, "The Fall and Galileo's Law of Falling Bodies: Geometrization vs. Observation and Describing Things in *Paradise Lost*," in Martin, *Milton and the New Scientific Age*, pp. 94–100; and, building on Trubowitz, Christopher Koester, "Mathematical Milton: Number Theory and Nesting Infinities in *Paradise Lost*," in *Locating Milton: Places and Perspectives*, ed. Thomas Festa and David Ainsworth (Clemson, SC: Clem-son University Press, 2021), pp. 101–23. Milton's conception of God as infinite is peculiarly quantitative, in contrast to many theological invocations of infinity: see Christian Tapp, "Infinity in Mathematics and Theology," *Theology and Science* 9, 1 (2011): 91–100.

218 MILTON'S THEOLOGICAL PROCESS

liberty, but well consist" (V.792–93). Hypocritical though Satan may be, he draws out the tyrannical, oppressive potential ("prostration vile," V.782) in a union of unequals. This potential is not limited to the occasion at hand; as John Rogers writes, "The logical fissure in Satan's reasoning points well beyond the circumscribed issue of his failing as a moral being. Satan's damning self-contradiction in his debate with Abdiel works rather to bring into relief the systemic lapses in coherence in the organizational discourse underlying all of Milton's poem."[28] Illustrative of the problem's systemic dimension, Paul's language of "slaves to God" in Romans 6, so central to Milton's thinking about Christian liberty in *De Doctrina Christiana*, carries the same potential.[29] What makes slavery to God qualitatively different from slavery to sin? Milton insists, discussing slavery to God in *De Doctrina Christiana*, that "Hence in religion we are freed from the judgements of human beings, much more [so] from coercion and judgement-seats," quoting James 2:12 to affirm that "God is going to judge us according to the law of freedom."[30] Slavery to God is, for Milton, paradoxically free.[31] Satan is thus, on the surface, wrong—God isn't like that, or at least doesn't have to be—but Satan nevertheless has an ecclesiologically useful point: he names the potential for coercion and dominion to enter into church life. Satan, in other words, isn't *necessarily* wrong: his wrongness depends on human choice, which means that he ends up being right plenty of the time.[32] The troublesome import of both Satan's accusations and Paul's metaphor cannot be avoided by argumentative special pleading—only by contrary living.

Precisely as an adversary, then, Satan has a place in Milton's church, which in a sense, needs someone like Satan right up until the moment when union with God becomes reality instead of aspiration.[33] Milton may not be of the devil's party, exactly, but his unwillingness to drive Satan by force from the church might understandably convey that impression. When William Empson writes that Milton "would hold the political scales sardonically even" by

[28] Rogers, *The Matter of Revolution*, 129.

[29] For an argument that Romans 6 includes Roman domestic slavery (and thus chattel slavery) in its conceptual ambit, see John K. Goodrich, "From Slaves of Sin to Slaves of God: Considering the Origins of Paul's Slavery Metaphor in Romans 6," *Bulletin for Biblical Research* 23, 4 (2013): 509–30.

[30] *DDC*, 333–34: "Hinc iudiciis hominum, multo magis coactione et tribunalibus in religione lib[e]ramur [...] in quibus si Deus nos iudicaturus est per legem libertatis."

[31] For a critique of this paradigm, see Adam Kotsko, *What is Theology? Christian Thought and Contemporary Life* (New York: Fordham University Press, 2021), Part III.

[32] Satan's error is recasting potentiality as actualized fact—an error, I am arguing, mirrored by those who would read the poem's theodicy as achieved. Err though he may, Satan, like Empson, is a useful heretic: dismissing either of them too casually is unwise.

[33] On Satan's necessary contribution to the Son's process of "invention" and self-realization in *Paradise Regained*, see Elizabeth Skerpan-Wheeler, "The Logical Poetics of *Paradise Regained*," *Huntington Library Quarterly* 76, 1 (2013): 49–50.

writing Satan in ways that reflect both Cromwell and Charles I, his point also applies to Milton's ecclesiology in that every church Milton encountered had something of Satan in it.[34] Keeping the scales even means that Satan gets to stay as a useful reminder of what the church still needs to do, and coercion would simultaneously expel him too soon and risk legitimating his complaint about tyranny. Milton depicts Satan's uncoerced expulsion from the church as the War in Heaven concludes with the rebel angels determining their own exit from Heaven: "headlong themselves they threw/Down from the verge of Heav'n, Eternal wrauth/Burnt after them to the bottomless pit" (VI.864–66). Heretics, Milton seems to be saying, will leave the church of their own accord when the choice presents itself between retaining their error and joining the collective union with God, no coercion required. Flaming wrath and the dread fury of the Son's chariot do invite the question of just what counts as coercion— or perhaps they suggest that Satan's usefulness as an unintentional provocateur against coercion did not expire with his exit from Heaven. It turns out that Hell, too, must be chosen again and again (as Satan does from Mount Niphates, in a speech buzzing with potentialities).

Potentiality and Internal Scripture

If the case of Satan suggests that Milton highly values adversarial work within the church, Satan's rebellion provides the occasion for a more complex case, in the (chronologically) first colloquy between the Father and the Son, where the Father speaks in error and the Son uses scripture to correct him. The Father initiates the conversation:

> Let us advise, and to this hazard draw
> With speed what force is left, and all imploy
> In our defence, lest unawares we lose
> This our high place, our Sanctuarie, our Hill.
>
> (V.729–32)

To which the Son replies: "Mightie Father, thou thy foes/Justly hast in derision, and secure/Laugh'st at thir vain designes and tumults vain" (V.735–37). When the Father seems in doubt of victory, the Son alludes (*avant la lettre*) to Psalm

---

[34] Empson, *Milton's God*, 82.

220 MILTON'S THEOLOGICAL PROCESS

2:4: "He that sitteth in the heavens shall laugh: the LORD shall have them in deri-sion" (KJV).[35] Anticipating the very text that speaks of his own coronation, the Son tells the Father that his worry is misplaced.

This exchange—the Father expressing worry and the Son using scripture to reassure him—offers a concise depiction of the process that grounds eccle-sial unity while also minimizing the threat posed by theological error. With rich irony, Milton portrays the Father getting a basic doctrinal point wrong by second-guessing his own supremacy and omnipotence. (Admittedly, the Father's status as less than fully actuated—on which more soon—calls his omnipotence into question.) Perhaps the Father is merely throwing the Son a theological softball, in a maneuver designed to get the Son to affirm what the Father already knows—not a real error, in other words, but a test or, perhaps worse, a play rehearsal or a chorus of "Forc't Halleluiah's" (II.243).[36] God again risks devolving into a tyrannical narcissist and the church into little more than a doting fan club. The result is something like Empson's claim that the angels "put up a timidly evasive but none the less stubborn resistance to dissolving themselves into God, like a peasantry under Communism trying to delay col-lectivization"; they have little enthusiasm for union that reifies inequality, and their enthusiasm (on this reading) diminishes the more inevitable such union seems.[37] A God who toys with inferiors precisely so that they will reaffirm his superiority undermines the prospect of their choosing union with him freely.

Read another way, however, the colloquy works to upset hierarchy. For one thing, Milton must surely be joking: watching an omnipotent being fret about the possibility of his impending defeat is, well, funny.[38] Making God's omnipo-tence the object of laughter seems like an especially risky form of punching up. The humor gains an additional edge from the Son's correction: God is supposed to be the subject, not the object, of laughter. Oddly, though, the Father's appar-ent mistake saves him from punching down in the gleeful way the Psalmist depicts. He does not respond to the Son's correction with approval or other-wise. Is the Son using scripture to correct the Father, or is the Father somehow correcting scripture by not acting (for the moment at least) in the derisively

---

[35] On *avant la lettre*, see Kerr, "Prophesying the Bible."

[36] In the manner of Stanley Fish, *Surprised by Sin* (London: Macmillan, 1967), which Michael Bryson finds Satanic; *The Tyranny of Heaven: Milton's Rejection of God as King* (Newark, DE: University of Delaware Press, 2004), pp. 24–25.

[37] Empson, *Milton's God*, 139.

[38] Empson reads the exchange as "one of God's jokes": *Milton's God*, 96. I am reading it as one of Milton's.

THE PROCESS OF *PARADISE LOST* 221

imperious manner it attributes to him?[39] (The Son may not be the only prac-
titioner of internal scripture in this exchange.) A tension thus runs through the
colloquy that unsettles the Father's supremacy. If the Son, quoting the Psalm,
is right about the Father, Satan may also be right about him, meaning that the
incipient rebellion is justified and that the Father is, in fact, in danger of losing
his position.

In the first colloquy between Father and Son, then, Milton uses a clever joke
to illustrate the difficulties of finding truth through noncoercive communal
practice. The foundations that might ground such a practice—including the
assumption that the Father is always right—slip into uncertainty. In the colloquy, the Father is neither clearly wrong nor clearly right, and the same holds
true of the Son. Quoting scripture to correct God does involve a certain amount
of chutzpah, after all. But perhaps their exchange nevertheless affords a good
model for church life. Indeed, the risk of using scripture to correct God animates Milton's interrelated theological and ecclesial projects: that risk informs
the constant churn of revisions to *De Doctrina Christiana*, and it drives Milton into the even more risky territory of internal scripture. But the Father does
not answer the Son—or Milton, or, in the event, Satan—by reasserting his
supremacy in Psalm 2 fashion and crushing error with his iron scepter. Such
a decisive assertion, Milton writes in *De Doctrina Christiana*, must await the
second coming: "**He conquers and subdues his enemies.** Ps. 2: 9, etc.: *you will
smash them with an iron rod*, namely, at the second coming."[40] Here, too, Milton is rethinking: he has amanuensis "A" insert "namely, at the second coming"
via the left-hand margin (see Figure 6.1). Church life, in the meantime, requires
that the Father's supremacy be suspended: not absent, but held in abeyance so
that those who would find union with him freely have the opportunity, until
the (possibly arbitrary) moment at which it becomes too late.[41] Then, either the

---

[39] Is God the mysterious κατέχον from 2 Thessalonians 2:6–7, the force holding back the day of eschatological reckoning, ironically with the aim of eliminating it? In Schmittian terms, perhaps God is gam-
bling on an everlasting discussion removing the need for his own dictatorial decision. See Carl Schmitt,
Political Theology: Four Chapters on the Concept of Sovereignty, trans. George Schwab (Chicago, IL:
University of Chicago Press, 2005), pp. 62–63.

[40] *DDC*, 204: "**Hostes vincit atque debellat.** Psal. 2. 9. &c; *confriges istos virgâ ferreâ.* secundo nempe
adventu." Milton also references, but does not quote, the verse on MS 447, where he uses it to support
the idea that Christ's reign will take place on the earth. Otherwise, notwithstanding the treatise's over-
whelming commitment to the Father's supremacy, it does not quote this verse, per Michael Bauman, *A
Scripture Index to John Milton's* De Doctrina Christiana (Binghamton, NY: Medieval & Renaissance
Texts & Studies, 1989).

[41] Empson suggests that the Father is considering abdication; *Milton's God*, 133–34. For Bryson, the
Son facilitates this morally necessary abdication; *The Tyranny of Heaven*, ch. 4.

Figure 6.1 Detail from *DDC*, 204 showing the belated second coming

Father's sovereignty re-emerges, revealing (in Schmittian fashion) that it underpinned the system all along—and that Satan was right—or the violent force of the smashing scepter becomes a metaphor (with the agency backwards) for the way that those who do not choose union are *ipso facto* excluded, just as the devils choose Hell over Heaven, again and again.[42]

Given the role of Psalm 2 in both this colloquy and the Son's elevation, perhaps the Son's rejoinder affords an attempt to reconcile the hierarchical structure of Arian Christology with freely chosen union. Together with its implication that the Son's elevation results from a divine decree that is not from eternity, the psalm affirms the Son's place below the Father and above everyone else in a hierarchy. This hierarchy is ontological, not orthodox Trinitarianism's freely chosen economic subordination.[43] In these terms, an Arian Son is less free than a Trinitarian one even as both are subordinate to the Father. Milton, however, both recoups and redefines the Son's freedom by having him use Psalm 2 to correct the Father. Even if the Son is wrong, and the psalm's imagery of divine mockery mischaracterizes God, and given that his own "Regal Power"

---

[42] Schmitt, *Political Theology*.
[43] See Bauman, *Milton's Arianism*, 120–26.

acquired from the Father will not, in fact, prove "dextrous to subdue" the rebel angels (V.739, 741), the Father remains content to let the truth (or otherwise) of these claims, grounded in scripture as they are, emerge in the course of events. Being wrong brings no divine reprimand, no forced acknowledgment of the Father's superior doctrine—in short, no act of groveling, disdained submission.[44] Empson reads the Father's acceptance of the angels' failed service as a tyrant's attempt to patch over their Sisyphean condemnation to an eternity of absurd make-work. By contrast, Milton's narrative of the Son suggests that the prospect of freely chosen union depends, in part, on a non-trivial freedom to be wrong and that the Father's commitment to union on those terms similarly depends on freely refusing to enforce a doctrinal norm by coercive means.[45]

At stake is the church's capacity to accomplish what Milton hopes it can: to arrive at truth through the vigorous conflict, "not without dust and heat," that brings the church into eventual unity.[46] But perhaps the church is like the War in Heaven, as described by the Father—"Whence in perpetual fight they needs must last/Endless, and no solution will be found:/Warr wearied hath perform'd what Warr can do" (VI.693–95)—and only a sovereign intervention can bring order. In theological terms, that sovereign intervention is atonement, necessitated by human fallenness, and the notion that the church might arrive at divine unity without atonement is Pelagian. A kind of cross-pressure thus emerges, with God's potentially tyrannical sovereignty on the one side and humanity's potential Pelagianism on the other.

From this cross-pressured place, the much-debated question of theodicy appears less as a question to be resolved (for or against) than as a productive tension to be navigated. Just as I have been arguing that the project of *De Doctrina Christiana* has more to do with the theological process it exemplifies than with its allegiances to any particular theological camp (Arminian, Socinian, etc.), so also the issue in *Paradise Lost* is not whether the Father turns out to be a tyrant or finally good but has rather to do with the process of attempting to enact a unity with God on terms that give the lie to Satan's claims. In this way, the ontological fact of God's goodness recedes behind an obscuring cloud, "Dark with excessive bright" (III.380). The question of God's goodness may not ultimately hinge on the church's success, but the church succeeds only to the degree that it freely manifests God's ontologically distinctive goodness. As with the relationship between the Father and the Son, Milton understands essential

---

[44] Thus Satan: "[No Pardon] left but by submission; and that word/*Disdain* forbids me" (IV.81–82; italics in original).

[45] Empson, *Milton's God*, 110, 139.

[46] Milton, *Areopagitica* (London, 1644), p. 12.

224 MILTON'S THEOLOGICAL PROCESS

or ontological union as entailing necessity. The church *in its ideal state* thus functions like the cloud, manifesting God's glory while obscuring the potential for divine dictatorship behind a veil of free obedience.[47] God may, in truth, not be a tyrant, but the manifestation of that fact in the human sphere depends on the church. From a human perspective, the argument is not ontological—how God *is*—but phenomenological—how God appears through the life of the church. Under these conditions, the decisive power of God's sovereignty drops out of the picture (until the second coming), and with it also falls away any firm foundation for establishing truth. The church therefore finds itself hoping to work out some kind of union with the divine while operating mostly in the uncertain world of internal scripture.

Still, Milton believes in speaking internal scripture boldly as a ward against the coercive potential latent in the process itself. The deep linkage between the concepts of tradition and tyranny in Milton's thought needs no additional comment except to say that submitting too readily to ecclesial process carries its own dangers. The church lives, if it is to live, on a structural indecision about whether what is coalescing under its care amounts to God or the rank idolatry of tradition. The closer that Milton's church moves to actuating God, the more urgent its need to remember that God remains—and will remain—essentially distinct from it. Satan's usefulness to the church escalates the nearer to God it becomes, as does the urgency of Milton's anti-trinitarianism.

Ontology and Freedom

To an even greater degree than *De Doctrina Christiana*, *Paradise Lost* grounds its ecclesiology in ontology. Milton uses the concept of "substance" to reconcile multiplicity with oneness by linking ontology, cosmology, anti-trinitarianism, and the church.[48] At the heart of this reconciliation is the relationship between Raphael's depictions of active, vitalist matter in Books V and VII and the passive,

---

[47] Compare III.372–89.

[48] I find ecclesiological ramifications in John Rogers's political account of Milton's materialism: *The Matter of Revolution*, ch. 4. Scholars occasionally link Milton's materialism and on his anti-trinitarianism: William B. Hunter Jr, C. A. Patrides, and J. H. Adamson, *Bright Essence* (Salt Like City, UT: University of Utah Press, 1971), pp. 15–25 accurately explains Milton's unorthodox distinction between *substantia* and *essentia*, only to pronounce it orthodox. For rebuttals, see Hugh MacCallum, *Milton and the Sons of God: The Divine Image in Milton's Epic Poetry* (Toronto: University of Toronto Press, 1986), pp. 41–43; Bauman, *Milton's Arianism*, 82–94; Hart, "Matter, Monism, and Narrative," 22–23. See further Rumrich, *Matter of Glory*; Gordon Teskey, *Delirious Milton: The Fate of the Poet in Modernity* (Cambridge, MA: Harvard University Press, 2006), ch. 5; Borris, "Milton's Heterodoxy of the Incarnation."

THE PROCESS OF *PARADISE LOST* 225

atomistic descriptions of Chaos in Books II and III.[49] The point of commonality between these apparently divergent views of matter is none other than the Father himself, in ways that keep the issue of freedom centrally in play:

> Though I uncircumscrib'd my self retire,
> And put not forth my goodness, which is free
> To act or not, Necessitie and Chance
> Approach not mee, and what I will is Fate.
>
> (VII.170–73)

In Milton's cosmos, only the Father has absolute freedom "to act or not" because the Father wills the origin of relationality by sending matter forth from himself. The Father's withdrawal of goodness produces Chaos, out of which he circumscribes a heaven and earth that are yet "Matter unform'd and void" (VII.233). *De Doctrina Christiana* holds that the matter from which Chaos derives is good ("For indeed that original matter is not to be thought of as an evil or worthless thing, but as a good thing, a seed bank of every subsequent good"), but the image of a seed bank [*seminarium*] suggests that what has not been extinguished is the *potentiality* for good.[50] In the epic's ensuing account of creation, Chaos, as pure potentiality, receives an infusion of "vital vertue" from the Spirit and becomes substance—or at least some of it does, as the "dregs/Adverse to life" (VII.238–39) remain cold and become first sediment and then excrement.[51] The difference between God and Chaos does not reside in goodness as moral quality—which the Augustinian language of "if not deprav'd from

[49] On Chaos, see Arthur Sewell, *A Study in Milton's Christian Doctrine* (London: Oxford University Press, 1939), pp. 124–34; Chambers, "Chaos in *Paradise Lost*"; Danielson, *Milton's Good God*, ch. 2; Regina M. Schwartz, *Remembering and Repeating: Biblical Creation in* Paradise Lost (Cambridge: Cambridge University Press, 1988), esp. ch. 1; Rumrich, *Milton Unbound*, ch. 6; Rogers, *The Matter of Revolution*, ch. 4; Teskey, *Delirious Milton*, ch. 4; William Dean Clement, "Milton, Thomas Hobbes, and the Problem of Chaos," *Studies in English Literature 1500–1900* 60, 1 (2020): 133–51. On contemporary debates about the theological valences of materialism, see David S. Sytsma, *Richard Baxter and the Mechanical Philosophers* (Oxford: Oxford University Press, 2017).

[50] *DDC*, 116: "neque enim materia illa res mala est, aut vilis existimanda, sed bona, omnisque boni postmodum producendi seminarium." Schwartz, *Remembering and Repeating*, 11: "I find the inference of an evil chaos so difficult to escape that it is not worth trying." For a rejoinder, see Rumrich, *Milton Unbound*, ch. 6.

[51] On the dregs as excrement, see Denise Gigante, *Taste: A Literary History* (New Haven, CT: Yale University Press, 2005), pp. 30–31. On Milton's broader interest in digestion and excrement, see Michael C. Schoenfeldt, *Bodies and Selves in Early Modern England: Physiology and Inwardness in Spenser, Shakespeare, Herbert, and Milton* (Cambridge: Cambridge University Press, 1999), ch. 4 (esp. pp. 143–45). On Chaos as "a state of *potency*, not of *privation*," see John P. Rumrich, "Of Chaos and Nightingales," in Pruitt and Durham, *Living Texts*, p. 222. I find the dregs, however, ontologically inferior to "the sort of material that went into God's creation of Hell"; Rumrich, "Of Chaos and Nightingales," 221–22. Beatrice Bradley contrasts the dregs with Adam's excremental sweat; "Creative Juices: Sweat in *Paradise Lost*," *Milton Studies* 62, 1 (2020): 107–35.

226   MILTON'S THEOLOGICAL PROCESS

good" (V.471) might suggest—but in goodness as the realization of a potentiality inherent in matter itself.[52] Chaos impedes the freedom "to act or not"
by paradoxically moving matter away from actuation: the "Battel" of "embryon
Atoms" leads to confusion rather than goodness as Chaos "by decision more
imbroiles the fray/By which he Reigns" (II.899–900, 908–909). If only God's
goodness remains free "to act or not," Chaos's "decision" indicates that the difference between God and Chaos is one of actuation and potentiality rather than
one of agency and necessity. "Necessitie and Chance" therefore name material
obstacles to the actuation of goodness, not the absence of agency per se. For Milton, God's freedom requires *potentia*, with the consequence that God remains
partly unactuated, eluding definition not just conceptually but materially as
well.

This all-pervading potentiality points to a capacity in prime matter to decide,
in quasi-Arminian fashion, whether to receive the spirit's vital infusion. It also
points away from the debates about whether or not Milton's ontology is monist
and toward seeing his account of matter as primarily a reflection on the problem
of community, with the concept of substance linking Milton's views on matter
and his anti-trinitarianism.[53] *Paradise Lost* does not therefore simply echo the
anti-trinitarianism of *De Doctrina Christiana* but expands it in response to the
new questions about freedom and ecclesiology that the epic raises through its
narrative demands. In keeping with Regina Schwartz's argument that creation
is redemptive, Milton's discussion of matter's egress from, and return to, God
gives his clearest articulation of what it means for the Son to be one with the
Father and for the church to be one both with itself and with God.[54] In these
terms, Milton's Chaos occupies one end of the spectrum of the church's ontological possibilities (as seen in the anti-Catholic Paradise of Fools, III.474–97),
with the incompletely actualized Father on the other end.

Again, for Milton, substance, not essence, provides a common basis for union
among the divine persons.[55] In Raphael's account of creation, Milton makes
the Father the material substrate of everything that exists: "because I am who
fill/Infinitude, nor vacuous the space" (VII.168–69). Prime matter is, in some

---

[52] As Rumrich argues, "Nor does privation itself always indicate *moral* evil": "Of Chaos and Nightingales, 222–23.

[53] See n 6 above.

[54] Schwartz, *Remembering and Repeating*, 35.

[55] Unlike Arians, Milton makes the Son consubstantial (but not coessential) with the Father; see
Barbara K. Lewalski, *Milton's Brief Epic* (Providence, RI: Brown University Press, 1966), pp. 141–46;
and Rumrich, *Milton Unbound*, 43. Both take aim at the claims of Milton's orthodox subordinationism
collected in Hunter et al, *Bright Essence*.

THE PROCESS OF *PARADISE LOST*   227

sense, God, while the Father himself represents one end on the spectrum of substance. Thus, both Chaos and the Father involve prime matter—the stuff with which God fills all that is. The way that prime matter both is and is not God introduces a core theological complication, illuminated by N. K. Sugimura's observation that "prime matter in Milton oscillates between potentiality and power," with the result that "it repeatedly eludes definition." Sugimura points out that the Latin *potentia* (like its predecessor in Aristotle's Greek, δύναμις) means both potentiality (in the sense of something's capacity to become other than it is) and power (in the sense of the force driving that becoming).[56] This tension or duality helps to clarify a curious claim in *De Doctrina Christiana*, presented amidst an argument about God's omnipotence:

> Hence it does not seem so suitable for God to be called "pure actuality" [*actus purus*], as—on Aristotle's authority—he usually is; for he will then have power to do nothing except what he does do, and he will do that of necessity, even despite the fact that he is all-powerful and has total freedom of action.[57]

In Reformed scholastic theology, the idea of God as *actus purus* is a linchpin whereby divine immutability preserves God's goodness and, with that, the possibility of faith and human salvation.[58] For Milton, however, God cannot be both good and powerful in the sense that God must remain free to actuate potentialities that are not already subject to some prior definition of the good.[59] It is in this sense that God's freedom requires *potentia* in the senses both of power and potentiality. Milton gives expression to the problem of

---

[56] Sugimura, *"Matter of Glorious Trial,"* 55.

[57] *DDC*, 14–15: "Hinc non ità commodè, actus purus, ut solet ex Aristotele, dici videtur Deus; Sic enim agere nihil poterit, nisi quod agit; idque necessario; cum tamen omnipotens sit liberrimèque agat." For useful context, see Yale, 145 n. 47; Danielson, *Milton's Good God*, 41–44; Rumrich, *Matter of Glory*, 62–63.

[58] As one instance, for Polanus, God cannot retain "passive potentiality [*passiva potentia*]" in any degree on the grounds that doing so would undermine divine simplicity and immutability (in the sense of moving from potentiality to actuality): Amandus Polanus, *Syntagma Theologiae Christianae* (Hanover, 1609), p. 966 (II.xiii); compare *PRRD*, III.278–79, 308–20.

[59] Oddly, Milton preserves the notion of God's power (in quasi-nominalist fashion) by rejecting a form of divine omnipotence. Perhaps unconsciously, Milton sides with Zeno against Aristotle's argument that infinities exist only *in potentia* and never in actuality. In the course of Miltonic creation and redemption, God moves from actually infinite to potentially infinite and then to a new kind of actual infinity, differentiated from the first by the presence of genuine plurality. On Milton's relationship to the contemporary debates about infinity, see Erin Webster, "Milton's Pandaemonium and the Infinitesimal Calculus," *English Literary Renaissance* 45, 3 (2015): 425–58; and Matthew Dolloff, "'Gabriel's Trumpet': Milton and Seventeenth-Century Conceptions of Infinity," in Festa and Ainsworth, *Locating Milton*, pp. 81–99. On infinity and Milton's God, see John Leonard, "Milton, Lucretius, and 'the Void Profound of Unessential Night,'" in Pruitt and Durham, *Living Texts*, p. 200. On the queer potentialities in Milton's approach to infinity, see Thomas H. Luxon, "Queering as Critical Practice in Reading *Paradise Lost*," in *Queer Milton*, ed. David L. Orvis (New York: Palgrave Macmillan, 2018), pp. 56–57, and Jason A. Kerr, "Eve's Church," Milton Quarterly 55, 2 (2021): 67–81.

228   MILTON'S THEOLOGICAL PROCESS

definition arising from God's enduring potentiality in Book II of *Paradise Lost*, when he offers a doubly ambiguous alternative to the confused mixtures of Chaos: "Unless th' Almighty Maker them ordain/His dark materials to create more Worlds" (II.915–16). "Dark" speaks to the unresolved potentiality, while "unless" names its dependence on the inscrutable externality of the divine will, although I will be arguing, in due course, that matter's own intrinsic capacity for decision yields an additional dimension of darkness and unknowability.

This material connection between freedom and *potentia* drives the poem's anti-trinitarianism, which aligns, in principle, with that on evidence in *De Doctrina Christiana* but which differs in the relation it bears to the project in which it is embedded. Whereas the treatise's anti-trinitarianism emerged messily in relation to that work's apparent intentions, culminating in the formal anomaly that is I.5, the epic proceeds more deliberately. The notion that God is not *actus purus*, rendered poetically in *Paradise Lost* by God's expropriation of prime matter into the *potentia* of Chaos, affords Milton a means of thinking about how the union between God and creation might happen freely, with the union between Father and Son as the prime example. It is in the nature of matter itself, through the double sense of *potentia*, that Milton thinks the complexity of freedom: as potentiality, matter remains susceptible to external action (such as the spirit's infusion of vital virtue, VII.236), while as power, matter has the capacity to respond to that external action, for instance, by accepting or rejecting the spirit's infusion—the capacity on some level to be otherwise than it is. Instead of a theodicy that preserves God's goodness by recourse to God's immutability, Milton presents a theodicy in which the goodness of God's eventual *actus purus* is contingent on matter itself freely participating. I am arguing that theodicy, for Milton, is a question that can only be settled in the event because God's *actus purus* can only be *bonus* or *malus* when it has been fully actualized, which depends heavily on the exercise of human freedom. For Milton, it seems, God is only as good as humans act. In other words, it was Stalin who made it possible for Empson to see Milton's God as Stalin because Milton's account of matter means that any life remakes God in its image—often without doing God any favors in the process.[60] Milton's primary contribution to the theodicy debates lies, therefore, in how profoundly he puts God's goodness into the hazard while yet imagining its possibility.

That hazard arises most potently in the case of the "black tartareous cold Infernal dregs,/Adverse to life": matter that gets "downward purg'd" (or purges

---

[60] Empson, *Milton's God*, 146. For Milton, *pace* Schmitt, discussion itself actuates praxis, even when the results tilt authoritarian. See Schmitt, *Political Theology*, 62–63.

itself?), perhaps to the point of elimination altogether from the equilibrium of being (VII.237–39).[61] In the dregs, we are invited to imagine some material that leaves God but does not return, possibly because it, Bartleby-like, would prefer not to.[62] I will be returning to the dregs later in the chapter, but I wish to draw attention to the problem they pose by suggesting that theodicy, if it is to be accomplished at all, may entail something like subtraction from God.[63] The eschatological *actus purus* might somehow be less than the initial state before God sent off matter from himself. What this might mean will haunt the argument going forward.

Matter and Atonement

The Son's role in actuating God offers a model for the church, but God's obscurity and refusal of definition make the prospect of the church's success seem vanishingly difficult. Milton, attentive to this problem, uses *Paradise Lost* to develop further the combination of satisfaction and moral exemplar theologies of atonement that he articulated in *De Doctrina Christiana*.[64] The epic does use language of satisfaction, as when the Father in Book III speaks of the need for "rigid satisfaction" (III.212), but it also addresses the problem of reconciling human incapacity with the call to imitative obedience through its material theology of creation. This theology recasts the Son's role in redemption from a satisfaction achieved by his death to a reconciliation achieved through his hypostatic union and his life, with hypostatic union reframed in terms of the spectrum of ontological possibility to encompass both actuality and potentiality.[65] In this way, Milton attempts to reimagine both atonement theologies within the unitary framework of a materialism that also explains the Son's ability to be one with, and yet distinct from, the Father.

---

[61] The blackness of the dregs suggests that Milton's materialism includes racial (and racist) potentialities. Reginald A. Wilburn suggests that reading Milton through the "uppity" responses of writers like Ishmael Reed and Toni Morrison can generate frameworks for thinking about his racial logics: "Getting 'Uppity' with Milton; or Because My Mom Politely Asked: 'Was Milton Racist?'" *Milton Studies* 62, 2 (2020): 266–79.

[62] See Rumrich, *Matter of Glory*, ch. 6.

[63] Marshall Grossman observes something like subtraction from God at the heart of the poem's creative and redemptive economy. "[W]hat God wants is himself: but not his whole self—which would collapse immediately into unity with its original—but rather, himself, as sufficiently different to be his other (self)": "The Genders of God," in *Milton and Gender*, ed. Catherine Gimelli Martin (Cambridge: Cambridge University Press, 2004), p. 106.

[64] See Borris, "Milton's Heterodoxy of the Creation"; and Chapter 5, pp. 173–83.

[65] John Rogers locates Miltonic satisfaction in the Son's pre-Incarnate priestly offering of himself: "Milton and the Heretical Priesthood of Christ," in *Heresy, Literature, and Politics in Early Modern English Culture*, ed. David Loewenstein and John Marshall (Cambridge: Cambridge University Press, 2006), pp. 203–20.

230 MILTON'S THEOLOGICAL PROCESS

Milton's account of creation involves all three divine persons operating in a non-Trinitarian fashion that produces an ontological *ordo salutis* for the collective church, as distinct from a kind of analogical social Trinitarianism or the explicitly Trinitarian model of church communion advocated by John Owen.[66] Returning to Milton's anti-trinitarian way of thinking about the difference between essence as a principle of individuation and substance as a principle of ontological commonality, the limits begin to appear of any analogy between the essential individualities of the Father and of the church's atomic elements. Essence similarly differentiates them from other beings with which they share a common substance, but they differ in that the Father's individuation is paradoxically compatible with dividing himself from his own substance, whereas other essences come into being by creative division from the common substance, as when the Son uses "the golden Compasses, prepar'd/In Gods Eternal store, to circumscribe/This Universe, and all created things" (VII.225–27). The Father has a hierarchical relationship to substance (at least on the level of will) and therefore also to all the essences that the Son individuates within it. These created essences, meanwhile, admit of "various forms, various degrees/Of substance" (V.473–74), which explains, among other things, the difference between angels and humans. These are different kinds of hierarchy: the Father's supremacy is absolute and unchangeable, but, as Raphael acknowledges, the hierarchy among created beings is subject to both stability and change, "Till body up to spirit work, in bounds/Proportiond to each kind" (V.478–79).

This change happens through the process of creation, whereby the Spirit transforms the inert atoms of Chaos into vital matter:

> but on the watrie calme
> His brooding wings the Spirit of God outspred,
> And vital vertue infus'd, and vital warmth
> Throughout the fluid Mass, but downward purg'd
> The black tartareous cold Infernal dregs
> Adverse to life.
>
> (VII.234–39)

The Father, then, provides out of himself the substance, the "embryon atoms" whose incessant collision contains the potential for goodness and order but not

---

[66] Owen's long title makes the point: *Of Communion with God The Father, Sonne, and Holy Ghost, Each Person Distinctly; in Love, Grace, and Consolation: Or The Saints Fellowship With the Father, Sonne, and Holy Ghost, Unfolded* (Oxford, 1657).

THE PROCESS OF *PARADISE LOST*   231

the necessity for it. The Son provides some order, using the golden compasses to divide the substance into distinct essences, which the Spirit then attempts to infuse with vital virtue.[67] Together, these creative acts make possible the church's transformation from chaotic matter to a body that is capable, in some measure, of refinement toward spirit.

Although the poem's language speaks of the Spirit, *De Doctrina Christiana* puts the Son back at the center of the process of ontological transformation toward life.[68] There, Milton identifies the Son as the agent of brooding in Genesis 1:2:

> **At another time** [it means] the father's power and virtue, especially that divine breath which creates and fosters all things: in which way many interpreters, both ancient and more recent, understand that verse Gen. 1: 2: *the spirit of God brooded.* There, however, the son seems rather to be understood, through whom the father is so often said to have created all things.[69]

"Spirit" thus seems to adumbrate a complex divine action in which the Son conveys a virtue deriving from the Father into creation. In these terms, "spirit" comes to signify the virtue or power of life itself, with the Son becoming the

---

[67] Milton's mathematical insistence on the indivisible unity of essence introduces a problem of scale. If the Spirit is infusing vital virtue at the atomic scale, followed by a process of atoms coming together into larger units ("then founded, then conglob'd/Like things to like," VII.239–40), readers are left to wonder whether essences can, in fact, admit some degree of composition such that a human or angel (whose being surely extends beyond a single atom) somehow counts as a single essence rather than a compound of billions, or if understanding God as an indivisible essence requires understanding God as an atom, in which case "atom" swerves wildly away from its Lucretian meaning. The problem points to the issues of continuity and divisibility illustrated in Zeno's paradox. Milton seems to intuit that the infinity of the continuous number line (Cantor's $\aleph_1$) is bigger than the infinity of the integers (Cantor's $\aleph_0$), neglecting (no doubt inadvertently, given his temporal location in the history of mathematics) that the set of real numbers contains the set of integers and so includes numbers that can be represented by division:

> But the answer which is usually given—that there can indeed be only one person of one finite essence, whereas there can be several persons of one infinite essence—is laughable; for because of the very fact that it is an infinite essence, all the more can it be of only one person [quod autem responderi solet, essentiae quidem unius finitae unam duntaxat posse esse personam, infinitae essentiae posse esse personas plures, ridiculum est; eo enim ipso quod infinita essentia est, tanto magis non nisi unius personae esse potest].

DDC, 62. The prospects of subtraction and division haunt Milton's mathematics of God. See Anselm's engagement with the problem of the continuum in ch. 22 of the *Monologion*, in Anselm of Canterbury, *The Major Works*, ed. Brian Davies and Gillian. R. Evans (Oxford: Oxford University Press, 1998), pp. 37–40; Anselm of Canterbury, *Opera Omnia*, ed. Franciscus Salesius Schmitt (Edinburgh: Thomas Nelson, 1940–61), I.39–41.

[68] On the Son's centrality to the poem's account of matter, see Russell M. Hillier, *Milton's Messiah: The Son of God in the Works of John Milton* (Oxford: Oxford University Press, 2011), ch. 3.

[69] *DDC*, 99: "**Nunc** patris potentiam atque virtutem, illum imprimis afflatum divinum omnia creantem ac foventem significari: quo modo locum illum Gen. 1. 2. *spiritus Dei incubabat*, multi intelligunt et antiqui et recentiores. Quanquam illic filius intelligendus videtur potius, per quem pater omnia creasse toties dicitur."

232 MILTON'S THEOLOGICAL PROCESS

means of infusing this virtue into matter through a literal or symbolic divine breath. Philippa Earle even identifies Jesus's brooding in *Paradise Regained* with his materialist process of growth in intellectual capacity, a self-creation that figures the restoration of paradise.[70]

The Son's creative brooding provides a model for vitalist agency in created matter with what John Rogers (building on VII.281) has called a "doctrine of the ferment" that proves "most radical in its unraveling of the authoritarian logic of early modern science."[71] The fermentation metaphor informs Milton's thinking about the church's progress toward unity with God, but in that context, the authoritarian implications prove harder to shake. Rogers finds the ferment at work in Satan's claim, against Abdiel, that he and the other rebel angels are "self-begot, self-rais'd/By our own quick'ning power" (V.860–61).[72] The parallel examples that Rogers adduces from creation, however, depend on the Spirit's infusion of vital virtue: God alienates the lump of matter from himself, the Spirit adds yeast, and only then do things take on lives of their own. In this sense, the Spirit provides a capacity on which the matter must make good—or not, in the case of the "black tartareous cold Infernal dregs." The question of the dregs' agency is complex. If they are like the seed in Jesus's parable that "fell among thornes: and the thornes sprung up, and choked them" (Matthew 13:7, KJV), then chance governs all, and the dregs are simply the victims of bad luck. The more likely parabolic intertext, though, is that most anxious of Miltonic scriptural passages, the parable of the talents, which would mean that matter, receiving the gift of life, incurs an obligation to multiply the gift.[73] This reading comports with Milton's treatment of renewal in *De Doctrina Christiana* I.17, where he argues that even the unregenerate give some signs of renewal (e.g., penitence) such that their failure to make good on the renewal leaves them truly without excuse while also making themselves, and not God, responsible for their exclusion from grace.[74]

Closer attention to the parable, along with Milton's sonnet responding to it, brings the potential for authoritarianism back into play, however. Both parable

---

[70] Philippa Earle, "'Till Body Up to Spirit Work': Maimonidean Prophecy and Monistic Sublimation in *Paradise Regained*," *Milton Studies* 62, 1 (2020): 169. Contrast Sewell, *A Study in Milton's* Christian Doctrine, 101–102.

[71] Rogers, *The Matter of Revolution*, 120. On fermentation as a postlapsarian phenomenon, see Charlotte Nicholls, "'By Gradual Scale Sublimed,'" in Martin, *Milton and the New Scientific Age*, pp. 173–75. The possibility remains of a positive ferment whose agent is spirit rather than yeast.

[72] Rogers, *The Matter of Revolution*, 124.

[73] On Milton and the parable of the talents, see Dayton Haskin, *Milton's Burden of Interpretation* (Philadelphia, PA: University of Pennsylvania Press, 1994), ch. 2.

[74] See *DDC*, 231.

THE PROCESS OF *PARADISE LOST* 233

and poem center the servant given one talent, who "digged in the earth, and hid his Lords money" (Matthew 25:18, KJV). Upon returning, the Lord orders his servants: "cast ye the unprofitable servant into outer darknesse" (Matthew 25:30, KJV). The unprofitable servant does not self-separate from the body of the faithful but must be forcefully ejected by the servants. The profitable servants can make new life, as it were, even in the Lord's absence; their church can operate according to an anti-authoritarian logic because the initial infusion of vital virtue proves sufficient. In the case of the unprofitable servant, though, even an authoritarian logic—"I knewe thee that thou art an hard man" (Matthew 25:24, KJV)—does not suffice to light a spark in lifeless matter, at which point, the Lord's servants forcibly expel the unprofitable servant. At issue is the servant's agency in her own receptivity, and the question of theodicy rests on the distributive justice of the Spirit's infusion. Milton's sonnet treats agency as a potentiality, arguing that the servant with the one talent only *looks* unfaithful: "they also serve who only stand and waite."[75] Accordingly, casting apparently inert matter into outer darkness would be premature: Patience is thus preventing God's murmur as much as the speaker's. The capacity itself can remain alive even when, to quote Milton's earlier poem on the same theme, "no bud or blossom shew'th."[76]

The mark of life, however, is slavery to God: "who best/Bear his milde yoak, they serve him best."[77] This image suggests, in contrast to the biblical parable, that the lord is never, in fact, absent but remains perpetually present in the yoke, however mild. In terms of the fermentation metaphor, though, the yoke is simply the infused vital virtue. What Rogers calls the epic's "political science" might more aptly be called its biopolitics in that the very condition of life entails a relationship of sovereign and subject.[78] But Milton notably presents the decision on life as not merely top-down. If the Spirit does, indeed, infuse vital virtue "throughout the fluid Mass" in a form of hypothetical universalism, the determination of some matter as "adverse to life" turns out to be more a matter of experimental outcome than predetermined result. The possibility remains that matter has the capacity, by virtue of the Spirit's infusing

---

[75] John Milton, *Poems* (London, 1673), p. 59.
[76] Milton, *Poems* (1673), 53.
[77] Milton, *Poems* (1673), 59.
[78] See the title of *The Matter of Revolution*, ch. 4. On biopolitics, see Giorgio Agamben, *Homo Sacer: Sovereign Power and Bare Life*, trans. Daniel Heller-Roazen (Stanford, CA: Stanford University Press, 1998), building on Michel Foucault, *The Birth of Biopolitics: Lectures at the Collège de France 1978–1979*, trans. Graham Burchell (New York: Picador, 2008).

234   MILTON'S THEOLOGICAL PROCESS

call, to decide on its own life, a decision that dispels any illusion of autonomy by acknowledging the relational facts—the ecclesial facts.[79] Raphael presents the ontological analogue to the theology of calling and renewal in *De Doctrina Christiana* I.17 when he explains that one stage of the process whereby matter progresses from body to spirit involves the generation of "Fansie and understanding, whence the Soule/Reason receives, and reason is her being" (V.486–87). Souls become essentially distinct once they receive reason, which has its own degrees (discursive and intuitive; V.487–90). Reason is a form of being that facilitates progression to further forms of being, all grounded in the shared substance and made possible by a capacity for choice. If all matter originated in the primal moment of alienation from God, then relation is a fact, but, intriguingly, Milton seems not to imbue this fact with necessity: God will not force matter that denies relationality to remain in relation.[80] On these terms, substance itself is the "milde yoak," and "service" means anything that furthers the Spirit's vital infusion. Indeed, Milton insists that service can take more than one form: "Thousands at his bidding speed/And post o're Land and Ocean without rest:/They also serve who only stand and waite." It is enough, Milton argues, for potentiality to go unrejected.

Milton treats unrejected potentiality as a guarantor of freedom, even in God, which helps to clarify the nature of the "milde yoak" and slavery to God. In his rejection of the notion that God is *actus purus*, undertaken in part to guarantee God's unbounded freedom, Milton nevertheless appeals to a form of necessity: "Indeed I do not even concede any necessity in God to act, but only that he is necessarily God."[81] God, it turns out, is yoked to life, to the potency of freedom. It is paradoxically necessary—and the yoke consists in this necessity—that God operate under conditions that are otherwise free from necessity. By contrast, the matter that God alienated from himself, to include humans, can be subject to necessity: slavery to sin, in Paul's sense, but also the metaphysical gravity that downward purges the life-averse dregs. The alternative—life—comes with the limiting condition that it requires freedom, and the author of the *Readie and Easie Way* certainly understands that freedom as a condition can be difficult to accept, let alone maintain.[82] Hence the yoke, but also the mildness.

---

[79] Grossman argues that Milton endows matter with a will that is "more *or* less a will toward God: more for matter moving along the line of progress 'up to God,' less for matter following the random and contradictory motions of its 'embryon atoms'": "The Genders of God," 101, citing Fallon, *Milton among the Philosophers*, 107. There, Fallon writes that "life is the usual condition of matter." I am arguing that matter's will consists in the decision on its own life, which means that not-life is (so to speak) a live option.

[80] Thanks to Deidre Nicole Green for shaping my thinking on this point.

[81] *DDC*, 21: "Verum nec in Deo necessitatem agendi ullam concedimus: sed esse quidem necessariò Deum."

[82] John Milton, *The Readie and Easie Way to Establish a Free Commonwealth* (London, 1660).

Ontology and Unity

Milton's theology of the church emerges from his ontological understanding of freedom as a decision on the Spirit's infusion of vital virtue into one's substance. If all beings (i.e., individuated essences) participate in a shared substance that, thanks to the Spirit's infusion, has the capacity to undergo a collective ferment, the decision on life always has consequences beyond those individuals themselves. Freedom entails participation in organic processes beyond any one person's individual control—indeed, perhaps beyond the control of any transcendent *arche*, including God. On these terms, unity becomes difficult to conceptualize, let alone achieve. Here too, Milton's primary model remains the Son, whose colloquy with the Father in Book III offers the practical corollary to what he achieves metaphysically through the hypostatic union (or the theological idea that the incarnate Jesus unites divine and human natures in a single person). The resulting metaphysics of speech—internal scripture—bring the complex contingency of church life into view, as indicated by the poem's treatments of human ecclesial practice in its depiction of Adam and Eve.[83]

Milton tackles the problem of union directly in the epic's treatment of the Son's mediation. If Milton refuses to unite the Father and the Son via a single shared essence, his account of the hypostatic union affords him a basis for nevertheless understanding the Son as in some sense divine. Milton's understanding that matter can progress—"Till body up to spirit work" (V.478)—affords crucial context for his perspective on the hypostatic union. Raphael's explanation treats the "various forms, various degrees/Of substance" as waystations on the roundabout path that begins with proceeding from "one first matter all" and culminates in a kind of ontological return to God (VII.472–74). Jesus, whose mediatorial function is as much a matter of ontology as office, embodies this path in its entirety, containing within his being both the procession and the return. In *De Doctrina Christiana*, Milton insists that the Son is fully human and defends this position against Zanchius's view that Christ assumed human nature instead of humanity proper.[84] For Milton, then, the Son in his humanity fully occupies one of the lower degrees of substance, while in his divinity he occupies a higher, "more refin'd, more spiritous, and pure,/As neerer to him plac't or neerer tending" (V.475–76).

The Son maintains in his person an ontological resistance to the progression of matter while doing so paradoxically—even mysteriously—in a manner that renders the need for such progression superfluous. The mystery of hypostatic

---

[83] See Kerr, "Eve's Church."
[84] *DDC*, 189–90. See the discussion in Chapter 5, pp. 184–85.

236   MILTON'S THEOLOGICAL PROCESS

union brings various forms and degrees into harmony with a kind of ontological union. Notably, however, the hypostatic is a different sort of union than the essential union posited by Trinitarian orthodoxy, as Milton also insists, observing that the scriptures describe the first as a mystery while nowhere mentioning the second.[85] The difference between these kinds of union turns on Christ's human nature. A human Christ, Milton avers, requires a distinction between the Son's essence and the Father's: "it could not coalesce into one person with man without the Father also being contained in the same union—without man, too, becoming one person with the Father, just as with the son, which is impossible."[86] Here, a return to "one first matter all" seems to smack of the potential for an appalling human assumption of the Father—by implication, the worst sort of *lèse-majesté*. In this sense, the distinction of persons, up to and including the subordinate Son, seems dependent on an ontological hierarchy that the Son nevertheless collapses in his own person. The hierarchy becomes all at once merely apparent and theologically necessary, offering a firm indecision on the question of hierarchy or equality.

A prospective body-spirit dualism thus lurks in the ontological distinction of persons, in the variety of forms and degrees that emerge from "one first matter all" but cannot ever quite be allowed to collapse back into it. William Walker offers a way of getting at this dualism when he argues that Milton's writings on ecclesiastical and civil power depend on a dualist distinction between external force (the province of the state) and internal freedom. Walker makes the case that Milton's thinking on this point owes to the tradition established by Luther's political thought. Milton's anti-trinitarian perspective on the hypostatic union offers an alternative possibility, however. In his person, the Son holds together divergent degrees of substance, corresponding to divergent degrees of freedom. Raphael says that humans operate by discursive reason and angels by intuitive, "Differing but in degree, of kind the same" (V.490). The Son embodies both poles of a similar, though presumably broader, difference between human "body" and divine "spirit." As Walker demonstrates, Milton makes bodies the province of civil power and spirits the province of ecclesiastical power. For Walker, the dualism arises from Milton's firm distinction between external body and internal spirit; these, he argues, are not differences of degree; the

---

[85] *DDC*, 187–88.

[86] *DDC*, 192: "eadem si esset, in unam personam cum homine coalescere non posset, quin pater etiam eadem unione contineretur, quin homo quoque eadem persona cum Patre haud secus atque cum filio fieret, quod impossibile est."

THE PROCESS OF *PARADISE LOST*   237

distinction marks "a difference between space and that which occupies and partitions space."[87] Milton does not use these terms in *A Treatise of Civil Power*, but the difference Walker describes could also be characterized as that between substance and essence, as Milton defines them, especially given his understanding of creation as an act of circumscription by the golden compasses (VII.225–26). In these terms, body is raw matter or substance, and spirit is the vital essence that arises in that substance from a decision on the life proffered by the Spirit's infusion.

Milton's ontological account of the hypostatic union casts the Son's exemplarity in ontological terms. Humans thus consist of both body and spirit, as does the Son in his human nature: the terms do not imply dualism per se but hierarchically distinct states or degrees of substance. Humans under the influence of spiritual renewal are a blend of more and less refined substance—a difference offering at least the appearance of dualism—and if this is the case, then it seems that the hypostatic union consists of a similar, though vastly more extreme, combination that encompasses both living ends of the spectrum (to the exclusion, presumably, of the dregs). By combining these extremes, the Son shows that life and freedom remain possible throughout the spectrum of being: no essence, no matter how lowly, is without promise or capacity, its growth contingent merely on accepting the Spirit's vital infusion and the resulting emergent order. The mystery of the hypostatic union exemplifies the potentiality active in every degree of substance, showing (but not determining) what could come of accepting the spirit's creative infusion. The Son simultaneously inhabits two ontological states: he is at once the matter alienated from God, a pure potentiality awaiting both the infusion and the subsequent decision, and the most completely alive of all created essences, a kind of pure actuality. This duality makes his exemplarity both possible and potentially redemptive. The decision on life that he models avoids the possibility of Pelagianism by demonstrating the creative potential of Spirit; he shows what redemption looks like and how to become it.

The Son's exemplary interplay with God's freedom and unknowability is on display in the colloquy in Book III, where the Son demonstrates internal scripture becoming effectual. The narrative drive of this exchange derives from the Son moving the Father from potentiality to actuality in a series of successive stages. The Father introduces the problem of passivity in his first speech:

---

[87] William Walker, "Milton's Dualistic Theory of Religious Toleration in *A Treatise of Civil Power, Of Christian Doctrine, and Paradise Lost*," *Modern Philology* 99, 2 (2001): 215.

238 MILTON'S THEOLOGICAL PROCESS

> What pleasure I from such obedience paid,
> When Will and Reason (Reason also is choice)
> Useless and vain, of freedom both despoild,
> Made passive both, had servd necessitie,
> Not mee.
>
> (III.107–111)

The passivity here pertains not to God but to humans, and yet humans consist of the divine matter that God alienated from himself. Ontologically, passivity would mean amounting to the dregs. Given that, for Milton, all things have their subsistence from God, a God conceived as *actus purus* could only have a relationship of utter necessity with creation. The Son himself therefore participates in God's potentiality, and he works to actuate God both through his own actions and through his redemptive relationship with humans, who are also ontologically involved in the process of actuating God.

The Book III colloquy finds the Son actuating God in this way. The Father's first speech lays out the conditions of human freedom, understood paradoxically as the product of "the high Decree/Unchangeable, Eternal, which ordain'd/Thir freedom" (III.126–28). The unchangeability of the decree suggests that it is a kind of *actus purus*, and that it is necessary in the sense that God's character requires it. And yet the decree of freedom, alongside Milton's account of creation, means that potentiality remains in the matter alienated from the Father. The Father, within the bounds that currently circumscribe him, is, in some sense, an *actus purus*, although the *actus purus* will become more complete as more matter moves from potentiality to actuality—a play on the idea that infinity plus one equals infinity, allowing change and changelessness to coincide. The Son, meanwhile, hearing the Father's decree that "Man therefore shall find grace" (III.131), understands that this decree rests on unactualized potentiality. This understanding appears in his recognition that the absence of grace would be a kind of uncreation: "wilt thou thy self/Abolish thy Creation, and unmake,/For him, what for thy glorie thou hast made?" (III.162–64). Without grace, matter would go the way of the dregs instead of returning to God, putting God's goodness into question: "So should thy goodness and thy greatness both/Be questiond and blaspheam'd without defence" (III.165–66). The Son's response articulates the risks implied by the Father's first speech in a way that suggests the need for action: he wonders how the grace will come about, given that God would cease to be God without it. When the Father says, then, "All hast thou spok'n as my thoughts are, all/As my Eternal purpose hath decreed" (III.171–72), he is not saying that the Son has said what

THE PROCESS OF *PARADISE LOST*   239

he (the Father) had already thought; rather, the present-tense "are" suggests that the Son's words have actuated a latent potentiality. By speaking in this way, the Father approves the Son's words as scriptural, showing how an internal scriptural response can become an external scriptural one.

The plan that subsequently emerges, and for which the Son volunteers, arises through a joint creation in which the Son actuates and repatriates the Father's expropriated matter. In this way, the Son becomes an agent of redemption in a strikingly literal sense, and this becoming manifests ontologically.[88] Before the first speech, the Son is already ontologically near to the Father—"in him all his Father shon/Substantially express'd" (III.139–40)—and the exchange concludes with the Father declaring that the Son will come to accomplish a new ontological feat in his exaltation: "thy Humiliation shall exalt/With thee thy Manhood also to this Throne" (III.313–14).[89] Humanity, which the Father described lines earlier in terms of the Son's "descending to assume/Mans Nature" (III.303–04), now occupies the exalted throne in the person of the Son, who "shalt Reign / Both God and Man, Son both of God and Man,/Anointed universal King" (III.315–17). Bringing humanity back into God's presence in the Son's exalted incarnate kingship is not the same as bringing all human beings into the presence, but the Son's combined redemption and example make a human ontological return possible:

> thy merit
> Imputed shall absolve them who renounce
> Thir own both righteous and unrighteous deeds,
> And live in thee transplanted, and from thee
> Receive new life.
>
> (III.290–94)

[88] For Danielson, the colloquy

> present[s] the reader, or a character, or both reader and character, with only a part of the truth, with only a limited view of reality, in such a way that questions are raised concerning divine justice or providence; and then, in one or more stages, to present further truths, a more complete view of reality, which serves at least in part to answer the question originally raised, and possibly to reevaluate the terms of the question.

Milton's Good God, 107. I suggest that Milton's account of substance-becoming-essence gives that unfolding a different ontological basis than the Platonism that Danielson assumes: the Truth needs to be instantiated, not merely uncovered. *Paradise Lost*, in other words, asks us to read it as though we did not already know how everything would turn out, notwithstanding the presumed familiarity of biblical narrative.

[89] On "Substantially express'd" as conveying both sameness and difference, see Antoinina Bevan Zlatar, "'The Image of Their Glorious Maker': Looking at Representation and Similitude in Milton's *Paradise Lost*," in *What Is an Image in Medieval and Early Modern England?*, ed. Antoinina Bevan Zlatar and Olga Timofeeva (Tübingen: Narr Francke Attempto, 2017), p. 115.

240 MILTON'S THEOLOGICAL PROCESS

"Transplanted" frames humans as seeds, capable of growth once their (already existent) potentiality has been replanted in the Son.[90] If they make the decision on life by renouncing their own deeds, they receive new life by the infusion of the Spirit and begin their ontological trajectory away from being lifeless dregs. "Imputed" might suggest "implanted," but "transplanted" emphasizes the process over the result.

With this concept of transplantation, an organic metaphor that expresses the material possibility of *imitatio Christi* runs alongside one of the poem's most forceful expressions of penal substitution. The metaphor begins by relocating the familiar image of Christ as "Virgin seed" (III.284) from the realm of human reproduction to that of plant reproduction, figuring Christ as a "second root" to replace Adam (III.288). Humans are then transplanted from death in Adam to life in Christ, a transplantation that reverses the logic of imputation: humans are put into Christ instead of Christ's merit being put into them. This process, which *De Doctrina Christiana* (I.21) calls "ingrafting into Christ [*insitio in Christum*]," produces the effects of "new life and growth."[91] This new life, one of whose effects is charity, happens "**Spontaneously and freely**. For our own effort is constantly required."[92] The cause of this charity does not reside in humans—Milton describes it as "**arising out of a sense of the divine love poured out into the hearts of the regenerate through the spirit**"—yet its maintenance requires human cooperation.[93] This effusion of the spirit [*per spiritum effusi*] bears a clear kinship to the infusion of vital virtue described in Raphael's account of creation. In both treatise and poem, it involves a divine gift of capacity that humans must then exercise.

Even the poem's depiction of satisfaction gestures, through its organic metaphor, toward the need for *imitatio Christi* in the larger project of reconciling humans to God. Transplantation enables humans to undergo the judgment of death together with Christ—*not* by substitution—and rise together with him. In the very moment of satisfaction, the poem inaugurates an organic process in which humans themselves must participate. Even though the next sentence of the poem speaks of humans as being "ransomed with his own [i.e., Christ's] dear life" (III.297), the passage also admits of the reading where humans, because of the ingrafting, participate not in an exchange of death for death but in a vital power that exceeds death. This participation is not meritorious on humans'

---

[90] See Claude N. Stulting, Jr, "*Theosis* and *Paideia* in the Writings of Gregory of Nyssa and the Prelapsarian Books of Milton's *Paradise Lost*," in Pruitt and Durham, *Living Texts*, pp. 148–49.

[91] *DDC*, 256: "Regenerationis simul et insitionis huius effecta communia sunt vita nova et auctio."

[92] *DDC*, 262: "**Sua sponte ac libere.** nostra enim opera passim requiritur."

[93] *DDC*, 260: "**charitas ex sensu divini amoris in corda regenitorum per spiritum effusi.**"

THE PROCESS OF *PARADISE LOST*   241

part, in that it depends wholly on Christ, and yet it is premised on a capacity for life and growth, framed in organic terms. Christ, as Man, shall "rising with him [i.e., 'man' in the generic sense of 'human'] raise/His Brethren" (III.296–97) such that humans become both participants in and recipients of life, the image of a resurrection from death to life operating alongside the image of a seed becoming a plant. The pre-renewal human state is, in these terms, only a figurative death, better understood as unactuated potentiality, sinful primarily in its tendency toward chaos, and the possibility of becoming the dregs.

Ultimately, the Son enacts human restoration (to use the umbrella term in *De Doctrina Christiana* for the processes of redemption and renewal) through an ontological love. This love consists in his being implanted with chaotic materials whose actions, though partly repudiated, are yet at odds with the ontological harmony that union with God entails. The notion of partial repudiation raises the question of the dregs, whose downward purgation suggests the possibility of total repudiation. By thinking of the dregs as divine excrement, though, Denise Gigante invites us to see salvation as a process of divine digestion—what John Rumrich calls "nutritional communion"—where the materials that come in are (mostly) transmuted into the greater life of an eventual divine *actus purus*.[94] Some materials, however, will not accept grace and so be destroyed, or expelled:

> So Heav'nly love shall outdoo Hellish hate
> Giving to death, and dying to redeeme,
> So dearly to redeem what Hellish hate
> So easily destroy'd, and still destroyes
> In those who, when they may, accept not grace.
>
> (III.298–302)

In death, the Son shows that the status of the dregs as adverse to life is not fated or inevitable but results rather from hellish hate.[95] As the case of Satan shows, hellish hate can be external and internal at the same time, and the dregs indicate the possibility that such is true on the basic level of matter itself. Because all matter comes from God, it all retains the potentiality for life. In these terms, love means a movement from actuality (God) to potentiality (humanity) in

---

[94] Gigante, *Taste*, 30–31; Rumrich, *Milton Unbound*, 122. See also Joanna Picciotto, *Labors of Innocence in Early Modern England* (Cambridge, MA: Harvard University Press, 2010), pp. 467–71.

[95] For Picciotto, innocent progress depends on a "distributed subjectivity," a "corporate subject of innocence" whose sundering into "discrete sensitive bodies [. . .]" coincides with that subject's fall from Paradise": *Labors of Innocence*, 472. On the dregs as a principle of separation and arelationality that resembles what God might have been like prior to the expropriation of matter that enabled the formation of other essences, see Kerr, "Eve's Church."

242 MILTON'S THEOLOGICAL PROCESS

order to present the possibility of actuation, understood as grace, or the transformative effects of digestion. The Father describes this kenotic action by the Son in terms indebted to Paul: "in thee/Love hath abounded more then Glory abounds" (III.311–12). In Paul's formula ("but where sinne abounded, grace did much more abound" [Rom: 5:20, KJV]). Milton replaces sin with glory and grace with love, and this replacement connects the kenotic reversal of "thy Humiliation shall exalt" with a non-coercive emphasis on love as freedom. The Son's preference for love over glory manifests in the Incarnation, in his redeeming humanity from the necessity of ontological inertness, and in his effecting human transformation through invited imitation rather than through force. Indeed, in a further reversal of Psalm 2, the Father envisions an eschatological end to coercion: "Then thou thy regal Scepter shalt lay by,/For regal Scepter then no more shall need,/God shall be All in All" (III.339–41). Perhaps the iron scepter will vanish simply because there are no more enemies to crush, but the Son's redemptive work suggests an alternative trajectory in which all of creation has, in love, fully realized its potential for life and thereby finally actuated God, while the dregs, actuating in themselves the potentiality of hellish hate, freely excrete themselves from the body of God, "downward purg'd" by the Spirit only in the sense that it occupies a space they refuse to enter (VII.237).

The divine colloquy thus affords a model of the church whose many members struggle to come together amidst the dust and heat of argumentative striving toward truth. The Father remains only partially actuated in that some matter remains alienated from him and not yet brought to life. The Son shows that creative responsiveness to the Father's speech can bring God more fully into actuation as a promised grace becomes ontological reality. The Son's redemption enables humans to participate in this responsiveness by welcoming the Spirit's vital infusion and then fermenting together toward greater and greater life. All this growth tends toward a moment, as yet unimaginable because still only *in potentia*, when God will be all in all. Whatever this state entails, it does not mean the incorporation of all creation into the divine essence, which Milton insists must remain singular and uniquely accessible to the Father. Rather, the substance that all creation derives from the Father forms the basis of unity, with the result that many fully realized essences sharing the same substance join together in one complete *actus purus*.[96] In that unity, modeled by the Son, Milton sees God and church find their ultimate reality in the same grand moment of consummation.

---

[96] On the idea that essences persist in the final "all in all," see Koester, "Mathematical Milton," 123.

Because the Son's participation in his conversations with the Father work to actuate God, they show the part that internal scripture plays in this consummation. Given that the relevant aspects of the Father remain as yet unactuated in the timeline of the poem, they cannot be expressions of external scripture in the way that modern readers equipped to hear biblical allusions in Milton's language might think. Rather, these exchanges show external scripture in the making as the Son's utterances succeed in actuating God. Human attempts at speaking scripture are less likely to meet with such ready success, but the Son's practice models both the speaking and the judging: what leads to greater life receives approbation, not just abstractly but materially, as God comes closer to being all in all. Milton has responded to the difficulty inherent in representing God by using his representation to think about the problem, all the while hoping that his words, too, have succeeded in actuating God.

Conclusion: Ontological Humility

Milton's hope that his words might actuate God certainly comports with his reputation for egotism, and yet his awareness of the problems of representation involved tends toward what I have been calling his ontological humility: his habit of speaking boldly but in the context of an ecclesiological process that will try his words. In that vein, I wish to consider briefly the epic invocations as church moments, building on the heft that the poem's material metaphors have lent to the word "ontological." Epic invocations require expressions of humility as a matter of convention—they explain the need for a muse—and as such, few readers are perhaps inclined to take them altogether seriously: the show of humility simply serves as a foil for the grandeur of the undertaking.

Nevertheless, moments in the invocations situate Milton within the ecclesial process this book has been tracing in ways that give substance to his humility. The invocations thus show in miniature how the epic genre of *Paradise Lost* afforded an opportunity to take up the project of *De Doctrina Christiana* and develop it in new directions. The poem's first invocation invites the Spirit that "with mighty wings outspread/Dove-like satst brooding on the vast Abyss/And mad'st it pregnant" to infuse Milton similarly with vital virtue: "What in me is dark/Illumin, what is low raise and support" (I.20–23). Anticipating the theology of substance and creation to follow, Milton frames himself as an imperfectly

244 MILTON'S THEOLOGICAL PROCESS

achieved being, with some of his substance not yet as alive as it might be and in need of the Spirit's "brooding" fermentation. The invocation in Book III continues this theme of substantial impediment, arguing at some length that, given light's association with the virtuous power of creation, Milton's blindness has consequently "wisdom at one entrance quite shut out," leaving him to plead that "Celestial light/Shine inward, and the mind through all her powers/Irradiate" (III.50–53). Milton directs his prayer toward his capacity to speak internal scripture; other modes of knowing have been closed off, but that one remains, if yet in need of divine illumination. The impediment grows cosmic in Book VII, which finds Milton singing "with mortal voice, unchang'd/To hoarce or mute, though fall'n on evil dayes" (VII.24–25). His plea is twofold: that there might be some community (or church) to counter his solitude ("fit audience find, though few," echoing, perhaps, the preference for small congregations expressed in *De Doctrina Christiana*), and that Urania might improve the substantial being of society itself ("drive farr off the barbarous dissonance," VII.31–32).[97] At stake are both Milton's own capacity to sing and the ecclesial capacity for his song to be heard, weighed, and sifted. He is not content to sing for himself! Book IX presents Milton's strongest claim in the poem to be speaking internal scripture:

> If answerable style I can obtaine
> Of my Celestial Patroness, who deignes
> Her nightly visitation unimplor'd,
> And dictates to me slumbring, or inspires
> Easie my unpremeditated Verse[.]
>
> (IX.20–24)

If Milton credits the "Celestial Patroness" as the source of his song, he nevertheless expresses doubts about his own capacities: "*If* answerable style I can obtaine." He is confident of his music's inspired source but less confident that his own capacities are up to the performance. He worries that he lives in an environment adverse to his own substantial development: "unless an age too late, or cold/Climat, or Years damp my intended wing/Deprest, and much they may if all be mine" (IX.44–46). Cognizant that his song requires substantial vigor and virtue, Milton finds himself somewhat sluggish or, perhaps, dreggish.

---

[97] *DDC*, 416. See the discussion in Chapter 3.

The invocations reveal a Milton aware of his own place on the spectrum of substance, powerfully capacitated, on the one hand, but in need of external aid on the other. Outside the invocations is the song itself, in all its complexity, awaiting evaluation from its readers, however fit we turn out to be. The invocations' blend of bluster and humility, along with the hope that they express for an audience able to hear, transform epic convention into a foundational ecclesial gesture. The church as Milton sees it rests on members' willingness to speak boldly the truth as they understand it, knowing that they might be wrong but not letting that possibility restrain their witness unduly.

Conclusion

On Milton and Theology

I conclude where I began by asking "Why should anyone read *De Doctrina Christiana*?" This book has responded with a sustained argument about *how* to read Milton's theological treatise, but the *why* question connects the particular, and perhaps narrow, work of this book to the larger matter of what it means to engage with theology in literary texts. One answer is simply to read theological texts as texts—as contingent, messy attempts to work out in language something that matters (at least to the people who wrote them). The gulf between poems and theological treatises is not so vast and unbridgeable as some have made it out to be.

The perceived gulf has, I think, to do with a question about doctrine and representation, or the perception that treatises record putatively stable doctrine while literary texts represent it, with all the complexities of representation that philosophers have been arguing about at least since Plato. The preceding chapters' sustained readings of *De Doctrina Christiana*—a book that proclaims doctrine as its subject—suggest that this binary is not tenable. To be sure, doctrinal writing exhibits what might be called a "will to stability," and it does not altogether fail to accomplish its ends, as the enduring influence of, say, Augustine attests. Nevertheless, I'd venture that few people (if any) now turn to Augustine as a secure repository of viable ideas about God and not just because his thinking shifted discernibly over the course of his career. Rather, people more usually read Augustine at the intersection of his mammoth influence and some sense of high-stakes disagreement with him. There is, to use the language of Pseudo-Dionysius, something at once cataphatic and apophatic about such reading. It's not that doctrine has dissolved into an amorphous blob devoid of internal distinction, but neither has it coalesced into some adamantine key to all mythologies.

So, theological texts are just texts, subject to the complexities that attend texts as such. Consequently, what Kimberly Johnson writes of seventeenth-century eucharistic poetry also pertains to theological treatises; she opts to locate the theological import of texts in poetics, defined as "*the way poems work as literary artifacts*," rather than in doctrine, or "whatever opinions concerning

---

Milton's Theological Process. Jason A. Kerr, Oxford University Press. © Jason A. Kerr (2023).
DOI: 10.1093/oso/9780198875086.003.0008

sacramental theology Renaissance literature seems to offer."[1] I have similarly found theology more at work in Milton's attempts to articulate doctrine than in the doctrine that he eventually articulates, precisely because attention to the attempts reveals the contingency of the results. There are compelling modern and postmodern ways of thinking about the constitutive instability of doctrine, but it is hardly a new phenomenon in the history of theology. As one instance, here is a famous passage from Anselm's preface to his *Proslogion:* "For I do not seek to understand so that I may believe; but I believe so that I may understand. For I believe this also, that 'unless I believe, I shall not understand' [Isaiah 7: 9]."[2] Anselm's formulation works to keep mystery at the heart of the enterprise: belief precedes understanding, not the other way around. This formulation thus stands as a counterbalance to the ensuing argument for God's existence, which cannot be reduced to philosophy, no matter how philosophical its language; that is, Anselm's arguments respond to a question that he knows he cannot answer, and he deliberately acknowledges the contingency of his undertaking.[3]

This book has primarily attended to the poetics at work in theological texts by closely tracking shifts in the linguistic surface of *De Doctrina Christiana.* Why did Milton first think of renewal as "external," and what led him to think that "natural" was a better word? These aspects of the text have conceptual implications, to be sure, but they also draw attention to the text as text, to the ways that *De Doctrina Christiana* locates doctrine in the work of representation itself instead of treating doctrine as the object of representation. I have argued that the concept of "internal scripture" articulates Milton's growing awareness of this situation, which seems to have been at some odds with his initial intention to gather the doctrine represented in scripture and re-represent it using Ramist logic.

A second way of attending to theological poetics emerges from the first: once Milton has acknowledged the contingency of his doctrinal expressions, they open up to responses and possibilities that he did not intend precisely

---

[1] Kimberly Johnson, *Made Flesh: Sacrament and Poetics in Post-Reformation England* (Philadelphia, PA: University of Pennsylvania Press, 2014), p. 1.

[2] Anselm of Canterbury, *The Major Works,* ed. Brian Davies and G. R. Evans. Oxford World's Classics. (Oxford: Oxford University Press, 1998), p. 87 [*Opera*, I.100]: "Neque enim quaero intelligere ut credam, sed credo ut intelligam. Nam et hoc credo: quia 'nisi credidero, non intelligam.'"

[3] Anselm's dictum might be read as limiting understanding to the in-group of believers, but this reading stands at odds with the uncertainty and reluctance with which he prefaces the *Proslogion* and *a fortiore* the earlier *Monologion.* As with Milton's epic invocations, the fact that these tropes are, on some level, conventional does not preclude taking them seriously and thinking about *why* they are conventional.

248 MILTON'S THEOLOGICAL PROCESS

because they need to do that if they are to accomplish their end. I have written elsewhere that Milton's representation of Eve in *Paradise Lost* inadvertently raises questions about the epic's materialist ecclesiology.[4] Fundamentally, the question is whether Milton imagines Eve as capable of evaluating his own internal-scriptural representation of her, to which I answer that he does but only in the part of the poem where he imagines her as the dregs, those materials that are "adverse to life" and are consequently "downward purg'd" (VII.237–39). This moment of alternative imagination occurs in Book X, where Milton depicts Eve as choosing to live childless with Adam until they both die:

> While yet we live, scarse one short hour perhaps,
> Between us two let there be peace, both joyning,
> As joyn'd in injuries, one enmitie
> Against a Foe by doom express assign'd us,
> That cruel serpent.
>
> (X.923–27)

By invoking the promised enmity between her seed and the serpent, and by hoping to enact that enmity together with Adam in the short time before their death, Eve all but explicitly frames their community as an alternative body of Christ. The quasi-ecclesial body that results is a queer community that refuses what Lee Edelman has called "reproductive futurism," the dependence of the future as such on the production of children.[5] Granted, the poem goes on to reject this vision of the church by having Eve accept childbearing, thereby making the eventual birth of Jesus possible. Nevertheless, by imagining a church aligned with the dregs, Milton gestures back to the God who inaugurated creation in an act of withdrawal that freed some erstwhile divine matter from necessity. Within the poem's materialist ecclesiology, some and perhaps most of that matter gradually works its way from body up to spirit until God is once again "all in all" (III.341), but without the dregs, this final all would somehow be less than the inaugural all. In this sense, God's "all in all" requires both the vitalist church and its queer cousin. *Paradise Lost* turns out to be theologically richer than its doctrinal intentions, in part because the possibility of God-talk requires

---

[4] The following paragraph summarizes Jason A. Kerr, "Eve's Church," *Milton Quarterly* 55, 2 (2021): 67–81.

[5] Lee Edelman, *No Future: Queer Theory and the Death Drive* (Durham, NC: Duke University Press, 2004), p. 2. I am indebted to forthcoming work by Lara Dodds that puts *Paradise Lost* (and especially Book X) in conversation with Edelman.

CONCLUSION 249

the presence of cracks in the representational structure, or else the poem risks becoming a theologically inert idol.

The prospect that the epic might become theologically inert touches (ironically) on a highly charged sense that devotional reading is incompatible with the kind of critical reading that informs professionally responsible literary criticism. Michael Bryson gave provocative expression to this concern when he wrote that "Milton *studies* have often threatened to turn into Milton *ministries*" in the course of a larger debate about whether Milton was a poet of "certainty" or one of "incertitude," on God's side or on Satan's.[6] An analogous professional pressure appears in the long effort to distinguish religious studies as a discipline from theology—the former aspiring to the outsider's view expressed in the dictum "know one, know none," meaning that those who know only one religion know nothing about religion, especially if the one religion they know is their own.[7] Theology, by implication, is insular, parochial, belying an investment more personal than public and therefore best kept to oneself. Religious studies is open and theology is closed, to invoke a distinction similarly made between *Paradise Lost* and *De Doctrina Christiana*. While allowing for the clearly evident possibility that theology can be narrow, crabbed, and exclusionary, as indeed both *De Doctrina Christiana* and *Paradise Lost* are at times, I hope that this book has demonstrated that such aspirations to closure founder on the very language with which they are undertaken.

The solution is not to dismiss the narrow and the crabbed in the name of some openness that allegedly exceeds it but rather to recognize that theological work resides in the interplay between these potentialities. In this way, to read Milton theologically is to read him in the interplay between our ossifying ideas of him (whatever they may be) and the parts of his oeuvre that work against them, including parts that seem at odds with his intentions or conscious self-fashioning. I recognize that I am not proposing some radically new way of reading, and yet here is where one reason to read *De Doctrina Christiana* resides. It occupies an awkward place in the Miltonic canon: accepted by most,

---

[6] Michael Bryson, *The Tyranny of Heaven: Milton's Rejection of God as King* (Newark, DE: University of Delaware Press, 2004), p. 23. For some of the sparks issuing from Bryson's firm grasp on the third rail, see David V. Urban, "Speaking for the Dead: C. S. Lewis Answers the New Milton Criticism; or, 'Milton Ministries' Strikes Back," *Milton Quarterly* 45, 2 (2011): 95–106; Peter C. Herman, "C. S. Lewis, David Urban, and the New Milton Criticism," *Milton Quarterly* 45, 4 (2011): 258–66; David V. Urban, "The Acolyte's Rejoinder: C. S. Lewis and the New Milton Criticism, Yet Once More," *Milton Quarterly*, 46, 3 (2012): 174–81. On Milton as a poet of incertitude, see Peter C. Herman, *Destabilizing Milton: Paradise Lost and the Poetics of Incertitude* (New York: Palgrave Macmillan, 2005).

[7] The dictum originates in F. Max Müller, *Introduction to the Science of Religion* (London: Longman, Green, and Co., 1873), p. 16. Its precise application has since shifted.

250 MILTON'S THEOLOGICAL PROCESS

questioned by some, read in depth by few. There may be other, stranger Miltonic byways (here's looking at you, *Accedence Commenc't Grammar* or *Brief History of Muscovia*), but none is so potently occupied with subjects of persistent interest to Milton while nevertheless remaining stubbornly inassimilable.[8] That resistance to assimilation, I am suggesting, is a feature rather than a bug. *De Doctrina Christiana* gives us a Milton who—on the literal material surface of the manuscript—was still figuring things out. Given the messiness of the manuscript, it should be little surprise that its contents align unevenly with Milton's published works.

For two centuries, this misalignment has been a nagging problem in Milton studies. Given that the preponderance of the material evidence connects the manuscript to Milton, the problem isn't going anywhere. The long tradition has been to treat this problem as a matter of doctrine: does the treatise's account of the Son align with that in *Paradise Lost*, or not? But perhaps the misalignment affords a theological opportunity in the way that it allows John Milton, the human being, to remain perpetually resistant to John Milton, the object of scholarly interest. Opportunities abound to make an idol of the author of *Eikonoklastes*: there is Milton, a soul so bookish as to follow his MA with an extended course of private study; there is Milton, defender of liberty against the tyranny of kings; and there is Milton, author of the greatest epic poem in the English language.[9] None of these images is wrong, exactly, and yet each is incomplete. We read *De Doctrina Christiana* not because it is a gloss on *Paradise Lost* but because it unsettles *Paradise Lost* by giving us a Milton whose doctrinal beliefs were still in process—by giving us a Milton, that is, who was (in spite of himself) a theologian.

---

[8] John Milton, *Accedence Commenc't Grammar* (London, 1669); *A Brief History of Muscovia* (London, 1682); see also *The History of Britain* (London, 1670).

[9] John Milton, *Eikonoklastes* (London, 1649).

APPENDIX

The Manuscript of *De Doctrina Christiana*

This book has argued that reading *De Doctrina Christiana* requires careful attention to the manuscript's materiality and especially to its chronology of revision. The recent Oxford edition represents manuscript details in a way unparalleled by earlier editions, but its account of the manuscript's chronological stratification remains limited to occasional notes. This appendix aims to fill that void with the hope that future scholars will improve on its work.

The manuscript's stratification emerges from its material construction. Each chapter was originally a *fascicule*, a gathering of one or more folios. A *folio* is a large sheet of paper folded in half to make two *leaves*, of which there are 380, numbered by an archivist. Each *leaf* has a *recto* (where the folded edge is to the left) and a *verso* (where the folded edge is to the right). I refer to each individual recto or verso as a *page*. There are 745 pages, numbered only to 735, due to mispagination in II.11; I indicate page numbers with a preceding *MS*. Most leaves are part of a folio, but I note the handful of exceptions.

The manuscript's current state obscures some of these details. In the National Archives, it is bound in three volumes, the first containing Daniel Skinner's recopied Epistle and I.1–13, the second containing Skinner's recopied I.14 and Picard's I:15–33, and the third containing II.1–17. A fourth volume contains papers pertinent to Robert Lemon's discovery of the treatise in 1823. This division into volumes seems to have been done in the 1930s—the volume covers have a label from the repairing department bearing the date "2.3.34" (presumably 2 March 1934)—at which time the leaves were cut from their folios, repaired or reinforced as needed, and pasted onto stubs that were then bound together in staggered fashion.[1] During their work on *Milton and the Manuscript* (2007), Gordon Campbell and Thomas N. Corns had access to the manuscript in an unbound state, which enabled them to examine the watermarks. It was subsequently rebound.

Campbell, Corns, and Jeffrey Alan Miller use *stratum* to describe a material stage of work on the manuscript. In this sense, Maurice Kelley understood Jeremie Picard's work as constituting a single stratum, with revisions in the hands of Picard and others constituting the next and Skinner's recopying constituting a final stratum.[2] Campbell and Corns expand on Kelley, noting the manuscript's division into fascicules and attending to the stratified quality of Picard's work. They posit three Picard strata: (i) a baseline fair copy of an earlier manuscript, divided into separate fascicules for each chapter; (ii) occasional leaves that have been recopied and tipped into the fascicules; and (iii) whole fascicules that have been recopied to accommodate revisions.[3] To these, Miller adds a fourth stratum, comprised of pages recopied and added to the already once recopied fascicules, and then a fifth stratum

---

[1] This repair work is mysterious; the Columbia edition, published in the same year the repairs were done, simply says that "In more recent times the manuscript has been bound in such a way as to conceal the edges of the text in many of the pages toward the end": Columbia, XVII.426–27. There is no mention of work to reinforce or repair the paper—evident in some form on nearly every page.

[2] Maurice Kelley, *This Great Argument: A Study of Milton's* De Doctrina Christiana *as a Gloss upon* Paradise Lost (Princeton, NJ: Princeton University Press, 1941), pp. 39–42. In his Yale introduction, Kelley still speaks of Picard's "original draft," acknowledging the possibility of subsequent recopying only in the case of the complexly paginated I.25; Yale, 23–27. Kelley uses the language of "strata" primarily regarding the later hands; see e.g., Yale, 32.

[3] *MMS*, 55.

252   MILTON'S THEOLOGICAL PROCESS

comprising Skinner's recopying of the first fourteen chapters (of which Miller, following Kelley but departing from Campbell and Corns, argues he recopied I.14 first).[4]

These definitions of *stratum* are grounded in material criteria that understand the manuscript as a layered phenomenon, but they do not account sufficiently for the chronological dimension needed to understand the manuscript's processes of revision. Even though text in two distinct parts of the manuscript might belong to the same material layer (e.g., the tipped-in pages of stratum ii), that text need not belong to the same temporal moment or stage of revision. In my view, Picard is more likely to have recopied individual fascicles as needed than to have undertaken a single, chronologically coherent recopying project. Surveying the manuscript has not persuaded me that stratum i exists as described above. Granted, the quantity of work on paper bearing watermark E and written in a broadly similar style seems to indicate a large copying project, but this did not necessarily extend to the entire manuscript. If Picard copied different fascicules at different times, the distinction between strata i and iii as described above begins to blur.

I use the term "stratum," therefore, to denote the material and chronological layering within a given chapter/fascicule. This layering tends to occur on the level of the folio, which seems to have constituted a working unit of the manuscript below the level of the fascicule. The clearest evidence of this practice appears in non-Picard cases, as when Amanuensis "A" recopied MS 549–52 and Skinner recopied MS 571–74, but Picard's tipped-in pages (strata ii/iv, as described above) also tend to come in folio-sized units, as in I.16's two-folio insertion. The result is segmentation within fascicules: the first and last segments of I.16 together constitute a single stratum. Noting the clear cases of working in folios offers insight into the murkier ones, evidenced by such things as text of increasing density on the last page of a folio so that the copied text will align neatly with the next folio, variations in catchword patterns, and shifts in handwriting style from folio to folio. Paper size is also a variable that could indicate an inserted folio, although the possibility remains that Picard was drawing from mixed stock such that variation in paper size alone need not indicate a distinct stratum. The same holds true of watermark evidence, which can weigh in either direction.

Attention to content further indicates that folios served as units of revision. To minimize recopying, Picard seems to have tried to align topics and folios as nearly as possible. Some overlap is difficult to avoid, but new topics frequently appear on the rectos of new folios, as with the doctrine of a twofold scripture and its ensuing discussion of textual corruption in I.30 (MS 394). This practice produces complex segmentation and stratification. For instance, of the five folios in I.28 that intervene between the same-stratum folios that bookend the chapter, the first two (each a distinct segment) discuss baptism and the last two (also distinct segments) discuss the Lord's Supper. Both topics are controversial, which helps to explain the apparent welter of revisions that produced the complicated material state of this chapter. The middle folio serves as a material bridge between these topics, and its extreme variation in density of text—where the least dense page in the entire manuscript has a very dense, much-revised verso—suggests a messy history of recopying to align this folio with its ever-shifting neighbors. A further case appears in II.4, where the topic of fasting mostly occupies a single folio (MS 527–30). The topic begins on the last verso of the preceding folio, and the last verso of this folio begins the discussion of vows, which makes the self-containment less than absolute but nevertheless potentially useful. Literary study can inform book history.

---

[4] Jeffrey Alan Miller, "Milton, Zanchius, and the Rhetoric of Belated Reading," *Milton Quarterly* 47, 4 (2013): 201–203, 205.

Distinctions in Picard's writing style may help to distinguish among segments or strata. Large hand is sometimes highly embellished (Figure A.1) and most often what I have called moderately embellished, which differs primarily in its less ornate initial letters (Figure A.2). Sometimes, the moderately embellished style appears without boldface (Figure A.3). Scriptural citations most often appear in a hand slightly smaller than that used for regular prose (Figure A.4). Sometimes, the small hand is significantly smaller (Figure A.5). Subtle variations in embellishment may carry evidentiary weight, but I omit them because such details can only be properly studied using the manuscript itself. The kinds of pattern-seeking on which this work depends may founder on the stochastic elements of Picard's scribal practice. How concerned was he really about keeping his style of majuscule P consistent, particularly as he became increasingly aware that he might find himself recopying the page at some point?

As the proliferation of variables might suggest, in this kind of work, the risk of question-begging seems high. Miller plausibly suggests that a greater degree of embellishment in Picard's hand indicates an earlier phase of his work. This is a reasonable conjecture, but it nevertheless behoves scholars to subject the rationales and assumptions that they use to determine chronology to strict scrutiny, for example, whether paper looks "older," assumptions about how writers used stocks of paper based on watermark evidence, etc. For instance, I have assumed that sections with extensive prose argument come later, but

Figure A.1 Highly embellished large hand; detail from *DDC*, 333

Figure A.2 Moderately embellished, boldface large hand; detail from *DDC*, 362

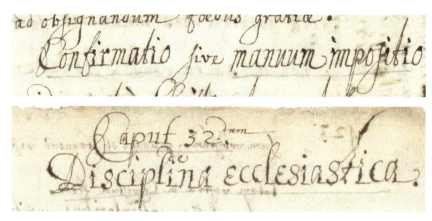

Figure A.3 Moderately embellished large hand without boldface; detail from *DDC*, 363, 422

Figure A.4 Small hand for scriptural citations; detail from *DDC*, 357

Figure A.5 Significantly smaller hand for scriptural citations; detail from *DDC*, 198

I believe that the material evidence (as in I.16 and I.27) bears this assumption out. Miller's dissertation work on II.7 provides a good example of this rigor as he carefully establishes the chronology of revisions within that chapter.[5] The work of establishing chronological bridges between segments appearing in different chapters will need to be similarly painstaking.

---

[5] Jeffrey Alan Miller, "Theological Typology, Milton, and the Aftermath of Writing," DPhil thesis, University of Oxford (2012), ch. 4.

Method

I proceed chapter by chapter (treating the epistle and I.1–13 as a single entity). Each entry lists the material segments of the chapter with explanations of the basis for determining them. Even where I think that discontinuous segments belong to the same stratum (as in I.16, with its tipped-in folios), I have listed them separately, using headnotes to connect segmentation and stratification where possible. The aim is not to overdetermine the results. I have also noted the manuscript's several attempts (generally in Skinner's hand) to divide the manuscript into parts (whether for theological or practical reasons is not entirely clear).[6] The three apparent endings of Part 4 (at the ends of I.17, I.22, and I.25) indicate some flux in the scheme. These have all been cancelled in the manuscript. Catchwords indicating the next chapter are generally in Skinner's hand, so I have omitted them from the descriptions below. Page measurements (width × height, in centimeters) are necessarily approximate, given wear to the pages, many of which seem not to have been quite rectangular in the first place (reflected in some measurements presented as ranges), and given that the folios have been cut so that individual leaves could be mounted to stubs for preservation.[7] The conservation and repair work completed in 1934 further complicates attempts at measurement. Width measurements are taken from the versos because, in most cases, the rectos have been pasted to the mounting stubs (made possible by the wide left-hand margins, a practice carried over from Milton's government work).

My work on the manuscript owes significant debts to prior work by Gordon Campbell, Thomas N. Corns, J. Donald Cullington, Waldo Hilary Dunn, John K. Hale, James Holly Hanford, Maurice Kelley, and Jeffrey Alan Miller. The following accounts of watermark evidence owe to Corns, who graciously shared information from his notes to supplement the material published in *Milton and the Manuscript*, whose watermark sigla I have adopted.[8] To allow for the possibility that pages without a visible watermark have been cut from a sheet with the watermark elsewhere, I have described them as "containing no watermark evidence."

Epistle, I.1–I.13 (MS 1–182)

Daniel Skinner recopied these pages as part of a single effort: chapters often begin midpage (e.g., I.2 on MS 9), unlike the fascicule method employed in the rest of the treatise.

---

[6] Oxford, xxxix.

[7] A further complicating factor is the discrepancy between the photocopied paper rulers available in the National Archives and more accurate rulers. The measurements given here have been adjusted, with 26.5 cm on the paper ruler equaling 25.0 cm on a better ruler. This ratio of 1.06 proved reliable at scale within the margin of error.

[8] *MMS*, 48–49. I was unable to examine watermarks for myself. In Ernest W. Sullivan, "Review of Gordon Campbell, Thomas N. Corns, John K. Hale, and Fiona J. Tweedie, *Milton and the Manuscript of* De Doctrina Christiana (Oxford: Oxford University Press, 2007)," *Review of English Studies* 60, 243 (2009): 153–54, Sullivan mentions his own work with the watermarks, yielding this conclusion: "My admittedly incomplete evidence suggested an erratic production of the manuscript over a substantial period of time, possibly beginning by 1625—a date that would preclude Milton's authorship of a manuscript not in his hand." Sullivan refers to a paper he presented at the 2001 Conference of the Modern Language Association that has not, to my knowledge, appeared in print. In any case, watermarks provide evidence as to the date of paper's manufacture, not its use. I concur that a clearer account of the watermark evidence in the manuscript would be bibliographically useful.

256   MILTON'S THEOLOGICAL PROCESS

The epistle (leaves 1–3) ends mid-page on a recto (MS 5), followed by a blank verso, so I.1 begins on a recto. I.1–I.13 consist of leaves 4–91, which measure 18.9–19.4 × 24.4–25.0 cm.

- MS 48 (end of I.4). End of Part 1.
- MS 110 (end of I.6). End of Part 2.
- MS 182 (end of I.13). End of Part 3.

I.14 (MS 183–96)

Skinner also recopied this chapter but separately from the preceding section: the paper is smaller (15.4–15.6 × 19.7–19.8 cm), and the chapter begins on a new page instead of after the mid-page ending of I.13 on MS 182. Kelley and Miller argue, persuasively, that Skinner recopied this chapter before deciding to recopy the first thirteen because its paper roughly matches the size of I.15 and not the other Skinner pages.[9] It contains leaves 92–98. Leaf 98 is unusually wide at 16.3 cm and is mounted on a larger than usual piece of paper.

I.15 (MS 197–204)

This chapter's single stratum includes two folios whose leaves (99–102) measure 15.5 × 19.8 cm and bear watermark W. Boldface large hand in the moderately embellished style marks the chapter title as well as the Ramist definitions and headings. Small hand distinguishes the scriptural citations. Several pages contain marginal revision, and catchwords appear on all pages.

I.16 (MS 205–20)

This chapter contains two strata, an older one comprising the first and last folios in the chapter and a newer one comprising the middle two folios, a paradigmatic case of tipped-in folios.

- MS 205–208. This segment includes a single folio whose leaves (103–104) measure 15.4 × 20.7 cm and bear watermark W. Boldface large hand in the moderately embellished style marks the chapter title as well as the Ramist definitions and headings. Some initial letters receive elaborate embellishment. A very small hand distinguishes the scriptural citations. Several pages contain revisions both marginal and interlinear, including MS 206, where Skinner has recopied the marginal insertion onto new paper and pasted it into the manuscript. Catchwords appear on all pages.
- MS 209–16. This segment includes two folios whose leaves (105–108) measure 14.6 × 19.3 cm and bear watermark A. Boldface large hand in the moderately embellished style marks the Ramist headings. Small hand distinguishes scriptural citations but less distinctly than in the preceding pages. These pages are densely written (especially MS 213–14), suggesting that they have been recopied to incorporate revisions to an earlier stratum. Catchwords appear on MS 212 and 216.

[9] Kelley, *This Great Argument*, 57; Miller, "Milton, Zanchius, and the Rhetoric of Belated Reading," 201–203, 205.

THE MANUSCRIPT OF *DE DOCTRINA CHRISTIANA*   257

- MS 217–20. This segment includes a single folio whose leaves (109–10) measure 15.2–15.8 × 20.6 cm and bear watermark W. Boldface large hand in the moderately embellished style marks the headwords, and initial letters sometimes receive elaborate embellishment. Small hand distinguishes the scriptural citations, but the distinction among Picard's three hands is less sharp than in the chapter's opening pages. These are the least densely written pages in the chapter, and they are free of revisions. Catchwords appear on MS 217–18.

I.17 (MS 221–35)

This chapter contains three distinct strata. The catchword evidence suggests that the final segment is the oldest, followed by the middle segment and finally by the first. Amanuensis "A" has revised all segments, however, suggesting that the chapter existed in its current segments for some period of the manuscript's working life.

- MS 221–24. This segment includes a single folio whose leaves (111–12) measure 15.8 × 20.7 cm and bear watermark B. Large hand is highly embellished, but bold face is inconsistent. Large hand is larger and bolder on MS 222–24 than on MS 221. An especially small hand distinguishes scriptural citations. These pages all contain revisions, most notably the deleted passage on MS 222–23 (deletion is a rare form of revision in a manuscript where most revisions are additive). The bottom of MS 224 becomes suddenly dense, and a mistake with the catchword (*videntur*, with "vi" in the last line of text and "dent[ur]" in the catchword space, where the next page begins with the entire word) suggests that these pages were recopied to align with the next stratum. Catchwords appear on all pages.
- MS 225–28. This segment includes a single folio whose leaves (113–14) measure 15.1 × 20.4 cm and contain no watermark evidence. Large hand is highly embellished and boldface, used for proper names as well as Ramist headings. Small hand for scriptural citations is likewise distinct. These pages carry only a few traces of revision. A catchword appears on MS 228.
- MS 229–35. This segment includes two folios whose leaves (115–18) measure 15.5–15.8 × 20.7 cm and bear watermark C. Large hand is embellished and boldface on the top of MS 230 but is less pronounced elsewhere in this stratum, including on the bottom of MS 230. By MS 232, embellishment alone distinguishes headwords. Revisions are concentrated on the stratum's first three pages. Catchwords appear on all pages. The chapter ends on a recto, followed by a blank verso.
- MS 235. First end of Part 4 (cf. MS 282, 304)—possibly: the cancelled words are difficult to make out.

I.18 (MS 236–39)

This chapter contains a single folio, with leaves (119–20) measuring 15.8 × 20.7 cm and containing no watermark evidence. Picard used a highly embellished large hand for the chapter title and headings, and the scriptural citations are in a distinctly smaller hand. Text is of similar, relatively high density throughout. Three of the four pages contain revisions, which are especially concentrated on MS 236. Catchwords appear on all pages.

258 MILTON'S THEOLOGICAL PROCESS

I.19 (MS 240–47)

This chapter's single stratum includes two folios bearing watermark C. The first folio (MS 240–43) has leaves (121–22) measuring 15.9–16.2 × 20.8–21.0 cm. The second folio (MS 244–47) has leaves (123–24) measuring 15.5–15.7 × 20.3–20.8 cm. Large hand is highly embellished and boldface, and small hand for scriptural citations is consistent. MS 244–45, however, do not use large hand for headings, although embellishment is present. The pages are fairly clean until MS 245, which has a deletion. The final page, MS 247, is densely written, with deletions and marginal insertions recopied by Skinner and pasted in. Catchwords appear on all pages.

I.20 (MS 248–55)

This chapter's single stratum includes two folios that contain no watermark evidence. The first folio (MS 248–51) has leaves (125–26) measuring 16.0–20.7 cm. The second folio (MS 252–55) has leaves (127–28) measuring 15.8–16.0 × 20.3–20.9 cm. Large hand is highly embellished and boldface. A very small hand distinguishes scriptural citations. The pages are mostly clean until the last leaf. MS 255 is especially dense. Catchwords appear on all pages.

I.21 (MS 256–67)

This chapter contains two strata. In the second segment, uneven embellishment of the hand and the greater density of the text suggest a later recopying.

- MS 256–59. This segment includes two folios, apparently drawn from mixed paper stock (there is no watermark evidence). The first (MS 256–59) has leaves (129–30) measuring 15.9 × 20.7 cm with catchwords on the versos. The second (MS 260–63) has leaves (131–32) measuring 15.5 × 19.6 cm with catchwords on all pages. The difference in catchword practice owes to cases of hyphenation. Large hand is highly embellished and bolder on the first page than elsewhere. The distinctiveness of small hand varies in this segment. Catchwords appear only on the versos. These pages contain a handful of revisions, with most on MS 256 and 261–62.
- MS 264–67. This segment includes a single folio whose leaves (133–34) measure 15.9 × 20.7 cm and contain no watermark evidence. Embellished, boldface large hand appears on MS 264, but headwords in the ensuing pages are distinguished only by embellishment (not even by size). The last three pages are especially dense (MS 267 particularly so) with the situation compounded by a large marginal insertion. The only catchword in this segment appears on MS 266.

I.22 (MS 268–82)

Consistency of the hand suggests that this chapter consists of a single stratum, with Picard drawing from mixed paper stock for its four folios. The first (MS 268–71) has leaves (135–36) measuring 15.8 × 20.7 cm. Leaf 135 bears watermark I, and leaf 136 contains no watermark evidence. The second (MS 272–75) has leaves (137–38) measuring 15.8 × 20.5 cm and bears watermark D. The third (MS 276–79) has leaves (139–40) measuring 15.8

THE MANUSCRIPT OF *DE DOCTRINA CHRISTIANA*   259

× 20.5–20.8 cm and contains no watermark evidence. The fourth (MS 280–82) has leaves (141–42) measuring 15.9–16.1 × 20.2–20.7 cm and bears watermark D. Large hand usage varies in these pages, appearing bold and somewhat embellished on MS 272 but often being distinguished only by embellishment. Small hand distinguishes scriptural citations. Catchwords appear on all pages except MS 270. MS 282 contains some text at the end that has been heavily blacked out. The chapter ends on a recto with a blank verso following.

- MS 282. Second end of Part 4 (cf. MS 235, 304).

I.23 (MS 283–86)

This chapter contains a single folio, with leaves (143–44) measuring 15.9 × 20.7 cm and bearing watermark D. Large hand is bold and embellished, but scriptural citations seem to be in the same hand as regular text. Aside from three small interlinear insertions, these are clean pages. Catchwords appear on all pages. The two leaves are bound out of sequence but numbered correctly.

I.24 (MS 287–90)

This chapter contains a single folio, with leaves (145–56) measuring 15.9 × 20.5 cm and bearing watermark D. Large hand is bold and embellished, but scriptural citations seem to be in the same hand as regular text. These are densely written pages, perhaps suggesting the need to incorporate extensive revisions while keeping the fascicule to a single sheet. Further revisions appear: interlinear changes on MS 287 and a marginal insertion on MS 290, which also has an addition to the end of the chapter crammed onto the bottom of the page.

I.25 (MS 291–304)

Page number offers a clue to this chapter's stratification. Picard numbered the pages of each fascicule, and Skinner often incorporated Picard's numbers into his own pagination of the manuscript as a whole: here, Picard's page 1 becomes Skinner's page 291. The complication emerges on MS 299, which Picard has also numbered p. 13 and subsequently scratched out. MS 300 has two canceled Picard page numbers: 10 and 14. MS 301 has "115," with the 5 apparently scratched out by Picard and the 11 crossed out by Skinner. MS 302 returns to having two Picard page numbers, 12 and 16, the latter scratched out by Picard. On MS 303, Skinner has incorporated Picard's 13 into his own page number; a scratched out 17 survives. MS 304 Picard has numbered 14 and 18, the latter scratched out. The gap between Picard's p. 8 (MS 298) and his page 9/13 (MS 299) suggests the possible excision of one folio from the fascicule. This potentiality may be borne out by the bottom of MS 298, where the catchword space reads "[coro-]nam tuam. Joan. 8.31," while the top of MS 299 begins with "8.31," suggesting that the preceding pages had been recopied to align with MS 299.[10]

---

[10] See the discussion in Kelley, *This Great Argument*, 44–45.

260   MILTON'S THEOLOGICAL PROCESS

- MS 291–98. This segment includes two folios that contain no watermark evidence. The first (MS 291–94) has leaves (147–48) measuring 14.8 × 19.9–20.0 cm. The second (MS 295–98) has leaves (149–50) measuring 14.8 × 19.7–19.9 cm. Large hand is embellished but not boldface in the chapter title, although some headings later on become moderately bold. Large hand emphasizes the word "paulum" (drawing attention to Milton's correction of other New Testament editors) and the name "Paulus" on MS 297. Small hand distinguishes scriptural citations. These pages (through MS 296) are extremely densely written, and several pages contain further revisions (such as the marginal insertion on MS 291). Catchwords appear on MS 294 and 298. On MS 298, Picard has needed the catchword space to finish out the line: "nam tuam. Joan. 8. 31." leads into "8. 31." at the top of MS 299. Skinner has incorporated Picard's numbering of these pages (1–8) into his own numbering.
- MS 299–304. This segment includes a folio and a leaf, all bearing watermark I. The folio's leaves (151–52) measure 14.5–14.7 × 19.1–19.3 cm. The leaf (153, not among the separate leaves listed by Campbell and Corns) measures 14.6 × 19.2 cm. Boldface, moderately embellished large hand emphasizes phrases like *Theologi Remonstrantes* on MS 302. Small hand distinguishes scriptural citations. A catchword appears on MS 302.
- MS 304. Third end of Part 4 (cf. MS 235, 282).

I.26 (MS 305–11)

Campbell and Corns count this chapter's first two leaves (MS 305–307a, leaves 154–55) among those not part of folios. The second of these contains MS 307a, by far the messiest, most revised page in the manuscript, and the only case of a single page that Skinner saw fit to recopy separate from the surrounding materials. I incline, however, to see these two leaves as part of a single folio. Neither contains a watermark, and they are very close in size: 14.7 × 19.0 cm and 14.6 × 19.1 cm, respectively. The primary variable that weighs in favor of separating them is the handwriting: the chapter title on MS 305 is moderately embellished without boldface, whereas large hand becomes boldface on MS 307 and highly embellished on MS 307a. Nevertheless, the hand also offers multiple points of continuity, especially when MS 307 is considered alongside its more famous verso, the chief of which is a highly distinctive majuscule F with embellishment on the top that occurs on both leaves.

Accordingly, this chapter contains a single stratum comprising two folios, with Skinner's page 308 (recopying MS 307a) placed in between them—tellingly with its blank recto allowing the recopied material to correspond to the original verso. Having described the first folio above, MS 308 (leaf 156, the recopied Skinner page) measures 14.6 × 18.9 cm and contains no watermark evidence. The second folio's leaves (MS 309–11, leaves 157–58) measure 14.3–14.5 × 18.3–18.4 cm and bear watermark FdLC. The chapter's only catchword is on MS 307a; the chapter ends on MS 311, with eight lines written in a later, unidentified hand; the verso is blank.

I.27 (MS 312–37)

This chapter, among the manuscript's more materially complex, contains five strata. It is unique in the prevalence of single sheets separate from folios: it contains three, two near the beginning and one at the end, each apparently a distinct stratum. The chapter's long

THE MANUSCRIPT OF *DE DOCTRINA CHRISTIANA* 261

middle section, comprising four folios, appears to be a later addition, as Miller has argued.[11] Beyond that, the chronology is difficult to determine.

- MS 312–15. This segment includes a single folio whose leaves (159–60) measure 15.3–15.6 × 20.0–20.2 cm and contain no watermark evidence. Large hand usage is uneven: the title and initial definition are distinguished more by embellishment than by thickness of stroke, but later headwords are bolder. (The paper is susceptible to bleed-through and has been heavily repaired, which affects perceptions.) Scriptural citations do appear in a smaller hand. MS 314 contains a marginal insertion, and this second leaf of the stratum is copied more densely than the first. A catchword appears on MS 315.
- MS 316–17. This segment includes a single leaf (161) that measures 15.1 × 20.9 cm and contains no watermark evidence. The paper is very worn, and conservation efforts have darkened it. Part of the top of the page appears to have been torn off and repaired, and the pasted edge is reinforced (uniquely, as far as I can tell) with what appears to be finely woven cloth. The rationale for treating this leaf as a distinct stratum instead of as part of a folio with MS 318–19 rests primarily on its style of large hand majuscule P, which is different to those on the preceding and succeeding leaves. The text on this leaf is also much denser than that on the next. Large hand is bold and moderately embellished, used for headwords, and a smaller hand distinguishes scriptural citations. There are no catchwords. Campbell and Corns do not include this leaf or the next in their list of leaves that do not belong to folios. The leaves are about the same size and so could belong to a folio, and the conservation efforts make the case difficult to determine, but the subtle changes in handwriting style and in density favor separating them.
- MS 318–19. This segment includes a single leaf (162) that measures 15.0 × 20.9 cm and contains no watermark evidence. Large hand is bold, moderately embellished, and used to mark only the proper name "Paulus" (no headwords appear on this leaf). Small hand distinguishes scriptural citations throughout, and a catchword appears on MS 319.
- MS 320–35. This segment includes four folios, drawn from mixed paper stock. Catchwords appear on all the versos except MS 329. The first two folios are on paper bearing watermark D and measuring 15.1 × 19.9 cm (MS 320–23, leaves 163–64) and 14.9–15.1 × 19.4–20.1 cm (MS 324–27, leaves 165–66). The second two folios are on paper bearing watermark E and measuring 15.1 × 20.3–20.9 cm (MS 328–31, leaves 167–68) and 15.1 × 20.7 cm (MS 332–35, leaves 169–70). These are densely written, mostly clean pages. An embellished, bold large hand emphasizes the proper name "Zanchius" on MS 320 and more proper names ("Zanchium," "Cameronis," "Polanus") on MS 329–31. These pages are mostly prose; in lieu of Ramist subheadings, they enumerate arguments with "Firstly [*Primùm*]" and a series of numerals that appear in large hand. A small hand distinguishes scriptural citations. Beginning on MS 332, large hand begins to distinguish headwords (the first that have appeared since MS 317), and the usage of proper names ceases. Other variables—paper stock, size, density of writing—suggest that this last folio continues the stratum otherwise occupied with the long prose insertion that fills the preceding three. MS 335 is much less densely copied than the other pages; MS 333 contains myriad revisions, both marginal and interlinear. The last phrase of MS 335 is "spicas vellerant," with "cas vellerant" in the

---

[11] Miller, "Milton, Zanchius, and the Rhetoric of Belated Reading."

262   MILTON'S THEOLOGICAL PROCESS

catchword space; MS 336 begins with "lerant." This circumstance suggests copying to fit with an already existing MS 336.

- MS 336–37. This single leaf (171) measures 15.1 × 19.5 cm and contains no watermark evidence. The word "Evangelium" appears in a boldface, embellished large hand; initial letters in paragraphs also receive boldface emphasis. The proper name "Paulus" has an embellished P but does not appear in large hand. A smaller hand distinguishes scriptural citations. A catchword appears on MS 336. Per Campbell et al., it is not part of a folio.[12]

I.28 (MS 338–65)

This is far and away the most materially complex chapter in the manuscript. It contains seven folios, of which the first and last seem to belong to the same stratum, with each of the five intervening folios apparently constituting its own distinct stratum. Piecing together the internal chronology of these strata is extremely difficult. The chapter's topic is the sacraments, and it seems that Milton kept interjecting or expanding polemical arguments about baptism and the Lord's Supper. The first and seventh folios are thoroughly Ramist, with the Ramist structure resurfacing on MS 347, 351, 353, and possibly also on 358 (which introduces the topic of administrating the sacraments). These pages are in the third, fourth, and sixth folios. The intervening spaces are filled with prose arguments of various kinds.

I hypothesize that the first and seventh folios are the oldest. The fourth folio serves as a hinge between the topics of baptism and the Lord's Supper; it seems to represent an older layer of both, with messy revisions on the first and last pages tying it into the surrounding polemics. That said, MS 352 is the least dense page in the manuscript, suggesting that this section was recopied at some point to fit, awkwardly, with parts of the chapter that may now be lost. Indeed, perhaps this folio's oddly variable density indicates recopying undertaken in the context of wildly shifting contents to either side, a strange bit of scribal bricolage that holds the larger chapter together. Working from the hinge (because ascertaining chronology across it is difficult, if not impossible), it seems, on the baptism side, that the second folio has been recopied to fit the third, which has, in turn, been recopied to fit the fourth. On the eucharist side, the fifth and sixth folios seem distinct on the grounds of handwriting style (majuscule P again), but clear chronological clues are difficult to discern except that the density of the penultimate page of the sixth folio before the resumption of Ramist structure on its last page suggests that it was copied to fit with the seventh folio. In short, even though this chapter uses the Ramist structure to advance the heterodox doctrine of believer's baptism, it offers the nearest material cousin in the surviving Picard pages to the complexity likely at work in I.5.

- MS 338–41. This segment includes a single folio whose leaves (172–73) measure 15.3 × 19.4 cm and bear watermark E. The chapter title appears in embellished large hand but not boldface, and Ramist headwords do not appear in large hand until "Credentium" on MS 341. A small hand unevenly distinguishes scriptural citations. Catchwords appear on all pages but the first. On MS 341, the catchword space continues the word *infantium*, but the catchword (*Qui*) that begins the next page appears only in a marginal insertion, cued to *infantium*, which also contains a reference to the discussion of vows in II.4 ("de quo infra l. 2. c. 4 ubi de Voto").

---

[12] *MMS*, 46.

THE MANUSCRIPT OF *DE DOCTRINA CHRISTIANA* 263

- MS 342–45. This segment includes a single folio whose leaves (174–75) measure 15.1 × 20.0 cm and bear watermark E. They are densely written and do not contain large hand, although initial letters occasionally receive embellishment. A catchword appears on MS 345.
- MS 346–49. This segment includes a single folio whose leaves (176–77) measure 15.3 × 19.4 cm and bear watermark E. They use a highly embellished, boldface large hand for Ramist headwords; a smaller hand distinguishes scriptural citations. They are mostly clean pages and much less densely written than the preceding section. Catchwords appear on all pages.
- MS 350–53. This segment includes a single folio whose leaves (178–79) measure 15.1 × 20.1 cm and contain no watermark evidence. They use an embellished, boldface large hand for both Ramist headwords and proper names, for example, "Joannis" and "Christi" as well as "Coena Dominica" on MS 350. The small hand is considerably smaller than the regular hand. The density of writing in these pages varies widely; MS 352 is the least dense page in the manuscript, whereas its verso is extremely dense. Two pages in this section, MS 350 and 353, include marginal insertions that Skinner has recopied and pasted in. A catchword appears on MS 353.
- MS 354–57. This segment includes a single folio whose leaves (180–81) measure 15.4 × 19.3 cm and contain no watermark evidence. A boldface, moderately embellished large hand emphasizes key words ("circumcisio" and "agnus" on MS 355). Small hand distinguishes scriptural citations. Marginal insertions appear on MS 356–57. A catchword appears on MS 357.
- MS 358–61. This segment includes a single folio whose leaves (182–83) measure 14.3 × 18.3 cm and contain no watermark evidence. No large hand appears in these pages, and "Paulus" uses the style of majuscule P found on MS 317. A significantly smaller hand distinguishes scriptural citations. The second leaf is written more densely than the first, and a catchword appears on MS 361.
- MS 362–65. This segment includes a single folio whose leaves (184–85) measure 15.4 × 19.3 cm and contain no watermark evidence. Large hand varies in boldness but is in the moderately embellished style; it sets off key words ("hoc est corpus meum") and Ramist headwords. Small hand distinguishes scriptural citations. Catchwords appear on MS 363–64.
- MS 365. End of Part 5.

I.29 (MS 366–81)

This chapter has two strata, the densely written final folio appearing to be the later.

- MS 366–77. This segment includes three folios (MS 366–69, 370–73, and 374–77) whose remarkably consistent leaves (186–91) measure 15.3–15.4 × 19.2–19.3 cm and bear watermarks E and E2 (which may not, in fact, differ).[13] The chapter title appears in large hand of the moderately embellished style. Ramist headwords and definitions do not appear in large hand until MS 374, after which they become pronounced. Revisions appear on half the pages. Catchwords appear on all pages except MS 371 and 374.

[13] *MMS*, 49.

264   MILTON'S THEOLOGICAL PROCESS

- MS 378–81. This segment includes a single folio whose leaves (192–93) measure 15.3 × 20.1–20.3 cm and contain no watermark evidence. They are extremely densely written. A boldface, embellished large hand emphasizes proper names, and a markedly smaller hand distinguishes scriptural citations. Three of four pages contain marginal insertions. There are no catchwords.

I.30 (MS 382–401)

I identify four strata in this moderately complex chapter. The last segment seems to be the latest; the hand is much less embellished than in the rest of the chapter. Catchword evidence suggests that the second and third were recopied, indicating that the first folio is the oldest in the chapter. The chronological relationship between the second and third segments/folios remains unclear.

- MS 382–85. This segment includes a single folio whose leaves (194–95) measure 15.5 × 19.3 cm and contain no watermark evidence. Boldface, moderately embellished large hand appears in the chapter title and is otherwise only used to distinguish between "canonici" and "apocryphi" books in a primarily prose section. Small hand distinguishes scriptural citations. Catchwords appear on all pages except MS 384 (the interior recto).
- MS 386–89. This segment includes a single folio whose leaves (196–97) measure 15.3 × 19.3 cm and contain no watermark evidence. This folio seems broadly similar in style to the preceding one, with the difference that its pages are more densely written, and the use of a catchword only on the final verso (MS 389) suggests that the entire folio has been recopied to fit existing material.
- MS 390–93. This segment includes a single folio whose leaves (198–99) measure 15.9 × 21.1 cm and contain no watermark evidence. They are densely written but with a larger script than the preceding sections. An embellished large hand appears only to emphasize certain words (especially "Jus" on MS 390) and the occasional initial letter. Use of small hand to distinguish scriptural citations is variable. A catchword appears on MS 393. This segment is distinguished in part by its preponderance of prose argumentation.
- MS 394–401. This segment includes two folios (MS 394–97 and 398–401) whose leaves (200–203) measure 15.2 × 19.3 cm and contain no watermark evidence (leaf 401 is 15.5 cm wide). These are mostly clean pages, with a marginal insertion on MS 398 and some eight lines in an unidentified hand at the end of the chapter on MS 401. Catchwords appear on each page of the first folio and on MS 398–99 in the second.

I.31 (MS 402–21)

This chapter's five folios seem to include two strata, divided after the third folio, which shows signs of recopying.

- MS 402–13. This segment includes three folios whose leaves (204–209) measure 15.8 × 20.8 cm and contain watermark E. The chapter title appears in boldface, moderately embellished large hand, but the definitions and headings at most appear in slightly larger script. Scriptural citations do appear in a smaller hand. These are very clean

THE MANUSCRIPT OF *DE DOCTRINA CHRISTIANA* 265

pages, with catchwords on every page. MS 411 contains several revisions, including a marginal insertion and a scratched out interlinear addition. On MS 413, Picard inadvertently skipped a paragraph, noticed his mistake after a few words, and started over—indicating recopying.

- MS 414–21. This segment includes two folios whose leaves (210–13) measure 15.8–21.0–21.1 cm and contain no watermark evidence. Large hand does not appear, although Ramist headwords often have their first letters embellished. A smaller hand distinguishes scriptural citations, especially on MS 421 as Picard condenses his copy to fit the page. Catchwords appear on versos.

I.32 (MS 422–31)

This chapter seems to consist of a single stratum drawn from mixed paper stock. It includes two folios and a single leaf. The first folio (MS 422–25) bears watermark E and has leaves (214–15) measuring 15.8 × 20.9 cm. The second folio (MS 426–29) contains no watermark evidence and has leaves (216–17) measuring 15.6–15.8 × 20.8 cm. The final leaf (MS 430–31, leaf 218) measures 15.8 × 21.1 cm and bears watermark I. Initially in the chapter, large hand appears in the moderately embellished style but without boldface. Embellishment decreases as the chapter proceeds such that large hand disappears in lieu of initial letters receiving some embellishment. Small hand distinguishes scriptural citations. These are mostly clean pages, with catchwords on every page.

I.33 (MS 432–61)

This chapter contains a single stratum comprising eight folios, all bearing watermark E. The first (MS 432–35) has leaves (219–20) measuring 15.6–15.9 × 20.9 cm. The second (MS 436–39) has leaves (221–22) measuring 15.6 × 20.8 cm. The third (MS 440–43) has leaves (223–24) measuring 15.8–16.0 × 20.9 cm. The fourth (MS 444–47) has leaves (225–26) measuring 15.8 × 20.8 cm. The fifth (MS 448–51) has leaves (227–28) measuring 15.8 × 20.8 cm. The sixth (MS 452–55) has leaves (229–30) measuring 15.8 × 20.8 cm. The seventh (MS 456–59) has leaves (231–32) measuring 15.6–15.8 × 20.8–21.2 cm. The eighth (MS 460–61b) has leaves (233–34) measuring 15.6–15.8 × 20.8 cm. Large hand appears in the moderately embellished style without boldface. Small hand distinguishes scriptural citations. Most pages are clean, with catchwords on all pages except MS 436, 442, 450, and 453. Of these, only MS 453 is a verso—one in the middle of a folio, where the catchword is less necessary.

- MS 461. End of Part 6.
- MS 461a. End of Book I. This leaf (blank on its verso) fills out the fascicule's final folio.

II.1 (MS 462–75)

This chapter presents a conundrum in its final section of six pages. The first two folios are easy enough to separate into distinct segments, based on watermark evidence and changing large hand practice. A six-page section, however, cannot be the usual four-page folio.

266   MILTON'S THEOLOGICAL PROCESS

Campbell and Corns posit that the chapter's final leaf (241) is the separate one.[14] They may be right. I suggest, however, that the middle leaf (240) might be tipped into a folio comprised of leaves 239 and 241. Its dimensions are slightly different, and it seems to be on different, dirtier paper than its neighbors (perhaps owing to the intense degree of revision on MS 472). The possibility nevertheless remains that these pages were part of a single six-page stratum because the internal continuity of content is fairly seamless, and the spine edges of the pages all manifest similar patterns of wear.

- MS 462–65. This segment includes a single folio whose leaves (235–36) measure 15.6–15.8 × 20.8–20.9 cm and contain no watermark evidence. Large hand appears in the moderately embellished style without boldface, but only in the title. Large hand is not used for the Ramist definitions or headwords. If a smaller hand distinguishes scriptural citations, the difference is not especially marked. These are mostly clean pages, with catchwords on every page.
- MS 466–69. This segment includes a single folio whose leaves (237–38) measure 15.6–15.9 × 20.9 cm and bear watermark E. Large hand in the moderately embellished style, without boldface, marks Ramist headings, and a smaller hand distinguishes scriptural citations. The middle two pages contain marginal insertions and other revisions; catchwords appear on all but the first page.
- MS 470–75. This segment includes six pages, a folio (leaves 239 and 241) with a separate leaf (240) in between. The outer pages (leaves 239 and 241) measure 15.8 × 20.8 cm. The middle leaf (240) measures 15.7 × 20.9 cm. None of these leaves contain any watermark evidence. Large hand appears in the moderately embellished style without boldface, although the proper name "Belshazzare" is embellished. Small hand distinguishes scriptural citations. All pages contain revisions, and MS 472 has a marginal insertion that has been recopied by Skinner and pasted in. All pages except the last contain catchwords.

II.2 (MS 476–90)

This chapter's single stratum includes four folios, all bearing watermark E. The first (MS 476–79) has leaves (242–43) measuring 15.6 × 20.8–21.0 cm. The second (MS 480–83) has leaves (244–45) measuring 15.6–15.8 × 20.8 cm. The third (MS 484–87) has leaves (246–47) measuring 15.6 × 20.3–20.5 cm. The fourth (MS 488–90) has leaves (248–49) measuring 15.7 × 20.3–20.9 cm. The chapter ends on a recto, leaving the last verso blank. Large hand appears in the moderately embellished style without boldface. A smaller hand distinguishes scriptural citations. Revisions appear on most pages, with the heaviest appearing on MS 485–87 in a discussion of sincerity. Catchwords appear on all pages except MS 478 (third page of the first folio), 480 and 482 (rectos in the second folio), and 488 (first page of the fourth folio).

II.3 (MS 491–506)

This chapter's single stratum includes four folios whose leaves (250–57) measure 15.6 × 20.8 cm (15.6 × 20.5 cm in the last folio, MS 503–506) and bear watermark E. Large hand appears in the moderately embellished style without boldface. A smaller hand distinguishes

[14] *MMS*, 46.

THE MANUSCRIPT OF *DE DOCTRINA CHRISTIANA*   267

scriptural citations. This chapter contains relatively little revision. Catchwords appear on every page except MS 497 (a recto in the middle of a folio).

II.4 (MS 507–36)

This chapter's complex material state may be related to that in I.28, where a marginal addition to MS 341 references its discussion of vows ("de quo infra l. 2. c. 4 ubi de Voto"). Whether this reference indicates that the chapter once bore the title *de Voto* instead of its extant *de Cultu externo* remains an open question. The content of the chapter may indicate some organizational uncertainty on this point. In the Ramist *divisio* that lays out the chapter's structure, on MS 511, the topic of "Invocation [*Invocatio*]" subdivides into "petition and thanksgiving [*petitio et gratiarum actio*]" and "oathtaking and decision by lot [*jusjurandum et sors*]." This latter resembles the title of II.5 as it appears on MS 537: "*de Iurerando et Sorte*." II.4 thus takes an unexpected turn when, after completing discussion under the final headword from the definition, it begins, on MS 522, to address topics unanticipated by the Ramist signposting. The first of these are questions of cursing and of the conditions under which God hears prayers. Bearing on the larger issue of the chapter divisions, though, are the topics of fasting and vows, which the *divisio* on MS 526 describes as "the supports of prayers [*Precum adminicula sunt ieiunia et vota*]." This language awkwardly fits these topics onto the existing logical structure by appending them to prayer, even though they were not included in the definition. A further bit of bridgework appears when the definition on MS 530 informs us (partly through an interlinear insertion) that a vow is "sometimes accompanied by an oath [*nonnunquam etiam cum iuramento facta*]." The discussion of vows in the final two folios of II.4 and of oaths in II.5 proceed down distinct paths, but it seems clear that, amidst the complex layers of revision in II.4, the Ramist organization might be better described as still settling than as finally settled.

The chapter comprises eight folios, of which all but the first bear watermark E. There appear to be five (or possibly six) distinct segments, as follows:

- MS 507–10. This segment includes a single folio whose leaves (258–59) measure 15.1–15.2 × 19.9–20.1 cm and contain no watermark evidence. Large hand appears in the moderately embellished style with boldface that might owe to this paper's susceptibility to bleed-through. Some letters appear in the highly embellished style (MS 507 has the word *Jehova* twice, once with a highly embellished J and h and once without). A significantly smaller hand distinguishes scriptural citations. These are mostly clean pages, with a catchword on MS 510.
- MS 511–14. These two leaves (260–61) may comprise a single, irregularly cut folio, or they may be separate leaves, in which case, they are two strata instead of one. Leaf 260 measures 15.8 × 20.7–21.1 cm, and leaf 261 measures 15.6 × 20.5–21.0 cm. Both bear watermark E. Large hand usage is variable. Ramist headwords on the recto of leaf 260 MS 511 (indicated by Sumner's pencil underlining) have, at most, slight embellishment of their initial letters. On the verso, MS 512, they receive a distinction of size and moderate embellishment. On leaf 261, headwords become larger still and appear in boldface, in the moderately embellished style. Small hand is similar on both leaves. Aside from a marginal insertion on MS 513, these are clean pages with catchwords on every page.
- MS 515–18. This segment includes a single folio whose leaves (262–63) measure 15.3 × 19.4–19.5 cm and bear watermark E. An embellished, boldface large hand appears in proper names on MS 518; ordinal numerals appear in boldface on MS 515, and some

268 MILTON'S THEOLOGICAL PROCESS

initial letters in paragraphs are embellished. A smaller hand distinguishes scriptural citations.

- MS 519–26. This segment includes two folios, both bearing watermark E. The first (MS 519–22, leaves 264–65) measures 15.6–15.8 × 20.8 cm. The second (MS 523–26, leaves 266–67) measures 15.6 × 20.4–20.9 cm. Large hand in the moderately embellished style with boldface marks the final Ramist heading from the definition of prayer but not the headings for the ensuing discussions of cursing, hearing prayers, or fasting (which includes a definition). A smaller hand distinguishes scriptural citations. These pages contain a few revisions, and catchwords appear on every page. Leaf 267 contains a tear on the fore edge that Picard has written around on the recto (it is in the margin on the verso).
- MS 527–30. This segment includes a single folio whose leaves (268–69) measure 15.6 × 20.9 cm and bear watermark E. Large hand is not in evidence, but initial letters occasionally receive slight embellishment. A smaller hand generally distinguishes scriptural citations. These pages contain relatively few revisions until MS 530, and catchwords appear on every page.
- MS 531–34. This segment includes a folio and a leaf, both bearing watermark E. The folio (MS 531–34, leaves 270–71) measures 15.6 × 20.6–20.8 cm. The leaf (MS 535–36, leaf 272) measures 15.6 × 20.7 cm. Leaf 271 contains a large repair of a tear that Picard had written around so no text is lost. Large hand is not in evidence, although initial letters often receive some embellishment. A smaller hand distinguishes scriptural citations. Per Campbell et al., leaf 272 is not part of a folio.[15]
- MS 536. End of Part 7.

II.5 (MS 537–59)

This chapter affords the clearest evidence that work on the manuscript included recopying and replacing folios because its fourth folio (of six) appears entirely in the hand of Amanuensis "A." As with I.16, which affords the clearest evidence of Picard's involvement in this practice, the rest of the chapter seems to be of a piece, albeit using mixed paper stock (the first section containing no watermark evidence and the last bearing watermark E).

- MS 537–48. This segment includes three folios that contain no watermark evidence. The first (MS 537–40) has leaves (273–74) measuring 15.7 × 20.8–20.9 cm. The second (MS 541–44) has leaves (275–76) measuring 15.6 × 20.8–20.9 cm. The third (MS 545–48) has leaves (277–78) measuring 15.6 × 20.8 cm. Large hand in the moderately embellished style appears but only in the title. A smaller hand distinguishes scriptural citations. A deletion carries over from the bottom of MS 540 (the last page of the first folio) to the top of MS 541, suggesting continuity. Deletions constitute a high proportion of the revisions in these pages. Catchwords appear on every page.
- MS 549–52. This segment includes a single folio whose leaves (279–80) measure 15.6 × 19.3–19.5 cm and contain no watermark evidence. Uniquely, this folio appears in the hand of Amanuensis "A." MS 552 contains further revisions by Amanuensis "N," which Skinner has deleted and recopied into the margin. Catchwords appear on all but the first page.
- MS 553–59. This segment includes two folios that bear watermark E. The first (MS 553–56) has leaves (281–82) measuring 15.6–15.9 × 20.5–20.9 cm. The second (MS

---

[15] *MMS*, 46.

THE MANUSCRIPT OF *DE DOCTRINA CHRISTIANA*   269

283–84) has leaves (283–84) measuring 15.8 × 20.8 cm. An embellished, boldface large hand emphasizes proper names. Small hand distinguishes scriptural citations. The leaf containing MS 555–56 is torn in the corner; Picard has written around the tear, but additional wear has eroded text at the edges, especially of the marginal insertion on MS 556. Catchwords appear on all pages but MS 555 (owing to the tear). The chapter ends on a recto, followed by a blank verso.

II.6 (MS 560–66)

This chapter's single stratum includes two folios that bear watermark FdLC. The first (MS 560–63) has leaves (285–86) measuring 14.3 × 18.0–18.2 cm. The second (MS 564–66) has leaves (287–88) measuring 14.3–14.5 × 18–18.3 cm. Large hand appears in the moderately embellished style, with a boldface that may owe to the paper's susceptibility to bleed-through. A significantly smaller hand distinguishes scriptural citations. Most pages are densely written, and the chapter contains no revisions or catchwords. The chapter ends on a recto, followed by a blank verso.

II.7 (MS 567–82)

This is another chapter with a folio that has been recopied and replaced, this time by Skinner.[16] In size, this folio more nearly resembles the paper used for I.14 than that used for the epistle and I.1–13, although even then it is slightly smaller. Whereas I.14 aligns closely in size with I.15, the four folios in II.7 are uneven, with only the first and last being of similar size (and therefore likely of the same stratum), so Skinner's added pages seem not to reflect an effort to match the surrounding pages.

- MS 567–70. This segment includes a single folio whose leaves (289–90) measure 15.6–15.8 × 20.4–21.1 cm high and contain no watermark evidence. Large hand appears in the moderately embellished style, without boldface, but only in the title and the proper name "Amesius" on MS 570; headwords may have their first letters embellished. A smaller hand distinguishes scriptural citations. Revisions are few, including the inserted "noster" regarding Amesius. Catchwords appear on every page.
- MS 571–74. This segment includes a single folio whose leaves (291–92) measure 15.1 × 19.2 cm. These pages have been recopied by Skinner and contain a catchword on MS 574.
- MS 575–78. This segment includes a single folio whose leaves (293–94) measure 14.3 × 18.4 cm high and contain no watermark evidence. They do not contain large hand, but initial letters are often embellished. Small hand distinguishes scriptural citations. A catchword appears on MS 578.
- MS 579–82. This segment includes a single folio whose leaves (295–96) measure 15.6–15.8 × 19.9–20.7 cm high and bear watermark E. A list of proper names at the end appears in a moderately embellished, boldface large hand. A smaller hand distinguishes scriptural citations. Catchwords appear on all pages.
- MS 582. End of Part 8.

---

[16] For a careful bibliographical reading of this chapter, see Miller, "Theological Typology," ch. 4.

270 MILTON'S THEOLOGICAL PROCESS

II.8 (MS 583–96)

This chapter's single stratum includes three folios and a single leaf (not among those identi-fied by Campbell et al.), all bearing watermark E. The first (MS 583–86) has leaves (297–98) measuring 15.6–16.0 × 20.9–21.4 cm. The second (MS 587–90) has leaves (299–300) mea-suring 15.6–15.9 × 20.8 cm. The third (MS 591–94 has leaves (301–302) measuring 15.8 × 21.0 cm. The leaf (MS 595–96, leaf 303) measures 15.6 × 19.8–20.3 cm. Boldface large hand in the moderately embellished style appears in the chapter title and the Ramist headings but not in the definitions. Small hand distinguishes scriptural citations. These are mostly clean pages with some revisions scattered throughout. Catchwords appear on all pages except MS 585 (a recto within a folio).

II.9 (MS 597–623)

This chapter's single stratum includes seven folios, all bearing watermark E. The first (MS 597–600) has leaves (304–305) measuring 14.6–14.7 × 19.8 cm. The second (MS 601–604) has leaves (306–307) measuring 14.6 × 19.3–20.5 cm. The third (MS 605–608) has leaves (308–309) measuring 14.6 × 19.8–20.3 cm. The fourth (MS 609–12) has leaves (310–11) measuring 14.7 × 19.8 cm. The fifth (MS 613–16) has leaves (312–13) measuring 14.6–14.8 × 20.0–20.8 cm. The sixth (MS 617–20) has leaves (314–15) measuring 14.6–14.8 × 20.0–20.3 cm. The seventh (MS 623–23) has leaves (316–17) measuring 14.6–14.8 × 20.0–20.1 cm. Boldface large hand in the moderately embellished style appears in the chapter title but not elsewhere. Small hand distinguishes scriptural citations. Revisions are scattered throughout, including in the chapter title. Catchwords appear on all pages. The chapter ends on a recto, followed by a blank verso.

II.10 (MS 624–30)

This chapter contains a single stratum comprising two folios bearing watermark I. The first (MS 624–27) has leaves (318–19) measuring 14.7–14.8 × 20.1 cm. The second (MS 628–30) has leaves (320–21) measuring 14.5–14.7 × 20.0–20.1 cm. Large hand in the moderately embellished style without boldface appears in the chapter title but not elsewhere, although "Patientia" on MS 628 is unusually embellished. Catchwords appear on the versos and on MS 628, the first recto of a folio. Small hand distinguishes scriptural citations. The chapter ends on a recto, followed by a blank verso.

II.11 (MS 631–42)

This chapter's single stratum includes five folios and a leaf, on paper bearing watermark E. Following MS 635 is a sequence of pages that Skinner (mis-)numbered 626–35; Kel-ley established the practice of numbering these 626b–35b. The first folio (MS 631–34) has leaves (322–23) measuring 14.6–14.7 × 20.1–20.2 cm. The second (MS 635–28b) has leaves (324–25) measuring 14.7 × 20.0–20.1 cm. The third (MS 629b–32b) has leaves (326–27) measuring 14.6–14.7 × 19.7–20.5 cm. The fourth (MS 633b–36) has leaves (328–29) mea-suring 14.6–14.7 × 19.8–20.1 cm. The fifth (MS 637–40) has leaves (330–31) measuring 14.6–14.7 × 19.8–20.0 cm. The leaf (MS 641–42, leaf 332) measures 14.6 × 22.9 cm; per

THE MANUSCRIPT OF *DE DOCTRINA CHRISTIANA*   271

Campbell et al., it is not part of a folio.[17] Large hand is embellished but not especially bold. It appears only in the title; in the chapter itself, headings, regular text, and scriptural citations appear with little distinction in the hand other than slight embellishment of the initial letter in a paragraph. An exception is on MS 632, where a Greek headword appears in boldface. Catchwords appear on all pages except MS 633, 635, and 633b.

II.12 (MS 643–50)

This chapter's single stratum includes two folios whose leaves (333–36) measure 14.6 × 19.8–20.4 cm (with similar variation on the inner leaves, 334–35) and contain no watermark evidence. Boldface large hand in the moderately embellished style appears in the chapter title; headwords receive varying forms of emphasis (compare "Placabilitas" on MS 645 to "Honestatis" on MS 649). Small hand distinguishes scriptural citations. The pages of the first folio are mostly clean, while the second contains revisions on every page. Catchwords appear on every page.

II.13 (MS 651–73)

This chapter contains four strata. A long prose argument about falsehood spans the first three folios, which use an especially elaborate large hand for initial letters. In the third and apparently earliest of these folios, this elaborate large hand comes to be used for proper names. This large hand is not on evidence in the three much more Ramist folios that follow, although a difference in handwriting and paper distinguishes the last of these from the preceding two.

- MS 651–62. This segment includes two folios that bear watermark E. The first (MS 651–54) has leaves (337–38) measuring 14.6 × 20–20.1 cm. The second (MS 655–58) has leaves (339–40) measuring 14.6 × 19.7–19.8 cm. Boldface large hand in the moderately embellished style marks the title, and initial letters are occasionally highly embellished, but key words and proper names are not. Small hand distinguishes scriptural citations. Revisions appear on a few pages and catchwords on all.
- MS 659–62. This segment includes a single folio whose leaves (341–42) measure 14.6 × 19.7–19.8 cm and bear watermark E. Boldface, embellished large hand marks proper names and key words, including the "-mum" of "Abrahamum," carried over in bolder script from the catchword on the preceding folio, where the name is not embellished (except perhaps in the catchword itself), suggesting that the preceding folios were copied to match this one. These are clean pages with catchwords on all but the second recto (MS 661).
- MS 663–70. This segment includes two folios (MS 663–66, 667–70) with leaves (343–44, 345–46) measuring 14.6 × 19.8 cm (the inner leaves) and 14.6 × 19.8–20.4 cm (the outer leaves), all bearing watermark E. Large hand does not appear, but initial letters receive slight embellishment. Small hand distinguishes scriptural citations. Some revisions appear in these pages, concentrated especially on the last. Catchwords appear on all pages but MS 664 (a mid-folio verso) and 667 (the first recto of a folio).

---

[17] *MMS*, 46.

272   MILTON'S THEOLOGICAL PROCESS

- MS 671–73. This segment includes a single folio whose leaves (347–48) measure 14.5–14.6 × 19.1–19.3 cm and contain no watermark evidence. Large hand does not appear, but initial letters receive slight embellishment. Small hand distinguishes scriptural citations. The last page is especially dense, which is odd, given that the chapter ends on a recto (with a blank verso following). There are no catchwords.

II.14 (MS 674–86)

This chapter contains two strata that are barely distinguishable, with different catchword practice and subtle handwriting changes marking the only differences.

- MS 674–81. This segment includes two folios that bear watermark E. The first (MS 674–77) has leaves (349–50) measuring 14.7 × 19.8–20.0 cm. The second (MS 678–81) has leaves (351–52) measuring 14.7 × 19.6–19.7 cm. Large hand in the moderately embellished style, without boldface, appears in the chapter title but not elsewhere; initial letters occasionally receive some slight embellishment. Small hand distinguishes scriptural citations. They contain a handful of revisions, and catchwords appear on all pages except MS 675 (the first verso of a folio).
- MS 682–86. This segment includes a single folio and a leaf, both bearing watermark E. The folio (MS 682–85) has leaves (353–54) measuring 14.6–14.7 × 19.4–19.5 cm. Per Campbell et al., the leaf (MS 686, leaf 355) is not part of a folio.[18] It measures 14.8 × 19.3 cm and contains writing only on the recto, with a blank verso. Large hand does not appear in these pages, but initial letters (especially majuscule H) receive slightly more embellishment than in the preceding pages. Small hand distinguishes scriptural citations. These are clean pages. A catchword appears on MS 685.
- MS 686. End of Part 9.

II.15 (MS 687–703)

This chapter contains three strata, with the second segment apparently added later. The chronological relationship between the first and third is unclear.

- MS 687–94. This segment includes two folios that bear watermark E. The first (MS 687–90) has leaves (356–57) measuring 14.7–14.8 × 19.4–19.6 cm. The second (MS 691–94) has leaves (358–59) measuring 14.6–14.7 × 19.4–19.5 cm. A highly embellished, boldface large hand marks the chapter title and two initial letters on the first page; after that, large hand does not appear, and initial letters receive slight embellishment at most. Small hand distinguishes scriptural citations. Catchwords appear on all pages but MS 689 and 693, both rectos inside folios.
- MS 695–98. This segment includes a single folio whose leaves (360–61) measure 14.6 × 19.3–19.5 cm and bear watermark E. Large hand is not on evidence, and initial letters receive only occasional embellishment. Small hand distinguishes scriptural citations. These are densely written pages with a catchword on MS 698.
- MS 699–703. This segment includes a leaf and a folio, both bearing watermark E. Per Campbell et al., MS 703 is not part of a folio, but I posit that the leaf, in this instance,

[18] *MMS*, 46.

THE MANUSCRIPT OF *DE DOCTRINA CHRISTIANA*   273

comes before the folio.[19] Two pieces of evidence support this conclusion. Leaf 362 (MS 699–700) measures 14.6 × 19.3 cm, while leaves 363–64 (MS 701–703) both measure 14.8 × 19.3 cm. Furthermore, MS 699 contains a catchword, perhaps as a means of keeping straight which side of leaf 662 is the recto. Whichever the case, these pages seem to be part of the same stratum. Large hand does not appear, although headwords stand out due to embellishment of initial letters. Small hand distinguishes scriptural citations. All these pages but the first and last contain revisions. Catchwords appear on MS 699 and 702, and the chapter ends with a blank verso.

II.16 (MS 704–11)

This chapter contains two strata, distinguished by large hand style.

- MS 704–707. This segment includes a single folio whose leaves (365–66) measure 14.6 × 19.3–19.4 cm and bear watermark E. Large hand appears in the moderately embellished style in the chapter title but not elsewhere. Small hand distinguishes scriptural citations. Catchwords appear on the versos.
- MS 708–11. This segment includes a single folio whose leaves (367–68) measure 14.7–14.8 × 19.3–19.4 cm and bear watermark E. The distinction between strata appears in the difference between the unembellished S in the catchword "Sine" on MS 707 and the embellished S that begins MS 708, signaling a larger shift in handwriting style. Embellished large hand likewise marks "Hospitalitas" on MS 710. Small hand distinguishes scriptural citations. A catchword appears on MS 708.

II.17 (MS 712–35)

This chapter contains three distinct strata across its seven folios. Perhaps owing to its position as the final fascicule in the manuscript, the first two leaves, along with the last, are quite worn and underwent heavy repair as part of the conservation project in the 1930s.

- MS 712–23. This segment includes three folios that bear watermark E. The first (MS 712–15) has leaves (369–70) measuring 15.8–16.0 × 20.8–21.3 cm. The second (MS 716–19) has leaves (371–72) measuring 15.7–15.9 × 20.7–20.8 cm. The third (MS 720–23) has leaves (373–74) measuring 15.8 × 20.6 cm. An embellished large hand, but not boldface, appears in the chapter title but not elsewhere, although "Pontius Pilatus" appears in boldface on MS 719. Small hand distinguishes scriptural citations. Most pages contain revisions. Catchwords appear on MS 714–16, 719, and 721–23— making the middle folio (MS 716–19) anomalous.
- MS 724–31. This segment includes two folios that contain no watermark evidence. The first (MS 724–27) has leaves (375–76) measuring 14.3–14.4 × 18.3–18.4 cm. The second (MS 728–31) has leaves (377–78) measuring 14.3 × 18.1–18.3 cm. The hand in these pages is more embellished than in the preceding pages, with large hand or boldface distinguishing initial letters, ordinal numerals, and key words (with some variation). Small hand distinguishes scriptural citations. Catchwords appear on the final versos (MS 727 and 731). These are clean, mostly densely written pages (MS 729 is less dense than the rest).

[19] *MMS*, 46.

274 MILTON'S THEOLOGICAL PROCESS

- MS 732–35. This segment includes a single folio whose leaves (379–80) measure 15.6–15.9 × 20.2–20.9 cm and contain no watermark evidence. Large hand does not appear in these pages, but small hand (barely) distinguishes scriptural citations. These are densely written pages with a few interlinear additions. A catchword appears on MS 734.
- MS 735. "Totius Operis Finis", that is, end of the tenth and final part.

Bibliography

Note: Early modern editions of primary texts have been accessed using *Early English Books Online* and *The Post-Reformation Digital Library* (prdl.org) unless noted otherwise.

Editions of *De Doctrina Christiana* (arranged chronologically)

De Doctrina Christiana. SP 9/61. National Archives, Kew.
A Treatise on Christian Doctrine, trans. Charles Sumner (Cambridge: Cambridge University Press, 1825).
A Treatise on Christian Doctrine, ed. Charles R. Sumner, Vols 4–5, in The Prose Works of John Milton, ed. James A. St. John (London: Bohn, 1853).
De Doctrina Christiana, ed. James Holly Hanford and Waldo Hilary Dunn, Vols XIV–XVII, in *The Works of John Milton,* ed. Frank A. Patterson (New York: Columbia University Press, 1934).
On Christian Doctrine, ed. Maurice Kelley; trans. John Carey, Vol. VI, in *The Complete Prose Works of John Milton,* ed. Don M. Wolfe (New Haven, CT: Yale University Press, 1973).
De Doctrina Christiana, ed. John K. Hale and J. Donald Cullington, Vol. VIII, in *The Complete Works of John Milton,* ed. Gordon Campbell and Thomas N. Corns (Oxford: Oxford University Press, 2012).

Other works by Milton

Accedence Commenc't Grammar (London, 1669).
An Apology against a Pamphlet (London, 1642).
Areopagitica (London, 1644).
Artis Logicae (London, 1672).
A Brief History of Muscovia (London, 1682).
The Doctrine and Discipline of Divorce, 2nd edn (London, 1644).
Of Education (London, 1644).
Eikonoklastes (London, 1649).
The History of Britain (London, 1670).
Paradise Lost (London, 1674).
Poems (London, 1673).
Of Prelatical Episcopacy (London, 1641).
Pro Se Defensio (London, 1655).
The Readie and Easie Way to Establish a Free Commonwealth (London, 1660).
The Reason of Church-Government (London, 1641).
Of Reformation (London, 1641).
The Tenure of Kings and Magistrates, 2nd edn (London, 1650).
A Treatise of Civil Power (London, 1659).
Of True Religion (London, 1673).

276 BIBLIOGRAPHY

Other editions of Milton

Bentley, Richard, *Milton's* Paradise Lost. *A New Edition* (London, 1732).
Darbishire, Helen, ed., *The Early Lives of Milton* (New York: Barnes and Noble, 1965).
Fletcher, Harris Francis, ed., *Milton's Poetical Works: Facsimile Edition*, 4 vols (Urbana, IL: University of Illinois Press, 1943–48).
Haan, Estelle, ed., *John Milton*: Epistolarum Familiarum Liber Unus *and Uncollected Letters* (Leuven: Leuven University Press, 2019).
Lewalski, Barbara K., ed., *Paradise Lost* (Oxford: Blackwell, 2007).
Patterson, Frank Allan, ed., *The Works of John Milton*, 18 vols (New York: Columbia University Press, 1931–38).
Poole, William, ed., *Manuscript Writings*, Vol. XI, in *The Complete Works of John Milton*, eds. Gordon Campbell & Thomas N. Corns (Oxford: Oxford University Press, 2019).
Toland, John, *A Complete Collection of the Historical, Political, and Miscellaneous Works of John Milton* (Amsterdam, 1698).
Wolfe, Don M., ed., *Complete Prose Works of John Milton*, 8 vols (New Haven, CT: Yale University Press, 1953).

Bibles [with descriptive titles for clarity]

Barker, Robert, [*KJV Bible*] (London, 1612).
Beza, Theodore, [*New Testament*] (Geneva, 1559).
Beza, Theodore, [*New Testament*] (Geneva, 1598).
Beza, Theodore, Franciscus Junius, and Immanuel Tremellius. [*JTB Bible*] (London, 1585).
Beza, Theodore, Franciscus Junius, and Immanuel Tremellius. [*JTB Bible*] (Hanau, 1623–24).
Beza, Theodore, Franciscus Junius, and Immanuel Tremellius. [*JTB Bible*] (Geneva, 1630).
Walton, Brian, ed., *Biblia Sacra Polyglotta*, 6 vols (London, 1657).

Primary Sources

Abelard, Peter, *Commentaria in Epistolam Pavli ad Romanos*, in *Petra Abaelardi Opera Theologica*, Vol. I, ed. Eloi Marie Buytaert, O. F. M., *Corpvs Christanorvm Continvatio Mediaevalis*, Vol. XI (Turnhout: Brepols, 1969), pp. 1–340.
Abelard, Peter, *Commentary on the Epistle to the Romans*, trans. Steven Cartwright (Washington, DC: Catholic University of America Press, 2011).
Ames, William, *Coronis Ad Collationem Hagiensem* (Leiden, 1618).
Ames, William, *Medulla S. S. Theologiae* (London, 1629).
Ames, William, *De Conscientia* (Amsterdam, 1631).
Ames, William, *The Marrow of Sacred Divinity* (London, 1642).
Amyraut, Moyse, *Brief Traitté de la Predestination* (Saumur, 1634).
Anselm of Canterbury, *Opera Omnia*, 6 vols, ed. Franciscus Salesius Schmitt (Edinburgh: Thomas Nelson, 1940–61).
Anselm of Canterbury, *The Major Works*, ed. Brian Davies and Gillian R. Evans. Oxford World's Classics (Oxford: Oxford University Press, 1998).
Aquinas, Thomas, *On Faith*, ed. Mark D. Jordan, in *Readings in the* Summa Theologiae, Vol. 1 (Notre Dame, IN: University of Notre Dame Press, 1990).

BIBLIOGRAPHY 277

Arminius, Jacobus, *Disputationes Publicae & Privatae* (Leiden, 1610).

Arminius, Jacobus, *Amica cum D. Francisco Junio de Praedestinatione* (Leiden, 1613).

Arminius, Jacobus, *Examen Thesium D. Francisci Gomari de Praedestinatione* (N.p., 1645).

Arminius, Jacobus, *The Writings of James Arminius*, 3 vols, trans. James Nichols and William R. Bagnall (Auburn, AL and Buffalo, NY, 1853; repr. Grand Rapids, MI: Baker, 1956).

Athanasius, *On the Incarnation*, trans. John Behr (Yonkers, NY: St Vladimir's Seminary Press, 2011).

Augustine, *De Doctrina Christiana*, trans. R. P. H. Green (Oxford: Oxford University Press, 1995).

Baxter, Richard, *A Christian Directory* (London, 1673).

Baxter, Richard, *Reliquiae Baxterianae* (London, 1696).

Baxter, Richard, *Reliquiae Baxterianae*, ed. N. H. Keeble, John Coffey, Tim Cooper, and Tom Charlton, 5 vols (Oxford: Oxford University Press, 2020).

Calvin, John, *Institutio Christianae Religionis* (Geneva, 1559).

Calvin, John, *Institutes of the Christian Religion*, ed. John T. McNeill; trans. Ford Lewis Battles (Louisville, KY: Westminster John Knox Press, 1960; repr. 2006).

Cappel, Louis, "*Spicilegium eiusdem argumenti*," in *Myrothecium Evangelicum*, ed. John Cameron (Geneva, 1632).

Cappel, Louis, *Critica Sacra* (Paris, 1650).

Cartwright, Thomas, *Christian Religion* (London, 1611).

Cartwright, Thomas, *A Treatise of Christian Religion* (London, 1616).

Cartwright, Thomas, *A Methodicall Short Catechisme* (London, 1623).

Cicero, *De Inventione*, trans. H. M. Hubbell. Loeb Classical Library (Cambridge, MA: Harvard University Press, 1976 [1949]).

Coleridge, Samuel Taylor, *Letters of Samuel Taylor Coleridge*, 6 vols, ed. Earl Leslie Griggs (Oxford: Clarendon, 1956–71).

Cyril of Alexandria, *On the Unity of Christ*, trans. John Anthony McGuckin (Yonkers, NY: St Vladimir's Seminary Press, 1995).

Downame, George, *P. Rami Veromandui Regii Professoris Dialecticae Libri Duo. Cum Commentariis Georgii Dounami Annexis* (London, 1669).

Erasmus, Desiderius, *De duplici copia rerum ac verborum* (Argentorati [Strasbourg], 1514).

Felbinger, Jeremias, *Politicae Christianae Compendium* (Bratislava, 1648).

Felbinger, Jeremias, *Demonstrationes Christianae* (N.p., 1653).

Felbinger, Jeremias, *Das Neue Testament* (Amsterdam, 1660).

Fenner, Dudley, *The Artes of Logick and Rethorike* (Middleburgh, 1584).

Fenner, Dudley, *Sacra Theologia, sive Veritas quae est secundum Pietatem* ([Geneva], 1586).

Junius, Franciscus, *De Theologia Vera* (Leiden, 1594).

Luther, Martin, *De Servo Arbitrio* (Wittenberg, 1525).

Mastricht, Petrus van, *Theoretico-Practica Theologia*, 2 vols (Amsterdam, 1682).

Melanchthon, Philipp. *Loci Communes Rerum Theologicarum seu Hypotyposes Theologicae* (Basil, 1521).

Owen, John, *Salus Electorum, Sanguis Jesu: Or The Death of Death in the Death of Christ* (London, 1648).

Owen, John, *Of Communion with God The Father, Sonne, and Holy Ghost, Each Person Distinctly; in Love, Grace, and Consolation: Or The Saints Fellowship With the Father, Sonne, and Holy Ghost, Unfolded* (Oxford, 1657).

Polanus, Amandus, *Syntagma Theologiae Christianae*, 2 vols (Hanover, 1609).

Poliandrus, Johannes, Andreas Rivetus, Antonius Walaeus, and Antonius Thysius, *Synopsis Purioris Theologiae*, 3rd edn (Leiden, 1642).

278 BIBLIOGRAPHY

Przpkowski, Samuel, *Catechesis Ecclesiarum quae in Regno Poloniae...Affirmant* (Racovia [London], 1651).

Pseudo-Dionysius, *The Complete Works*, trans. Colm Luibheid. The Classics of Western Spirituality (New York: Paulist Press, 1987).

Ramus, Petrus, *Institutionum Dialecticarum Libri Tres* (Lyon, 1553).

Rupp, E. Gordon, and Philip S. Watson, eds, *Luther and Erasmus: Free Will and Salvation* (Philadelphia, PA: Westminster John Knox, 1969).

Smalcius, Valentin, *The Racovian Catechism* (Amsterdam, 1652).

Spanheim, Friedrich, Sr, *Disputationum Theologicarum Syntagma* (Geneva, 1652).

Synod of Dort, *The Ivdgement of the Synode Holden at Dort* (London, 1619).

Terence, *Heauton Timorumenon*, in *Terence: In Two Volumes*, Vol. I, ed. and trans. John Sargeaunt. Loeb Classical Library (Cambridge, MA: Harvard University Press, 1912), pp. 113–229.

Westminster Assembly of Divines, *Articles of Christian Religion* (London, 1648).

Wilson, Thomas, *The Arte of Rhetorique* (London, 1553).

Wolleb, Johannes, *Compendium Theologiae Christianae* (Cambridge, 1642).

Wolleb, Johannes, *The Abridgment of Christian Divinitie*, trans. Alexander Ross (London, 1650).

Zanchius, Girolamo, *Operum Theologicorum*, 3 vols (Geneva, 1619).

Secondary Sources

Agamben, Giorgio, *Homo Sacer: Sovereign Power and Bare Life*, trans. Daniel Heller-Roazen (Stanford, CA: Stanford University Press, 1998).

Ainsworth, David, *Milton and the Spiritual Reader: Reading and Religion in Seventeenth-Century England* (New York: Routledge, 2008).

Ainsworth, David, "Milton's Holy Spirit in *De Doctrina Christiana*," *Religion & Literature* 45, 2 (2013): 1–25.

Auger, Peter, "The Poetics of Scriptural Quotation in the Divorce Tracts," *Milton Quarterly* 54, 1 (2020): 23–40.

Backus, Irena, and Aza Goudriaan, "'Semipelagianism': The Origins of the Term and Its Passage into the History of Heresy," *Journal of Ecclesiastical History* 65, 1 (2014): 25–46.

Bangs, Carl, *Arminius: A Study in the Dutch Reformation*, 2nd edn (Grand Rapids, MI: Francis Asbury, 1985).

Barnaby, Andrew, "'The Form of a Servant': At(-)onement by Kenosis in *Paradise Lost*," *Milton Quarterly* 52, 1 (2018): 1–19.

Bauman, Michael, *Milton's Arianism* (Frankfurt am Main: P. Lang, 1987).

Bauman, Michael, *A Scripture Index to John Milton's* De Doctrina Christiana (Binghamton, NY: Medieval & Renaissance Texts & Studies, 1989).

Bentley, Richard, *Dr. Bentley's Emendations on the Twelve Books of Milton's* Paradise Lost (London, 1732).

Bevan Zlatar, Antonina, "'The Image of Their Glorious Maker': Looking at Representation and Similitude in Milton's *Paradise Lost*," in *What Is an Image in Medieval and Early Modern England?*, ed. Antonina Bevan Zlatar and Olga Timofeeva. SPELL: Swiss Papers in English Language and Literature 34 (Tübingen: Narr Francke Attempto, 2017), pp. 109–33.

Blacketer, Raymond A., "Arminius' Concept of Covenant in Its Historical Context," *Nederlands Archief voor Kerkgeschiedenis/Dutch Review of Church History* 80, 2 (2000): 193–220.

Borris, Kenneth, "Milton's Heterodoxy of the Incarnation and Subjectivity in De Doctrina Christiana and Paradise Lost," in Pruitt and Durham, *Living Texts* (2000), pp. 264–82.

Bourne, Claire M. L., "*Vide Supplementum*: *Romeo & Juliet, Hamlet*, and Seventeenth-Century Collation as Play-Reading in the First Folio," in *Early Modern English Marginalia*, ed. Katherine Acheson (New York: Routledge, 2018), pp. 195–233.

Bourne, Claire M. L., and Jason Scott-Warren, "'Thy Unvalued Booke': John Milton's Copy of the Shakespeare First Folio," *Milton Quarterly* 56, 1–2 (2022): 1–85.

Bowers, A. Robin, "Milton and Salmasius: The Rhetorical Imperatives," *Philological Quarterly* 52, 1 (1973): 55–68.

Bradley, Beatrice, "Creative Juices: Sweat in *Paradise Lost*," *Milton Studies* 62, 1 (2020): 107–35.

Brower, Jeffrey E., "Trinity," in Brower and Guilfoy, *The Cambridge Companion to Abelard* (2004), pp. 223–57.

Brower, Jeffrey E., and Kevin Guilfoy, eds, *The Cambridge Companion to Abelard* (Cambridge: Cambridge University Press, 2004).

Bryson, Michael, *The Tyranny of Heaven: Milton's Rejection of God as King* (Newark, DE: University of Delaware Press, 2004).

Buckham, Rebecca, "Milton's Strange Angels," in Donovan and Festa, *Milton, Materialism, and Embodiment* (2017), pp. 111–36.

Burgess, Thomas, *Milton Not the Author of the Lately-Discovered Arian Work* De Doctrina Christiana (London, 1829).

Butler, Todd, *Literature and Political Intellection in Early Stuart England* (Oxford: Oxford University Press, 2019).

Campbell, Gordon, "*De Doctrina Christiana*: Its Structural Principles and Its Unfinished State," *Milton Studies* 9 (1976): 243–60.

Campbell, Gordon, "Milton's *Index Theologicus* and Bellarmine's *Disputationes De Controversiis Christianae Fidei Adversus Huius Temporis Haereticos*," *Milton Quarterly* 11, 1 (1977): 12–16.

Campbell, Gordon, and Sebastian P. Brock, "Milton's Syriac," *Milton Quarterly* 27, 2 (1993): 74–77.

Campbell, Gordon, and Thomas N. Corns, *John Milton: Life, Work, and Thought* (Oxford: Oxford University Press, 2008).

Campbell, Gordon, and Thomas N. Corns, "*De Doctrina Christiana*: An England That Might Have Been," in *The Oxford Handbook of Milton*, ed. Nicholas McDowell and Nigel Smith (Oxford: Oxford University Press, 2009), pp. 424–35.

Campbell, Gordon, Thomas N. Corns, John K. Hale, and Fiona Tweedie, *Milton and the Manuscript of* De Doctrina Christiana (Oxford: Oxford University Press, 2007).

Chambers, A. B., "Chaos in *Paradise Lost*," *Journal of the History of Ideas* 24, 1 (1963): 55–84.

Channing, William Ellery, *The Character and Writings of John Milton* (Boston, MA, 1826).

Chaplin, Gregory, "Beyond Sacrifice: Milton and the Atonement," *Publications of the Modern Language Association of America* 125, 2 (2010): 354–69.

Chaplin, Gregory, "Milton's Beautiful Body," in Rumrich and Fallon, *Immortality and the Body* (2017), pp. 91–106.

Clark, Gregory, *Civic Jazz: American Music and Kenneth Burke on the Art of Getting Along* (Chicago, IL: University of Chicago Press, 2015).

Clawson, James M., and Hugh F. Wilson, "*De Doctrina Christiana* and Milton's Canonical Works: Revisiting the Authorship Question," *Renaissance and Reformation* 44, 3 (2021): 151–98.

280 BIBLIOGRAPHY

Clement, William Dean, "Milton, Thomas Hobbes, and the Political Problem of Chaos," *Studies in English Literature 1500–1900* 60, 1 (2020): 133–51.

Coffey, John, "A Ticklish Business: Defining Heresy and Orthodoxy in the Puritan Revolution," in *Heresy, Literature and Politics in Early Modern English Culture*, ed. David Loewenstein and John Marshall (Cambridge: Cambridge University Press, 2006), pp. 108–36.

Connor, John T., "Milton's *Art of Logic* and the Force of Conviction," *Milton Studies* 45 (2006): 187–209.

Corns, Thomas N., "Milton's Churches," in *The Church and Literature*, ed. Peter Clarke and Charlotte Methuen (Woodbridge: Boydell, 2012), pp. 185–201.

Crane, Mary Thomas, *Framing Authority: Sayings, Self, and Society in Sixteenth-Century England* (Princeton, NJ: Princeton University Press, 1993).

Creaser, John, "'Fear of Change': Closed Minds and Open Forms in Milton," *Milton Quarterly* 42, 3 (2008): 161–82.

Danielson, Dennis Richard, *Milton's Good God* (Cambridge: Cambridge University Press, 1982).

DeVine, Charles F., "The 'Blood of God' in Acts 20:28," *Catholic Biblical Quarterly* 9, 4 (1947): 381–408.

Dobranski, Stephen B., and John P. Rumrich, *Milton and Heresy* (Cambridge: Cambridge University Press, 1998).

Dolloff, Matthew, "'Gabriel's Trumpet': Milton and Seventeenth-Century Conceptions of Infinity," in Festa and Ainsworth, *Locating Milton* (2021), pp. 81–99.

Donnelly, Phillip J., "'Matter' versus Body: The Character of Milton's Monism," *Milton Quarterly* 33, 3 (1999): 79–85.

Donovan, Kevin J., and Thomas Festa, eds, *Milton, Materialism, and Embodiment: "One First Matter All"* (Pittsburgh, PA: Duquesne University Press, 2017).

Duhamel, P. Albert, "Milton's Alleged Ramism," *Publications of the Modern Language Association of America* 67, 7 (1952): 1035–53.

Earle, Philippa, "'Till Body Up to Spirit Work': Maimonidean Prophecy and Monistic Sublimation in *Paradise Regained*," *Milton Studies* 62, 1 (2020): 159–89.

Edelman, Lee, *No Future: Queer Theory and the Death Drive* (Durham, NC: Duke University Press, 2004).

Eisenring, Albert J. Th., *Milton's De Doctrina Christiana: An Historical Introduction and Critical Analysis* (Fribourg: Society of St Paul, 1946).

Ellis, Mark A., *Simon Episcopius's Doctrine of Original Sin* (New York: Peter Lang, 2006).

Empson, William, *Milton's God*, rev. edn (Cambridge: Cambridge University Press, 1981).

Ettenhuber, Katrin, "Milton's Logic: The Early Years," *The Seventeenth Century* 36, 2 (2021): 187–212.

Evans, Bill, *Conversations with Myself* (Los Angeles: Verve Records, 1963).

Falcone, Filippo, "More Challenges to Milton's Authorship of *De Doctrina Christiana*," *ACME* 63, 10 (2010): 231–50.

Falcone, Filippo, "Irreconcilable (Dis)Continuity: *De Doctrina Christiana* and Milton," *Connotations* 27 (2018): 78–105.

Falcone, Filippo, "Milton's Consistency: An Answer to Jason Kerr," *Connotations* 29 (2020): 125–28.

Fallon, Stephen M., *Milton among the Philosophers: Poetry and Materialism in Seventeenth-Century England* (Ithaca, NY: Cornell University Press, 1991).

Fallon, Stephen M., *Milton's Peculiar Grace: Self-Representation and Authority* (Ithaca, NY: Cornell University Press, 2007).

BIBLIOGRAPHY   281

Fallon, Stephen M., "John Milton, Isaac Newton, and the Life of Matter," in Martin, *Milton and the New Scientific Age* (2019), pp. 211–37.

Feingold, Mordechai, "English Ramism: A Reinterpretation," in *The Influence of Petrus Ramus: Studies in Sixteenth and Seventeenth Century Philosophy and Sciences*, ed. Mordechai Feingold, Joseph S. Freedman, and Wolfgang Rother (Basel: Schwabe, 2001), pp. 127–76.

Festa, Thomas, "Eve and the Ironic Theodicy of the New Milton Criticism," in *The New Milton Criticism*, ed. Peter C. Herman and Elizabeth Sauer (Cambridge: Cambridge University Press, 2012), pp. 175–93.

Festa, Thomas, and David Ainsworth, eds, *Locating Milton: Places and Perspectives* (Clemson, SC: Clemson University Press, 2021).

Fish, Stanley, *Surprised by Sin* (London: Macmillan, 1967).

Fish, Stanley, *Self-Consuming Artifacts: The Experience of Seventeenth-Century Literature* (Berkeley, CA: University of California Press, 1972).

Fish, Stanley, "Wanting a Supplement: The Question of Interpretation in Milton's Early Prose," in Loewenstein and Turner, *Politics, Poetics and Hermeneutics* (1990), 41–68.

Fixler, Michael, "Ecclesiology," in *A Milton Encyclopedia*, Vol. II, ed. William B. Hunter, Jr (Lewisburg, PA: Bucknell University Press, 1978), pp. 190–203.

Fletcher, Harris Francis, *The Use of the Bible in Milton's Prose* (Urbana, IL: University of Illinois Press, 1929).

Foucault, Michel, *The Birth of Biopolitics: Lectures at the Collège de France 1978–1979*, trans. Graham Burchell (New York: Picador, 2008).

Fulton, Thomas, *The Book of Books: Biblical Interpretation, Literary Culture, and the Political Imagination from Erasmus to Milton* (Philadelphia, PA: University of Pennsylvania Press, 2021).

Gigante, Denise, *Taste: A Literary History* (New Haven, CT: Yale University Press, 2005).

Gilson, Erinn Cunniff, "Vulnerability and Victimization: Rethinking Key Concepts in Feminist Discourses on Sexual Violence," *Signs: Journal of Women in Culture and Society* 42, 1 (2016): 71–98.

Goldberg, Jonathan, *The Seeds of Things: Theorizing Sexuality and Materiality in Renaissance Representations* (New York: Fordham University Press, 2009).

Goodrich, John K., "From Slaves to Sin to Slaves of God: Considering the Origin of Paul's Slavery Metaphor in Romans 6," *Bulletin for Biblical Research* 23, 4 (2013): 509–30.

Grafton, Anthony, *Joseph Scaliger: A Study in the History of Classical Scholarship*, Vol. 1 (Oxford: Clarendon, 1983).

Green, Ian, *Print and Protestantism in Early Modern England* (Oxford: Oxford University Press, 2000).

Gregory, Tobias, "How Milton Defined Heresy and Why," *Religion & Literature* 45, 1 (2013): 148–60.

Gregory, Tobias, *Milton's Strenuous Liberty* (Forthcoming).

Grossman, Marshall, "The Genders of God," in *Milton and Gender*, ed. Catherine Gimelli Martin (Cambridge: Cambridge University Press, 2004), pp. 95–114.

Guibbory, Achsah, *Ceremony and Community from Herbert to Milton: Literature, Religion, and Cultural Conflict in Seventeenth-Century England* (Cambridge: Cambridge University Press, 1998).

Hale, John K., "Points of Departure: Studies in Milton's Use of Wollebius," *Reformation* 19, 1 (2014): 69–82.

Hale, John K., *Milton's Scriptural Theology: Confronting* De Doctrina Christiana (Leeds: Arc Humanities Press, 2019).

282 BIBLIOGRAPHY

Hale, John K., and J. Donald Cullington, "*Universis Christi Ecclesiis*: Milton's Epistle for *De Doctrina Christiana*," *Milton Studies* 53 (2012): 3–15.

Hammond, Paul,. *Milton and the People* (Oxford: Oxford University Press, 2014).

Hardy, Nicholas, *Criticism and Confession: The Bible in the Seventeenth Century Republic of Letters* (Oxford: Oxford University Press, 2017).

Hart, David Bentley, "Matter, Monism, and Narrative: An Essay on the Metaphysics of *Paradise Lost*," *Milton Quarterly* 30, 1 (1996): 16–27.

Haskin, Dayton, *Milton's Burden of Interpretation* (Philadelphia, PA: University of Pennsylvania Press, 1994).

Headley, Alrick George, *The Nature of the Will in the Writings of Calvin and Arminius: A Comparative Study* (Eugene, OR: Wipf and Stock, 2017).

Helm, Paul, *Reforming Free Will: A Conversation on the History of Reformed Views on Compatibilism (1500–1800)* (Fearn: Mentor, 2020).

Heppe, Heinrich, *Schriften zur Reformirten Theologie*, 2 vols (Elberfeld: R. L. Friderichs, 1860).

Herman, Peter C., *Destabilizing Milton*: Paradise Lost *and the Poetics of Incertitude* (New York: Palgrave Macmillan, 2005).

Herman, Peter C., "C. S. Lewis, David Urban, and the New Milton Criticism," *Milton Quarterly* 45, 4 (2011): 258–66.

Hessayon, Ariel, and Nicholas Keene, eds, *Scripture and Scholarship in Early Modern England* (Aldershot: Ashgate, 2006).

Hillier, Russell M., *Milton's Messiah: The Son of God in the Works of John Milton* (Oxford: Oxford University Press, 2011).

Hirschfeld, Heather, *The End of Satisfaction: Drama and Repentance in the Age of Shakespeare* (Ithaca, NY: Cornell University Press, 2014).

Hogg, David S., "Christology: The *Cur Deus Homo*," in *The Oxford Handbook of Christology*, ed. Francesca Aran Murphy and Troy A. Stefano (Oxford: Oxford University Press, 2015), pp. 199–214.

Honeygosky, Stephen R., *Milton's House of God: The Invisible and Visible Church* (Columbia, MO: University of Missouri Press, 1993).

Hopkins, Jasper, *A Companion to the Study of St. Anselm* (Minneapolis, MN: University of Minnesota Press, 1972).

Hopkins, Jasper, "God's Sacrifice of Himself as a Man: Anselm of Canterbury's *Cur Deus Homo*," in *Human Sacrifice in Jewish and Christian Tradition*, ed. Karin Finsterbusch, Armin Lange, and K. F. Diethard Römheld (Leiden: Brill, 2007), pp. 237–57.

Huguelet, Theodore Long, "Milton's Hermeneutics: A Study of Scriptural Interpretation in the Divorce Tracts and in De Doctrina Christiana." PhD dissertation, University of North Carolina (1959).

Hunter, William B., Jr, "The Theological Context of Milton's *Christian Doctrine*," in *Achievements of the Left Hand: Essays on the Prose of John Milton*, ed. Michael Lieb and John T. Shawcross (Amherst, MA: University of Massachusetts Press, 1971), pp. 269–87.

Hunter, William B., Jr, *Visitation Unimplor'd: Milton and the Authorship of* De Doctrina Christiana (Pittsburgh, PA: Duquesne University Press, 1998).

Hunter, William B., Jr, C. A. Patrides, and J. H. Adamson, *Bright Essence* (Salt Lake City, UT: University of Utah Press, 1971).

Iliffe, Rob, "Friendly Criticism: Richard Simon, John Locke, Isaac Newton and the Johannine Comma," in Hessayon and Keene, *Scripture and Scholarship* (2006), pp. 137–57.

Johnson, Kimberly, *Made Flesh: Sacrament and Poetics in Post-Reformation England* (Philadelphia, PA: University of Pennsylvania Press, 2014).

Keene, Nicholas, "'A Two-Edged Sword': Biblical Criticism and the New Testament Canon in Early Modern England," in Hessayon and Keene, *Scripture and Scholarship* (2006), pp. 94–115.

Kelley, Maurice, "Milton's Debt to Wolleb's *Compendium Theologiae Christianae*," *Publications of the Modern Language Association of America* 50, 1 (1935): 156–65.

Kelley, Maurice, *This Great Argument: A Study of Milton's* De Doctrina Christiana *as a Gloss upon* Paradise Lost (Princeton, NJ: Princeton University Press, 1941).

Kelley, Maurice, "On the State of Milton's *De Doctrina Christiana*," *Modern Language Notes*, 27, no. 2 (1989): 42–48.

Kerr, Jason A., "Prophesying the Bible: The Improvisation of Scripture in Books 11 and 12 of *Paradise Lost*," *Milton Quarterly* 47, 1 (2013): 13–33.

Kerr, Jason A., "*De Doctrina Christiana* and Milton's Theology of Liberation," *Studies in Philology* 111, 2 (2014): 346–74.

Kerr, Jason A., "Milton and the Anonymous Authority of *De Doctrina Christiana*," *Milton Quarterly* 49, 1 (2015): 23–43.

Kerr, Jason A., "Shifting Perspectives on Law in *De Doctrina Christiana*: A Response to Filippo Falcone," *Connotations* 28 (2019): 129–41.

Kerr, Jason A., "Eve's Church," *Milton Quarterly* 55, 2 (2021): 67–81.

Kerr, Jason A., and John K. Hale, "The Origins and Development of Milton's Theology in *De Doctrina Christiana*, I. 17–18," *Milton Studies* 54 (2013): 181–206.

Koester, Christopher, "Mathematical Milton: Number Theory and Nesting Infinities in Paradise Lost," in Festa and Ainsworth, *Locating Milton* (2021), pp. 101–23.

Kolbrener, William, *Milton's Warring Angels* (Cambridge: Cambridge University Press, 1997).

Kotsko, Adam, *What Is Theology? Christian Thought and Contemporary Life* (New York: Fordham University Press, 2021).

Lehnhof, Kent R., "Deity and Creation in the *Christian Doctrine*," *Milton Quarterly* 35, 4 (2001): 232–44.

Leonard, John, "Milton, Lucretius, and 'The Void Profound of Unessential Night'," in Pruitt and Durham, *Living Texts* (2000), pp. 198–217.

Leonard, John, *Faithful Labourers: A Reception History of* Paradise Lost, *1667–1970*, 2 vols (Oxford: Oxford University Press, 2013).

Lewalski, Barbara K., *Milton's Brief Epic* (Providence, RI: Brown University Press, 1966).

Lewalski, Barbara K., *Protestant Poetics and the Seventeenth-Century Religious Lyric* (Princeton, NJ: Princeton University Press, 1979).

Lewis, Charlton T., and Lewis Short, *A Latin Dictionary* (Oxford: Oxford University Press, 1879).

Lewis, C. S., *A Preface to* Paradise Lost (Oxford: Oxford University Press, 1960).

Lieb, Michael, *Theological Milton: Deity, Discourse and Heresy in the Miltonic Canon* (Pittsburgh, PA: Duquesne University Press, 2006).

Loewenstein, David, "Rethinking Political Theology in Milton," *Journal for Early Modern Cultural Studies* 18, 2 (2018): 34–59.

Loewenstein, David, and James Grantham Turner, eds, *Politics, Poetics and Hermeneutics in Milton's Prose* (Cambridge: Cambridge University Press, 1990).

Loewenstein, Joseph, *The Author's Due: Printing and the Prehistory of Copyright* (Chicago, IL: University of Chicago Press, 2002).

Luxon, Thomas H., "Queering as Critical Practice in Reading Paradise Lost," in Orvis, *Queer Milton* (2018), pp. 45–63.

MacCallum, Hugh, *Milton and the Sons of God: The Divine Image in Milton's Epic Poetry* (Toronto: University of Toronto Press, 1986).

Mandelbrote, Scott, "English Scholarship and the Greek Text of the Old Testament, 1620–1720: The Impact of Codex Alexandrinus," in Hessayon and Keene, *Scripture and Scholarship* (2006), pp. 74–93.

Marmion, Declan, and Rik van Nieuwenhove, *An Introduction to the Trinity* (Cambridge: Cambridge University Press, 2011).

Martin, Catherine Gimelli, ed., *Milton and the New Scientific Age: Poetry, Science, Fiction* (New York and London: Routledge, 2019).

Masson, David, *The Life of John Milton and History of His Time*, 6 vols (London: Macmillan, 1859–80).

McDonald, Grantley, *Biblical Criticism in Early Modern Europe: Erasmus, the Johannine Comma and Trinitarian Debate* (Cambridge: Cambridge University Press, 2016).

Miller, Jeffrey Alan, "Reconstructing Milton's Lost *Index Theologicus*: The Genesis and Usage of an Anti-Bellarmine, Theological Commonplace Book," *Milton Studies* 52 (2011): 187–219.

Miller, Jeffrey Alan, "Theological Typology, Milton, and the Aftermath of Writing," DPhil thesis, University of Oxford (2012).

Miller, Jeffrey Alan, "Milton, Zanchius, and the Rhetoric of Belated Reading," *Milton Quarterly* 47, 4 (2013): 199–219.

Mineka, Francis E., "The Critical Reception of Milton's *De Doctrina Christiana*," *Studies in English* 23 (1943): 115–47.

Mortimer, Sarah, *Reason and Religion in the English Revolution: The Challenge of Socinianism* (Cambridge: Cambridge University Press, 2010).

Müller, F. Max, *Introduction to the Science of Religion* (London: Longman, Green, and Co., 1873).

Mueller, Janel, "Milton on Heresy," in Dobranski and Rumrich, *Milton and Heresy* (1998), pp. 21–38.

Muller, Richard A., *Post-Reformation Reformed Dogmatics*, 2nd edn, 4 vols (Grand Rapids, MI: Baker Academic, 2003).

Muller, Richard A., *Dictionary of Latin and Greek Theological Terms*, 2nd edn (Grand Rapids, MI: Baker Academic, 2017).

Muller, Richard A., *Divine Will and Human Choice: Freedom, Contingency, and Necessity in Early Modern Reformed Thought* (Grand Rapids, MI: Baker Academic, 2017).

Myers, Benjamin, *Milton's Theology of Freedom* (Berlin: Walter de Gruyter, 2006).

Nagel, Ernest, and James Newman, *Gödel's Proof*, ed. Douglas R. Hofstadter (New York: New York University Press, 2008).

Nicholls, Charlotte, "'By Gradual Scale Sublimed': Chymical Medicine and Monist Human Physiology in John Milton's Paradise Lost," in Martin, *Milton and the New Scientific Age* (2019), pp. 167–91.

Nuttall, Geoffrey F., *The Holy Spirit in Puritan Faith and Experience* (Chicago, IL: University of Chicago Press, 1992 [1946]).

Nuttall, Geoffrey F., "Milton's Churchmanship in 1659: His Letter to Jean Labadie," *Milton Quarterly* 35, 4 (2001): 227–31.

Ong, Walter J., S. J., *Ramus: Method, and the Decay of Dialogue* (Cambridge, MA: Harvard University Press, 1958).

Orvis, David L., ed., *Queer Milton* (Cham: Palgrave Macmillan, 2018).

Patrides, C. A., *Milton and the Christian Tradition* (Oxford: Clarendon Press, 1966).

BIBLIOGRAPHY 285

Patrides, C. A., "Paradise Lost and the Language of Theology," in Hunter, et al., *Bright Essence* (1971), pp. 165–78.

Patterson, Annabel, *Milton's Words* (Oxford: Oxford University Press, 2009).

Picciotto, Joanna, *Labors of Innocence in Early Modern England* (Cambridge, MA: Harvard University Press, 2010).

Poole, William, *Milton and the Idea of the Fall* (Cambridge: Cambridge University Press, 2005).

Poole, William, "Theology," in *Milton in Context*, ed. Stephen B. Dobranski (Cambridge: Cambridge University Press, 2010), pp. 475–86.

Porter, H. C., "The Nose of Wax: Scripture and the Spirit from Erasmus to Milton," *Transactions of the Royal Historical Society* 14 (1964): 155–74.

Potts, James B., Jr, "Milton and Augustine: The Rule of Charity," *Explorations in Renaissance Culture* 16 (1990): 101–10.

Potts, James B., Jr, "Milton's Two-Fold Scripture," *Explorations in Renaissance Culture* 18 (1992): 93–110.

Pruitt, Kristin A., and Charles W. Durham, eds, *Living Texts: Interpreting Milton* (London: Associated University Presses, 2000).

Raamsdonk, Esther van, *Milton, Marvell, and the Dutch Republic* (London: Routledge, 2020).

Rajan, Balachandra, Paradise Lost *& The Seventeenth Century Reader* (London: Chatto & Windus, 1962).

Raleigh, Sir Walter Alexander, *Milton* (New York and London: G. P. Putnam's Sons, 1900).

Rashdall, Hastings, *The Idea of the Atonement in Christian Theology* (London: Macmillan, 1919).

Raymond, Joad, *Milton's Angels: The Early-Modern Imagination* (Oxford: Oxford University Press, 2010).

Roebuck, Thomas, "Milton and the Confessionalization of Antiquarianism," in *Young Milton: The Emerging Author, 1620–1642*, ed. Edward Jones (Oxford: Oxford University Press, 2013), pp. 48–71.

Rogers, John, *The Matter of Revolution: Science, Poetry, and Politics in the Age of Milton* (Ithaca, NY: Cornell University Press, 1996).

Rogers, John, "Delivering Redemption in *Samson Agonistes*," in *Altering Eyes: New Perspectives on* Samson Agonistes, ed. Mark R. Kelley and Joseph Wittreich (Newark, NJ: University of Delaware Press, 2002), pp. 72–97.

Rogers, John, "Milton and the Heretical Priesthood of Christ," in *Heresy, Literature, and Politics in Early Modern English Culture*, ed. David Loewenstein and John Marshall (Cambridge: Cambridge University Press, 2006), pp. 203–20.

Rogers, John, "Orson Pratt, Parley Pratt, and the Miltonic Origins of Mormon Materialism," in Donovan and Festa, *Milton, Materialism, and Embodiment* (2017), pp. 157–88.

Rosenblatt, Jason P., *Torah and Law in* Paradise Lost (Princeton, NJ: Princeton University Press, 1994).

Rumrich, John P., *Matter of Glory: A New Preface to* Paradise Lost (Pittsburgh, PA: University of Pittsburgh Press, 1987).

Rumrich, John P., *Milton Unbound: Controversy and Reinterpretation* (Cambridge: Cambridge University Press, 1996).

Rumrich, John P., "Milton's Arianism: Why It Matters," in Dobranski and Rumrich, *Milton and Heresy* (1998), pp. 72–92.

Rumrich, John P., "Of Chaos and Nightingales," in Pruitt and Durham, *Living Texts* (2000), pp. 218–27.

286 BIBLIOGRAPHY

Rumrich, John P., "Does Milton's God Play Dice with the Universe?," in Martin, *Milton and the New Scientific Age* (2019), pp. 108–26.

Rumrich, John, and Stephen M. Fallon, eds, *Immortality and the Body in the Age of Milton* (Cambridge: Cambridge University Press, 2017).

Saurat, Denis, *Milton: Man and Thinker* (New York: Dial Press, 1925).

Schmitt, Carl, *Political Theology: Four Chapters on the Concept of Sovereignty*, trans. George Schwab (Chicago, IL: University of Chicago Press, 2005).

Schoenfeldt, Michael C., *Bodies and Selves in Early Modern England: Physiology and Inwardness in Spenser, Shakespeare, Herbert, and Milton* (Cambridge: Cambridge University Press, 1999).

Schwartz, Regina M., *Remembering and Repeating: Biblical Creation in* Paradise Lost (Cambridge: Cambridge University Press, 1988).

Schwartz, Regina M., "Citation, Authority, and De Doctrina Christiana," in Loewenstein and Turner, *Politics, Poetics and Hermeneutics* (1990), pp. 227–40.

Scott-Craig, T. S. K., "Milton's Use of Wolleb and Ames," *Modern Language Notes* 55, 6 (1940): 403–07.

Sellin, Paul, "'If Not Milton, Who Did Write the DDC?': The Amyraldian Connection," in Pruitt and Durham, *Living Texts* (2000), pp. 237–63.

Sewell, Arthur, "Milton and the Mosaic Law," *Modern Language Review* 30, 1 (1935): 13–18.

Sewell, Arthur, *A Study in Milton's Christian Doctrine* (London: Oxford University Press, 1939).

Shitaka, Hideyuki, "Degeneration and Regeneration of Man's Language in *Paradise Lost*," *Studies in English Literature [Japan]* 62, 1 (1985): 17–33.

Shore, Daniel, *Milton and the Art of Rhetoric* (Cambridge: Cambridge University Press, 2012).

Shuger, Debora, *The Renaissance Bible: Scholarship, Sacrifice, and Subjectivity* (Berkeley, CA: University of California Press, 1993).

Simpson, Ken, *Spiritual Architecture and* Paradise Regained: *Milton's Literary Ecclesiology* (Pittsburgh, PA: Duquesne University Press, 2007).

Skerpan-Wheeler, Elizabeth, "The Logical Poetics of *Paradise Regained*," *Huntington Library Quarterly* 76, 1 (2013): 35–58.

Sloane, Thomas O., *Donne, Milton, and the End of Humanist Rhetoric* (Berkeley, CA: University of California Press, 1985).

Smith, Samuel, "Milton's Theology of the Cross: Substitution and Satisfaction in Christ's Atonement," *Christianity and Literature* 63, 1 (2013): 5–25.

Snobelen, Stephen D., "'To us there is but one God, the Father': Antitrinitarian Textual Criticism in Seventeenth- and Early Eighteenth-Century England," in Hessayon and Keene, *Scripture and Scholarship* (2006), pp. 116–36.

Specland, Jeremy, "Unfinished Exegesis: Scriptural Authority and Psalm 2 in the Miltonic Canon," *Milton Studies*, 62, 1 (2020): 48–77.

Sprunger, Keith L., *The Learned Doctor William Ames: Dutch Backgrounds of English and American Puritanism* (Urbana, IL: University of Illinois Press, 1972).

Stanglin, Keith D., and Thomas H. McCall, *Jacob Arminius: Theologian of Grace* (Oxford: Oxford University Press, 2012).

Strier, Richard, "Milton against Humility," in *Religion and Culture in Renaissance England*, ed. Claire McEachern and Debora Shuger (Cambridge: Cambridge University Press, 1997), pp. 258–86.

Stulting, Claude N., Jr, "Theosis and Paideia in the Writings of Gregory of Nyssa and the Prelapsarian Books of Milton's Paradise Lost," in Pruitt and Durham, *Living Texts* (2000), pp. 144–61.

Sugimura, N. K., "*Matter of Glorious Trial*": Spiritual and Material Substance in Paradise Lost (New Haven, CT: Yale University Press, 2009).

Sullivan, Ernest W., "Review of Gordon Campbell, Thomas N. Corns, John K. Hale, and Fiona J. Tweedie, Milton and the Manuscript of De Doctrina Christiana (Oxford: Oxford University Press, 2007)," *Review of English Studies* 60, 243 (2009): 153–54.

Sytsma, David S., *Richard Baxter and the Mechanical Philosophers* (Oxford: Oxford University Press, 2017).

Tapp, Christian, "Infinity in Mathematics and Theology," *Theology and Science* 9, 1 (2011): 91–100.

Teskey, Gordon, *Delirious Milton: The Fate of the Poet in Modernity* (Cambridge, MA: Harvard University Press, 2006).

Todd, H. J., *Some Account of the Life and Writings of John Milton* (London, 1826).

Trubowitz, Rachel J., "Body Politics in *Paradise Lost*," *Publications of the Modern Language Association of America* 121, 2 (2006): 388–404.

Trubowitz, Rachel J., "The Fall and Galileo's Law of Falling Bodies: Geometrization vs. Observation and Describing Things in Paradise Lost," in Martin, *Milton and the New Scientific Age* (2019), pp. 79–107.

Urban, David V., "Speaking for the Dead: C. S. Lewis Answers the New Milton Criticism; or, 'Milton Ministries' Strikes Back," *Milton Quarterly* 45, 2 (2011): 95–106.

Urban, David V., "The Acolyte's Rejoinder: C. S. Lewis and the New Milton Criticism, Yet Once More," *Milton Quarterly* 46, 3 (2012): 174–81.

Urban, David V., "John Milton, Paradox, and the Atonement: Heresy, Orthodoxy, and the Son's Whole-Life Obedience," *Studies in Philology* 112, 4 (2015): 817–36.

Urban, David V., *Milton and the Parables of Jesus: Self-Representation and the Bible in John Milton's Writings* (University Park, PA: Pennsylvania State University Press, 2018).

Urban, David V., "Revisiting the History of the *De Doctrina Christiana* Authorship Debate and the Its Ramifications for Milton Scholarship: A Response to Falcone and Kerr," *Connotations* 29 (2020): 156–88.

Urban, David V., "The Increasing Distance between *De Doctrina Christiana* and Milton's Poetry: An Answer to John K. Hale," *Connotations* 32 (2023): 1–10.

van Asselt, Willem J., J. Martin Bac, and Roelf T. te Velde, eds, *Reformed Thought on Freedom: The Concept of Free Choice in Early Modern Reformed Theology* (Grand Rapid, MI: Baker Academic, 2010).

Waldock, A. J. A., Paradise Lost *and Its Critics* (Cambridge: Cambridge University Press, 1959 [1947]).

Walker, William, "Milton's Dualistic Theory of Religious Toleration in *A Treatise of Civil Power, Of Christian Doctrine*, and *Paradise Lost*," *Modern Philology* 99, 2 (2001): 201–30.

Webster, Erin, "Milton and the Infinitesimal Calculus," *English Literary Renaissance* 45, 3 (2015): 425–58.

Wilburn, Reginald A., "Getting 'Uppity' with Milton, or Because My Mom Politely Asked: 'Was Milton Racist?,'" *Milton Studies* 62, 2 (2020): 266–79.

Williams, Thomas, "Sin, Grace, and Redemption," in Brower and Guilfoy, *The Cambridge Companion to Abelard* (2004), pp. 258–78.

288 BIBLIOGRAPHY

Wilson, Emma Annette, "Mapping Milton's 'Great Argument': The Literary Significance of the Argument Sections in *Paradise Lost*," in *Milton Through the Centuries*, ed. Gábor Ittzés and Miklós Péti (Budapest: L'Harmattan, 2012), pp. 125–36.

Wilson, Emma Annette, "The Classical Sceptical Origins of John Milton's Logic Terms," *Notes and Queries* 60, 1 (2013): 61–63.

Zachman, Randall C., "The Christology of John Calvin," in *The Oxford Handbook of Christology*, ed. Francesca Aran Murphy and Troy A. Stefano (Oxford: Oxford University Press, 2015), pp. 284–96.

General Index

Abelard, Peter, 170, 174–76, 182
ad explorandum, 53–55
Adam, 72, 87, 95–96, 198, 216, 235, 240, 248
Amanuenses
"A", 29, 73, 99–100, 104, 221, 268
"B", 45, 177
"M", 52, 56, 104. *See also* Picard, Jeremie; Skinner, Daniel
Ames, William
and ecclesiology, 112
Milton's interlocutor, 8–9, 25–27, 67–68, 204, 269
on ministers, 130
and scripture, 69, 74–92, 104, 106, 118–21, 128
and the Trinity, 144–47, 150–57, 160, 162, 164
Amyraldianism, 15, 180
Amyraut, Moyse, 179–80
Anabaptists, 11
angels, 173, 216–20, 223, 230, 232, 236
Anselm of Canterbury, 170, 231, 247
Aquinas, Thomas, 16, 96
Arabic, 53
Aramaic, 23
Aristotle, 17, 22, 39, 227–28
Arminianism, 11, 15, 68–73, 95–98, 103–6, 180, 224, 226
Arminius, Jacob, 71–72, 95–98, 105–6
atonement
and ecclesiology, 169–72
and incarnation, 197
and matter, 229–34
and Pelagianism, 223
and process of Christian doctrine, 172–83
on behalf of all, 177, 179, 188
moral exemplar, 170–72, 174–75, 181–82, 229

penal substitution, 170–81, 188, 190, 140
satisfaction, 170–73, 176–84, 188, 198, 229, 240
Augustine, 5, 38, 56, 64, 108–9, 124, 132, 169, 186, 225, 246
authority
authoritarianism, 233
of Christology, 4
dialectics of, 56–64
ecclesiological, 5, 65, 108–11, 114, 127–31, 132–38, 169
of individual within church, 132–35
of scripture, 4
scriptural, 22, 37, 44, 48–50, 66–67, 107, 124–25
speech, 5, 43
theological, 10, 73, 138, 144
and the Trinity, 192

baptism, 144, 252, 262
Baptists, 10
Basil of Caesarea, 214
Bauman, Michael, 13, 173, 178–79
Baxter, Richard, 10–11, 17, 124, 216
benedictione, 87–88
Bernard of Clairvaux, 174
Beza, Theodore, 46, 52–55, 72, 78–79, 82, 89, 97–98, 103, 136, 166
Bible
biblical theology, 6, 116–17, 122, 148
citations, 5, 8, 14, 22–27, 47, 52, 55, 58, 60, 81, 85–91, 99, 104, 106, 151, 184
commentaries, 16
in *DDC*, 22–24
Latin, 52
and literary form, 49–50, 54–58, 109, 155–58, 199
and *Paradise Lost*, 7, 204, 210
on penitence, 104
scholarship on, 67, 113

290 GENERAL INDEX

Bible (*Continued*)
  text, 44, 48, 136
  and the Trinity, 153, 169, 171, 193, 195,
    243. *See also* Junius-Tremellius-Beza
    Bible (JTB); King James Bible
biopolitics, 233
Bradshaw, William, 24
Burgess, Thomas (Bishop of Salisbury), 1,
  8–13, 138, 178–79, 204

calling, 66–85, 88–94, 99–100, 104, 108,
  127, 130, 179, 234
  and internal scripture, 55
  and Milton's interlocutors, 81–92
  natural/supernatural renewal, 74–80,
    93–94
  and renewal, 66–73
  special calling, 76, 81–85, 88, 90, 106
Calvinism, 11, 15, 24–27, 68–73, 86, 181
  anti-Calvinism, 67
Calvin, John, 16, 51, 68, 71–72, 98, 182
Cameron, John, 62, 261
Campbell, Gordon, 28–31, 127–28,
  251–52, 255, 260–61, 266, 270, 272
Cappel, Louis, 46–47, 179
Cartwright, Thomas, 24–25
Channing, William Ellery, 10
Chaos, 217, 225–28, 230
Chappell, William, 26
Christ's College, Cambridge, 17, 26
Christian liberty, 4, 38, 42, 52, 63, 66, 171,
  174, 218, 250
  freedom from, rather than freedom
    to, 133, 191
Christology
  in *DDC*, 1, 4, 12, 21, 32, 144, 164, 205
  and ecclesiology, 7, 210
  hypostatic union, 185–87, 229, 235–38
  and the rule of faith, 199
  and the Trinity, 153, 216, 223
church militant, 24–25
Church of England, 12
church
  as body of interpreters, 131
  church of one, 115, 126, 132–35, 137,
    197–98, 213
  universal, 41, 116, 126, 131, 195, 199
  visible, 109–12, 126–27, 131–36, 199,
    211, 215, 217. *See also* ecclesiology

Cicero, 4, 19–21, 39
Coercion (coercive), 6, 70, 194–95, 198,
  210, 218–24
  non-coercion, 190, 194, 213, 242
community (communal)
  and ecclesiology, 112–14, 117, 131, 133,
    211, 230
  and freedom, 48
Corns, Thomas N. ix, 6n20, 7n21, 11–12,
  26n92, 28–29, 31, 162n61, 175n22,
  205n6, 251–52, 255, 260–61
Council of Chalcedon, 199
Council of Nicaea, 12, 199, 213
creation
  ex Deo, 210, 212
  Fenner on, 25
  of humans, 71, 81, 96–98, 104, 170, 191
  and materialism, 229–32
  in *Paradise Lost*, 206, 241
  and the Son, 213–14
  and the Trinity, 146–49, 226–28, 237–44
  as withdrawal, 248

Dati, Carlo, 47
David, 151–53
De Doctrina Christiana
  authorship, 1, 9, 12–13, 138, 143,
    178–79, 204–5
  chronology, 4, 28, 30, 112–13
  as literature, 2
De Doctrina Christiana manuscript
  complex material state, 4, 116, 251–54
  dating, 6
  discovered, 1, 28, 138, 251
  folios, 4, 29–31, 63, 73–74, 144
  fonts, 29, 253–54
  messiness, 250
  not static, 203–4
  reading the manuscript, 28–31
  revisions, 9, 24–25, 59, 68–69, 73, 77,
    92, 99–100, 139
  and theological process, 2–3
devils, 218, 222. *See also* Satan
Dionysius Alexandrinus, 42–44
  Pseudo-Dionysius, 246
discernment, 78–80, 94, 97–98, 105–7,
  111–13, 116, 139, 144–45, 162, 169–71

dispositio, 18–22, 38–39, 42, 44, 50, 82,
    92, 120–23. *See also* Keckermann,
    Bartolomaeus; Ramism
duntaxat, 56–59, 120–22, 133–34
  potissimum, 56–57

ecclesiastical concerns, 5, 108–11, 126,
    135, 209, 211, 236
ecclesiology (ecclesial)
  church of one, 115, 126, 132–35, 137,
    197–99, 213
  Christ as model for, 187
  and coercion, 218
  and Congregationalism, 27, 115, 198
  defined, 108
  and exploration, 55
  fallibility, 169–70
  materialist, 248
  not ecclesiastical, 5
  and ontology, 224–26, 235, 236, 243–45
  in *Paradise Lost*, 209–13, 219–21, 24
  political-ecclesial, 123, 216–17
  process, 7, 111–18
  and the rule of faith, 64
  and scripture, 38, 43, 48, 62, 65, 108–11,
    126–40
  of the Son, 145, 158, 169, 196–98
  and speech, 32, 118–19
  theological foundations of, 209–10, 245
  and the Trinity, 194–95. *See also* church
Election (Elect)
  and calling, 72–85, 88–91, 97, 100, 103,
    180
Erasmus, 19, 46, 136
Eve, 96, 198, 235, 248
external scripture
  and atonement, 177
  and certainty, 136–38
  and critical judgment, 44
  and ecclesiology, 109–11, 124–25,
    132–35, 169, 194–95
  and freedom, 47, 104–5, 228, 237
  and internal scripture, 48, 51–61
  and intuition, 41
  and liberty, 63–64
  and literary form, 31, 37, 49–51
  and Milton's interlocutors, 81–84,
    87–89, 92
  and rhetoric, 5, 56, 66, 167

and the Son, 32
and speech, 4, 7, 38
and the Trinity, 146–49, 158, 199–200,
    239, 243

Fall, the, 7, 69–72, 96–98, 212
fanatics, 51
Felbinger, Jeremias, 13n39, 178n38
Fenner, Dudley, 24–25
freedom
  and Christ's freedom, 183–84, 187–97,
    210–13, 218–24, 235, 237–38
  of debate, 114
  and God's calling, 72–73, 86, 100
  human, 4, 69
  ignorance is not freedom, 46–47, 59
  and judgment, 42, 44, 56
  love as, 242
  and ontology, 224–29
  and scripture, 47–48. *See also* Christian
    liberty

genre
  in *DDC*, 6, 8, 14–23, 26, 118
  epistolary, 112–13
  in *Paradise Lost*, 200, 215, 243
  Ramist, 63, 200
  and rhetoric, 3, 204
Gentiles, 58–59, 86
God (Father)
  attributes, 156–59
  calling, 83
  divine encroachment, 190–91
  and ecclesiology, 126, 213–19
  external efficiency, 22, 147, 149, 161, 163
  Jehovah, 40, 78, 154, 156
  judgment of, 72, 99, 179, 218, 243
  love of, 60–61, 174–75, 241–42
  Pater, 155–56
  and sin, 71–73, 97, 191
  subject of laughter, 220
  unknowability, 211, 237
  will of, 63, 90
  yoke of, 110, 133, 234
God (Son). *See* Son, the
God (Spirit). *See* Holy Spirit
grace
  acceptance of, 241–43
  and Arminianism, 95–97
  and atonement, 174–75, 179–82, 238

292   GENERAL INDEX

grace (*Continued*)
  and Calvinism, 71–72
  of gifts, 197–98
  and human capacity, 196
  and Milton's interlocutors, 81–91
  Milton on, 98–99
  and nature, 95
  and perseverance, 103
  and regeneration, 170, 232
  and renewal, 69, 75, 78
  and scripture, 64
Greek (language), 23, 52–54, 89, 108, 152,
      165, 177, 185, 214, 227
  Greek New Testament, 136–37

Hale, John K., 2–3, 21n74, 24n82, 26n95,
      27n100, 56n59, 79n27, 113n21,
      135n26, 139n106, 143n2, 165n69, 167,
      179n39, 204n3, 255
Hebrew (language), 23, 45, 52, 154
Hebrew Scriptures, 45–47
Hebrews (Israelites), 123
heresy (heretics), 1, 8–13, 42–43, 50, 67,
      116, 145, 196, 219
Hillier, Russell M., 172–74, 231
Hobbes, Thomas, 67
Holy Ghost. *See* Holy Spirit
Holy Spirit
  and critical judgment, 42–44
  and ecclesiology, 5
  ferment, 232–35, 243–44
  and freedom, 106
  is God, 147
  infusion of virtue, 232–35, 240, 243
  and justice, 93
  power of life itself, 231
  and preaching, 105
  relationship to Father and Son, 146–50,
      155–57, 166, 214, 231–38
  and renewal, 82
  and scripture, 11, 41, 51, 75, 82, 124,
      127, 129, 139
  sin against, 90
  and the Son, 146–51
  and substance, 214
  as surer guide, 46, 48, 109
human (humanity)
  fallibility, 5, 11, 169–71, 196
  "merely" human speech, 4, 135, 138

restoration of, 176–77, 180–83, 241
  as sons of wrath, 81, 85, 92, 94, 97, 106
  unsaved state of, 69, 97
Hunter, William B., 8–9, 12–13, 26n94,
      173n9, 216n25, 224n28

imitatio Christi, 32, 62, 172–73, 181–83,
      195–98, 240–41
infralapsarianism, 16
internal scripture
  authority, 58, 136
  and charity, 61–62
  and critical judgment, 37, 42–50, 54–56
  defined, 3–5
  diverse, 56
  and ecclesiology, 32, 37–42, 108–13,
      169, 171, 195, 198–99
  and Eve, 248
  as foundation of theology, 12, 14, 31–33,
      37, 56, 66, 118–30, 144, 171
  and freedom, 104, 200
  and hate, 242
  and literary form, 31, 155, 168
  and potentiality, 168, 210–12, 219–30
  prolegomena, 118, 121, 128
  and renewal, 69, 74–84, 87–99, 106–7
  and representation, 247
  as rule of faith, 109, 137–38
  and the Son, 145–49, 158–67
  and speech, 134–38, 209, 235, 244
  and the Trinity, 215, 238–39, 243
intuition, 39–43, 55, 234, 236
invention (*inventio*), 4, 18–21, 42, 67, 69,
      82
Israel (Israelites), 56–59, 78

Jesus Christ. *See* Son, the
judgment
  church's collective, 5, 108–11, 117, 127,
      131, 137, 169, 195–96, 199, 213
  critical judgment, 37, 64
  and ecclesiology, 114–17, 123
  of God, 72, 99, 179, 218, 243
  human capacity of, 92, 104–5
  and intellect, 71
  and internal scripture, 44–50, 54
  intuitive, 39–41, 55–56
  and rhetoric, 167
  and the Spirit, 41–44

Junius, Franciscus, 52, 55, 95–97, 152, 154, 156
Junius-Tremellius-Beza Bible (JTB)
    1585 edition, 152–54
    1623/24 Hanau *vs.* 1630 Geneva edition, 154, 157, 166, 189
    Milton quotes from, 52–55
justification, 72–75, 81, 91–94, 174, 176, 179–82, 191

Keckermann, Bartolomaeus, 17
Kelley, Maurice, 1, 6–7, 12–13, 26–32, 120, 203, 209, 251–52, 255–56, 259n10
kenosis, 173, 181, 186, 242
King James Bible (KJV), 14, 53, 82, 109, 220, 242

Law of Moses (Mosaic Law), 45–46, 56, 60–61, 192
Lemon, Robert, 1, 28, 251
Lewis, C.S., 10–12, 172–73, 204
liturgy, 128, 183
Livy, 54
logic
    and atonement, 179, 240
    and internal scripture, 5, 38–41, 49–50, 64, 92, 95, 135
    logical *dispositio*, 18–22, 38, 82, 122–23
    and renewal, 69–70, 89–90
    and rhetoric, 3, 17–22, 37, 40, 66–67, 137, 165–66
    of Satan, 218
    and self-reference, 165
    The Art of Logic, 17–18, 38–41
    and the Trinity, 22, 146–47, 157, 164–66, 186, 232–33. *See also* Ramism
Lord's Supper (Eucharist), 144, 246, 252, 262
love
    of God, 60–61, 174–75, 241–42
    of humans, 170
    ontological, 241
    unity in, 187–97
Luther, Martin, 64, 70–71, 75–76, 95, 130, 236
Lutheran, 11, 70

magisterium, 5–6, 14, 48, 66, 125, 131
marriage, 10, 61, 193
Mary, 185, 213
materialism, 2, 205, 230, 232, 248

Melanchthon, Philipp, 14, 16
methodology (method)
    defined, 8
    and ecclesiology, 108–9, 112–13, 169, 197
    and headings and passages, 61, 92, 144–47
    over doctrine, 11
    of Milton, 27–32, 67–68, 150
    and *Paradise Lost*, 206–9
    for reading *DDC*, 2–7, 15, 17, 21–22, 203
    and the rule of faith, 163, 165
    and scripture, 37–41, 48–54, 118–22, 135–37, 151, 154, 163, 167, 200
    and the Trinity, 148, 156–61
Miller, Jeffrey Alan, 24, 28–29, 251–56, 261, 269n16
Milton, John
    An Apology, 182–83
    Areopagitica, 42–44, 54, 113, 115, 121, 183, 196, 210
    Art of Logic, 17–18, 38–41
    A Treatise of Civil Power, 212, 237
    and the Celestial Patroness, 244–45
    Eikonoklastes, 32, 250
    inaccurately labeled as narrator, 139
    "Index Theologicus", 17, 114
    individual faith, 114, 139
    Lycidas, 212
    Of Reformation, 143
    Of True Religion, 11–12, 62
    scrivener's son, 111
    "The Passion", 172, 205
ministers, 128–31, 149, 209
morals, 73, 94–96, 182, 218
More, Alexander, 6–7, 205
Mormons (Latter-day Saints), 10
Muller, Richard A., 5n15, 14, 33n109, 50n42, 71n12, 94n85, 95n91–92, 99n106, 109n6, 118n37, 128n78, 135n98, 146n10, 152n29, 153n35, 155n42, 163n65–66, 178n35, 184n56, 191n83, 197n102, 215n18, 227n58

nature (natural)
    Calvinist definition, 71–72
    natural dialectic, 39

294   GENERAL INDEX

nature (natural) (*Continued*)
  renewal (natural person), 69, 74–82,
    86–100, 104–6, 108, 180, 182, 247
  natural theology, 95
  supernatural renewal, 69, 72–74, 80,
    87–88, 94–99, 104–6, 108, 180, 182
New Testament, 46, 52, 147, 159, 181, 185
  Greek, 136–37

obedience
  human capacity for, 174
  humans and, 11, 57, 72, 173–74, 212
  and the Son, 178, 187–91, 216–17, 230
  and will, 224, 238
Old Testament, 45, 47, 145, 147, 154–55
ontology
  and creation, 230–31
  and ecclesiology, 213, 225–29
  and freedom, 103
  ontological humility, 196, 243–45
  and renewal, 234
  and the Trinity, 4, 173, 178, 195, 210–13,
    223–24, 235–43
orthodoxy
  and action, 193
  heterodox, 10, 32, 106, 146, 167, 169,
    171, 197, 216
  Milton's, 1, 8–15, 67–68, 181
  Reformed, 146, 172
  and renewal, 105
  Trinitarian, 147–48, 160, 164, 167, 173,
    178, 181, 214–15, 222, 236
  unorthodox, 98, 166, 173, 175, 196, 210

Paradise Lost
  and atonement, 229–34
  colloquy, 210–11, 215, 219–23, 235,
    237–39, 242
  and *DDC*, 1–2, 6–13, 16, 20, 32, 146,
    164, 173, 198, 203–13, 248–50
  DDC as gloss to, 1, 6–7, 12–13, 20, 250
  dregs, 206, 217, 225, 229–42, 244
  on God, Satan, and the Church, 213–19
  and ontology, 224–29, 235–45
  and potentiality, 219–24
Patrides, C.A., 12, 172–73, 205–6
Pelagianism, 55, 70–73, 88, 106, 181, 188,
  223, 237
  Semipelagian, 70, 98, 171

Perkins, William, 25–26
perseverance, 82, 103, 174
Phillips, Edward, 25
Picard, Jeremie, 6, 28–31, 56–57, 80, 94,
  100, 138, 144, 159–60, 177, 251–54,
  256–74
Placaeus (Josué de la Place), 156, 179n59
Plato (Platonic), 199, 246
  Neoplatonic, 186
poetics, 246–47
Polanus, Amandus, 62, 162, 261
politics, 58, 123, 133, 151, 216, 218, 237
Poole, Matthew, 210
Pratt, Orson, 10
prayer, 11, 25, 197–98, 244–45
preaching
  and atonement, 171
  and the elect, 73–76, 80, 84, 127
  and Melanchthon, 14
  and the natural/supernatural, 104–6,
    108
  and renewal, 92, 98
  and scholarship, 67
predestination, 72, 79, 83, 87–88, 91, 98,
  146–47, 180
Protestantism (Protestant)
  and individuality, 114
  Milton as, 5
  scholastic theology, 9–10, 14, 45, 50, 62
  and scripture, 44, 49, 66, 124, 127, 129,
    132, 135
  tradition, 12
  unity, 11
Psalm 2, 21, 145, 151–55, 157–58, 162–64,
  200, 205–6, 221–22, 242
  hodie, 152–54, 157, 162
purification, 180–81, 189
Puritanism (Puritans), 10, 26, 124

Ramism
  and calling, 106
  and *DDC*, 3, 16, 18, 21–24, 32, 49, 63,
    127, 176, 204, 247
  and ecclesiology, 108, 128
  and Milton, 8, 17, 42, 74
  and interpretation of scripture, 64, 99,
    121, 135, 158–67, 169
  and Milton's interlocutors, 24, 26
  and nature, 92

and scripture blocks, 37, 41, 50, 58, 64, 81, 143, 167

and the Trinity, 145–50, 155–57, 167, 199–200

Ramus, Petrus (Pierre de la Ramée), 8, 17–18, 38–39, 42

Raphael, 7, 206, 216, 224, 226, 230–31, 234–37, 240

Reformation, the, 14, 17, 143

Reformed
and atonement, 170, 172, 177, 182
and calling, 72
and God's will, 163
and human will, 103
and nature, 95
and renewal, 67, 98–99
and scripture, 4, 31–33, 49, 51, 69, 203
and Trinity, 186, 227
Westminster Confession, 146
Wolleb as, 25, 27

regeneration, 72–84, 89–94, 99, 104–8, 127, 170, 182, 191, 241
unregeneration, 52, 75, 108, 233

renewal
and atonement, 172, 176–77, 182, 184, 247
calling and, 69–73, 127
distinction between external and natural, 69, 99–107
and externality, 69, 74–80, 92–95, 99–100, 182, 247
and the Fall, 96
and freedom, 183, 190–91
and grace, 170–71, 180, 196, 233
human, 67
Milton's contexts, 69–80
and Milton's interlocutors, 81–92
of mind, 53, 55
and obedience, 188
and reason, 234
and scripture, 97–99

Restoration (monarchy), 6, 116

rhetoric
and ecclesiology, 112, 131, 133
and external scripture, 56
and internal scripture, 5–6, 38–41, 48–50, 64, 69, 136–38, 169
and literary form, 37–38

and logic, 2–3, 17–23, 42, 59–60, 66–67, 82

and scriptural interpretation, 66–67, 70, 82, 92, 145, 199

and speech, 108

and theological treatise as genre, 15, 21, 138–39

and the Trinity, 4, 158–61, 164–67, 204

Roman Catholicism, 11, 42, 45, 129, 132
anti-Catholic, 226
magisterium, 5, 48, 66
Roman Index, 45

rule of faith
Augustinian practice, 5
and ecclesiology, 108–9, 124–34, 169, 171
and scripture, 11–12, 38, 45, 47, 56, 60, 63–64, 135–38, 160–65, 205
and the Trinity, 189, 197–200

Sabbath, 27, 61, 193
anti-Sabbatarianism, 31, 203

Saumur
hypothetical universalism, 16, 179, 234
theologians, 179n39. *See also the Saumur theologians*; Amyraut, Moyse; Cameron, John; Cappel, Louis; Placaeus

sanctification, 72–75, 81–84, 88–94

Satan, 209, 213, 217–21, 223, 232, 241, 249

Scaliger, Joseph, 47

Schleiermacher, Friedrich, 15

scripture
disruptive force of, 151–55
and ecclesiology, 126–31
foundation of theology, 14, 31–32, 66, 128, 135, 197, 203
governs, 109
speaking of, 135–38
theology of, 4, 13, 22–23, 31, 37, 64, 145, 168
twofold nature, 37
as Word of God, 11–12, 44, 105, 114, 136. *See also* scripture, external; scripture, internal

Selden, John, 47

Septuagint, 45

Sewell, Arthur, 56n59, 143n3, 183n55, 225n49, 232n70

296   GENERAL INDEX

Shakespeare, William, 47
Simon, Richard, 67
sin
  against Holy Ghost, 90
  boldly, 64
  death through, 86
  enslaved to, 52, 96, 174, 188–89, 218,
    234
  and externality, 87
  glory replaces, 242
  God and, 71–73, 97, 191
  original sin, 72, 191
  penalty for, 170, 175–76
  and sanctification, 84, 89, 94
Skinner, Daniel, 28–31, 56, 113, 116, 144,
  148, 150, 160–61, 251–52, 255–56,
  260, 269
slavery (enslaved person), 52–53, 56, 66,
  171, 174, 188, 218, 233–34
Smith, Samuel, 172–73
Socinianism, 11, 95, 97, 170–71, 175–77,
  180–82, 188, 223
sola scriptura, 14, 44, 49–50, 113, 122, 124,
  129, 135
Son, the
  begetting of, 145–46, 151–54, 157, 166,
    178, 186
  blood of, 172, 174, 178
  body of, 130–31, 145, 198, 233–34, 242
  body-spirit dualism, 237
  as Creature, 163, 213
  decretum, 152, 154, 157
  golden compasses, 230–31, 237
  human with divine power, 183–87
  incarnation, 177–79, 183–87, 197, 235,
    240, 242
  as *logos*, 2, 185
  and transplantation, 240–41
  mediator, 173, 178, 185–90, 194–95, 236
  oblatio Christi, 84
  as theological foundation, 32, 197, 203
  two natures, 162, 183–86
  as vicegerent, 217
sovereignty, 73, 221, 223–24, 234
speech
  and authority, 70, 73, 107, 111, 134
  and ecclesiology, 32, 115

  and logic, 18
  metaphysics of, 235
  public discourse, 41
  and scripture, 4–7, 38, 41, 61, 113, 118,
    123, 135
  spirit-driven, 145. *See also* rhetoric
Spinoza, Baruch de, 67
Sumner, Charles, 1, 8–9, 13–14, 52, 267
supernatural, 69–74, 80, 87, 94–99, 104–6,
  108, 180, 182. *See also* natural
supralapsarianism, 72, 97
syllogism, 17–18, 22, 39–41
Syriac, 23, 53, 178–79

theodicy, 210–13, 216, 223, 228–29, 233
tradition
  Christian, 11–12
  and doctrine, 11
  and ecclesiology, 116, 124–25, 132, 162
  and nature, 95
  Reformed, 31, 49–50, 163, 182, 203
  and scripture, 55–56, 109, 169
  and theology, 5
  and tyranny, 224
Trinity (Trinitarian)
  anti-trinitarianism, 22, 145–46, 151,
    158, 160, 174–77, 210, 224–25, 228,
    230, 236
  communion of, 192–94, 197, 221
  essence, 153, 157–58, 163–64, 177,
    184–92, 199, 213–17, 230–31, 235–38,
    242
  homoousios, 150, 158, 162–63, 199, 214
  and oneness, 144, 210, 214–15, 224
  orthodoxy, 147–48, 160, 164, 167, 173,
    178, 181, 214–15, 223, 236
  and substance, 146, 193, 210–17, 224,
    226–227, 230–31, 234–38, 242–45
  united in love and speaking, 187–97
tyranny, 66, 210, 216, 218–20, 223–24, 250

uncertainty, 92–99, 125, 134, 148, 159,
  171, 195, 221, 224
Unitarian, 10
universalism, 85, 99, 106
  hypothetical universalism, 16, 179–80,
    234
Urban, David V., 1n3, 2n5, 13, 68, 173,
  178n34, 204–6, 249n6

virtue, 96, 183, 228, 231–35, 240, 243–44
vivificavit, 86–90
vocation. *See* calling
Vulgate, 53, 89, 154

War in Heaven, 7, 212, 219, 223
Westminster Confession, 146
will
  and freedom, 70–71, 96, 103–6, 163
  of God, 63, 90, 96, 163
  and grace, 86
  and renewal, 100
  voluntas, 70–71, 87. *See also* agency
William of St. Thierry, 174
Williamson, Joseph, 28
Wilson, Thomas, 19–20
Wolleb, Johan

and agency, 79–80, 103–4
Milton's interlocutor, 8–9, 25–27, 67–69, 204
and ministers, 128–30
and renewal (sanctification), 74–78, 88–92, 104, 106
and nature, 92–94
and the rule of faith, 162
and scripture, 81–85, 128–31, 151
and theological process, 112, 118–22
and the Trinity, 144–47, 150–52, 155–60, 166

Zanchius, Hieronymus (Zanchi, Giro-lamo), 24, 62–63, 85–88, 95, 98, 184–85, 235, 261
Zohar, 10

Index of Biblical Passages

OLD TESTAMENT/HEBREW BIBLE

Genesis 1:2, 231
Exodus 19:5-6, 57
Psalms 2, 21, 145, 151-53, 158, 163-64, 200, 205-6, 221-22, 223, 242
Psalms 2:1-2, 151
Psalms 2:4, 151, 219-20
Psalms 2:6, 151
Psalms 2:7, 145, 151-57, 160, 162, 166, 189
Psalms 2:9, 151
Psalms 2:10, 151
Psalms 2:12, 151
Psalms 19, 95
Psalms 147:19-20, 56, 58
Isaiah 7:9, 247
Isaiah 59:21, 44
Jeremiah 31:33, 51
Jeremiah 31:33-34, 44
Daniel 3:16, 123

NEW TESTAMENT

Matthew 10:18, 85
Matthew 13:7, 232
Matthew 13:52, 68, 121
Matthew 24:26, 189
Matthew 25:18, 233
Matthew 25:24, 233
Matthew 25:30, 233
Mark 2:27, 61
Mark 13:32, 189
John 1:1, 124
John 3:16, 146, 152
John 8:58, 205
John 10:30, 159, 191
John 10:38, 192
John 14:10, 192
John 14:20-21, 192
John 14:23, 193
John 15:19, 195
John 15:26, 150

John 17:21-23, 192
Acts 5:32, 44
Acts 13:32-33, 160
Acts 13:46, 85
Acts 14:16-17, 58
Acts 15:10, 110
Acts 17:27-30, 58
Acts 20:27, 122
Acts 20:28, 178
Romans 2:4, 58
Romans 2:20, 122
Romans 4:25, 175
Romans 5:18, 179
Romans 5:20, 242
Romans 6:14-15, 60
Romans 6:17, 121
Romans 8:35, 195
Romans 9:8, 76
Romans 12:2, 48, 52-55, 81-82, 89-92, 100, 106
Romans 12:6, 109
1 Cor 1:26, 78-79
1 Cor 2:12, 44
1 Cor 7:12, 61
2 Cor 4:16, 81, 89, 92, 95, 99, 104-5
2 Cor 5:14, 179
Gal 4:26, 110
Eph 1:3,5, 81
Eph 1:11, 189-90
Eph 2:3, 86, 92, 94, 97
Eph 2:3,5, 81, 85
Eph 2:12, 58
Eph 2:14, 58
Eph 3:18-19, 195
Eph 4:23-24, 81
Philippians 2:12, 103
Philippians 2:12-13, 103, 106
Colossians 2:8, 123
Colossians 3:10, 81, 89
1 Thess 5:19-20, 51

INDEX OF BIBLICAL PASSAGES   299

1 Tim 3:16, 184
2 Tim 1:9, 78–79, 100
2 Tim 1:13, 121–22
Titus 2:14, 180
Titus 3:5, 81–84, 99
Heb 1:3, 214

Heb 6:1–3, 121
Heb 6:4,6, 8, 82
James 2:12, 218
1 John 1:3, 6–7 193
1 John 5:7, 54, 159, 193
Rev 5:12, 188